Advance Praise for *A House Divided* by Mark Gerzon

"Gerzon gives us an original and compelling analysis of a problem critical to every American. Perhaps more important, he provides practical steps that will enable each of us to become part of a solution. When I finished *A House Divided,* I felt a surge of optimism."

—Allen Grossman, CEO, Outward Bound USA

"A House Divided is a unique, well-conceived analysis of America's divisions and provides a powerful program for its renewal."

—Michael Murphy, co-founder of Esalen Institute

"Mark Gerzon's insightful portrayals of Americans' belief systems are unfailingly engaging even when they make us angry. This perceptive book will draw many into helping create a civic renaissance in our country."

—William S. Edgerly, chairman emeritus, State Street Bank;
chairman, Foundation for Partnerships

"It's a mature society that can honor its differences and still work toward and celebrate its community. *A House Divided* offers role models and practices for realizing this balance."

—Ram Dass, author and lecturer

"Mark Gerzon adds to the growing literature of hope with his insightful analysis of the nation's crippling ideological divisions and his commonsense suggestions for healing them. Any resident of our divided house, no matter where he or she starts, can find here ways to move toward reconciliation without surrendering core values."

—Davis Merritt, editor of the Wichita *Eagle;*
author, *Public Journalism and Public Life*

"Read this book at your own peril! *A House Divided* challenges us to listen sympathetically to the fellow citizens we love to judge, and inspires us with courageous stories of those working to realize the twenty-first-century age-old American dream of *E pluribus unum.* "

—William Ury, author, *Getting to Yes* and *Getting Past No*

"If you believe it's enough to fight for your values—right or left—this book is for you. Gerzon argues that unless we learn to step beyond the boundaries of our particular worldviews—to listen to the viewpoints of others—we Americans can't solve our worsening problems. And he shows how some Americans are learning to transcend those limiting boundaries. *A House Divided* is an arresting and challenging book. Jump in and think!"

—Frances Moore Lappé and Paul Martin DuBois,
co-authors, *The Quickening of America*

"If you're looking for a road map to an American renaissance, look no further. *A House Divided* is the real thing—provocative, passionate, and profound. I believe it may well become *the* bible of good citizenship for the new century, a must-read for every politician and voter who cares about our nation's future."

—Jon Cowan, co-author, *Revolution X: A Wake-Up Call for America*

"More than any analysis to date, *A House Divided* lays bare the roots of the crisis confronting America today. It provides a framework for healing our nation, calling each of us to enlist together in a personal, practical crusade to renew America's destiny as the world's leading democracy."

—John Vasconcellos, member of the California Legislature

"No less than it did over two centuries ago, this nation faces a crisis of unity. Can we reinvent a democracy built firmly on common ground or will we continue to sink in the quicksand of divisiveness, clinging ever more tightly to our own belief system? Mark Gerzon lets us view the world through the eyes of others and, thereby, begin to discover ourselves. More important, he offers hope and help to every citizen who aspires to participate in our renunciation."

—Wendell J. Walls, president and CEO,
National Association for Community Leadership

A House Divided

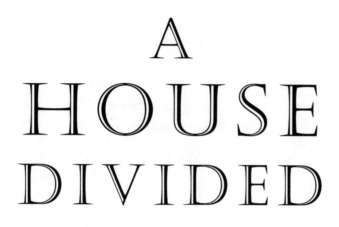

A HOUSE DIVIDED

Six Belief Systems
Struggling for America's Soul

MARK GERZON

A JEREMY P. TARCHER/PUTNAM BOOK
published by G. P. PUTNAM'S SONS *New York*

This book is dedicated to my three sons,
Shane, Ari, and Mikael,
and to their twenty-first-century generation.
May they help bring
a new patriotism to America.

Most Tarcher/Putnam books are available at special quantity discounts for bulk
purchases for sales promotions, premiums, fund-raising, and educational needs.
Special books or book excerpts also can be created to fit specific needs.

For details, write or telephone Special Markets, The Putnam Publishing Group,
200 Madison Avenue, New York, NY 10016; (212) 951-8891.

A Jeremy P. Tarcher / Putnam Book
Published by G. P. Putnam's Sons
Publishers Since 1838
200 Madison Avenue
New York, NY 10016

http://www.putnam.com/putnam

Library of Congress Cataloging-in-Publication Data

Gerzon, Mark.
A house divided : six belief systems
struggling for America's soul / Mark Gerzon.
p.   cm.
"A Jeremy P. Tarcher / Putnam book."
Includes bibliographical references and index.
ISBN 0-87477-823-9 (alk. paper)
1. Political culture—United States.   2. Ideology—United States.
3. Patriotism—United States.   4. United States—Politics and government.   I. Title.
JA84.U5G389   1996
306.2'0973—dc20   95-21049 CIP

Design by Lee Fukui

Printed in the United States of America
1   3   5   7   9   10   8   6   4   2

This book is printed on acid-free paper. ∞

ACKNOWLEDGMENTS

BEFORE ACKNOWLEDGING the colleagues, friends, and family who shared in the vision of this book, I must first thank those who did not. Because this book explores divergent belief systems, it depended even more on the help of those who do not share my views than those who do. Even though many of them suspected that I was not "one of them," scores of American citizens confided in me some of their deepest thoughts and feelings. They invited me into their meetings, their churches, their homes, and sometimes even their hearts. I thank the more than one hundred fellow citizens I interviewed, whether identified by name in these pages or not, for trusting me enough to let me inside their beliefs. (For the names of specific individuals who assisted me in developing certain chapters, please see the appropriate section of the footnotes.)

Without the support of my publisher, editor, and friend, Jeremy Tarcher, I would not have undertaken the years of research that culminated in this book. Just as *A House Divided* challenged my beliefs, so I knew it would challenge those who worked on it with me. To his credit, Jeremy did not flinch when he found his own worldview challenged in these pages. Throughout the process, in addition to bringing his lifelong editing experience to bear on the text, he was fair-minded toward beliefs even when they conflicted with his own.

Five other people also provided significant editorial advice that immeasurably improved this book. In Boston, Jill Kneerim of the Palmer & Dodge Agency, who has been my agent and friend for many years, provided vital guidance throughout the project. In New York, Irene Prokop and Gene Stone reviewed and helped me redesign the structure of the book in ways that helped correct my own blind spots. Here in Colorado, during the early chaotic stages of the project, Donna Zerner helped research and strengthen the early versions of the manuscript. During the final year, Matthew Moseley persevered with me in the interviewing, rewriting, and fact-checking that were required and invested his special enthusiasm in the project.

Many friends and colleagues provided extremely useful reactions to the manuscript in progress, including Harry Boyte, Senator Bill Bradley, David Chrislip, Lawrence Chickering, Jon Cowan, Peggy Dulany, Mike Eichler, James Gibson, Michael Lerner, Robert Levi, John Parr, Jeff Peters, Bob Samples, and Marta Tellado. I also received useful counsel from many colleagues at the Rockefeller Foundation, particularly Peter Goldmark and Terri Potente, as well as from my colleagues around the country who helped develop the set of projects known as the Common Enterprise. I also benefitted enormously from the critical support of William Ury, who not only repeatedly reviewed the manuscript but provided me with a writing hideaway. Finally, I am deeply grateful to John Steiner, whose faith in me and in this book never wavered and who challenged me to become more aware of how my own beliefs affected my perceptions of those of others.

I am most indebted, of course, to my own family: my wife, Shelley Kessler, and our sons, Shane, Ari, and Mikael. In their own way, each of them has taught me a lesson that goes to the heart of being part of a family *and* of a country. Being different from one another can lead to fear and distance, but it can also yield a deep mutual respect and profound intimacy that is as precious as life itself.

Contents

PREFACE

And if a kingdom be divided against itself,
that kingdom cannot stand.
And if a house be divided against itself,
that house cannot stand.

MARK 3:24–25

IF YOU WALK down Philadelphia's cobblestone streets past the Liberty Bell and Constitution Hall, you arrive at the site of the first Continental Congress in 1774. There stands a plaque erected by the National Park Service which bears the words of the man who is perhaps America's most famous patriot, Patrick Henry:

> The distinction between Virginians, Pennsylvanians, New Yorkers, New Englanders are no more. I am not a Virginian but an American.

At first glance, Patrick Henry's words could be dismissed as irrelevant. To care so much about a particular state seems like a horse-and-buggy anachronism. Now that we all move around so much, loyalty to our respective geographic states has waned enormously.

But look what happens if we change the wording of Patrick Henry's phrase slightly, to make it refer not to where we live, but what we *believe:*

> The distinctions between liberal Democrats, conservative Republicans, Religious Right, and New Age secular humanists are no more. I am no longer loyal to any of those belief systems, but pledge allegiance to the whole of which they are all parts.

So reworded, this patriot's message from two centuries ago is as urgent and timely as tomorrow's headlines. The civic struggle is no longer geographical, but ideological. The competition is not between loyalty to the American nation versus loyalty to a particular state, but between fealty to our country and fighting for our personal beliefs.

Can a nation whose citizens hold fundamentally different beliefs remain united? Is the United States becoming the Divided States? Or, from the ashes of a fragmenting and polarized "pluribus," is a new "unum" arising?

To raise these questions cuts to the heart of what it means to be an American today. So many kinds of people now claim to be "real patriots" that the concept of patriotism in peacetime has become nearly meaningless. When Americans were asked the question "How patriotic are *you?*" two out of three Americans—66 percent—described themselves as "extremely" or "very" patriotic. Yet the same group of randomly sampled adults were much more skeptical about other people's patriotism. When the interviewers asked "Do you believe that Americans today are more patriotic or less patriotic than Americans in previous decades?" almost three out of four—73 percent, to be precise—said that Americans are *less* patriotic than in previous decades.[1]

On the one hand, then, the vast majority of Americans believe that they themselves love their country deeply. Yet an even larger majority feel that their fellow citizens do not. What are we to make of this paradox? Are we overestimating our own patriotism—or underestimating our neighbors'?

After talking with hundreds of Americans in cities and towns across the country during the past few years, I believe that neither conclusion is correct. What was at issue in this poll, and what is dividing America today, is the meaning of patriotism. The vast majority of Americans consider themselves patriotic because they meet their own standards of patriotism. But when they apply their standards to others, they believe most of their fellow citizens fall short. Whether Americans are more or less patriotic now than before depends on what patriotism means—and, as the statistics reveal, it means different things to different people.

To some degree, this has always been true. A writer for the *Hartford Courant,* for example, once warned his readers about the impact that a new administration would have on the nation:

> Neighbors will be enemies of neighbors, brothers of brothers, fathers of their sons, and sons of their fathers. Murder, robbery, rape, adultery, and incest will be openly taught and practiced, the air will be rent with the cries of distress, the soil soaked with blood, and the nation black with crimes.[2]

We can take some comfort from the fact that the year was 1800, and the new administration which so terrified this forecaster of doom was Thomas Jefferson's.

Although it is true that we Americans have always had our political differences, it is not true that the civic spirit is as strong as ever. What united us in the past was faith in our public institutions, and that faith is eroding far more rapidly than we dare to admit. When I was a boy growing up in Indiana during the fifties, the citizens of this country widely believed that our country was on the right track and that our leaders were trustworthy. When pollsters asked adults back then whether they believed that government could be trusted most of the time to "do the right thing," almost three out of four said yes.

The America which my three sons' generation is inheriting has lost that confidence. Today, when Americans are asked the same question, only one out of eight says yes.[3] The vast majority have become cynical—not only about government, but about every major institution of our society. Americans are in "a foul mood," concludes experienced public opinion analyst Daniel Yankelovich, and "it is likely to last for a very long time, perhaps even degenerating into class warfare, generational warfare, increased racial hostility, demagoguery." As one veteran political observer summed it up: "The country has about as much cohesion as a dropped jigsaw puzzle."[4]

From one end of the political spectrum to the other, Americans believe we are a nation sinking deeper and deeper into quicksand. Liberal Democrats such as Senator Bill Bradley warn that our "civic society is collapsing" and that our "disconnected families, disconnected children, and disconnected communities . . . are headed for trouble." Conservatives like William Bennett argue that the moral fiber of the country is weakening and will continue to do so unless we radically alter the direction of our country. "It is impossible to maintain civilization," says the Speaker of the House, Newt Gingrich, "with twelve-year-olds having babies, with fifteen-year olds killing each other and seventeen-year-olds dying of AIDS, and with eighteen-year-olds getting diplomas [who] can't even read."[5]

To make matters worse, political leaders are not lifting us out of the quicksand but pulling us under. Campaigns have reached new lows in their willingness to defame and defile. No leader is sufficiently respected, and no candidate decent enough, to avoid being dragged through the mud by their opponents. Even the authority of the president is so compromised that a leading senator warns him not to visit his state without a bodyguard. In this venerable democracy, half a billion dollars were spent in the last mid-term election on advertising, the primary purpose of which was to denigrate opponents.

It should not surprise us then, that the vast majority of Americans lack confidence in public and private institutions and question each other's patriotism. After all, that is precisely what our leaders do. The truth is that we no longer trust our institutions, our leaders, or each other.

The statistics cited here all predate the infamous attack by home-grown terrorists on the federal building in Oklahoma City which killed more than 160 of their fellow citizens and ignited national debate about the hate and paranoia within our borders. But the extremists who dot the American landscape, destructive as they can be, cannot be blamed for the erosion of shared values among the vast majority of Americans. The Branch Davidians in Waco, Texas, or the right-wing militias in Idaho, Michigan, and other states are a symptom of our cultural fragmentation, not its cause. The ultimate threat to the security of the United States is that the rest of us are divided too.

In 1858, the day before the Republican convention in Illinois at which he would be nominated for the U.S. Senate, Abraham Lincoln called a dozen of his closest friends together in a small room at the state library and read to them the speech he intended to give the following day. "A house divided against itself cannot stand," Lincoln began, citing from the Bible. In a few passionate paragraphs, he explained why our great nation had to come to agreement about slavery. "I do not expect the house to fall," he said, "but I do expect it will cease to be divided. It will become all one thing, or all the other." His decision to stand boldly against slavery, and to begin his speech with scriptures, was a decision rooted deeply in his soul. As he told a friend later: "I know there is a God and he hates injustice and slavery. I see the storm coming. I know His hand is in it. If He has a place and work for me—and I think He has—I believe I am ready. I am nothing, but the truth is everything."

Almost all of Lincoln's listeners told him that delivering such an outspoken speech would be a serious mistake and would cost him the election. But Lincoln did not waver. He delivered the speech. Two years later, he became president of the United States and saved the Union. He prepared for the coming storm, and helped the nation weather it. So, more than a century later, must we.

As in President Lincoln's time, a struggle is being waged for America's soul. Just as the issue of slavery was fundamental to the destiny of our country, so are scores of issues that divide us today. But now we are not divided into two armies wearing blue or gray uniforms and fighting over slavery. Rather we are fragmented by conflicting belief systems which turn almost any issue into flash points for bitterness, anger, hatred, and often violence. The range and intensity of these disputes has become almost overwhelming. With the exception of combating foreign dictatorships, almost no cause commands consensus. Instead of healthy, constructive debate about fundamental issues, we hear divisive, destructive charges and countercharges, all too often about trivia. The media, the courts, the political campaigns—all have become gladiators' arenas. Trust between citizens has been replaced by fear; and the more Americans fear each other, the weaker we become. At a point in history when no nation on earth is powerful enough to defeat us, we may defeat ourselves. No longer able to portray Moscow as the Evil Empire, some of our fellow citizens now portray Washington that way. Since the end of the Cold War, we often act as if we are our own worst enemies.

Fortunately, the outbreak of civil war has not yet begun. As in the 1850s, America today is "a house divided," but not yet an armed battlefield. As James Davison Hunter observed in *Before the Shooting Begins,* "culture wars always precede shooting wars." But we cannot afford another Gettysburg: a civil war today would destroy America. The battle of beliefs, therefore, is being waged without cannons; divisive issues are being resolved off the battlefield. On the eve of the twenty-first century, we are being challenged to discover more civil forms of combat, and a deeper, more embracing kind of patriotism.

This book is an invitation to witness some of the battles about beliefs that are being waged in America—battles about what we and our country hold sacred. We are all participants in these battles, whether we admit it or not: even if one stands on the sidelines and does nothing, one is involved. In a democracy whose vitality depends on participatory self-governance, passivity is a political act.

We are in a struggle about our deepest values and our most cherished beliefs. Writing this book has challenged me to confront my own beliefs as well as beliefs different from my own; to retain what is of value and to discard what is not; in other words, to be a citizen.

"Souls are like athletes that need opponents worthy of them," wrote Thomas Merton, "if they are to be tried and extended and pushed to the full use of their powers." May you and I, and the scores of fellow citizens we meet in these pages, be worthy adversaries when we disagree. Let us face our differences, respect them, and learn from them. Only by doing so can Americans reunite our divided house and save America's soul.

MARK GERZON
September 1995

∞

INTRODUCTION

American democracy is in much deeper trouble than
most people wish to acknowledge. Behind the reassuring facade,
the regular election contests and so forth, the substantive
meaning of self-government has been hollowed out.
What exists behind the formal shell is a systemic breakdown
of the shared civic values we call democracy.

WILLIAM GREIDER
Who Will Tell The People?

TO WRITE FAIRLY about belief systems is a humbling task. Since we observe the beliefs of others through the lens of our own, we can never be certain that our observations are accurate. How often have you heard someone refer to their own beliefs as "values" or "principles," and then call someone else's beliefs "prejudices" or "biases?" Clearly, before we can be trustworthy observers of the beliefs of others, we must be aware of our own.

Twenty-five years ago, when I first began studying the power of belief systems to shape personal identity and political behavior, I was fortunate to be a student of one of the masters of the subject, the late Erik H. Erikson. As my professor and thesis advisor at Harvard, this renowned psychohistorian taught me that our personal life history and history itself are intimately intertwined. The perspective that each observer brings ("identity") influences what we observe and record ("history"). So it was clear to me that in order to study the clashing belief systems of our times, my first responsibility was to be clear about my own.

Confused by the clash of values between the Hoosier heartland of the fifties in which I was raised and the Harvard campus of the sixties, I dealt with what Erikson called my "identity crisis" by turning my confusion into prose. The result was *The Whole World Is Watching*, a book about the generation gap first published in 1969. Even at a young age, unconscious as I was of the ways in which my experience had formed my views, I somehow knew that "truth" was something far larger than I could claim to possess. I dedicated the book:

To the members of my generation, who as an act of patriotism, went into the jungles of Vietnam, and to those who, as an act of conscience, went into the jails of America. May they unite and work together for a better society where future generations will not have to make either sacrifice.

Unfortunately, as the next quarter century would teach me, I was not yet worthy of my own vision. For Americans to "unite and work together" would require more than lofty sentiments: the hard soul-work of recognizing the ignorance and the wisdom present on both sides of most profound disagreements.

In the seventies, I learned this lesson again on a global scale when I cofounded and edited *WorldPaper*, a monthly publication with a global perspective. As coordinator of a team of associate editors from every major region of the world and as managing editor of a periodical that was read in several languages on several continents, I was constantly surrounded by fundamentally different points of view. My job was to listen to the associate editors and to ensure that the varied voices of this small planet had a fair hearing. While we occasionally succumbed to parochial American perspectives, sometimes we really succeeded in finding a global voice. Thus in 1980, for example, when the Soviet Union invaded Afghanistan, my colleagues and I assembled a set of articles so unique (including Russian, Chinese, Afghani, African, and Asian writers as well as representatives of the U.S. State Department) that they were widely reprinted in newspapers at home and abroad.

By then, I was also a husband and father, two roles which plunged me into a personal clash of belief systems. My wife Shelley had taught women's studies at several colleges and was an articulate and thoughtful feminist. Although I overtly supported the movement for women's rights, I nevertheless felt threatened by its hostility toward men and its scapegoating of the "patriarchy." The power struggle in our marriage was an intimate clash of two belief systems, each of us eager to prove that our view was right and the other's was wrong. Once again, to understand the roots of this conflict, I turned to writing. Now, more than a decade later, *A Choice of Heroes: The Changing Faces of American Manhood,* the book which I wrote with Shelley's invaluable counsel, is still being read by men seeking a way of thinking and living that honors both feminine and masculine within each of us.

The years I spent researching gender catalyzed my interest in the family, where, for better or worse, men and women seek common ground. Resuming my earlier studies in clinical psychology, I trained as a family therapist. The training taught me a lesson that I have found useful ever since: if you want to help the whole, don't become allied with only one part of it. Nothing is less useful to most families than a therapist who, consciously or unconsciously, aligns himself with one member of the family against the other members. To do so may resolve a short-term problem, but in the long run it will only make the house more divided. Although I often personally liked one person in a family better than another, professionally I learned to commit myself to the well-being of the *whole* family.

By the mid-eighties, my career took a different turn. I became president of a small film company in Los Angeles specializing in stories that dealt with important national and international social issues, including the threat of nuclear war. With movies like *Rambo, Rocky, Red Dawn,* and scores of others raking in millions by demonizing the Soviet Union, it was clear that entertainment was exacerbating the Cold War rather than helping to end it. With the support of my board directors, I launched the "Entertainment Summit," a not-for-profit initiative which called attention to the lies in both Soviet and American films about the "other side." Bringing influential delegations from Moscow and Hollywood to each other's studios, and building face-to-face working relationships between them, changed the mood. A few years after the Cold War died in fiction, it also died in fact.

At first, like most Americans, I was relieved that the superpower hostility and the accompanying threat of nuclear war had abated. After a generation of living under the threat of a mushroom cloud, it was a blessing to look ahead to the nineties without a nuclear clock poised ominously at a few minutes to midnight. But as the Berlin wall fell and the Cold War faded into memory, other conflicts immediately became more visible and volatile. If the world was no longer to be policed by rival Soviet and American armies, what would take its place? Could diverse global perspectives find common ground?

Because of the success of the Entertainment Summit in building partnerships across the barricades, I was funded by the Rockefeller Foundation and others in the late eighties to address these questions by assembling a global team to develop new strategies for approaching complex international problems. An American and a Soviet citizen were on the team, of course, but it also included a Chinese communist rocket scientist, the son of an African chief, an Argentinean economist, a German environmentalist, a proponent of global government from New Zealand, and an Indian journalist. For three years the members of this team met together, fought with each other, learned to respect each other, and ultimately launched projects together. For me it was a powerful lesson about "E pluribus unum" on a global scale. The difficulties of creating a whole out of disparate parts were enormous—but so were the rewards.

By the early nineties, I knew that it was time to try the same experiment here at home. The end of the Cold War presented Americans with the challenge of facing our own diversity. When Americans lost the superficial unanimity that came from having a fearsome external enemy, we become more aware of the sharp divisions within our own society. While the brief military campaigns in Panama, Grenada, and the Persian Gulf temporarily boosted our national self-confidence, the lift did not last. Headline after headline brought home the fact that within our own borders, we were not at peace with each other. On the contrary, violent debate about virtually every issue—from gun control to deficit reduction, from health care reform to campaign finance reform, from abortion to euthanasia, from affirmative action to school prayer—proved that we had become a nation divided against itself.

Determined to tackle this thorny problem, my colleagues at the Rockefeller Foundation and I began designing projects to revitalize citizenship, rebuild community, and develop civic leadership. The president of the foundation, Peter Goldmark, called these projects "The Common Enterprise." In his view America was in danger of losing its shared vision; and the purpose of the projects was to reconnect diverse groups of Americans who were often in conflict with each other and assist them in finding "common enterprises" in which they could join hands.

This community-building work in cities around the country, as well as the interviews and research for this book, allowed me to witness firsthand the struggle for America's soul. I traveled across America seeking out citizens who held beliefs very different from each other's—and from my own. I encountered people in cities all across America who feared and sometimes hated each other: blacks and whites in Kansas battling over school desegregation; religious fundamentalists and secular humanistic educators in Arizona struggling for control over the public schools; affluent white suburbanites and Hispanic leaders in California battling over immigration; Christian activists and homosexuals in Colorado battling over a gay rights amendment; Hollywood stars and the "family values" movement battling over the content of films and television; and, of course, liberals and conservatives in Washington, D.C., battling over nearly everything.

In Tucson, Arizona, for example, I spent the morning at a press conference featuring a high school teacher who had been fired for allowing her students to rehearse a controversial play. She was flanked by Hollywood stars, liberal advocacy groups from Washington, and several supportive students, all eager to defend freedom of speech. I then spent the afternoon at another press conference a few miles away featuring the school administrator who had fired the teacher. He was flanked by members of conservative organizations and by sympathetic parents proud that he had imposed moral discipline. Both press conferences were powerful, moving, and heartfelt—but each was filled with bitter animosity and suspicion toward opponents who, conveniently, were not in the room. Each gathering had a fundamentally different view of what education in a democracy should be. The problem was not that the two sides had differences, but that they never met together to explore them. The message to their children was a bitter one: we are a nation divided.

In controversy after controversy, I have found the diversity of beliefs and the hostility among those who hold them to be astounding. The truths I learned as a child—that Columbus discovered America; that budgets should be balanced; that boys are better at math; that newspapers report the facts; that anyone who works hard can get ahead; that a Latino immigrant should learn English; that praying to God is good and cussing is bad—have turned into controversies. What is acceptable to adherents of one belief system is immoral to another. What one parent considers educational, another finds obscene. And to make matters worse, we do not seem to know how to discuss our growing differences, much less resolve them.

In 1993, for example, my colleagues at the Rockefeller Foundation and I convened a meeting of the heads of major membership organizations whose purpose was to engage citizens in public affairs—ranging from liberal organizations such as Common Cause to conservative ones such as the Christian Coalition. Two of the participants were bitter enemies: a top leader from People for the American Way, a liberal organization in Washington, D.C., founded by Norman Lear to defend freedom of speech against the "Religious Right"; and a high-level executive from Focus on the Family, a fundamentalist Christian group based in Colorado Springs with three million members nationwide. The two organizations had been at war for several years, and had fought against each other repeatedly in cities across the country. Their representatives at our meeting had frequently felt attacked and personally maligned by each other.

Prior to the meeting, we had asked participants to bring with them a physical object that somehow symbolized the meaning of their work. Although the request was unorthodox, they complied. After the participants had all introduced themselves, I asked them to place their objects on a table in the center of our circle. The Focus on the Family official placed the Holy Bible on the table and explained that the purpose of his work is to expand the Christian faith in American life. A few moments later, the representative of People for the American Way, an organization depicted by its adversaries as the staunch defender of secular humanism, reached inside his shirt and removed a gold chain from around his neck on which hung the Christian cross. He stepped up to the table and laid the cross beside the Bible.

The sight of the cross and the Bible, placed on the table by representatives of two feuding organizations, was as powerful as it was unexpected. It was as if two champion boxers had entered the ring, looked in each other's faces, and discovered that they were brothers. As moderator of the discussion, I paused to let the group ponder the questions raised: What does the Christian faith mean to each man? How has it led them to reach opposite conclusions on matters of public policy? And how does their faith influence their attitude toward non-Christians?

The silence was quickly broken. Within seconds, the two men had resumed hostilities. Exploring common ground was too threatening; it was easier just to continue fighting.

As I have studied the landscape of American conflict—interviewing more than a hundred Americans and working with hundreds more to resolve conflicts in communities across the country—that moment remains in my mind. For I have witnessed countless times the same missed opportunity. In Congress or on "Nightline," in street demonstrations or at public hearings, during national elections, or in city council debates, two citizens may stand face to face bitterly opposed to each other over a volatile issue. An opportunity appears for them to reach out to each other, to speak from their hearts, and to rediscover their common bond as Americans. They see the opportunity, they lean toward it—and then turn away.

In such moments, I have felt America's pulse weaken, our nation's arteries harden, and the hearts of my fellow citizens grow cold. My faith in myself and in my country has been shaken. I want to believe in America as the "land of the free and the home of the brave." But when I see citizen turn against citizen, I do not feel free but paralyzed, not brave but afraid.

Had my experience ended at that point, I would have concluded that bitter and increasingly violent struggle among American citizens is inevitable. Fortunately, however, that is not the end of the story. As I report in Part II of this book, I have also encountered scores of Americans who are taking action to heal America's wounds and make our nation whole. Wherever they live—from Spartanburg, South Carolina, to Portland, Oregon; from Taos, New Mexico,

to the inner city of Baltimore; from Milwaukee to San Antonio—they are working to reunite America. Everywhere I have traveled, I found farsighted, hardworking citizens who were building a new culture.

This movement has neither a single name, nor a single leader, nor a single
goal—but it *is* a movement. Larger and more vibrant than even its participants
know, it is a movement for the revitalization of America. Thousands of men
and women, many of whom feel isolated and overwhelmed, are in fact part
of this grass-roots resurgence, which is happening—and can only happen—
spontaneously, in our own communities. They are reaffirming the right of self-
governance, rededicating themselves to the core values of our country, and
ensuring, in Lincoln's memorable words, "that government of the people, by
the people, and for the people shall not perish from the earth."

The Civil War was a time of crisis when the nation had to decide its destiny. The multiple conflicts now raging among our citizens are bringing us to
another such crisis. How this struggle for America's soul will end is still un-
clear, but its urgency is undeniable. I have seen scores of children—black and
white, affluent and impoverished, across town and in my own neighborhood,
total strangers and my own flesh and blood—caught in the cross fire. The
venom and hostility affects us all: how we drive on the freeway; whether we
take a walk after dark; what we feel about our child's school; why we must
numb ourselves to watch the evening news; and so on. We know that we are
witnessing a culture at war with itself and that, unless something changes, it
will fragment beyond repair. As David Broder, the *Washington Post*'s veteran
political commentator, observed: "Somehow we have to hit the brakes on this
downhill plunge—and soon."[1]

But how? one immediately wonders. Can an organized, grass-roots movement of ordinary citizens—or "everyday heroes," as *Newsweek* calls them—turn
the country around? What can we *do?*

The first step toward halting this plunge toward self-destruction, I
believe, is to stop pretending that we can convince other Americans to adopt
our particular beliefs, and to begin seeking new common ground. In every dispute I have witnessed around the country, the combatants were always brimming over with their own opinions, and convinced that their ideas were right
and their adversaries' were wrong. The first thing we can do to stop "this
downhill plunge" is to put aside our own opinions temporarily and just listen
to other people's.

This sounds easy but it's not. If we hear voices that confirm our cherished
opinions, then of course we are flattered and eager to listen. But what we need

is to hear opinions we do not agree with. As citizens on the eve of the next millennium, in a nation exploding with diversity, our challenge is to listen to fellow citizens who anger us, disturb our thoughts, expose our preconceptions, and even impugn our integrity.

Instead of covering our ears, let us open them. Instead of turning our backs on our adversaries, let us face them. They are, after all, our neighbors.

The

DIVIDED
STATES
of
AMERICA

One wonders: will the center hold?
Or will the melting pot give way
to the Tower of Babel?

ARTHUR C. SCHLESINGER, JR.
The Disuniting of America

THE DIVIDED STATES of America can be found anyplace and everyplace in our nation. Each of these states is comprised of Americans who are bound together not by where they live, but by what they believe. In terms of how they behave as citizens of the United States, what counts is not their ZIP code, but their belief code. For citizens of the Divided States, personal beliefs are more important than anything else. Their belief systems are the prisms through which they may view their fellow citizens and their country.

Before we can repair and reunite a nation divided against itself, we must understand these Divided States: what they are, who lives in them, and why they are at war. Few Americans are willing to sacrifice their life for the state where they live, but many will die—and some, unfortunately, will kill—for their beliefs.

Citizens of each Divided State share a worldview that binds them together, separates them from, and often puts them in conflict with other citizens. A stockbroker working in a glass skyscraper in San Francisco or Seattle has more in common with his colleagues in Atlanta or Manhattan than with the new immigrant standing right outside his building searching for day labor. A born-again, fundamentalist Christian in Miami or Los Angeles shares more of a common culture with her like-minded sisters in Indianapolis or Dallas than she does with the New Age meditation instructor whose office may be right next door to the church where she worships. Despite a two-thousand-mile separation, the residents of riot-torn South Central Los Angeles and Chicago's impoverished South Side have more in common with each other than they do with the gentrified city-dwellers whose expensive condos may stand just across the tracks.

In a nation with a population approaching 300 million, countless belief systems exist. From junk bond dealers on Wall Street to gamblers in Las Vegas; from followers of turbaned gurus on Oregon ashrams to Branch Davidians in Waco, Texas; from highly paid lobbyists on Capitol Hill to crackheads on skid row; from an Ivy League math whiz to a pregnant high school dropout in the inner city—the variety of beliefs among these subgroups is infinite. But the purpose of this book is not to examine all of them—every ashram, every protest group, every extremist sect. Rather, it is to understand the overall dynamics of the conflict between the major belief systems struggling for America's soul.

After listening to scores of citizens explain their beliefs about themselves and their country, I have constructed composite descriptions of six adversary belief systems that, taken together, provide an overview of the hostility that exists in our country today. All six of them directly and profoundly influence the national consciousness. They are prevalent and powerful enough to have an impact on the lives of virtually all Americans. These composite belief systems, which I call the Divided States, are described in the chapters that follow. We will travel through each of them in turn.

Look closely at any major conflict in America today and you will find two or more of these Divided States at war:

PATRIA: *The Religious State*

CORPORATIA: *The Capitalist State*

DISIA: *The Disempowered State*

MEDIA: *The Superstate*

GAIA: *The Transformation State*

OFFICIA: *The Governing State*

Distinguishing between competing belief systems in America can of course lead to a variety of typologies. This map of the Divided States could be redrawn in many other ways, and involve many more pieces. (Indeed, in earlier drafts of this book, other Divided States were included, such as Academia, Militia, Technia, Gerontia, etc.) But after careful analysis, these six emerged as a useful microcosm of the belief systems seeking to dominate discourse in America today.

I recognize that reducing the range of belief systems to six required me to sacrifice some complexity, but it is nevertheless far more illuminating than the black-and-white dichotomies that prevail in so much public discourse. "Right" vs. "left," "conservative" vs. "liberal," "culture" vs. "counterculture"—this tired, simplistic, either-or language is still used with alarming frequency to describe a nation which clearly cannot be reduced to such stark dichotomies. The typology of the six Divided States is valuable because it helps illustrate how they break out of this one-dimensional world and symbolize more accurately the enormous diversity of views and values that coexist so precariously in our country today.

I have given each state a new, Latinized name for two very simple reasons: First, it is easier to refer to them by these simple names than by the complex, multifaceted belief systems for which they stand. Second, by coining a new name, it compelled me—as I hope it will also compel the reader—to examine the beliefs held by that State's citizens with a fresh eye and an open mind.

As different as these Divided States are from one another, their belief systems have one important common feature: they are belief *systems.* Unlike personal beliefs, held privately by individuals, belief systems are interlocking sets of belief held by large groups of citizens and represented by organizations designed to promote their particular ideology.[1]

Belief systems are to beliefs what security systems are to security. When one needs the former, it means that the latter has been lost. Just as we need a security system when we no longer feel safe in our own homes, so do we need a belief system when we no longer feel secure with our own beliefs. While beliefs explain *some*thing, belief systems claim to explain *every*thing. Unlike a belief, which leads us to learning, belief systems are turnkey operations. They come prefabricated and preassembled. They are ready-made systems that in effect do our thinking for us.

At the heart of its belief system, each of the six Divided States has a set of *core beliefs* that form its foundation. These core beliefs will be shown in **boldface** type. Individual citizens of a Divided State may vary in the intensity of militancy of their adherence to these core beliefs, but their behavior is nevertheless affected by them. These core beliefs set the boundaries between them and their enemies.

Each Divided State also has *sacred texts,* ranging from the Bible to Adam Smith's *The Wealth of Nations* to Malcolm X's *Autobiography.* Each State also has its *channels of communication,* through which its citizens speak to each other and share information supporting their beliefs. Each state has its own *advocacy groups* that defend criticism and challenge the belief systems of opponents. To some degree, each Divided State even has its own *language,* including words and catchphrases that epitomize the belief system itself. And of course each State has it own *leaders,* some of whom are regarded as heroes, who expound and defend the belief system.

As we travel through these Divided States, be prepared to feel disoriented. From watching nightly news reporting on fluctuations in the Dow Jones and the vicissitudes of electoral campaigns, we are accustomed to viewing the world in terms of political and economic factors. But beliefs are also powerful, and rapidly becoming more so. They permit otherwise law-abiding Americans to assassinate doctors who perform abortions or to blow up government buildings and kill hundreds of innocent people. In other cases, some of these beliefs enable citizens to risk death to protect their country and to devote their life to serving their neighbors and their communities. Systems of belief, put simply, can strengthen America or weaken it. Distinguishing between constructive and destructive belief systems, and the complex combinations of the two, is one of the primary purposes of this book.

Although the six belief systems will be identified as separate, embattled

5

States in the following chapters, they do overlap and intermingle in us—and in America. They are struggling for our souls just as they are struggling for our country's. Most Americans are not captives of one of these belief systems, but have multiple citizenship in more than one of the Divided States. So as we visit each of these States in turn, observe not only the struggle for America's soul, but the struggle within your own.

You will meet people whom you hate—or who hate you. You will witness behavior you consider indecent and hear ideas you consider dangerous, deranged, and even demonic. Because what you encounter will at times frighten and anger you, you must find the empathy within to enter that world and the courage to listen with an open heart. As much as possible in Part I, let your own opinions take a temporary rest. Let the citizens of the Divided States describe how they view America, who they think their friends and enemies are, and how they feel toward the citizens of the other States. Listen to them and take them seriously, as if you were sitting in their living room or their church, their boardrooms or their newsroom.

But please don't align yourself with any one Divided State until you have visited them all. Wait until Part II before you decide to which state, if any, you will pledge your allegiance.

1

PATRIA

The Religious State

Core belief:	Faith in Jesus Christ as Lord and Savior should shape every aspect of American Life.
Defining events:	Supreme Court ban on school prayer (1962); Pat Robertson presidential campaign (1988).
Sacred text:	The Bible.
Primary organization:	The church.
Spokespersons:	Ralph Reed, Paul Weyrich, Phyllis Schlafly, Bill Kristol, William Bennett, Dan Quayle, Gary Bauer, Pat Robertson, Rush Limbaugh, Tim and Beverly LaHaye, Dr. James Dobson, Pat Buchanan.
Electronic media:	Christian Broadcasting Network, National Empowerment Television.
Periodicals:	*Christianity Today, Christian America, Guideposts, The Weekly Standard.*
Educational institutions:	Religious universities, Bible colleges.
Advocacy groups:	Christian Coalition, Focus on the Family, National Association of Christian Education, Heritage Foundation, Traditional Values Coalition, Free Congress Foundation, Family Research Council, The Eagle Forum, The American Family Association, Concerned Women of America, Morality in Media, Christian Defense Coalition, numerous pro-life organizations, The National Religious Broadcasters, and The American Center for Law and Justice.
Ultimate authority:	God.
Quote:	*"Onward, Christian soldiers,* *Marching as to war,* *With the cross of Jesus* *Going on before."* —FROM THE HYMN *"Onward,* *Christian Soldiers" (1866)*

Y OU KNOW YOU are entering Patria when you see the four flags framing the main entrance to Focus on the Family's new $30 million national headquarters in Colorado Springs. To the left fly the Stars and Stripes and the Colorado state flag. To the right, flapping in the Rocky Mountain wind, is the flag of the Religious State (a red cross set against a blue background) and a flag emblazoned with the Focus on the Family emblem.

The magnificent complex of buildings, which staff members refer to as "the campus," is the hub of a national and international communications system that is unique in the world. A world map in the main hallway is covered with multicolored pins indicating where the organization's radio broadcasts are received. North America is covered by a sea of pins, each one indicating a radio station which carries one or more of Dr. James Dobson's radio programs. But beyond our borders, the former Soviet Union is also covered with white pins, as are southern Africa, much of Latin America, and various portions of Europe and Asia—4,000 radio facilities worldwide. While radio is the core of the organization's outreach, it is complemented by a book and videocassette distribution operation; a warren of dozens of telephone operators who provide direct advice to 2,000 callers each day; and a correspondence program which responds to mail arriving in volumes up to 10,000 letters a day, which is more than the White House normally receives.

"It is pain mail," observes Tom Minnery, Focus's vice president for public policy. "We feel that in it we can see the moral decline of our culture and the search for a new moral foundation."

As millions of parents in the State of Patria pray for guidance and support in strengthening their Christian marriages and raising Christian children, Dr. James Dobson, the founder of Focus on the Family, seems like an answer to their prayers. "Be in the studio, Lord. Speak through us," says Dr. Dobson before each taping of his program, which goes out instantaneously to over 1,600 radio stations nationwide.

Although Dobson has a doctorate in psychology and is familiar with academic studies and scientific data, his primary text is the Bible, which he calls "the word of God." The letters and phone calls received daily by Focus on the Family's 1,200-person staff are from troubled Patrians seeking guidance that is grounded above all in Christian values. Dr. Dobson and his colleagues provide it—by phone and by mail, on radio and TV, in books and audiocassettes.

On the wall of the main hall are photographs tracing Dr. Dobson's life, which began as the son of a Church of the Nazarene pastor, continued through his training as a child psychologist and associate clinical professor of pediatrics at the University of Southern California School of Medicine, and culminated with the founding of Focus on the Family and its growth. As head of the three-million-member, $90-million-a-year organization, Dr. Dobson can frequently be found sitting with presidents. Beside a photograph of Dr. Dobson and then-president Ronald Reagan side by side at the table where meetings of the cabinet are held, a letter from Reagan thanks him for his counsel and concludes that "your participation . . . will be most welcome." Other photographs show Dr. Dobson with George Bush, Oliver North, William Bennett, and other stalwart leaders of the State of Patria. (A caption adds that as yet President Clinton has not called.)

As the scriptures mounted in enormous letters in the main hall remind viewers daily: "Unless the Lord build the house, the workers labor in vain (Psalms 127:1)." Despite the organization's name, Dr. Dobson is frank about its purpose. Enter the beautiful new theater, which airs an interview with the founder throughout the day, and you will hear him say that strengthening the family is the means, but serving the Lord is the ultimate goal. The four cornerstone beliefs—the importance of evangelism, the permanence of marriage, the value of raising children, and the sanctity of life—are enshrined everywhere, including the main lobby of the Welcome Center. The annual report concludes, not with a financial statement, but with a "statement of belief," which reads in part:

> We believe the Bible to be the only infallible, authoritative Word of God.
>
> We believe that there is only one God, eternally existent in three persons: Father, Son, and Holy Spirit.
>
> We believe in the deity of our Lord Jesus Christ, in His virgin birth, in His sinless life . . . in His bodily resurrection, in His ascension to the right hand of the Father, and in His personal return to power and glory.

This, simplified, is the constitution of the State of Patria. It is, Patrians believe, the gospel truth. In a secular nation that is spiritually lost and morally declining, the simple work of God seems alien. Just referring to America as a "Christian nation" can create a fire storm of controversy.

While Other Faiths Will Be Tolerated,
America Is and Must Remain a Christian Nation.

How was Governor Kirk Fordice to know he would stir up such a fuss by saying that America was a "Christian nation?" After all, from his perspective, it was a simple fact of life. The governor of Mississippi made the statement at a safe setting: a national meeting of Republican governors in 1993 in Fontana, Wisconsin. But it caused such a ruckus that the national media picked up the story.

Fordice couldn't understand why his words were so controversial, because he thought of himself as a citizen of Mississippi. In fact, he is a citizen of the Divided State "Patria," otherwise known as the Religious State. Citizens of Patria consider their religious beliefs to be their lives' foundation. From the Patrian perspective, those beliefs should also be the moral cornerstone of American society and should inform every dimension of our lives—not just private and familial issues, but also economic, legal, political, and even foreign policy issues.

Seen through the Patrian lens, America is caught in a downward spiral of moral deterioration. Although thoughtful Patrians recognize the economic, political, and ecological factors that underlie our current predicament, they believe that the root cause of the crises in our society is the corrosive, and often explosive, moral decline. Gang murders, teen pregnancy, drug abuse, gay rights, homelessness, media violence, federal gridlock, the deficit—however far-ranging the symptoms may be, they are all part of the same disease: amorality.

Moral Decline Is the Root Cause
of What Is Wrong with America.

The Patrian prescription for what ails America, consequently, is a return to the bedrock of moral values rooted in the Judeo-Christian tradition. Patrians believe that the United States of America is a "Christian nation." Older Patrians nostalgically recall a time when all Americans could be called together in the name of Jesus Christ, our Lord and Savior. They dream of a society in which shared moral values will once again bind together Americans—men and women, black and white, rich and poor—into one great congregation.

According to the Patrian vision, America's problems will be solved when the citizens of this nation return to their spiritual origins. Patrians have different names for their vision—revival, reformation, restoration, renewal, reawakening—but the underlying meaning is the same. A secular democracy, they believe, is better than atheistic totalitarianism; but a secular democracy is not enough. We need at last to fulfill the vision of a republic which is "one nation, indivisible, *under God."*

The citizens of Patria are numerous and increasingly vocal. According to demographic data, one out of four Americans embraces a belief system based on intense, devout, conservative Protestantism. Whether they call themselves evangelicals, Pentecostals, fundamentalists, or simply "born-again," the ranks of these Christians are swelling in number and growing in impact. Unlike liberal wings of the Christian faith, which have been declining since 1965, these conservative Protestants are now a larger percentage of the American population than ever before.[1]

Other signs of Patria's continuing strength include:

- A sharp increase in enrollment in primary and secondary schools based on Christian principles.

- Rapid growth in the more than $1 billion Christian publishing trade, including expanded membership in the Evangelical Press Association and the Christian Booksellers Association.

- The continuing expansion of membership organizations, such as Dr. James Dobson's Focus on the Family and Pat Robertson's Christian Coalition.

- The visible and tangible presence in politics of thousands of outspoken advocates of Christian perspectives on school boards and city councils, in state government, and in the U.S. Congress.

- The explosive growth of Pentecostal Christianity, which, according to Harvard theologian Harvey Cox, has made it the fastest-growing religious denomination in the world.[2]

- Enormous support in Congress for the Christian Coalition's "Contract with the American Family," which according to Speaker of the House Newt Gingrich is aligned with the beliefs of 85 percent of the country.[3]

Despite the increase in organizational power, Patrian leaders recognize that this secular, materialistic nation will not be brought back to Christ overnight. Because Patria has lost control over American values, the power of their

State has eroded. To reclaim America as a Christian nation will require years of hard work. In a pamphlet titled "Taking Your City for Christ," Christian activists suggest the following ten-year timetable:

- Developing leadership: one year.
- Forming networks/strategies: six months.
- Prayer/research/church preparation: one year.
- Evangelism: six months.
- Reformation: seven years.

What Patrian activists mean by "reformation" is a leadership network "from the fields of law, government, business, education, the media, the arts, science, etc." This leadership network will be strictly "for those who have a vision and a burden to see all of society impacted by the principles of the Bible, that the Lord's Prayer may be fulfilled to get God's will done on earth as it is done in heaven."[4]

Using churches as organizing tools, Patrian activists are fighting to defend the core values for which they believe our country stands. They are not going to let their State forfeit leadership of America without a battle, and they are ready to go to war. "The first thing that is required to win a war is *soldiers*," exhorts a political manual prepared by Focus on the Family. "Churches must begin with a program of recruitment, or more plainly, discipleship. Secondly, an army needs intelligence. Where are the battles raging? Who is involved? What is the nature of the conflict and the size of the enemy? Questions like these must be answered in order to direct the efforts of your soldiers."

One of the generals of Patria—Ralph Reed, executive director of the Christian Coalition—knows exactly how big the program must be and how much it will cost. His goal: ten workers in each of America's 175,000 precincts. That's an army of 1,750,000 soldiers, using as their base of operations 100,000 churches nationwide with an annual budget of up to $100 million. When Reed reaches that goal, he says, "we will be larger and more effective and will reach more people than the Democratic and Republican parties combined."[5]

What most motivates this Patrian army of orthodoxy is a fervent belief that God's place in every citizen's life and in the life of this nation must become central once again. One of the forty-two statements in the "Essentials of a Christian World View," a document signed by scores of Patrian leaders throughout the country, reads: "We affirm that God is the source of all right and just values and that they reflect His moral character." Another statement in this catechism is: "We affirm that the ultimate source of authority is God. (We deny that man has the authority to create his own moral standards.)"[6]

True Christians Must Apply the Word of God in the Marketplace and in the Polling Booth.

Believing firmly that the time is near when they can return to power, many Patrians gain strength from their faith that God is on their side and that, with His help, they can reverse the visible decline that is weakening America's moral foundations. To accomplish this task, they must run for school boards and city councils, establish radio stations and TV networks, and gain new footholds of power throughout America. Their children must go to schools where the Christian values of prayer, faith, and reverence for God are honored rather than banished. "The thing we are beginning to understand—and I didn't understand this for years," said Carolyn Sundseth, former president Ronald Reagan's director of public liaison"—is that if Jesus Christ is going to be your Lord in every area of your life, He has to be the Lord of your politics, too."[7]

Just as the core belief of Christians is that truth is absolute, immutable, and rooted in faith in Jesus Christ as our Lord and Savior, today's Patrians believe that being a "Sunday morning Christian" is not enough. They believe faith should shape every aspect of their lives: their attitudes towards birth and death and everything in between. In the following four sections, we will explore the Patrian belief system regarding the *family, education, media, and politics.* As different as the issues are, all are grounded in the bedrock of their Christian beliefs.

So let us now meet citizens of Patria who live in Michigan, Iowa, Texas, California, Florida, and other states. But remember: those geographic states are simply where they *reside.* The State of Patria is where they actually *live.*

The Family |
"IT'S TIME TO DRAW THE LINE"

A few years ago, feminist organizations such as the National Organization of Women (NOW) targeted Iowa as the most likely state to reignite the national Equal Rights Amendment (ERA) campaign. Polls in Iowa showed a consistent 70 percent support for the amendment, and political insiders were sure that pro-ERA forces would win.

But Marlene Elwell didn't agree. Although she lives in Farmington, Michigan, she was a political veteran in Iowa. She had coordinated Pat Robertson's 1987 straw poll victory which helped to establish him as a credible candidate for the presidency of the United States. That campaign taught her that Iowans were fair-minded people willing to change their views, and she was convinced that if they really knew what damage the ERA would do, they would turn against it. "I'm a mother with five children," she says, "and I couldn't even imagine someone having an abortion."

*We Must Be Ever Vigilant Against Those
Who Seek to Replace God's Laws with Their Own.*

For Marlene and many other Patrians, the ERA isn't about equal rights at all. "As a woman, I am certainly for equal rights for women," Marlene says. "But that's not the agenda. There's a hidden agenda to the Equal Rights Amendment, and that's the message we had to get to the people." According to most Patrians, ERA is a Trojan horse that will unleash an army of immoral causes if it enters God's country. Although different Patrian organizations use different words to describe the ERA—"cover," "conspiracy," "con job," "trick," or simply "lie"—their fears are similar. They are afraid that it will lay the groundwork for taxpayer-funded abortions, special privileges for homosexuals, more support for two-worker families and state-run child care, and ultimately the dissolution of the family.

Marlene faced an uphill battle in Iowa. On the surface, the actual changes that the ERA amendment proposed in the Iowa constitution (indicated in italics) sounded incredibly innocuous:

> All men *and women* are, by nature, free and equal, and have certain inalienable rights—among which are those of enjoying and defending life and liberty, acquiring, possessing and protecting property, and pursing and obtaining safety and happiness. *Neither the states nor any of its political subdivisions shall on the basis of gender, deny or restrict the equality of rights under law.*

To defeat the ERA forces and the national lobby that was supporting them, she would have to demonstrate to the people of Iowa that this deceptively ordinary language was in fact dangerous.

Marlene began by forming an alliance of five organizations, each of which assigned one staff person to work with her to form the Iowa Committee to Stop ERA: Concerned Women for America, Iowa Right to Life, Christian Coalition, Eagle Forum, and Iowans for Life. By the time they started they had less than six months to turn the tide. "When you do this kind of campaign, coming in at a late hour," Marlene says, "you have to have a ton of money; and if you don't, you have to have an army of people." Since the Iowa Committee to Stop ERA did not have much money, they had no choice but to take the second option. They decided to form an army of volunteers to ring every doorbell in Iowa. With chairpersons in each of Iowa's ninety-nine counties, they flooded the state with door-to-door canvassers who distributed a brochure detailing the ERA's dangers, including tax-funded abortions, special rights for homosexuals, higher insurance rates for women, and even the abolition of veterans' benefits.

A week before the election, according to a *Des Moines Register* poll, 57 percent still favored the ERA amendment versus 29 percent who were opposed. By election day, the pro-ERA lead had shrunk by eight percentage points—from 48 to 40 percent. The margin in favor, though smaller than ever, was still so comfortable that the pro-ERA forces declared certain victory. On Election Day, Marlene recalls, the media came to her office and asked for her concession statement. But she refused.

The next day, ERA was defeated in Iowa by 58 to 42 percent. As one of Marlene's colleagues put it: "The polls didn't pick up the grass-roots opposition. When you reach the grass roots, you can beat the ERA."

One of the people touched by Marlene's anti-ERA campaign was Jim Rohlfsen. A white, conservative, middle-aged farmer who tends his 240 acres of corn and soybeans in the small town of Le Mars, Jim is a grass-roots citizen of Patria who knows what he stands for and speaks his mind.

"Farming is the original occupation," Jim says. "We need food and fiber. For the time being, it's going to come from the soil. I get satisfaction from starting with nothing every year and producing a crop. There's creation going on—and that doesn't happen in a lot of occupations. Those paper-pushing jobs, accountants and lawyers, don't create anything. Besides, I work for myself. I pay for my mistakes and I reap my own rewards. It works better that way."

Folks in Le Mars, a "conservative" town according to Jim, either farm or work in one of the two large food processing plants. Although he believes his children's economic future is precarious, Jim's greatest worries about his kids concern deteriorating morals. "The world I grew up in—believing in God and raising a family that believes—is disappearing. Because of two-income families, there's not as much volunteerism, and the churches are suffering. Nobody's got time for it anymore. We're all too tired to do it. Sunday morning comes around, and people feel: 'Hey, this is the only morning I can do nothing.' So they stay home."

Jim doesn't belong to any political organizations, but considers himself a conservative. "I don't think we can legislate the answers to our problems," he says, echoing Ronald Reagan and George Bush, both of whom he voted for. "It has to come from ourselves; we have to look after each other. Even here in Le Mars, we've relied too much on government to take care of our problems when we should have looked to each other. What happens with entitlements is that it's easy to say, 'Yes, these people need a chance.' But should they have a *better* chance than the rest of us? Do we need to keep legislating more rights to some people than others? Women have been mistreated, so now we're going to make these laws so that they have a better chance than men. That's going overboard. They're taking rights away from one person in order to give rights to somebody else. Should a woman have a better chance to get a job than a man? That's what happened with civil rights, with quotas and all that." Jim's wife, who is a schoolteacher, agrees, he says, because "she knows that there are differences between girls and boys. You can't legislate that they be the same."

Like many anti-ERA voters, Jim's religious beliefs remain in the background of his conversation. But when they do arise they come forth with emotion. "It's easier *not* to believe now, *not* to have a religion," he says. "People don't think it makes any difference. The churches have contributed to the decline in belief by watering down their beliefs. Take abortion. They used to say flat out it was wrong; now they say, 'Well, maybe it is all right.' The Lutheran church I go to is like that. When I grew up, there was more fire and brimstone. You had to do certain things if you were to have salvation. Now it's watered down; the grace of God will save you no matter what. Well, if you're going to be saved anyway, what's the difference?"

With the decline of religion, Jim thinks too many people are out for themselves. "What worries me most is that people are too concerned about their own individual selves. I see that a lot. That kind of selfishness is definitely on the increase. Even farmers—we're looking at what's good for us, not the country. Everybody cares about what's going to happen to them immediately. That's why Congress has so much trouble passing a law. Everybody has their own lobby. So nothing gets done. Religion used to be a common ground, but not anymore."

By joining to kill the ERA, Jim Rohlfsen felt he was helping to preserve that common ground. Marlene and her colleagues reached Jim Rohlfsen and other Patrians scattered across Iowa and mobilized them to victory. They did so knowing that in every city and town across America other citizens of Patria were praying for their victory. For in the Religious State, "family values" is not a political slogan, but a way of life.

"Family Values" Symbolize Everything Right, True, and Good.

From the perspective of Dr. James C. Dobson and Focus on the Family's affiliates in thirty states, the mother-child bond is "absolutely vital" to the healthy development of children and it must be protected against all the forces which are combining to weaken it. In response to a question from one of his readers, who asks him what happens to kids raised in "various child-care settings," Dobson cites experts, both liberal and conservative, who argue that the role of the mother at home with young children is, and always will be, absolutely crucial.

To those confused women who "are struggling to convince themselves that the state-sponsored child-care centers offer a convenient substitute for the traditional family concept," Dr. Dobson has unequivocal and passionate advice: "It will not work!" Lamenting that in less than a generation "the term 'housewife' has become a pathetic symbol of exploitation, oppression and—pardon the insult—stupidity," he criticizes both radical feminists and the media for "this pervasive disrespect shown to women who have devoted their lives to the welfare of their families."

To varying degrees, Patrians accept what Pat Robertson calls the "biblical model of the family":

> The first head of the family is Jesus Christ. We believe in headship.
> Now, under Jesus is the husband, and the husband is to be the high
> priest of the family. Now the concept of headship . . . is repugnant
> to many in our age, especially those who want to create a unisex so-
> ciety. They say, male equals female, female equals male, therefore
> they are equal and there is no difference. Well, that's not what the
> Bible says.[8]

From this model emerge many of the core Patrian beliefs concerning the rights and wrongs of sexuality, abortion, homosexuality, teenage pregnancy, women's rights, parent-child relationships, child care, and other highly charged social issues.

Since the husband is the "high priest" in the family, it follows logically that his role in the church is also more elevated. The Mormons, for example, haven't hesitated to excommunicate women leaders who have challenged the church's all-male priesthood. "I am an orthodox, believing Mormon and a feminist," said Lavinia Fielding Anderson, one of those excommunicated, "and my church has informed me that those are incompatible categories." The president of the Mormon Women's Forum, Lynn Whitesides, was "disfellowshipped" (one step short of excommunication) for the role her 2,000-member organization played in challenging Mormonism. "If you excommunicate one of us, there will be ten more to step up and take her place," said Ms. Whitesides. "Ex-communicate those ten and there will be a hundred to take their places."[9]

*Decisions About Every Issue, Political As Well As Personal,
Must Be Based on the Holy Word.*

Most Patrian women face such feminist heresies with equanimity. Like Marlene Elwell, they understand that because some women have faced various kinds of discrimination in their lives, they may occasionally succumb to the feminist propaganda so prevalent in the media. But even those who are willing to tolerate feminism feel compelled to draw the line when it comes to homosexuality, which they see not merely as a heresy but as an abomination before the Lord.

"Who does Barbra Streisand think she is, coming here to Colorado and calling me a bigot?" says Warren Miller, infuriated by the Hollywood star's lobbying on behalf of an amendment in Colorado that Warren thought granted privileged status to homosexuals. Even though he was angry, Warren didn't raise his voice, for his years in the oil and gas exploration game, with its cycles of boom and bust, have taught him to keep his emotions under control. But he is confident that media superstars can't get Christians to change their minds.

"She and these other Hollywood hotshots fly in here and tell me and every other Coloradan who voted for Amendment Two that we're bigots. They zip around Aspen and Vail, doing fund raisers and going to parties. They just don't understand the situation, that's all! I got nothing against gays, but sometimes you just have to draw a line. Nowadays, just about everybody is an interest group: blacks, Hispanics, Asians, and Indians. I had no problem with that; I figure they deserve a break. But now there's women too, who want a better shot at jobs and everything. And the handicapped. But when I saw this Amendment Two thing coming down the pike, I said: No way. The way I read it, if that thing passed, then an ordinary guy like me going in for a job would get passed over for a gay guy. And that's going too far. I mean, it's getting to the point where the only folks who don't get special treatment are straight, white guys like me."

Warren is particularly sensitive to the issue of jobs because, after fifteen years in the oil and gas business, he was laid off. To make ends meet, he started driving a cab while going to night school studying heating and refrigeration. He hoped to find a job soon, but the economy had him worried. So he didn't want to be standing at the back of the line, with all the "minorities" ahead of him. "The way I see it," he says, "we used to be one country. We're all citizens, all in this together. But now everybody's climbing onto their own particular bandwagon, trying to get a jump on everybody else. I'm tired of it, and I figure now's the time to draw the line."

Like Warren Miller, Patrians refuse to be intimidated by those who portray them as insensitive, dogmatic, narrow-minded bigots. For instance, gay rights activists and others concerned about the AIDS crisis portray Patrians as indifferent to the suffering of the victims of this cruel epidemic. The truth is, say Patrians, they care profoundly about this health crisis. They believe that if only gays adopted Christian morals and stopped being sinners, the AIDS crisis could be solved very quickly.

Adopting precisely this line of reasoning, Focus on the Family took out full-page ads headlined "In Defense of a Little Virginity." In the ads, the organization charges that network executives "are wringing their hands about this terrible epidemic of AIDS. They profess to be very concerned about those who are infected with sexually transmitted diseases, and perhaps they are sincere. However, TV executives have contributed mightily to the existence of this plague. For decades, they have depicted teens and young adults climbing in and out of each other's beds like so many sexual robots. Only the nerds were shown to be chaste. . . . It all looked like so much fun. But what a price we are paying now for the lies we have been told."[10]

The homosexual movement strikes at the very heart of this "biblical model" of the family. Every aspect of moral family life—marriage, sexuality, parenting, gender roles—is undermined by the gay rights agenda. Even liberal theologians such as Martin Marty, professor of divinity at the University of Chicago, are made uncomfortable by gay demands for legalized, church-sanctioned marriages for lesbian and gay couples. "Call it something else," pleads Marty. "Let them covenant, let them bond, let them promise."[11]

For the most part, Patrians consider the homosexual threat a major assault on their belief system. When the Presbyterian Church (U.S.A.) voted in 1993 to maintain their ban against ordination of homosexuals, they did so to protect the very integrity of their spiritual world view. "What we're talking about here isn't a simple up-or-down matter of one minor part of the church's constitution," said Linda B. Team, an elder at the Central Presbyterian Church in Austin, Texas, who headed the committee that drafted the resolution. "These are issues that touch on every important theological component of our faith from our doctrine about creation to how we use scripture."[12] For this reason, Patrians have fought determinedly to exclude outspoken gays—not only from the U.S. military but from any public gathering in which a homosexual presence would desecrate traditional religious values. Thus the Ancient Order of Hibernians, who host the traditional St. Patrick's Day parade in New York City, and the American Zionist Youth Foundation, who hosted a recent Salute to Israel parade, both tried to exclude homosexual groups from joining in the proceedings.

The homosexual cause represents "the most vicious attack on family values that our society has seen in the history of our republic," according to Republican Congressman William Dannemeyer from California. The desire by gays and lesbians for legal status, not to mention legal protection as a minority, strikes at the heart of Patrian beliefs because it lays the groundwork for homosexual "families." Similarly, the movement for the ERA threatens a direct government assault on this "biblical model" of the family. As we have seen, Marlene Elwell and her fellow citizens believe that the real purpose of ERA is not to help women at all. "Not women as a sex but lesbians and homosexuals need the ERA; and believe me, that's what it's really all about!" writes Patrian crusader Tim LaHaye in *Battle for the Family*. "Homosexuals and lesbians . . . decided early that the feminist movement and the ERA provided them with a handy vehicle to ride piggyback upon women's rights and achieve homosexual rights. Fortunately, citizens who suddenly realized how close we were to the city limits of Sodom and Gomorrah successfully resisted. . . ."[13]

Just As Family Must Fit the Biblical Model, So Must Sexuality, Pregnancy, and Child Care.

At Bob Jones University in Greenville, South Carolina—one of the leading institutions of higher education based on traditional Christian values—home economics professor Diane Hay tells her women students to follow "God's dress-for-success program." This means focusing men's attention on their character, not their legs. "A man's eyes travel from the floor up," says Professor Hay. "A Christian woman wants to do everything she can to draw his eye to her face, because that is where her character is revealed."[14]

A woman's beauty, like her sexuality, should be in the service of God. Thus Focus on the Family placed full-page ads in over 400 newspapers for the purpose of advocating abstinence as the only recommended form of birth control because the group believes that sex before marriage violates God's will. As far as sex education is concerned, Patrians think it is the parents' responsibility, not the schools'. Similarly, the Southern Baptist church, with a membership of almost 15 million—the largest Protestant denomination in the country—devoted much of its 1993 convention in Houston to a highly publicized campaign promoting virginity. Its goal was to have 100,000 pledge cards with the heading "TRUE LOVE WAITS" signed by teenagers within the first year. The pledge card reads: "Believing that true love waits, I make a commitment to God, myself, my family, those I date, my future mate, and my future children to be sexually pure until the day I enter a covenant marriage relationship."

"It's awesome to be a virgin," says seventeen-year-old Baptist David Medford, who signed the pledge in Houston. "I want to give that gift to my wife. I want it to be special, not something I do just to fit in. I think there's a lot of people that are virgins, but they're afraid to come out." Echoed Laura McCalman, also seventeen, who also joined the "TRUE LOVE WAITS" program: "I think a lot of people will be very curious, and it will be very popular. It will become a thing to do. Once you know a hundred kids can do it, you know another kid can do it. It's positive peer pressure."[15]

Although some Patrians favor the use of birth control by married couples to control the number or timing of children they have, they believe that for teenagers abstinence is the only way to prevent unwanted pregnancies. For adult women and teenage girls alike, once a new life has begun inside their womb, it belongs not to them, but to God.

Starting from that premise, destroying one of God's children is murder. It is a sin against the Almighty. Although they do not condone killing abortion doctors or fire bombing abortion clinics, they consider such acts of moral outrage to be inevitable. Faced with the wholesale slaughter of innocent life, some Christian soldiers are bound to respond with violence. But most pro-lifers are not "violent, crazy people," says Nancy Piccione, a spokeswoman for the National Right to Life Committee. They are just people who want America to follow God's word.[16]

The family, in short, is Patria's battle cry. As the Christian Coalition's "Contract with the American Family" makes clear, protecting the American family—as interpreted by Patrians—has implications for almost everything. It provides a basis for changing the school curriculum; abolishing the U.S. Department of Education, the Corporation for Public Broadcasting, and the National Endowments for the Arts and the Humanities; changing the tax code; limiting abortion; denying access to sexually explicit materials; and even rejecting the United Nations Convention on the Rights of the Child.

"Parents have the right to raise their own children," announced Representative Mike Parker (D-Miss.) at the Christian Coalition's press conference in Washington, D.C. Anyone who threatens that basic right will find themselves at war with Patria.

Education |
"A GREAT WAR IS BEING WAGED."

Citizens of the Religious State want to abolish the Department of Education because it symbolizes the secular government's attempt to mold their children's minds. Patrians believe that an anti-Christian bias pervades the public schools. As evidence, they point to studies by government organizations, such as the National Institute of Education (NIE), which concur that public school textbooks "commonly exclude the history, heritage, beliefs, and values of millions of Americans." Particularly, "those who are committed to their religious tradition . . . are not represented." Or, as Dan Quayle put it more graphically, "God has been expelled" from America's schools.[17]

Citizens of the Religious State have responded by trying to take control of their schools. When Patrians in New York became alarmed over what they considered a pro-gay, pro-condom, multicultural liberalism taking over the schools, they launched a drive to elect fellow Christians to the school boards. As part of their strategy, the Christian Coalition of New York asked every candidate to fill out a "candidate issues survey" which would reveal whether or not they subscribed to Patrian beliefs. The first of the four sections on the questionnaire were devoted not to academic or policy issues, but to "parent's rights:"

1. Legislation that grants parents the right to inspect instructional materials and methods.
   _____ Support _____ Oppose _____ Undecided

2. Informing parents on changes in curricula, in writing.
   _____ Support _____ Oppose _____ Undecided

3. Notification of parents before psychologically evaluating a student.
   _____ Support _____ Oppose _____ Undecided

4. Legislation allowing parents to withdraw their children from classes teaching material contrary to their moral values.
   _____ Support _____ Oppose _____ Undecided

5. Parental consent for students to receive condoms in school.
   _____ Support _____ Oppose _____ Undecided

6. Parental consent for students prior to dispensing [sexuality and reproductive health] information to students.
   _____ Support _____ Oppose _____ Undecided

Any candidate who opposed these measures or was undecided—as well as those who refused to complete the questionnaire—was considered by Patrians to be unfit for office.

Parents in Patria feel that they began to lose control over their children's education in 1962 when the Supreme Court—in a session of the Court that opened with a prayer—ruled that prayer in public schools violated the United States Constitution. Widespread public outrage and vehement opposition in the Senate (including the angry protests of Senator A. Willis Robertson, Pat's father) were of no avail. Then came busing to achieve desegregation. To many Patrians, the government seemed determined to steal their children and destroy their neighborhoods, all for the elusive goal of creating some kind of "racial balance." But what outraged Patrian parents even more was government harassment of Christian schools.[18] Unless they did something to stop the encroachment of a godless government in schools, many Patrian parents feared that they might be the last generation of Christians in America.

God-Fearing Parents Must Take Back
Control of the Classroom.

"Read it," Mike Wallace insisted, pointing to a stack of school materials which contained offensive passages.

"No, I won't," Norma Gabler said, pushing aside the materials.

Sitting in Norma and Mel Gabler's living room, flanked by his "60 Minutes" camera crew, Wallace was determined not to let this Texas housewife stonewall him.

"Read it," Wallace repeated.

"No. I won't."

"Read it!"

"No, I won't!"

Frustrated by his war of wills with this woman, Wallace finally handed the book to someone else on the staff. The passage was so obscene, however, that the staff person's reading could not be aired on television.[19]

Mel and Norma Gabler of Longview, Texas, were among the first citizens of Patria to mount the barricades to protect traditional values in education. Their long crusade to bring education back to its Christian roots began in 1961, when they looked at their sixteen-year-old son Jim's textbook and founded it riddled with bias and inaccuracies. When they complained to the superintendent of the Hawkins School District, they learned that local schools were compelled to choose their textbooks from a list approved by the state of Texas.

So the Gablers began organizing. They began speaking up on radio call-in shows. They began writing letters to school officials. Using their 300-person Christmas card list, they sent out their first alert and asked for donations. Before long, concern about textbooks escalated in the state to the point that the Texas House of Representatives appointed an investigative committee and invited the Gablers—Mel, Norma, and their son Jim—to present their testimony. And so began the Gablers' donation-supported organization, Educational Resource Analysts, and with it a crusade for Christian education that continues to this day.

While many citizens in the other Divided States ridicule the idea of a Christian education, Patrians believe that thousands of young people are in desperate need of clear, faith-based training and that the schools should pro-

vide it. One of these young people was a young teenager named Becky Delmonico, who says she once had no purpose in life except partying. She would
drink too much and have a good time, but she realized that she could not go on
with such a valueless existence forever. Then one of her friends joined a Christian organization called The Way.

"My friend was real happy all of a sudden, real peaceful," Becky recalls.
"But I thought she was a religious freak, so I wanted to have nothing to do with
her. She got married, knowing that she couldn't conceive a baby because something was wrong with her. For years, she had made love with men not using
contraceptives because she believed what the gynecologists had told her. But a
couple of months after the wedding, before she knew it, she was pregnant. She
couldn't believe it. Neither could I. It was really a miracle!"

Following in her friend's footsteps, Becky started attending The Way
classes and immediately felt a surge of self-confidence. "It helped me get control over my life. I never felt they were brainwashing me. They were helping
me. I didn't feel like I had to censor what I was feeling. If I felt something, I said
it. My family was thrilled to see the changes in me—just thrilled. They questioned the ministry part of it, but they knew my friends and liked them. They
were just so pleased that I had gotten myself together."

Becky then committed herself further by going to New Knoxville, Ohio,
and joining the Word Over the World (WOW) program. Sent to do her missionary work in a small town in the state of Washington, she discovered that
she could live away from her family and flourish. She was proud to discover
that she was a resilient, independent, responsible person who could go anywhere on her own and make it.

Her real family, however, was worried. Part of her agreement with The Way
was that she would remain exclusively in Washington for one year. Consequently, when her first niece was born, she did not go home to visit. When her
brother graduated from medical school, she was the only one who missed the big
event. She didn't even return home for Christmas. Her repeated absences made
her parents and her brother wonder what was happening to Becky.

When she did go home after the year of mission work, she wanted to be
out on her own. Her life seemed boring, her job held no interest for her, and
she found herself drifting back into her old bad habits. So she returned to the
"family" that she knew best: The Way.

"I really liked the concept of The Way," she says. "I liked the values, the
principles of living, being in tune with God and at peace with myself. I like
the Bible teachings—not always the people, who could be rather arrogant, but

the teachings were beautiful. So I packed up my car and just set out on my own. I would could call up headquarters in Ohio and ask if there was a Way ministry in whatever town I was heading toward. There almost always was. I would be welcomed by loving people, treated like a friend, and after a couple of days I would be on my way again. I traveled around for almost a year having a wonderful time. And I felt blessed to have this network that welcomed me wherever I went. My family had a hard time with it, but they realized that The Way had turned my life around and so they accepted it."

Becky was only one of tens of thousands of young people for whom The Way provided a spiritual education. Like many other Patrian youth organizations, The Way claims to do so in order to protect the minds and souls of children, and although it sometimes divides child against parent, an organization like The Way believes that following the Savior is more important than family ties. Despite their advocacy of "family values," Patrians believe that a Christian education outside the family is better than a secular education within it.

Case studies of school districts, researched and reported by highly respected organizations such as the New York–based Public Agenda Foundation, demonstrate that parents across the country feel increasingly distant and disconnected from their children's public education. "The majority of educators are fearful of the parent who is actually involved," says one parent in the South. Echoes another parent in a suburb of New York City: "The [school] administration is looking to have less involvement by the parents, not more." Parents feel shut out of their children's schooling, and increasingly suspicious of the bureaucrats and teachers who are in charge. The title of the Gablers' book—*What Are They Teaching Our Children?*—says it all. Parents are in one camp; school administrators in the other.

"New Age" Ideas Are Infiltrating Classrooms and Turning Children Against God.

After watching government push Christianity out of the schools, many Patrians now watch aghast as a hodgepodge of half-baked mystical ideas, pseudo-psychological methods, and so-called "spiritual values" enter the vacuum in the classroom. They are shocked to see how, in the words of one Patrian critic of the "Gaian agenda," ecology is becoming "a sacrament, while shamanism, pantheism, feminist spirituality, and science form its foundation." To many Patrians, it seems as though pagan spiritualists are trying "to replace Christmas

Day with Earth Day" and to replace the true God in heaven with the pagan worship of earth goddesses, such as Gaia.[20]

"Environmentalism is the new paganism," says Alan Gottlieb of the Center for the Defense of Free Enterprise in Bellevue, Washington. "Trees are being worshipped and humans sacrificed at its altar. It is evil. And we intend to destroy it." People for the West, an organization with forty local chapters throughout the mountain states, is fighting the Clinton administration's "pro-environmental" policies on land use. They are joined by loggers in Oregon, miners in Nevada, cattle ranchers in the Plains states, as well as scores of snow-mobile clubs, motorcycle dealers, and corporations involved with mineral re-sources and timber. Many Patrians believe that ecology is paganism because it turns nature into an idol to be worshiped, replacing God as the supreme being and opening the door to satanism and witchcraft.

Those Patrians who have carefully researched the literature of the New Age, such as Pat Robertson, clearly recognize the threat that it poses to Chris-tian education. Robertson isolates three "particular ends" advocated by New Age thinking:

1. The subversion and denial of divine revelation.

2. The deification of the self.

3. The submersion of the individual personality.

"Suppose," Robertson says, "that a powerful spiritual being, a supernat-ural force such as Satan, a being who is contrary to God and opposed to what-ever He does, wanted to overthrow the kingdom of God and to install himself in the seat of power. What would be his agenda? How would he go about im-plementing such a plan?" Robertson argues that these three New Age premises— denying God's teaching; turning the individual into God; and then making the individual part of larger whole—are precisely the steps that the forces of Satan would need in order to take over the mind of humanity. And there is no better starting point, of course, than the classrooms of America.[21]

"It is the day of the gods of the occult," warns Robert Simonds, who spearheads both Citizens for Excellence in Education and the National Associ-ation of Christian Educators. "New Age religions are teaching our children how to worship gods other than the true and living God." To fight these forces of godlessness, Simonds has a battle plan for Patrians, which is already under way across America:

> There are 15,000 school districts in America. When we get an active parents' committee in operation in all districts, we can take complete control. . . . This would allow us to determine all local policy: select good textbooks, good curriculum programs, superintendents, and principals.

With more than a thousand chapters across the country, Simonds's Costa Mesa-based organization is one of the most active across the country in making this vision of Christian-controlled education a reality. According to their own data, they have elected 3,500 new school board members who support their cause across the nation in the last five years, and have already had major triumphs in many cities, including New York and San Diego.

In New York, a coalition of Patrian organizations, including the Christian Coalition and Focus on the Family, decided to block adoption of the "Children of the Rainbow" curriculum. Promoted by then New York City schools chancellor Joseph Fernandez—whom Christian groups described as a "darling of the educational elite" and a $195,000-a-year bureaucrat—the curriculum was opposed by Patrians for many reasons. Their most publicized objection was to a fifteen-page section about sexuality, which included the following mandate to teachers and administrators:

> Classes should include references to lesbians/gay people in all curricular areas. . . . Children need actual experiences via creative play, books, visitors, etc., in order for them to view lesbians/gays as real people to be respected and appreciated. Educators have the potential to help increase the tolerance and acceptance of the lesbian/gay community.

A wide coalition of Patrian groups, including the Catholic church and a number of Hispanic and black religious and civic leaders, decided to work together to kill the curriculum and oust chancellor Fernandez. And they did.

As Mary Cummins, president of a local school board and a sixty-one-year-old grandmother, put it, the curriculum backed by Fernandez as well as New York City mayor David Dinkins was "promoting the idea that sodomy is acceptable, virginity is weird." She sent out 22,000 letters to parents inviting them to a demonstration in front of the Board of Education headquarters at 110 Livingston Street in Brooklyn. Then, on the heels of her successful protest, the

Hispanic community organized another demonstration a few weeks later to demonstrate their opposition to Fernandez's leadership. "I do not want them to have that kind of education," Damaris Ortiz, a Brooklyn mother of two, told a reporter. "As a Hispanic, Fernandez should know better." Within a few months, Fernandez was out of a job, and the Rainbow curriculum was dead.[22] Patria had won another battle.

Meanwhile, in San Diego, Patrians moved from opposition to actual control. Again, a coalition—including Simonds's organizations, the Christian Coalition, the California Pro-Life Council, and the Traditional Values Coalition—joined forces to run a slate of "pro-family candidates" for school boards across the country. They campaigned primarily in churches and in other settings sympathetic to their cause. As Steve Baldwin, the young political consultant who helped design their strategy, explained, "There are enough Christian voters out there to win most races if they register and vote for whom they're supposed to vote for."[23]

Of the eighty-eight candidates who ran on the "pro-family" slate in the 1990 election, sixty were elected—a triumph that echoed through every corner of the State of Patria. It gave Christians hope that once again they might live in a nation in which Christian values were honored in every public school classroom in America.

The Media |
"ON YOUR FAVORITE CHRISTIAN STATION"

Seated in the control booth of radio station WSEB, John Higgins swivels his chair in front of the microphone. "Partly cloudy, seventy degrees, winds from the south at ten miles per hour," says Higgins in a deep, bass voice. "Tomorrow, high in the upper seventies. This is WSEB, where you can find music of the world on your favorite Christian station, ninety-one-point-three FM."

Turning back to his guest, he recalls the strange chain of events that brought him to this control room on the west coast of Florida. While not raised in a churchgoing home, Higgins was "born again" at the age of twenty-one. He soon married, had children, and found work with the National Guard in Massachusetts working as a technical advisor, which permitted him time with his family and for his faith. He lived a quiet life until 1982, when—repulsed by the "spiraling taxation and bigger government"—he "sought guidance from the Lord" and was led here to the small town of North Port. Jobless, he prayed to the Lord and asked for guidance, and was told to start "his ministry" in his own backyard. He waited for a sign as to what this ministry should be, and it came, finally, through an incident at his daughter Rebecca's school.

Public Institutions in America Today Discriminate Against Christianity and Favor Secular Humanism.

A fifth-grader at Venice Elementary School, Rebecca asked if she could do a book report on Revelations, the final book in the Bible. Given permission, she decided, as part of her presentation, to give each of her classmates a copy of the New Testament. She received an A on her report, passed out her gifts, and left class proud of herself for doing such a good job. Her next class was mathematics where, according to John, the teacher confronted Rebecca and told her that passing out Bibles was "against the law." Soon the principal became involved, supported the math teacher's position, and prevented Rebecca from passing out Bibles.

The incident caused some of John's neighbors to suggest that he run for mayor. He did, was elected, and was immediately faced by a recall committee formed by citizens terrified by the prospect of having a hardcore Christian running the government. Unable to oust him from his elected position, they changed their strategy: they abolished his office. Instead of having a mayor, the committee put all administrative control in the hands of a seven-person commission, thus reducing John's role to one of seven commissioners.

But John was indefatigable. As the Board of Commissioners of the small town of North Port, Florida, bowed their heads, commissioner John Higgins invoked the Holy Father and asked Him to "guide and direct" their work. "May there be a good spirit among all of us here," John prayed, "as we go about doing the will of the people for the city of North Port. We pray this in Jesus' name. Amen."

The reaction was swift and furious. "After the meeting," John says, "a Jewish lady and an atheist who was a member of the local Unitarian Universalist Church came up and told me that I couldn't do this. 'If you don't cease and desist,' they threatened, 'we will call the ACLU [American Civil Liberties Union] and get their help.' "

The *Tampa Tribune* gave John's critics a chance to be heard. "It's wrong for a commissioner to use his seat as a pulpit for his particular brand of religion," said Charles V. Miller, the man whom Higgins had referred to as an atheist. "It's inappropriate, offensive, and arrogant." Rita Moore, who is Jewish, concurred. "If he wants to proselytize, then let him do it in a proper setting, like a church," she told the reporter. "He can do it on a street corner, if he wants to, but at a public building, just like at a public school, it should be restricted."

But John was defiant. Refusing to be "intimidated by the ACLU or anybody else," he would not excise Jesus' name from his prayers, because, he said, doing so would be "extremely out of character." The other commissioners, however, did not share his convictions (or, if they did, they were unwilling to stand up for them). At their next meeting, the commission chairman insisted on a "neutral-type prayer," i. e., without any reference to a particular religious tradition. John refused to go along with the plan, so the commissioners took a vote and agreed that only the chairperson could pray at every meeting—a prayer, insisted the city attorney, that had no reference to "any particular religious symbol."[24]

John Higgins was not about to be silenced by these legalities. "I feel Jesus Christ, the son of God, is not a symbol," Higgins replied publicly. "He is God." Only the commission's decision to reserve the right to pray to the chairman alone put an end to the controversy. While John remained on the Board of Commissioners, the part-time, underpaid position was not enough to support his family. Besides, he felt he had to find another way to serve the Lord. "Miraculously," he says, he was offered the job of station manager of WSEB.

The Christian station carries a host of commentators, including Dr. James Kennedy, Chuck Swindoll, Dr. James Dobson, Cal Thomas, Reed Irvine, and the Radio Bible Class—all of whom spread the message of the gospels. Seated in front of shelves overflowing with albums, tapes, and CDs of religious music. John's job allows him to spread the Holy Word, support his family, and reflect on the turbulent events he has managed to survive. "I know some people would say that the whole incident was a waste of time. 'Why not just skip the prayer?' they ask. Well, I think it's important that we set a spiritual tone. We are here to do the people's business. We have been entrusted with their faith. It is only fitting that we ask for spiritual guidance. And don't get me wrong. I don't care if a rabbi comes, or a minister or a priest. I'm not going to censor *them*. I just don't want somebody censoring *me.*"

A mild-mannered, soft-spoken man, John prides himself on his openness to non-Christians. He does not want to ostracize those who do not share his faith in Jesus Christ. On the contrary, he says: "They're welcome, of course. But the country that was created by the Founding Fathers was set on a Christian foundation. We *are* a Christian nation. From that point in time, of course, other groups have come in and have become part of our national life. But our country's foundation isn't Buddhist, or Muslim, or Hindu. It's Christian. It was founded on the Holy Bible, not the Koran. There is only one true God, only one Bible. And that is the foundation of our government. God has given us a road map for everything—for finances, for marriage, for everything! All we need to do is follow it."

He sticks in a new tape, gives the station identification, and turns back to his visitors, shaking his head in disbelief. "Can you believe it? The Russians are calling *us* now, asking for missionaries to come and teach about Christianity in their public schools. They're asking us to send Bibles—can you believe it?—when we're not allowed to have them in our own schools! So we extract Christianity from the public schools, and look what happens. Guns coming into the schools. Rapes happening. Unbelievable acts now occur in the classrooms and hallways. It's an outrage! There is only one solution. We must return to godly principles!"

The Mainstream Media Are Motivated by Greed, Rather Than the Holy Word.

The Christian tradition itself is based on words, both spoken and written; on stories told by one generation to the next over the centuries; on hymns sung to the glory of God; and on images, sacred visions of the Lord and Savior Jesus Christ, of the Holy Virgin Mary, and of other religious figures. These words, stories, songs, and images are the vital communications link which have sustained the Christian faith for two millennia. Anyone who traffics in these media is trespassing on sacred ground, Patrians believe, and must be prepared to answer to God.

Patrians know that their children are growing up in a technological, media-saturated environment which bombards their children from every direction and is endangering their souls. "Why is there a dramatic breakdown of morality in our society?" writes Ted Baehr in *Crosswinds,* a magazine dedicated to persuading "Christians everywhere [to do] all they can in the power of the Holy Spirit." His answer, like the answer of most Patrians, is the godless mass media. By titling his article "Reclaiming Lost Territory," Baehr makes clear that the citizens of Patria, using organizations like the Atlanta-based Christian Film and Television Commission, must take back the Word and the Image from the commercial hustlers and put them back in the service of God.[25] They must fight back and smite the serpent before it strikes.

Ken Forester, a retired government worker turned Patrian pamphleteer, is outspoken concerning his feelings about some of the nation's best-known journalists. "Tom Brokaw, Dan Rather, Peter Jennings—they are near deities. But what they're doing has no place for God. So they walk a fine line. They don't want to offend Christians like me. They know they can't push us all the way out because I would ban the box from my house. But now we've got Rush [Limbaugh] on our side, and they're scared of him. Those moguls in entertainment, the press, TV—the biggest threat to them is talk radio. You're going to get more objective viewpoints expressed on talk radio than anywhere else."

Forester was one of 30,000 fans of radio talk show host Rush Limbaugh who descended in the spring of 1993 on the quiet little town of Fort Collins in the foothills of the Rockies for an event called Dan's Bake Sale. The event was triggered in March 1993 by a call to Limbaugh from an unemployed Fort Collins man, Dan Kay. Complaining about being unemployed, Dan said that he simply couldn't afford the $29.95 cost of Limbaugh's newsletter. Always a promoter of free enterprise and self-reliance, Limbaugh suggested that Dan hold a bake sale and told him that he was sure other listeners in the area would help out. And the rest is history.

"*USA Today,* CBS, NBC—all of them ran something on the Bake Sale," Forester says. "A lot was accomplished. Thirty thousand people got sixty million dollars' worth of free advertising. I'd say we're turning the tables on 'em, wouldn't you? Yep, we're fighting fire with fire. It's our media against their media—and we're playing to win."

Next to Bill and Hillary Clinton, the biggest enemy at Dan's Bake Sale was clearly the media, and Limbaugh's fans made it clear that they considered him their White Knight battling the dragons of the mainstream communications industry. One T-shirt illustrated Rush's heroism by depicting a seesaw, with "ABC • CBS • NBC • CNN" on one side, and "RUSH" alone on the other. Underneath was a one-word message: "BALANCE."

Again and again, when Patrians tell the story of what awakened them to action, the catalyst was outrage about the mind-poisoning media. When Pat Robertson tells the story of the birth of his Christian Broadcasting Network, for example, the moment of truth came when he and his fifteen-year-old daughter turned on the television one night to find "scenes of a young man romping in bed with two scantily clad girls." Robertson flicked the television off. "I was infuriated by having this sick behavior invading our home," he wrote in a fundraising letter to his subscribers. "Surely you feel as I do that this sort of thing is *wrong!!*"[26]

Whether in song lyrics on the radio, on billboards by the roadside, in stories plastered across the front page, in prime-time TV movies, or in feature films, Patrians are incensed that the words and images of our culture are not turning us to God but turning us to sin.

The Media Corrode Faith in God and Promote Violence, Lust, and Adultery.

What woke up Dr. Richard Neill, a dentist in Forth Worth, Texas, was the birth of his first child. Before then he seldom watched TV. "I would see this stuff and say, 'This is disgusting,' click off the TV, and fume," Neill recalls. But the birth of his daughter made a difference. He realized that he could defend himself against the onslaught, but that she couldn't. She was young and vulnerable. She needed protection. Richard's first target was "Donahue," which outraged him, not just because of the content, but the timing: nine o'clock in the morning, when small children are often watching TV. "What parent, Christian or non-Christian, would bring a homosexual marriage ceremony or seventy-year-old strippers or lesbian go-go dancers into their home and let the children watch?" Richard asks, dumbfounded. "That's exactly what parents are doing when they let their kids watch 'Donahue.'"

Millions of fellow Patrians have felt the same way. But Richard took action. He began early one summer by contacting the advertisers on the show and asking them to stop supporting it. To strengthen his case, he distributed a twenty-two-minute videotape showing the advertisers the filth he felt they were helping to distribute to the people of America. His modest goal was to cause four sponsors to drop the show by the end of the summer. He now has over ninety letters from local and national companies saying that they won't advertise on "Donahue."

"My friends think this is out of character for me," says Richard. "I'm actually very quiet and shy. I had never been an activist. But the Lord has helped me develop boldness. I'm having a ball."[27]

Patrian activists like Richard naturally consider themselves underdogs when confronting the multimedia multinationals who control the information flow. As the National Right to Life Committee put it in one of their direct mail fund-raising letters: "ABC, CBS, and NBC [have] declared war . . . on the movement. . . . We cannot let a handful of network executives and Hollywood writers, actors, and directors poison America with their godless attitudes, which are anti-religion, anti-family, and anti-life."

35

Viewed from Patria, the news and entertainment media are alien powers, controlled by materialistic, cosmopolitan liberals living in Manhattan or Hollywood who are removed from the ordinary communities in which down-to-earth Americans live their lives. Patrians believe the executives in the communications industry are openly hostile toward them. The only time the news bothers to portray Christian leaders at all is when a scandal erupts. And the only dramas that deal with ministers or priests are those with story lines involving sexual infidelity, corruption, or some other violation of Christian conduct.

The problem, according to Michael Novak, Roman Catholic author and scholar at the American Enterprise Institute, is that the media suffer from "Christophobia." They are afraid of genuine religious feelings. He tells the story about Michael Medved, a movie critic who sympathizes with Patrian concerns, who went to Hollywood parties and asked people what percentage of Americans attended church. Some guessed 1 or 2 percent; others estimated the figure at 10 percent. The actual is number is 43 percent. "But Hollywood doesn't know that," Novak remarks—and, even worse, they don't *want* to know.[28]

The Faithful Must Create Their Own Media, To Spread the Holy Word.

Many Patrians today are members of national organizations guarding against media abuse. Organizations like Morality in Media (founded in 1962 by three clergymen), Accuracy in Media (founded in 1969), and the Parents' Music Resource Center (established in 1985 to monitor rock lyrics) are hard at work trying to stem the tide of misinformation inundating communities across the country. Perhaps the media's most outspoken challenger is Reverend Donald Wildmon, whose American Family Association (and the affiliated Christian Leaders for Responsible Television, or CLEAR-TV) has spearheaded many of the campaigns to boycott shows or otherwise curb media bias. Backed by a membership of "1,700,000 families," Wildmon's American Family Association regularly placed full-page ads in major newspapers exhorting readers to "clean up TV" by boycotting advertisers whose programs have anti-"family values" themes.[29]

In addition, most Christians can now tune in at almost any time of day to religious radio stations and at least one television station providing programming exclusively of, by, and for Patria. Although the organization called National Religious Broadcasters was founded in 1944, it was not until the mid-1980s that it became a powerful market force, with over 1,000 members and reaching an audience estimated in the tens of millions.[30] Pat Robertson's popular Christian talk show "The 700 Club" alone reaches a daily audience of 4.4 million. And despite scandals surrounding individual televangelists, the audience numbers continue to grow.

Every form of communications—newspapers, television, children's books, entertainment parks—is being utilized in Patria to provide alternatives for Christians. Thus Patrians avoid Las Vegas when they want musical and theatrical entertainment, and instead visit Branson, Missouri, where Loretta Lynn, Johnny Cash, Merle Haggard, Roy Clark, and other performers with traditional values come to perform. The shows invariably include gospel segments, as well as old favorites like "God Bless America" and the national anthem. "Branson gets down to the basics of family values," says Louise Mandrell, a singer who appears at the luxurious 4,000-seat Grand Palace in the heart of town, "and it's because a lot of the theaters here are run by families." When one of the taverns brought in some male strippers, recalls Peter Herschend, co-owner of the Silver Dollar City amusement park in Branson, "the sheriff was at the front door saying, 'We don't want that here,' and within seventy-two hours they were gone. We've told our legislators, don't even think about giving this area the authority to have gambling. We're offering squeaky-clean family entertainment, and the public is responding."[31]

Patrians are creating their own electronic and print information flows because they know that it is their sole means of protecting their way of life. Without communication channels, their State is at the mercy of outsiders who at best do not care about their values, and at worst actively seek to undermine them. Pointing to the *New York Times* and the *Washington Post*, Patrians make clear that they do not share the high regard that these publications enjoy elsewhere. They feel the press is not only indifferent to Patria, but is often downright hostile. No incident has been recounted more often in Patria in recent years than the 1993 *Washington Post* story about the Religious Right which referred to Christian activists as "poor, uneducated, and easy to command." The *Post* received 1,500 outraged letters, forcing the writer of the article to apologize and lamely defend himself for having repeated "universally accepted" opinions.

Patrians feel this is not an isolated incident. They believe Christians are frequently slandered by reporters who not only disagree with them, but fundamentally disrespect them too. Patrians avoid the *Village Voice,* for example, because they know it represents fundamentally anti-religious values, and they cannot fail to notice how that newspaper refers to Christians. In one recent article dealing with a successful Christian school board campaign, the writer explained the election results by resorting to stereotypes. He characterized the families in the town—Vista, California—as "middle-class, pull-up-the-drawbridge" types who moved to the "selfish demimonde" of San Diego County to escape big city problems. "Frightened, confused, and angry accountants, real estate brokers, and investment bankers," they are in the writer's view "people who care only about their own comfort and nothing about the nation."[32]

These articles are but two examples of a widespread phenomenon called "Christian-bashing," according to Don Feder, who writes a syndicated column distributed by the Creators' Syndicate. No reputable newspaper today would dare a print a news article, writes Feder, in which Jews were described as "conniving, covetous, and clannish" or blacks were stereotyped as "loutish, lazy, and rhythmical." Arguing that "Christians are the only target left," Feder challenges the media to stop its Christian-bashing once and for all, which he defines as: "(1) ridiculing conservative Christians as benighted and sheeplike; (2) suggesting there's something sinister about political ideas based on scriptural standards, or (3) implying that clergy forfeit their constitutional rights when they don a clerical collar."[33]

Politics |
"PEOPLE WHO THINK JUST LIKE YOU!"

Back at Dan's Bake Sale, two shirtless, muscled college students turned their backs into placards: "RUSH IN '96" was scrawled on Ken Philbrick's back, while his buddy Vince Soteolo's back sported an even bolder message, which seemed to amuse everybody: "RUSH is GOD." If Rush Limbaugh was in heaven that day, it was clear who was in hell: Bill and Hillary Clinton and their liberal cohorts. For the first time in a generation, virtually no mention was made of the Soviet Union or the threat of communism. In it place was a tirade of insults, ranging from sarcastic humor to blunt denunciation, aimed at Washington, D.C.

Politics Is the Struggle Between Good and Evil,
and Christians Are on God's Side.

Despite the political messages, however, the mood was upbeat and lighthearted. "This is just the greatest feeling," said Greg Strope of Saratoga, New York. "Where else could you be among all these people who think just like you?" A quick scan of the crowd supported this view, because everywhere were buttons reading "DITTO HEAD" and subscription flyers for the "DITTO Digest." "DITTO" is now an integral part of the Limbaugh lexicon, which was born on his talk show. "DITTO HEAD" came from a woman who called to say she was in complete and total agreement with him, and said: "I guess I'm just a ditto head."

The other phrase that saturated Dan's Bake Sale was "Ought to Be," which has become Limbaugh's trademark. Many folks were signing up to become members of the "Ought 2 B Society," a nonprofit organization based in Otley, Iowa, which promises to "donate nonoperating funds to charities benefiting conservative, family, and evangelistic organizations."

These amateur efforts only served to emphasize the professional polish of *The Limbaugh Letter,* the publication which ignited Dan's Bake Sale in the first place. In each issue, Limbaugh opens with a long essay challenging one of the Big Government myths he claims are promoted by the mainstream media. In the issue of *The Limbaugh Letter* sold at Dan's Bake Sale, for example, Limbaugh's essay was entitled " 'Neglected' Cities: The Big Lie." Limbaugh debunks the liberal ploy to rip off law-abiding, hardworking citizens. He ridicules federal officials like Housing and Urban Development secretary Henry Cisneros for wanting to give poor Americans an "economic lift" ("They have to lift themselves," admonishes Limbaugh). He scoffs at liberal journalists and government officials for their willingness to promote the big lie that urban problems are a result of federal neglect during the Reagan years.

> As is so typical of liberalism, we are handed a complex and disheartening problem—as defined by them—without any possibility of solving it. The only thing we can possibly do is feel very, very bad. "We're sorry. Sob! Please forgive us! We were heartless and greedy, but now we know better! Tax us, tax us, pleeeeease!"

The problem he says, isn't federal money, but social values. "Why have so many of the things that hold society together crumbled?" Limbaugh asks.

> We have allowed the values that permit people to seize opportunities—self-discipline, hard work, responsibility—to be ridiculed. Instead, we have handed people excuse after excuse: they have been victims, they have been oppressed, they have been disadvantaged. And, naturally, what is needed is more dollars.

Don't be fooled by complicated, convoluted arguments about how to rebuild America's "declining infrastructure," he warns his readers, because such phrases are just another liberal effort to separate them from their hard-earned money. He concludes: "My friends, when you hear this administration using the term 'infrastructure' watch out. It's a very long way to spell pork."

Limbaugh's ardent fans also admire him, of course, because America loves an underdog. In their view, their hero is outnumbered a thousand to one by the media establishment. Like Rambo alone against a squadron of Viet Cong guerrillas, Rush is facing an army of high-tech mainstream liberal journalists, and speaks out fearlessly in the face of what seem to be the overwhelming odds.

Politicians Can't Be Trusted—
But Conservatives Are Less Dangerous Than Liberals.

Though votes from many of the geographical states are needed to put someone in the White House, Patrians like those in Fort Collins were responsible for electing three consecutive Republican administrations. With the help of the other Patrians we have met—Jim Rohlfsen and Marlene Elwell in Iowa, John Higgins in Florida, the Gablers in Texas, and their friends across the country—Ronald Reagan and George Bush gave Patria a strong and powerful voice in Washington.

"When a person goes into the voting booth," George Bush said during the heat of the 1988 election, "they're going to say, Who has the values I believe in?"[34] With the exception of the 1992 election, which took place during a sharp recession, the Republican Party has been far more successful than the other parties in targeting the values of America as a whole, and Patria in particular.

The Heritage Foundation, an influential Washington think tank, focused a recent fund-raising letter around three themes which directly touch the heart of Patria:

1. Congress Doesn't Represent You Any More.

2. The Media and Cultural Elites Hold You in Contempt.

3. Government Education is a Total Disaster.

As the Heritage fund-raising letter indicates, the politics of Patria draws on the energy of its citizens' desire—in the fund-raising letter's phrase—to have "effective representation in Washington *for the principles you believe in.*"

Unlike the eighties, when scandals toppled such leading Patrians as James Bakker and Jimmy Swaggart, today ordinary citizens of the State of Patria are asserting their power. Some are doing so at the local and state level; others as national spokespersons for major organizations like the Christian Coalition, Forum for the Family, the National Council of Christian Educators, Concerned Women of America, and the Eagle Forum. But at whatever level they may choose to work, activists in the state of Patria are clear about their goal. It is not, they say, to achieve personal power, but to express their faith in God.[35]

From the perspective of Patria, it is not their State which is trying to impose its belief on others, but the converse: those who are anti-Christian are imposing their secular, amoral views on God-fearing, law-abiding families. "It's important sometimes to remember just who's pushing whom," wrote Tom Minnery, vice president for public policy at Focus on the Family, in an editorial for that organization's magazine *Citizen,* in which he itemizes the ways in which Patrians feel they have been pushed around by the other States. It was not Christians, he argues, who imposed their anti-abortion views on all the States by a single decision in 1973. "No, it was the Supreme Court." It was not Christians who have tried to impose the view that "full-time motherhood is a life of drudgery from which all progressive women must escape." It is not Christians who told children that they "cannot start the day in prayer and the Ten Commandments cannot hang on classroom walls." It is not Christians who advocate "constitutional protection to bizarre forms of sex, men with men and women with women, even when these practices spread diseases, one of which is lethal and the others debilitating." And he concludes:

> Christians are not imposing their views on society. Christians are seeking to restore to society the traditional views that have, until now, undergirded the country, but are being eroded by philosophical viewpoints carried into the marketplace by those who reject Christian values. . . . We are not pounding Christianity into people. The Christian faith is worthless if it is not voluntary. But it is the shared national values that stem from Christian tradition that all must assent to if the country is to remain vital.[36]

The Secular State Is Not Legitimate,
and Good Christians Must Resist Its Authority.

Let us not confuse the State of Patria with the local militias. The differences between them are crucial. While the Christian militias and mainstream citizens of Patria share a powerful common bond—belief in the Bible—their attitudes toward violence and democracy differ sharply.

For hard-core militia members, voting conservative is an empty gesture. While they may sympathize with Patrians' desire to rebuild the government on a Christian foundation, this militant minority believe that the political system has become so corrupted and so secular that it no longer deserves the allegiance of true Christians. They further believe that democracy is in crisis and that armed warfare may be required to restore it.

Long before anti-government terrorists killed 164 Americans in Oklahoma City, groups calling themselves Christian Patriots were organizing across the nation, particularly in the Midwest and West. "This is probably where the war is going to begin, right here in Montana," a member of the Militia of Montana told a visiting journalist. A member of a "Christian covenant community" just across the border in Idaho fears the godless government bears the "mark of the beast," a phrase from Revelations, the last book of the Bible, signifying forces aligned with the Devil. James (Bo) Gritz, a leading figure in the militia movement, named his Christian Patriots community in Kamiah, Idaho, "Almost Heaven" because, its residents believe, they are one of the outposts of Christianity in an otherwise secular state. In his speeches and newsletters, this former Green Beret, whom the *New York Times* called "perhaps the closest thing the militias have to a true leader," combines scriptures and survivalism, the Holy Word and high-tech weapons.[37]

Like the original patriots who liberated America from British tyranny, the Christian Patriots believe that armed insurrection is a legitimate tool in the defense of liberty. When a bag of explosives ripped a hole through the headquarters of the Bureau of Land Management in Reno, Nevada, and when a few months later a pipe bomb exploded at an office of the U.S. Forest Service just around the corner from the state capitol in Carson City, these events received little news coverage. In the big cities, they were dismissed as the isolated actions of cowboy ranchers against government regulation of Western lands. But in fact, the resentment runs far deeper.

"This is a war and we're choosing up sides," Gene Gustin told 350 men, women, and children at a "Win Back the West" rally in Elko, Nevada. Chairman of the public lands advisory board, Gustin told the cheering crowd that what was at stake is "whether we'll live as a free society." Echoes Nevada rancher Wayne Hage: "It's the same old battle of 1776 and before, whether free people will exist or we'll be serfs under an elite class that is destined to rule."[38]

Many of the Christian Patriot militias believe that there will soon come a time, according to their reading of Revelations, when those who wear the "mark of the beast" will try to dominate ordinary, God-fearing Christians. When this time of apocalypse comes, decent law-abiding Christians must be prepared to pick up their rifles, and like the Minutemen who fired the "shot heard 'round the world," defend their land and their liberty. The difference between the unarmed Patrians and their armed brethren in the militias is one of strategy, not philosophy. When militia leader Ralph Turner tells ABC News that he and his confederates are part of "the army of the Lord" which is "God's front line against a godless federal government," he takes his military metaphor literally. Ordinary Patrians don't.[39] Unlike many militia members, Patrians neither seek or expect massive violence. But far more than the citizens of the other Divided States which we are about to visit, they understand and empathize with the frustration that leads militant Christians to take up arms.

Religion Should Not Be Separate from the State;
It Should Be the Foundation of the State.

Traditionally, when builders laid the foundation for a house, the first stone that was placed in the earth was called the "cornerstone." It was the stone from which all other measurements would follow. Based on its position, the other corners of the structure could be determined accurately and a sound, stable foundation could be constructed.

If Patrians were to describe their State's calling in the simplest terms, they would see it as a cornerstone. This State believes its mission is to rebuild the foundation of America so that once again it is aligned with a cornerstone of morality. This is why Patrians do not apologize for their moralism, but are in fact proud of it. They do not believe progress and permissiveness, tolerance and open-mindedness, humanism and "alternative life-styles" will ever make a strong foundation for society. At every level of the social order—from the individual and family to the community and the nation—a strong foundation based on fundamental moral precepts is essential.

43

If the cornerstone is misaligned or is missing altogether, the social structure will never be sturdy or safe. No matter how much the GNP may grow, no matter how big our army or how sophisticated our technology may be, the United States of America can never fulfill its destiny if its very foundation is flawed.

In many different walks of life, and with many different voices, Patrians are calling Americans back to this Christian cornerstone. They are exhorting the citizens of the other States to remember the place of morality in our lives, and warning them of the punishment and pain that awaits them if they do not see the light. They yearn for a resurrection of religious faith as the guiding force in public life as well as private. They want all Americans—not just Christians, not just conservatives, but everyone—to subscribe to their view of public morality. Pragmatically, they do not expect 100 percent obedience. But they expect a high enough percentage of Americans to agree with their agenda—"75, 80, 85 percent," as Newt Gingrich put it—so that they will be able to make the country follow Jesus' footsteps. They are fighting for what they believe and to achieve their goal in the halls of power: to ensure that God's word will be heeded on earth as it is in heaven.

2

CORPORATIA

The Capitalist State

Core belief:	Economic growth enriches society and makes progress possible.
Defining events:	Industrial, Technological, and Telecommunication revolutions.
Sacred text:	Adam Smith, *The Wealth of Nations;* George Gilder, *Wealth and Poverty.*
Primary organizations:	The corporation.
Spokespersons:	Warren Buffett, Bill Gates, Louis Rukeyser, Malcolm Forbes, Jr., Lee Iacocca, and other corporate CEOs and successful entrepreneurs.
Electronic media:	CNBC, Blumberg Financial, the stock "ticker."
Periodicals:	*Fortune, Forbes, Wall Street Journal, Inc.*
Advocacy groups:	U.S. Chamber of Commerce, National Association of Manufacturers, American Management Association, American Enterprise Institute, The American Petroleum Institute, American Tobacco Institute, and other industry associations, corporate lobbyists.
Educational lobbyists:	Wharton School of Management, Harvard Business School, and other business schools.
Ultimate authority:	Annual report, the balance sheet, the stock indexes, price/earning ratio.
Quote:	*"If there is a power elite in the United States, perhaps the most interesting thing about it is that anyone with sufficient talent can join."*
	—Henry Steele Commager, *Freedom and Order*

I N CORPORATIA, the Capitalist State, the citizens believe that a free market based on growth, competition, and profits is the economic wellspring
of a humane, progressive civilization. Without a free market, they warn,
our civilization will be undermined. Capitalism succeeds not just for the benefit
of individuals, but for the benefit of society as a whole. Therefore, Corporatians think, their core beliefs should be the foundation of our society. Because
the private sector is the engine of progress, according to citizens of the Capitalist State, the leaders of the private sector should set the country's course.

From Henry Ford to Lee Iacocca, from CEOs of multinational corporations
to successful pioneers of small start-up enterprises, the leaders of Corporatia consider themselves to be creators of value. While the beliefs of mainstream corporate executives and small-scale entrepreneurs differ in important ways, they both
share a faith in capitalism. They work with the raw materials of our economy—
money, people, and resources—to make the whole more valuable than the sum of
its parts. Consequently, products and services created by the enterprises of Corporatia have emerged victorious in marketplaces throughout the world.

Corporatia is a State which believes in its heroes. Although some of the heroes are well known in history, such as Rockefeller, Carnegie, Ford, and Mellon,
many others, like J. R. Simplot of Idaho (who became a millionaire potato
farmer) and Richard Warren Sears of Minnesota (who co-founded Sears, Roebuck) are not. Today, names like those of MicroSoft's Bill Gates and Chrysler's
Lee Iacocca are known far beyond the borders of Corporatia itself. But thousands
more—like Mary Rodas, a Latina teenager whose marketing genius with toys
made her a millionaire, or Steve Davies, the owner of a computer repair company
who helped his clients postpone costly new purchases—have become highly successful entrepreneurs, even during hard times, without public notice.[1]

Whether famous or unknown, the citizens of Corporatia share the can-do
philosophy of *The Little Engine That Could,* the children's story about a train
engine that, against all odds, pulled a heavy load of toys up a steep hill, and of
Horatio Alger's heroes, who, through perseverance and sweat and toil, pulled
themselves up by their bootstraps. Their philosophy is well expressed in the
advice given by an old Italian immigrant to his grandson Lido: "You could be
anything you want to be, if you want it badly enough and are willing to work for
it." The grandson, Lee Iacocca, went on to work his way up to the presidency
of Ford Motor Company, revive the Chrysler Corporation from near bankruptcy, rescue the Statue of Liberty from disrepair, and write a best-seller. The
values of Corporatia are also exemplified by executives such as Peter Ueber-

roth, who built a $300 million company from scratch, organized the highly profitable 1984 Olympics, became commissioner of baseball, and then tackled the Herculean job of rebuilding riot-scarred South Central Los Angeles; and by Steve Jobs, who built Apple Computer and became a multimillionaire before the age of thirty.[2]

Our Beliefs Are Not Just Theoretical; They Are Practical and Produce Results.

From the perspective of their capitalist State, these Corporatian entrepreneurs have made their fellow citizens an extraordinary gift: they created value and fueled progress. Corporatian belief systems are grounded in real results: they put bread on the table; they create cars that run faster and sell for a lower price; they manufacture clothes that last longer and look better; they create roads that don't crack, roofs that don't collapse, and buildings that weather earthquakes. They create computers that accelerate learning and pharmaceuticals that save lives. They provide jobs for workers, stock options for executives, and wealth for an entire society. In their opinion, Corporatia generates the riches and the opportunity on which all the other States depend.

In addition to the legions of executives of major corporations, Corporatia's citizens include the thirty million hardworking entrepreneurs and business people who made post–World War II America the world's greatest economy. They are the men and women who start more than half a million new companies annually. As George Gilder salutes these entrepreneurs in *The Spirit of Enterprise,* "they are the heroes of economic life . . . movers and shakers, doers and givers, brimming with visions of creation and opportunity." They are visionaries "who see in every patch of sand a potential garden, in every man a potential worker, in every problem a possible profit." Although they clearly have an economic self-interest, says Gilder, they are "impelled by their curiosity, imagination, and faith." They are "the hope of the poor and . . . the redemption of an oppressed and desperate world."[3]

For rendering this service to humankind, the leading citizens of Corporatia are rewarded by living well and building personal wealth. According to the Claritas Corporation's forty-category "PRIZM cluster system" of American life-styles, successful Corporatians live in the top three zip codes, putting them in the top quarter of the American population in terms of income, home value, and educational level. The areas they live in, which Claritas calls by such names as "Blue Blood Estates," "Money and Brains," and "Furs and Station Wagons," are enclaves of success.[4]

Success Is a Ladder, Society a Hierarchy, and Getting to the Top Is the Most Sensible Goal.

The Claritas zip code analysis is a vertical ranking of all communities, clustering each in one of forty categories ranging from the most attractive and successful (ZQ #1: "Blue Blood Estates") to the poorest, least successful and least desirable (ZQ #40: "Public Assistance"). As Michael Weiss (who lives in a "Money and Brains" neighborhood in Washington, D.C.) analyzes the communities in *The Clustering of America,* they form a ladder with rungs ascending from the bottom to the top, from the worst communities to the best. In an appendix called "Where Do You Fit In?" he helps his readers figure out where their communities stand in his ranking. "One day . . ." Weiss says, "you may live in the millionaires' enclave of Blue Blood Estates and no longer wonder how you measure up. You'll know you've reached the top."[5]

From the Corporatian perspective, no segment of the population contributes more to society than the executives of the Capitalist State. Successful entrepreneurs feel they should therefore live in good-quality neighborhoods; should enjoy the comforts of country clubs and health clubs; should eat expensive food and subscribe to high-end periodicals. They have to take care of their bodies and their minds because they are leaders. They are producing the new ideas, products, and organizations that bring prosperity. No matter where they live—be it a ranch in Montana or a houseboat in Key Largo—they view themselves as the economic backbone of America.

The core beliefs of the Capitalist State coalesce around several key concepts: *growth,* a belief in economic expansion; *competition,* a belief in the efficiency of free markets and ever-changing technology; *profit,* a belief in entrepreneurial control over capital; and *liberty,* the freedom to buy and sell without outside interference.

Although these four interlocking beliefs may be expressed in the language of economics, they reach into every aspect of American life. The fourth belief, liberty, is particularly important to small-scale entrepreneurs, who often dislike big business as much as they dislike big government.

Growth |
"EVERY TIME A CASH REGISTER RINGS"

When Henry Ford doubled workers' wages in 1914 to an unprecedented level—$5 a day—stockholders chastised him for being too generous. The *Wall Street Journal* mocked him for "putting Biblical teachings in places where they don't apply." But Ford did it anyway. While raising wages, Ford lowered the price of an automobile farther and faster than anyone else could possibly imagine. He was able to do so for one main reason: growth.

Although economic models can become so complex that economists lose their way, the moral of Henry Ford's story is easy to grasp: economic growth helps everyone. For example, each year between 1909 and 1917, the number of Model T cars rose, and their price fell:

YEAR	NUMBER	PRICE
1909	12,292	$950
1910	19,293	$780
1911	40,402	$690
1912	78,611	$600
1913	182,809	$550
1914	260,720	$490
1915	355,276	$440
1916	802,771	$360

Ford made this possible by reducing the time required to assemble the 500 different components of the Model Ts from twelve and a half hours to two hours and thirty-eight minutes, and did so within one year. In following years, the time was reduced to an hour and a half.[6]

Although Gottlieb Daimler invented the car engine in Germany, and the French first put such an engine in a car frame, it was Henry Ford and his associates who brought cars to the people. By 1926, 85 percent of the world's cars were made in America. Henry Ford's ideas were superior—and the fortune he made proved it. Like Ford, the aim of Corporatians is to prove that their business methods are more efficient, more productive, and more profitable than any others. What better evidence is there of their success, they say, than dollars and cents?

Economic Growth Is the Practical Foundation
on Which Human Values Depend.

The marvels of economic growth, Corporatians argue, depend on optimism and confidence, which fuel expansion. The news that a major company is coming to town, for example, can bring almost automatic growth to the area. When Mercedes-Benz decided to open a $300 million manufacturing plant in Vance, Alabama (population 248), the town immediately began attracting other new businesses. Land prices doubled overnight. The same process occurred in Spartanburg, South Carolina, when BMW decided to open a major manufacturing plant there. Previously inexpensive agricultural land was suddenly selling for $20,000 to $30,000 an acre. Similarly, after Toyota announced the opening of its plant in Georgetown, Kentucky, the price of farmland once valued at $1,000 to $2,000 an acre went as high as $50,000. Such skyrocketing land prices are but one signal that the promise of growth can, in Corporatia, be a self-fulfilling prophecy.[7]

"Every time a cash register rings," concludes one of the perennial Mobil Oil Corporation advertisements, "it creates a ripple that eventually builds into a tidal wave of economic activity." More than 10,000 Mobil ads have appeared weekly in more than one hundred newspapers for the past quarter century. They clearly articulated the Corporatian philosophy of economic growth to an audience of millions. As this particular ad underscores, this "tidal wave of economic activity" helps everybody. In a five-year period, Mobil grossed almost a hundred billion dollars. This fortune did not stay in Mobil's pockets, the ad copy explains. On the contrary, $9 billion went to salaries for its employees across the country; over $10 billion went to vendors, who in turn paid their own employees; almost $6 billion went out in dividends to Mobil's 200,000 U.S. shareholders; and $600 million was paid to federal and state governments, on its employees' behalf, in unemployment and Social Security taxes.

These figures, argues Mobil executive Ray Vaughn, a forty-year veteran at the company who is responsible for Mobil's innovative "advertorial" program, demonstrate that growth is just as good for America as it is for Mobil Oil. In the words of another of their ads, "Growth is not a four-letter word."

Big Business Yields Great Benefits for All,
Yet the Public Takes It For Granted.

"Most people just don't understand large corporations," Vaughn says. "They look at big business as if it is a giant, amorphous, impersonal thing. But a company like Mobil is, in fact, thirty thousand ordinary, individual people. They live in your neighborhood; their kids play with your kids; they coach your Little League teams. When they come to work, they do what the company needs to do to meet its responsibility to its stockholders."

Vaughn has long battled anti-business stereotypes. "If you were asked on a poll if you wanted to help (a) big business or (b) small business, which box would you check? You'd check (b), right? In America nowadays, if it's big, it's bad. And that's truly unfortunate, because, as we've tried to make clear in our columns, the money that comes in to Mobil goes right back out again. The dollar and change that you pay for a gallon of gasoline doesn't stay in our pockets. It moves right back out into every corner of our society."[8]

In another ad, entitled "Facing Facts," Vaughn and his colleagues challenge the government to follow the Corporatian philosophy. The ad explains that expenditures by the U.S. government from 1980 to 1992 increased by 137 percent, while during that same period revenues increased only 95 percent. The Corporatian authors of the ad are clear: the government should not raise taxes; it should stop spending so much.

"It's tragic that in our country business and government are in such adversarial positions," Vaughn says. "In Japan and Germany, they work more in concert than we do. I don't know why. Maybe it goes back to the Great Depression, when government felt that it needed to get in the face of business. I understand that. Early in the century, big business made mistakes. Regulation was needed. But now we've gotten the message that we have to more careful. And we are—not just in terms of the environment, but also regarding the community. We—Mobil—spend $1 billion a year protecting the environment. We do a lot—and still the government and the media try to portray us as just out for ourselves."

*The Private Sector Creates Values;
the Public Sector Feeds Off It.*

"When it comes to taxes, our position is clear: we think we manage money better than the government does," says Mr. Vaughn. "We know we are more efficient. A dollar that stays with us will be better used than a dollar that goes to Washington. Unfortunately, 'profits' has become a political word. 'Windfall profits' is even more of a red flag. People forget that our profits are reinvested, not just in R and D, but in new equipment, new exploration, and so on."

Naturally Corporatians dislike being perceived as so mesmerized by profits they care nothing about society at large. As evidence, they point to the way in which remarks by arbitrageur Ivan Boesky, in his University of California commencement address, were taken out of context. "I think greed is healthy," Boesky said. "I think you can be greedy and still feel good about yourself." As Boesky later explained, success allows one to "take the role that nobility played in ancient times, by becoming involved in the arts, politics, science, and culture for the betterment of mankind." Greed breeds growth and progress.[9]

When the U.S. Food and Drug Administration (FDA), eager to crack down on what it saw as unfair claims by pharmaceutical companies, charged that the corporations involved were motivated by greed, not the health of consumers, *Forbes* magazine immediately jumped to the industry's defense. "The FDA's David Kessler wants to liberate us from greedy corporations," ran the article's opening line. "But who will liberate us from the FDA?"[10]

The word "liberate" reveals much about Corporatia's perspective, because it underscores the widespread belief in this State that government undermines the genius and productivity of the private sector. Unlike government, which Corporatians see as lazy and inefficient, the private sector—the institutional backbone of Corporatia—is hardworking and highly efficient. The difference, from the Corporatian perspective, is simple: competition.

Competition |
"THE HIGHEST POINT OF EFFICIENCY"

Every modern society wants economic growth, but not every society achieves it, and the primary reason is competition. Too many societies, argue citizens of this State, are top-down societies, with dictators, tribal chiefs, or socialist bureaucrats making decisions. Societies that don't have free markets, based on competition, become stagnant and inefficient. Only economies that pit one enterprise against another can be assured of growth, and only economies that allow the strongest enterprises to eliminate the weakest will become truly prosperous. It is a war of markets, with both casualties and victors. Instead of battlefields, the marketplace. Instead of scouts, innovators. Instead of generals, CEOs.[11]

From the top brass at corporate headquarters to the middle-level manager to the worker on the assembly line, Corporatians believe in competition. They believe in it because it fosters profits, growth, and innovation.

Competition Inspires Greatness, Punishes Laziness,
and Makes the System Work.

During the mid-eighties, Rich Tosi was cost-reduction coordinator at the AC Rochester plant in Milwaukee. A division of General Motors (GM), the AC plant's job was producing catalytic converters. "Because of the environmental pressures, it was one of the biggest growth industries in automotive components," says Tosi, who began working there in 1973. "I felt this was a great place to work, not just because we were working for a prestigious American corporation, but because we were helping to clean up the air."

Faced with increasing competition, particularly from the Japanese, the AC plant became panicked because it was consistently running over budget. One day Rich's boss said to him, "We're overspending our budget. Would you take on the challenge of reducing our costs?"

"We were driven by the fear that if AC was losing money," Rich says, "GM would go elsewhere to get the converters, and we'd go under." So Rich agreed to become cost-reduction coordinator, and began what he feels was the most exciting time of his twenty-year career at GM. A former Marine, with ten years in uniform including a tour of duty in Vietnam as an airborne electronic countermeasures officer, he knew how to put together a team and eventually persuaded representatives from each of the plant's major areas to target specific goals to reduce costs.

"We set a goal of saving half a million dollars a month," Rich says. "We had regular meetings every Friday afternoon. It became the fun meeting, and we got stuff done." The "stuff" they did saved the AC plant $5 million to $10 million a year, which amounted to about 5 percent of the operating budget. The news traveled like wildfire throughout the GM system. "From across the country, top GM brass started arriving to check out what was happening. One week it was a plant manager from Texas. The next week it was a group of divisional accountants from Flint. Everybody was coming around, amazed at what we were doing. It felt great to be recognized and honored by other men who were so high in the corporation. I was chairman of the whole operation. I felt I had achieved something significant."

The experience made Rich proud to be part of Corporatia because it was a victory for everybody, not just for himself. For the people who worked in Milwaukee, it meant job security. For the consumer, the catalytic converter would now cost less. And for the company, Rich's achievement taught the corporation "how to do it better." As Rich says, "We had proven ourselves."

When he retired from his position as a competitive analyst at GM after twenty years with the company, Rich Tosi was still proud he had risen to the challenge. "A lot of people talk about how competition is destructive. But my experience then was that competition was not only necessary but good. Without competition, you can get lazy and fat. Competition keeps you on your toes, moving, learning. Although the fear that you will get eaten up if you're not competitive can be uncomfortable, it inspired us. It inspired us to be the best we could be."[12]

From the top to the bottom of industry, a belief in competition as the ultimate economic cure-all guides behavior. When asked why the private sector is so much more efficient than its government counterparts, Mobil's Vaughn replies: "Competition, plain and simple. The feds don't have to be efficient; they have a monopoly on the services they provide. If we don't improve our efficiency and our competitor does, he'll put us out of business. If the government isn't efficient, it just raises our taxes."

Henry Ford said in his autobiography that what makes the American economy great is not just the raw materials and the technology, but our belief system. Reflecting on his achievement, Ford wrote:

> Our policy is to reduce the price, extend the operations, and improve the article. . . . Although one may calculate what the cost is, and of course all of our costs are carefully calculated, no one knows what a cost *ought* to be. One of the ways of discovering . . . is to name a price so low as to force everybody in the place to the highest point of efficiency."[13]

Dig beneath the surface of any business success story, say citizens of Corporatia, and you will find someone spurred on by competition to find this "highest point of efficiency."

By the time Iacocca retired in 1992, he symbolized American competitiveness. "Some guys operate best in a crisis," Iacocca told reporters at a farewell gathering celebrating his retirement. "When you're near death, you're focused."

Iacocca was referring to his rescue of the Chrysler Corporation from bankruptcy. First, he secured a $1.2 billion loan to keep Chrysler from going bankrupt. Then, in record time, he built it back into a highly profitable company and along the way spearheaded the minivan explosion, which led to Chrysler accounting for 55 percent of all minivan sales in the U.S.

Iacocca believes so deeply in competition that he has become convinced his major mistakes occurred when things became too easy. When Chrysler had become profitable and he was a household name, he slowed down. As he put it: "When you get into an up-cycle you don't keep up the heat as much; you get a little fat." What makes a company great, and what makes a man aspire to greatness, is competition—when the "heat" is on. Otherwise, a person—like the economy as a whole—can get lazy and fat.[14]

Growth, Competition, and Efficiency
All Depend on Constant Innovation.

"I love my work," says H. Donald Nelson, president of United States Cellular Corporation. "I'm creating freedom. I'm creating choices. A farmer out on his tractor in the middle of a field in Iowa can now talk to anybody, can be *connected* to anybody. If I want to watch a ball game, I can watch a ball game whenever I want. In almost any city there's a ball game on at almost any time. I'm not being programmed from any central authority. I'm making my own free independent choices. The global village is finally coming to everybody. The world is opening up. Our horizons are global. Everybody has access to everything."

Don is a man with a mission, one which began more than a quarter century ago when he visited the New York City Coliseum and saw Sputnik, the Russian satellite. He was amazed, he recalls, "that even in that oppressive environment they had that kind of intensity and creativity."

Early in Don's career, he started up Texas Instruments' calculator business, which taught him a lesson he never forgot. "People always go crazy when it comes to technology. Even the calculator people were opposed to it. Teachers would say, 'This is horrible. Now children won't learn their times tables.' But people have to adapt. There's nothing wrong with a calculator. I've been to the Consumer Electronics Show for the last thirty years. Change and innovation—that's *the* game."

Fortunately for U. S. Cellular, Don is an expert at the game. U. S. Cellular had annual revenue increases of 68 percent over the last three years, and although the cellular industry is only nine years old, it now serves over eleven million customers and generates over $7.8 billion in revenue. In the spring of 1993 U. S. Cellular celebrated a major milestone: its 200,000th customer. Considering that operations began only in June of 1985, and that in May of 1990, the company had reached only its first 50,000 customers, this is a remarkable growth rate. This growth is further evidence to Don that his work is the wave of the future. In the consumer electronics field, cellular telephones and VCRs are the "fastest-growing products ever."

Don believes progress is part of his family background. "My grandparents never got past elementary school. My parents were immigrants—laborers—and never got past high school. I'm a Northwestern MBA. That's progress, isn't it? Sure, we pay a price for progress, but it's a price worth paying. We know that there are risks involved with things like smoking or nitrates in our foods, but we still use them. My father, even after he knew he had cancer, had to have bacon and eggs fried in butter every morning. He was a common man in the Chicago stockyards. At four-thirty he'd start the day with three eggs and four pieces of bacon. That was a risk and he took it."

Although Don considers himself a religious person, he says that he simply "can't buy the fundamentalists' arguments most of the time." Born and raised a Lutheran, he fell in love with and married a Presbyterian. "Since we had to merge our beliefs, we decided to become Methodists. The fundamentalists have to evolve. Things change. We have to change with them. I've read [Alvin] Toffler's *Future Shock* and [John] Naisbitt's *Megatrends*. The message is clear. You have to throw out the old and welcome the new. It's the only way."

As a CEO, Don has personally experienced the deep resistance to innovation in some parts of our culture. Although the industry is young, U. S. Cellular weathered its first storm when it withstood what Don calls a "smear campaign" spreading the idea that cellular phones are health hazards. What causes the many false alarms about technology's dangers, Nelson believes, is fear of change. "There are always rumors about the dangers of new technologies. They're almost always bullshit. I know that cellular phones present no risk at all."

*The Costs of High Technology Are Vastly Outweighed
by Its Extraordinary Benefits.*

Recently Don received a letter came from David Shipler, a Pulitzer Prize–winning journalist who lives part of the year in his summer home overlooking Mackerel Cove in Ellsworth, Maine. His letter was a plea asking Don to remove, or lower, a 300-foot transmitting tower that U. S. Cellular had installed, on Swan's Island. It had flashing lights, and it disrupted David's view and that of his neighbors. Shipler argued that the tower destroyed the skyline, which consisted of spruce trees, a church steeple, and the lighthouse.

Although Don had a secretary draft a conciliatory note, he felt little sympathy for David, who he thought was more interested in the past than the future.

"My wife is an antique dealer," Don says. "We love going out to antique shows and seeing the beautiful old things from previous eras. But it's not reality. We love the past, but we *really* love the future. What I wonder about Mr. Shipler and people like him is: are they facing the future or the past? Whenever we find a new technology, we have to change. But some people can't change, or won't. Everything new creates problems. I visited the Henry Ford Museum recently and was reminded of all the resistance to the automobile. Of course when we got rid of the buggies and went to cars, it created problems. But it also brought us a whole new world. To people like that writer I would say: 'Think not of thyself, think of the children and grandchildren.' "

*Technology Is Not a Dangerous, Alien Force,
But a Vital and Healthy Part of Our Lives.*

Once centralized in places like California's Silicon Valley and Boston's Route 128, the high-tech lifeblood of Corporatia now runs throughout the American landscape. Across the country, from central Florida to Minneapolis–St. Paul to suburban Philadelphia and Salt Lake City, new growth regions are blossoming because of new technologies. Innovation-based economic booms are sprouting wherever new ideas and new capital take root.[15]

The products of high-tech companies, particularly in computers and telecommunications, have enabled other parts of Corporatia to change their ways of doing business. Whether in investment or in R and D, executives and researchers can now live almost anywhere. An options trader or brokerage-firm executive can work in a mountain chalet in Great Falls, Montana (where brokers at D. A. Davidson handle $2.7 billion a year), or minutes from the Rockies in Denver, Colorado (where Janus Funds manages its $19 billion in assets). Scores of other major financial firms, from Kansas City's Twentieth Century Mutual Funds ($20.5 billion) to Minneapolis's IDS Financial Services ($87 billion), have brought Wall Street to Main Street.[16] Similarly in high-tech research and development, a network of research parks now dot the landscape. The 145 members of the Association of University-Related Research Parks (AURRP) are high-tech city-states that crisscross America. From the 6,800-acre tract of North Carolina pine forest that is now the Research Triangle Park to the University of Utah's Research Park in the "Biomed Mountains," state-of-the-art laboratories and design facilities are now as much a part of the American landscape as the amber waves of grain.[17]

Free Markets + High-tech = The Most Productive, Advanced Society.

Peter Feinstein, whose consulting company has been involved with the advance of biotechnology since its earliest days, believes that the heroes of high-tech business are those who can identify most quickly and accurately what he calls "opportunity holes." These visionary entrepreneurs, according to Feinstein, are "the people who understood the power of a technology early on. They knew that biotechnology was one of the opportunity holes that appear in the cosmos from time to time and, if you leap through it, you can make a tremendous contribution."

From the Corporatian perspective, biotechnology is simply one of the latest waves in commercialization of basic research. Riding this wave has its dangers. The stocks of some of the biggest names in biotechnology have left investors severely burned. Somatogen, U. S. Bioscience, Synergen, Immune Response, Cytogen, Centocor, Alliance Pharmaceuticals, Greenwich Pharmaceuticals, XOMA, ICOS—all of these stocks have experienced at least a 75 percent decline from their all-time highs. But while some companies lose their luster, others are being eyed by stock trackers as best bets. Day by day, analysts at companies such as Oppenheimer and Company and at Fidelity's $700 million Select Biotechnology Fund track which companies are sound investments and which are not. Should an investor pick Amgen, Biogen, Celtrix Pharmaceuticals, and Liposome Technology? Or should one place bets on Cephalon,

Cor Therapeutics, and Creative BioMolecules? These are the questions which make Corporatia tick. The answers to these questions, Corporatians argue, will—and should—shape the future.[18]

What to many critics of Corporatia appears to be a ruthless and meaningless game of real-money Monopoly is, within the State, an almost sacred ritual. The flow of investment dollars determines how society will unfold. It gives life to some enterprises and condemns others to slow, often painful deaths. It decides with almost divine wisdom what the next phase of creation will be.

Profits |
"WE DESERVE TO BE REWARDED."

As director of Boston Scientific Corporation, John Abele believes in the power of profits. The company he cofounded saves lives—and saves money.

One of the products Abele's company produces is a dilation balloon that is used with patients suffering from heart disease. "It's a medical device," Abele explains, "that can be used to open up a narrow artery anywhere in the body." Until recently, a narrowed artery that could cause a heart attack could be treated only by surgery: "Five days in the hospital, four weeks to recover; costing in the range of $15,000." Using Abele's products, however, doctors now have a procedure that takes two days, allows the patient to be back at work in "five to ten days max," and costs half as much as surgery.

Of course there were other companies who were also trying to develop alternatives to surgery. One of Abele's competitors, for example, was experimenting with the use of lasers. "The downside of lasers is that they are expensive to buy," Abele notes, "and require extra personnel to manage. Even if they achieved the same objectives as our dilation balloon, they would have been an inferior solution. And remember: there is no free lunch. If some people are getting these sexy lasers, then someone else is probably not even getting the basics. Our product fits with our belief: the greatest good for the greatest number."

For the patient, Abele says, the difference between dilation and surgery is "the difference between night and day. From our perspective, this particular aspect of medical technology enhances the quality of health care and reduces the costs at the same time. We are using technology to empower the patient. That's our job—to do more for less."[19]

That, in a nutshell, is the potential Corporatian recipe for profit: doing more for less. And anyone who questions the legitimacy of making a profit in the Capitalist State is asking for a fight.

"I was appalled at what Hillary Clinton said about the insurance industry in yesterday's paper," says Compton Chase-Lansdale, referring to a speech that the First Lady had delivered in 1994 to the American Academy of Pediatrics in which she declared that the health-insurance industry "has brought us to the brink of bankruptcy because of the way they have financed health care." She also charged that the industry "likes being able to exclude people from coverage because the more they can exclude, the more money they can make. It is time that we stood up and said, 'We are tired of the insurance companies running our health-care system.' "

What infuriated Compton was his sense of Hillary Clinton's anti-business bias.[20] "She thinks profits are bad," says the forty-five-year-old executive, a regional sales director for Nutrasweet, a wholly owned Chicago-based subsidiary of the chemical giant Monsanto. "She thinks that there's a fair level of profits, and the government will decide what's fair. I think she's dead wrong. It's absolutely good if we make a lot of profits. It rewards our effort. It rewards our creativity. Who has the right to tell us that our annual rate of return should be 10 percent, or any other defined figure? Certainly not the government."

Corporatia feels the government routinely charges one industry after another with making "excess profits." In addition to the health insurance industry, for example, the First Lady also challenged the pharmaceutical industry for reaping unfair profits and driving up the costs of health care. She based her attack in part on a study by the Office of Technology Assessment which showed that the profit levels in the drug industry are consistently higher than in other high-tech, high-risk industries that depend on scientific research. The report prompted Representative Henry Waxman, chairman of the House Health and Environment Subcommittee to conclude: "Competition simply does not work in the market for prescription drugs." But looking at the same set of figures, Robert Allnut of the Pharmaceutical Manufacturers Association reached the opposite conclusion. "High financial returns are necessary to induce companies to invest in researching new chemical entities," he said. "The study comes to inaccurate conclusions that simply do not pertain to the marketplace or industry today."[21]

Siding with the industry group, Compton believes that public sector bureaucrats need a lesson in economics. "Government officials' attitude that making money is bad is a very destructive mentality," he says. "It shows remarkably poor understanding of basic economics. Incentives are important. Without incentives, without a payoff, you lose many things—you lose the ability to galvanize creativity. Everybody looks for an advantage. The only way I'm going to sell my product is if it has a basis for differentiation. What's the competitive advantage of my product? If it has advantages, I'll have a superior level of profitability. And I deserve those profits!"

The media are part of the reason Corporatia is misunderstood by the public. "I'm very frustrated every time I read or see in the media how critical they are about profitability," says Compton. "Maybe they're jealous. But they're subject to the same market forces we are. It makes good copy to bash corporations. But why? I think it probably has to do with a fundamental weakness that people have. We like to be taken care of. We want the government, the paternalistic government, to be like a king who takes care of us—who knows what's best for us. But that's just not the way it is."

"Nutrasweet is a for-profit company. Profit maximization takes place within a set of rules, a set of boundaries. For example, we can't take products to the marketplace that aren't approved by the FDA. Fine! We have to report our finances accurately to the IRS. Fine! We have to treat our employees equally, without regard to race and gender. Fine! But where this kind of interference goes too far is when taxes are raised so high that they don't reward our work. If you tax corporations too heavily, so that they cannot earn high rates of return, people like me won't work here because we aren't being adequately rewarded. The concept of excessive profit is invalid. If we're especially clever or able, we deserve to be rewarded."

Profits Lead to Opportunity— the Only Sound Basis for Equality.

Citizens of the Capitalist State feel frustrated by the ignorance of those who don't share their faith in profits. Corporations have experienced the power of profits to bring growth, wealth, creativity and joy into people's lives. They care about profits because it's a vital part of the "pursuit of happiness." Corporations care about inequality, poverty, injustice, and other social ills, but they believe that the only genuine way to cure those ills is through private profit-making, not public giveaways.

Most Corporatians acknowledge that blacks and other racial minorities have been victims of discrimination, and that women haven't had the same access to power as men. But they believe that Corporatia has the best solution: keep the economy growing and there will be room for everyone, including the poor. African–Americans, Asians, and Latinos are already swelling the ranks of their middle classes to a size many civil rights activists never thought possible. Those willing to work can move up the ladder of success, no matter what color their skin.

Women have made even more striking progress. According to the National Association of Women Business Owners, firms owned by women now employ more workers than all the Fortune 500 companies combined. Seven million women now run their own businesses, according to *Entrepreneur* magazine editor Rieva Lesonsky, and are generating $500 billion in revenues (up from just $98 billion a decade ago). In most major cities, there are Women in Business Yellow Pages or other women-only organizations that provide aspiring women with their own version of the "old boys" network.[22]

Great Wealth Is Evidence of Generosity, Not Greed;
a Sign of Virtue, Not Vice.

Wealthy entrepreneurs, who've made their money in the marketplace, are heroes in Corporatia. When Jack Schwager, who was director of futures research and trading strategy at Prudential Securities, went out to interview the most successful traders, his goal was to understand the nature of their genius. Like a boy who watches in wonder as pro basketball players perform their acrobatic feats on the court, Schwager wanted to get a front row seat in the lives of those who made fortunes in the market. So he went to visit the world's most successful traders, men who "amassed millions of dollars in a year—or sometimes in hours." As Schwager introduces them in his book *Market Wizards,* these Corporatian heroes include:

- "Michael Marcus, who turned a $30,000 account into $80 million.
- "Michael Steinhardt, whose fund has averaged a 30 percent annual return over a twenty-one-year period.
- "Tom Baldwin, who left a managerial job at a meat packing plant with $250,000 in hand and now trades up to $2 billion worth of T-bond futures in a day.
- "Paul Tudor Jones, whose funds have registered triple-digit gains five years in a row.

- "Ed Seykota, who realized an astounding 250,000 percent return on his accounts over sixteen years."

Almost all these men suffered great losses early in their careers. They worked hard and invested their earnings, but often lost as much as they won. However, they learned, and they persevered. Quietly and patiently, they developed an ability to distinguish between productive and unproductive ventures. Ultimately, they became legends—not because they sought fame, but because they had performed a service to society.[23]

If one visits them in their homes, the luxury and comfort their wealth makes possible is striking. They can afford the seaside Malibu estates and the panoramic Manhattan penthouses about which others can only fantasize. Citizens of other States may see them as greedy, immoral, or worse. But to citizens of Corporatia, the lives of luxury that such entrepreneurs can enjoy is part of the ethical symmetry of capitalism. To those who give much, much is given. To those who create value, rewards are received. To those who enrich society, riches are returned.

John D. Rockefeller, Edward Harriman, and Andrew Carnegie were, from a Corporatian perspective, paragons of generosity. They all started at the bottom: Rockefeller as a clerk in a commission merchant's house; Harriman as a $5-a-week office boy; and Carnegie as a $1.20-a-week bobbin boy in a Pittsburgh cotton mill. They started with nothing, and in the end had everything. They were not "robber barons," as ill-informed outsiders called them; they were benefactors of humankind. The true heroes of Corporatia did not inherit their wealth; they made it.[24]

But instead of being heralded for their extraordinary leadership, wealthy business leaders complain that they are portrayed as greedy and corrupt, depicted by environmentalists as insensitive to nature, stereotyped in Sunday morning sermons as indifferent to spiritual values, and denounced by liberals and other champions of "social justice" for ignoring the needs of the poor. As Irving Kristol once lamented in the *Wall Street Journal,* the cultural environment is obviously hostile toward business, as evidenced by the frequency with which corporate executives are depicted as "pure villains" in the media. Instead of being heroes, the top business leader is "the only unadulterated bad guy."[25]

For Corporatians, however, business tycoons are heroes, not villains. These men are proof that the rags-to-riches story is not just fiction. By providing their customers with the best possible deals, they have attracted more and more customers. By giving, they received. By strengthening the free market, they protected our liberty.

Liberty |
"NOBODY CAN TELL ME WHAT TO DO."

"I had a dream of being able to do whatever I wanted," recalls Brenda French, a clothing designer. "But that was impossible given how the big corporations in the fashion industry were set up. To be free, I had to set up my own factory—which is just what I did."

Brenda began with a $500 knitting machine in her spare bedroom. Today, seventeen years later, her company, French Rags, runs a 40,000 square foot factory, owns a million dollars of state-of-the-rag knitting machines, and has a 100-person work force plus 68 agents across the nation selling its products. "It's an entire business that revolves around creativity," Brenda says proudly. "There is nobody telling me what to do; there are no limits; there are no nos."

Brenda loves her freedom. "It's different from corporate life because there are no rules. It's problem-solving: that's all it is. Everything changes all the time. All those financial plans, and all that stuff—it's pretty useless. I make my living as a creative person. What I've learned is that the creativity is in the air. You channel it. When you're creating, you don't know what it will look like. When an artist picks up paint and a brush, he doesn't know how it will end. The thing you're creating takes you over. It teaches you. It's all based on creativity. We are all peddlers—even IBM, although they forget it."

Although Brenda is a citizen of Corporatia, she doesn't share some of big business's biases. Her business is based on selling custom-made women's clothing directly to her customers around the country, and she's appalled at how the industry as a whole operates. "Fashion has nothing to do with what I do," she says. "It's ridiculous. It's nothing more than fads. Don't get me wrong: women love clothes, and we love looking lovely. That will never change. But we're sick of fads. We're sick of being treated as if we're fifteen. The top-down fashion industry bypasses real women. It tries to tell us what we like rather than letting *us* tell *them*."

When she started out, Brenda thought that success meant following what she calls "the big business ethic." She spent a fortune on consultants. She made costly business plans. "It didn't work," she says. "Now I do it differently. I'm constantly learning. I think for myself. I don't really care about how big it gets. That's not the issue. The issue is doing what I do the best I can, enjoying it, and making sure the people who work with me enjoy it. That's the momentum that pushes us forward, not balance sheets."

Unlike corporate giants like Monsanto and Mobil, entrepreneurs like Brenda French are driven by a personal vision. They read *Inc.* magazine, not *Fortune.* They see themselves as creative renegades, not as hired executives. They echo the belief mentioned earlier that government should not intrude in their affairs. But they push that belief even farther by applying it to the private sector as well. They believe that corporations can become so big and bureaucratic that they stifle productivity. The antidote, they argue, is liberty—the right to express one's creative vision without interference.

According to Joel Kotkin, who writes frequently about business, "People running large organizations dislike anything that is disruptive, and entrepreneurs are fundamentally disruptive. If I'm IBM and I am trying to carve out my turf, we don't want a Michael Dell coming up with a completely different strategy for selling computers. Entrepreneurs accelerate change in ways that are unpredictable and out of control. The corporate mind-set wants a controlled environment. The executive avoids risks; the entrepreneur seeks out risks. Executives climb up the organizational ladder; entrepreneurs strike out on their own."

Nothing symbolizes the small-scale entrepreneur better than his magazine of choice, appropriately entitled *Inc.* In little more than a decade, it rose from nowhere to achieve a circulation of 640,000 and a readership of almost three million. The magazine's ranking of the fastest-growing small private companies, called the Inc. 500, is now as closely watched as the older listing of more established, larger corporations compiled by *Fortune.* As editor-in-chief George Gendron notes in his column, "the Fortune 500 may provide a record of America's economic history, but the Inc. 500 has become a window on its future."

Liberty Means Keeping Government Out of People's Business.

Despite these differing attitudes toward corporate life, executives and entrepreneurial citizens of Corporatia share their commitment to liberating the private sector from government interference. Whether the business is small and newborn like French Rags or big and established like General Motors, they stand together in opposition to federal red tape and bureaucratic meddling. "Land of the free" means being free to start a business and make money; "home of the brave" means having the courage to take the risks, work hard, and make it happen.

"I call myself a libertarian," says one wealthy trader in commodities futures, who prefers to remain anonymous. "Most of what the federal government does is unnecessary. Sure, we need to coordinate fire protection, police, road maintenance, and a few other vital services. But most of it is just freeloading. If we cut back on the fat, we could have an 8 percent flat tax and everybody would be better off."

Not surprisingly, Corporatians are frequently aligned with conservative politics, and against Big Government; with the Republicans' Contract with America and against liberal social welfare programs. Because of their core belief in economic liberty, they are opposed to anything that prevents French Rags, Monsanto, or Mobil from doing whatever they want to generate wealth. From the Corporatian perspective, the freer business enterprises are to make money, the more productive they will be, and the more productive they are, the stronger America will be. They believe that patriotism based on the pocketbook has made America the world's preeminent power today and that people who generate wealth are the backbone of America. Government, media, churches, welfare recipients, New Age gurus—all of them depend on the wealth of the private sector for their survival. In return, Corporations demand that the core beliefs of the Capitalist State—growth, competition, profits, and liberty—be honored.

Corporatia is known for producing wealth, but it also contributes to social progress. Its entrepreneurs make life better—not just for the wealthy, but for everyone in the economic system. The men and women in this chapter believe in Corporatia because it has worked for them. That Mr. Chase-Lansdale's salary is in six figures (or that Mr. Iacocca's was well into the millions) is not to them evidence of exploitation, but of the incentives of the marketplace. That Nutrasweet generates millions of dollars in profits does not mean the profits are excessive but shows that the system works. Those who generate wealth—that is, those who create value for the whole society—are the ones who have the moral right and the economic wisdom to decide how best to invest that wealth.

The genius of Corporatia, according to its citizens, is that their State turns dreams into reality. Their belief system does not just pontificate or theorize about the American Dream: it actually makes the dream come true. Out of concern for the well-being of citizens in the other Divided States, Corporatians want their fellow citizens to be more like them. They want the rest of us to wake up and, as they say at their management training seminars, "get with the program."

The "program" is the generation, accumulation, and reinvestment of wealth. They want citizens of the other Divided States to become more productive; to contribute more to the economy and thereby get more in return; and, by producing and consuming more, to help raise the American economy to even higher levels. To citizens of the Capitalist State, this agenda is not an ideology, but a practical, nuts-and-bolts strategy for improving the lives of all Americans.

3

DISIA

The Disempowered State

Core belief:	The exploitation and oppression in American society must be resisted by any means necessary.
Defining events:	Slavery, Chicago Seven trial, Nineteenth Amendment, Stonewall riots, civil rights movement, women's liberation movement, anti–Vietnam War movement, gay rights movement, anti-poverty movements.
Sacred texts:	*Autobiography of Malcom X, The Other America, And the Band Played On, The Feminine Mystique.*
Spokespersons:	Jesse Jackson, Louis Farrakhan, Jonathan Kozol, Barney Frank, Betty Friedan, Noam Chomsky.
Electronic media:	Minority radio stations, Handsnet.
Periodicals:	*Race & Poverty Action Coalition, Ms., The Advocate, Dissent, Mother Jones.*
Advocacy groups:	National Association for the Advancement of Colored People (NAACP), National Organization of Women (NOW), National Lesbian and Gay Task Force, American Indian Movement, The Rainbow Coalition, Citizen Action, Industrial Areas Foundation, and Progressive Unions.
Educational institutions:	The street, the prison system.
Quote:	*"Here in Subcity, life is hard . . . Government and business hold the purse strings . . . I am at the mercy of the World."*[1] —TRACY CHAPMAN, *"Subcity"*

For Disians—whom Jesse Jackson at the 1984 Democratic Convention called "the desperate, damned, disinherited, disrespected, and despised"[2]—history is a chronicle of exploitation and oppression, the story of the victims, not the victors; of the forgotten, not the famous; of those who were pushed to the bottom, not those who clawed their way to the top; of those who were, in the jargon of today's ghetto, "dissed." Like a slave on an auction block, an Indian on a reservation, or a single mother on welfare unable to feed her children, Disians feel trapped in a system designed to destroy their body and spirit.

The subterranean State which now exists in America is often referred to simply as the ghetto. But its ten million or more people can be found in every city and in most rural areas of the continent.[3] The Vietnamese child in the shack in Long Beach, California; the Mexican youth on the corner in El Paso seeking day labor; the white teenage mother in Illinois, waiting impatiently for her welfare check; the Salvadoran maid who cleans houses in Virginia—all are citizens of the State of Disia. It is invisible, except in crisis. Suddenly, without warning, this State can erupt and explode.

Although Disians are divided in many respects, they share the conviction that they are victims. Disians decry the price they and their forebears have paid in order to make America what it is today. Disians were always the ones who suffered. Economic growth was achieved on their backs. Market competition destroyed their culture and values. Technological innovation displaced their jobs and communities.

For some citizens of this State, the primary concern is how the rich oppress the poor. For others, it is how whites oppress blacks and other minorities. For still others, it is how men oppress women or heterosexuals oppress gays and lesbians. But for all citizens of Disia, oppression and exploitation of the weak by the strong are the heart of their story. They feel underrepresented everywhere: in the halls of power on Capitol Hill; in the citadels of finance on Wall Street; in the TV networks and film studios and newspaper offices.

Of course Disia tries to fight back against the more powerful States which surround it. One of the ways they try to keep their beliefs alive is through a network of independent bookstores that promote dissident thought. In Santa Monica, California, for example the Midnight Special bookstore displays in its front window books on poverty such as *Malign Neglect: Homelessness in an American City; The Other America: Poverty in the United States;* and *The Mole People: Life in the Tunnels Beneath New York City.* Disia also spreads the word through con-

71

sciousness-raising journals that include *Mother Jones; Covert Action Quarterly; The Boycott Quarterly; Living Marxism; International Trotskyist; Off Our Backs: A Women's Newsjournal;* and *Multinational Monitor* (a Ralph Nader publication). Like the Midnight Special bookstore, its counterparts around the country—such as Revolution Books and Black Books Plus in New York City, A Different Light in San Francisco, and New Words in Cambridge—struggle to sustain radical thinking. Mainstream books on "Eurocentric" subjects by "establishment" authors are not carried; instead, shelf space is offered to all those who challenge the ruling ideology.

To tell their story, Disians do not harken back to Columbus's "discovery" of the New World or to George Washington's cherry tree. Their "people's" history begins elsewhere: in the cages on West African shores where young black men and women were held for loading onto slave ships; on the Bahamian Islands, where the Spanish sailors under Columbus's command encountered the docile, peaceful native Indians; in the coal mines of West Virginia, where the owners lived in hilltop mansions, intimidated union organizers, and brought in troops to break strikes; on the railroads, were Chinese laborers bordering on starvation were paid less than a third the wage of white laborers. The history of Disia is not recounted in Horatio Alger's novels, but in smuggled notes from the underground railroad; not in *Gone With the Wind,* but in *The Autobiography of Malcolm X.* It is told by the victims, not the victors.[4]

The Battle of Wounded Knee is to some Disians what Auschwitz or Pearl Harbor is to others: a defining moment that established lasting themes. Near this small town in South Dakota, four days after Christmas in 1890, the Sioux were finally surrendering after encountering Major Samuel Whiteside and his Seventh U.S. Cavalry. More than 100 Sioux men and 230 women and children raised the white flag and agreed to halt at Wounded Knee Creek. Whiteside ordered the Sioux to turn over all their weapons, and they did. But the soldiers wanted more. They proceeded to search every tent and gathered axes, knives, even tent stakes; still not satisfied, they ordered the Sioux warriors to open their blankets to be searched. Despite the humiliation, the Sioux complied. Only one brave, Black Coyote, who was deaf, resisted. He raised his Winchester toward the sky and shouted that he had bought the rifle and it belonged to him. The soldiers grabbed him, spinning him around. As they tried to grab the rifle, it fired into the air.

Then, using not only their rifles, but also the rapid-fire Hotchkiss guns mounted on the hillside, the cavalry opened fire. Women and children were shot as they fled into the ravine. "We tried to run," Louise Weasel Bear recalled, "but they shot us like we were buffalo. I know there are some good white people, but the soldiers must be mean to shoot women and children. Indian soldiers would not do that to white children."

"When I look back now from this high hill of my old age," Black Elk said many years later, "I can still see the butchered women and children lying heaped and scattered all along the crooked gulch and plains as when I saw them with eyes still young. And I can see that something else died there in bloody mud, and was buried in the blizzard. A people's dream died there."

The few survivors were taken by wagon to nearby Pine Ridge, where the only available shelter was the mission. As the frozen, bleeding Sioux entered the church, Christmas decorations still hung on the walls. Above the pulpit hung a banner: PEACE ON EARTH, GOOD WILL TO MEN.

History Books Tell the Story of the Oppressors;
the Story of the Oppressed Is Covered Up by Lies.

Just as Patrians name their children after disciples and saints, Disians like Bernardine Dohrn, the former leader of the radical underground group the Weathermen, name their children after their State's pantheon of heroes. Dorhn's oldest son was named Zayd Osceola—after Zayd Shakur, the Black Panther killed in a New Jersey shoot-out with police and after the Seminole chief who sheltered runaway slaves. Her second son she named Malik Cochise, after one of Malcolm X's middle names and after the Apache chief who resisted encroachment by white settlers. Although these children's namesakes lived in different times and places, they have something important in common: their lives embody the core Disian belief that the ruling culture is destructive and oppressive and must be resisted at all costs.[5] Their hope, as Tracy Chapman sings in "Revolution," is that one day: "Poor people gonna rise up and get their share / Poor people gonna rise up and take what's theirs."

If the enemy of Disia were reduced to an archetype, it would be a white (probably Anglo-Saxon) Protestant heterosexual male born into affluence and raised in a family that has resided in this country for several generations. "To be 'all-American,' " observes Manning Marable, chairman of the African-American studies department at Columbia University, "is to be an English-speaking, upper to middle class white male." Or, as social critic Harold Cruse put it, America is "a nation of minorities ruled by a majority of one—it thinks and acts as if it were a nation of white Anglo-Saxon Protestants."[6]

The more closely a person resembles this elitist ideal, according to Disians, the more he is untouched by the indignities of immigration, the persecution of racial discrimination, the inequality of sexism, the injustice of poverty, and the corrosive slurs of religious animosity. Instead, the affluent WASP male lives securely amid the comfort and amusements of the ruling class. From cradle to grave, he is tended by others: by women, who serve him at home, at work, and at play; by minorities, who clean his toilets and gather his garbage; and by the poor, who, visibly or invisibly, subsidize his splendor.

The affluent WASP male is a symbol of villainy because he exemplifies three of the key tenets of Disian belief: racism, exploitation, and sexism (including sexual orientation). These three forces conspire to produce the fourth and final core belief of Disians: oppression.

Racism |
"TO KILL THE MINORITY"

Seventeen-year-old Sherwood Sanders lay paralyzed from his neck down in a hospital bed in Camden, New Jersey, the victim of a brutal police beating. "I don't remember a lot of despair about never being able to walk again," he recalls. "I just remember being in a holding pattern. I remember the officer who arrested me wanting me to be handcuffed to the bed just in case I would recover movement in my body. Since the doctors in the hospital said nothing to me, I sort of lived in my own world. I had a lot of time to think."

Sherwood's childhood consisted of poverty, racism, and neglect; of segregation and welfare checks; of dehumanizing schools and condemned apartments that he remembered as a life of oppression. His only window on the wider world, ironically, was books. Suffering from asthma and often absent from school, he spent hours at a local library that had been financed during the depression and was beautifully constructed. He remembers walking in the main door and seeing "ceilings higher than a house. They had all these classics there, that I had never seen or heard of. I started with the A's and went straight through. The things that stuck most in my mind were Russian folk tales. Suddenly the world was at my doorstep. I would try to talk to other kids about what I was reading, but they would just laugh."

After he had read every book in the children' section, the librarian let him upstairs. He started with the A's again, but before long his health had improved and he returned to school. It was, unfortunately, the end of his education.

His sixth-grade teacher at the Broadway Elementary School would give her class a five-page story, tell them to read it, and then wait with their hands folded until every child was finished. "The slowest child was Jerome Walker," Sherwood says, "I would finish in a minute; most kids would take five or ten minutes; Jerome would take half an hour. The teacher would police the aisles with a ruler in her hand, under no circumstances allowing students to read ahead." Unfortunately, Sherwood loved reading ahead, and if the book was good, he would forget to stop reading and his teacher would catch him. "Suddenly, a ruler would come down straight across my fingers. She was punishing me for loving to read."

Before long, Sherwood shared virtually all of the basic beliefs of Disia. "I believed, in essence, that there was a white power structure that existed off the blood, sweat, and tears of black people. I didn't think about other races much at the time. It was a kind of modern, urban slavery. Whites, as I saw it, were either evil or incapable of feeling. They don't know, or don't want to know, the pain and suffering that they are causing. The checks that came to our mailbox were not proof that they cared, but proof that they didn't. It wasn't enough to live on, but it was enough to keep us in our places. I would never have thought of saying 'thank you' for it, of feeling any gratitude. It was a self-serving act, a symbol of the system wanting to keep us exactly where we were.

"I heard other people say that because the white man had stolen everything from us, we could steal from him. If you robbed somebody, or took something from the department store, it didn't matter. It was really ours anyway. I heard other people say that drugs were a plot to keep us in our place. That was one of the reasons the whites gave us money—so we would buy drugs and stay powerless."

In seventh grade, Sherwood was invited to a meeting at a nearby church. As he neared the building, Father Donald Otto Griesman saw him and pulled him aside. "We called him D.O.G.," Sherwood says. "He told me he wouldn't tell me not to go, but that he wanted me to know that I'd be followed home in a car and that I'd be watched from that point on. He told me not to walk alone again, and to stay on well-lit streets. He assured me that he was telling me all this not because he wanted to scare me, but because he wanted me to know that I was making a serious choice."

Inside the church a group of African-American activists were starting "The Black People's Unity Movement." Sherwood remembers being impressed with what these "deadly serious black dudes" were saying. Just being there made him feel important. Since he had never had a father, it was exhila-

rating sitting among men who seemed to care about him. "They all swore to se-
crecy, which made it even more exciting. But I was more interested to find out
if Father Griesman was right about what would happen next. It turned out that
D.O.G. was dead right." An unmarked police car followed Sherwood home,
and from that moment until he lay paralyzed in the hospital, Sherwood was
tracked like an animal.

Over the next few years, Sherwood became head of the Movement's youth
organization. By 1967, when Sherwood was about seventeen, the Movement
had grown rapidly, now occupying the entire community center and providing
classes on how to deal with police dogs, batons, and other devices. Members
were trained by veterans from World War II and from a strange place he had
never heard of: Vietnam. As the Movement became more influential in the
community, the rumor began circulating that the police were determined to
eliminate its leadership. But the demonstrations continued.

"At City Hall one day, there were three or four hundred of us demonstrating against false media reports that the leadership of our organization was
involved in the heroin trade." Everyone knew that this was a common "disinformation" strategy: destroying a grass-roots organization by defaming its leadership. But Sherwood, convinced the media were lying, was eager to be part of
the demonstration that stood up for the truth.

For the first time, the police had their new fiberglass riot sticks.

Sherwood managed to disarm one policemen. But another officer stepped
forward, held his baton horizontally, and smashed it with full force into Sherwood's chest. The blow pushed him several feet back, disoriented him, and
knocked off his brand-new sunglasses. Then Sherwood made the mistake that
almost cost him his life: he let down his guard, and rather than protect himself
from the cop, he reached for his sunglasses. The next memory he had was waking up in the hospital, unable to move.

The doctors told him that he had received several powerful blows of
a blunt instrument on his skull. His paralysis, they told him, was due to brain
damage. He might recover full use of his body, or he might be paralyzed for life.

As he began his slow recovery, one of his first decisions was to change his
name. He would no longer be Sherwood Sanders, which was a slave name. He
would take his own name, Sharif Abdullah, as a symbol of taking control of his
own life.

Anyone Who Stands Up Against the System of Oppression
Risks Assassination or Imprisonment.

From the perspective of Disia, it was not chance that Sharif was almost killed. Any person of color who stands up against the system of oppression risks death. The history of the State is filled with such martyrs.

Snoop Doggy Dogg, the top-of-the-charts rap artist charged with murder, is the kind of hero many Disians trust. He talks in Disian language and he lives by Disian rules. "He tells it like it's supposed to be told," says seventeen-year-old Taneika Archer, who is talking about her hero at his old hangout, Toney's #3 World Famous Chili, Burger, and Hotdogs. Located less than a block from Polytech High School in Long Beach, California, Snoop's alma mater, Toney's is frequented by Snoop fans who defend him no matter what "the system" says he did. "People will always try to bring you down no matter what you do," says Taneika. All Disians know about the famous assassinations of Malcolm X and Martin Luther King, Jr. But they talk about scores of lesser-known murders too. Virtually every leader of the state, from American Indian Movement (AIM) founder Russell Means to the black crusader Louis Farrakhan, has been the target of police plots. But those are only the most prominent and publicized of the thousands of murders and attempted assassinations in Disia. Every year hundreds more activists and organizers are intimidated, incarcerated, libeled, maimed, or killed. As soon as any organization threatens the Establishment in any significant way it becomes the target of harassment.

"Why are we attacked?" asks Russell Means. "Anytime the Eurocentric males perceive that a Native American male is developing any power independent of the system, they attack. They are ruthless. There have been eight assassination attempts on my life. They are trying to destroy us."

Not far from AIM headquarters, Means is standing on a stage surrounded by five bodyguards. He is speaking to a primarily white, standing-room-only crowd that has spilled out into the surrounding building on a recent Columbus Day, a holiday Means despises "because we don't want to celebrate a despot."

Means is no stranger to conflict. He was picketed in the seventies by the John Birchers, who accused him of being a lackey for communism. In the eighties, he tells the crowd, he was picketed by the Left because he took a strong stand against Marxism and the Sandinistas, and his speeches at Berkeley and Stanford were canceled. Now, in the 1990s, Means says, the Italians are taking shots. "They're picketing AIM because we have a different view of the discovery of this country than they do, and we're making noise. The fact is, when you're a quiet Indian, no one pays attention, no one listens, no one cares."

Means's voice momentarily softens when he explains why he gave up violence as a strategy. "I tried to pick up the gun in the seventies," he says. "I urged my people to go to war. I said that it was better to die free than to live a slave. Let's get our guns and blow them away. Let's take out some judges. Let's kill. But my people wouldn't respond. I went all over the country and they wouldn't follow me. Down in the Everglades amongst the people whites call the Seminoles, I began to have my awakening. The Seminoles there were in love with life. They're indigenous people. They understand immortality. They are close to the earth. It was clear to me that they wouldn't pick up guns. I felt ridiculous. I realized we had to change another way. An elder there told me: 'The white man is like a child. You have to have a lot of patience.' I thought about it. I put down the gun and began to listen to my elders. I understood a little more about how change happens."

Fame has not softened Means's determination to defend the rights of his people and the other oppressed peoples of the Americas. "So now it's Clinton, is it? I worked in Hollywood—all pro-Clinton. The New Age—the political guru—the Messiah. Bullshit! It was all the same. First thing he does is appoint [Lloyd] Bentsen, the man who brought you the S and L debacle. The guy should be in prison, not secretary of the treasury. He was the architect of the theft. He's the head, the don. Yeah, that's Clinton, your savior! Don't be fooled by it. FBI, DEA, IRS, all the alphabet—none of them respect your rights. All they interview in the media is government or ex-government officials. It's a totalitarian state, Orwellian to the max. The government hacks give their 'expert' position. The Demapublicans—it's all a show."

After pausing briefly to punctuate his point, Means hammers it home: "You have no freedoms. The United States of America is becoming one huge Indian reservation. The Constitution has been ripped to shreds."[7]

The audience gives Means a standing ovation, and then flows out of the auditorium, past the "Seeds of Change" exhibit, which has been traveling through public libraries across the nation to honor the wisdom and beauty of Native American cultures. It includes a portrait of the Aztec chief Montezuma, accompanied by a statement attributed to Cortez. "I and my companions suffer from a disease of the heart, which can only be cured by gold."

The White Man Stole the Land from the Native Americans and Christened the Continent with Blood.

For many Disians, the annihilation of the cultures native to American soil is the beginning of the history of their State. These indigenous people, whom Columbus called "Indios," were considered morally righteous even by their conquerors. The Spanish explorer who "discovered" America wrote to the king and queen of Spain that the people he encountered in the New World were peaceable; that they "loved their neighbors as themselves"; that their discourse was "sweet and gentle"; and that their manners were "decorous and praiseworthy." Summoning his strongest language, Columbus wrote: "I swear to Your Majesties there is not in the world a better nation." Yet for over the next four hundred years, in almost every state of the ever-expanding union, the native peoples were exterminated.[8]

From the Disian perspective, American history is written in the blood of racial genocide. While many other citizens hold South Africa up to the world as an example of racial injustice, Disians know better. The only reason why America is not facing the same dilemma, they argue, is that the Americans were more brutal and killed off the native populations.

Black Disians, the descendants of slaves, share the outrage of this continent's native people. Manacled by their necks and legs to the floor with barely enough space to turn from side to side, fifty million Africans were packed like animals in ships and forced to endure weeks of agony crossing the storm-tossed Atlantic. More than one out of three died. According to observers, many more were "driven to frenzy" by their inhumane conditions. When the ships finally docked and the corpses and live bodies were removed from their floating torture chambers, they were "so covered with blood and mucus that it resembled a slaughterhouse."[9]

Racism Runs So Deep in America That No Law Can Eradicate It.

Although more than a century has passed since slavery was officially abolished, its legacy continues. Despite the many obstacles to advancement, minority citizens of Disia admit that a growing black middle class now exists. Twelve percent of blacks twenty-five years and older have four years of college or more. Seventeen percent have jobs that are professional/managerial; 12 percent have family incomes of over $50,000; 1 percent over $100,000. But so deep is racism in America, according to the Disian view, that even blacks who achieve professionally and financially and reach the middle or upper class are treated by the larger society with disdain.[10] As Malcolm X said: "You don't stick a knife in a man's back nine inches and then pull it out six inches and say you're making progress."[11]

Nevertheless, those who think blacks should quit complaining and pull themselves up by their bootstraps habitually cite successful members of minorities—usually entertainers and sports heroes like Michael Jackson, Oprah Winfrey, Michael Jordan, or Whitney Houston—to prove that opportunity exists today for anyone who wants it. When a black enters the ranks of the successful, those in other States claim he has crossed the borders out of Disia. But blacks themselves reach a different conclusion. They believe that racism still afflicts the vast majority of Americans. One-third of blacks interviewed by the *Los Angeles Times* felt that most white people do not want minorities to get a better break, but rather, want "to keep minorities down," or simply "don't care." Fewer than one out of four blacks felt that white people actually wanted to see them make it in American society.[12]

Black Rage, Black Crime, Black Vulgarity— All Are a Consequence of Racism.

Thelma Malone walks a group of visitors through her community in Atlanta's south side, not far from the church where Martin Luther King began his ministry. She points out an area that symbolizes the plight of blacks in Disia today. On one corner is the Lakewood GM plant, which once bustled with the manufacture of automobiles and where many of the employees were black. The wages were low, but the money kept black families out of poverty and kept black men off drugs. The plant is now closed, the jobs eliminated or moved overseas.

The results of this, Thelma points out, are visible across the street. There sits the U.S. penitentiary, now being expanded and modernized, with a new, top-security wing to house more inmates, who are predominately black. The men, who once might have been gainfully employed across the street at the GM plant, now have no way to make a living and turn to drugs and crime, leading many directly to prison, which some have called "the American gulag." That one out of four African-American males between the ages of nineteen and twenty-eight is now behind bars or on parole is further evidence of what former NAACP president Reverend Benjamin Chavis calls the "lingering vestiges of American apartheid.[13] The result is the highest rate of incarceration in the world, higher than formerly racist states like South Africa (which is second) and totalitarian states like the former Soviet Union (which is third).[14]

Chavis played a leading role in Kansas City, Missouri, where gang leaders met for a "gang summit" in May 1993 to begin to lay out their views for the public. Although many gang members were open to the dialogue and enjoyed being treated like celebrities, many were suspicious of all the non-Disians. Keith Peddler, for example, wouldn't even consider calls for turning in guns. "I'm tired of black Uncle Toms telling us to lay down our guns when the police are out there killing us," he said, at which other gang members applauded enthusiastically. "I'm not dumb. Check this out: if you are going to go out and fight a war for the white man, you better sure as damn stand up and fight for yourself."[15] Or, as the rap group N.W.A. (Niggers With Attitude) puts it:

A young nigger got it bad . . .
Some police think they have the authority to kill the minority.

In Disia, lyrics such as these, which sound outrageous to many outside the state's borders, simply reflect the reality of racism, which is as old as the slave ships.

The Myth of the "Melting Pot" Is Dead,
Destroyed by Racism.

When Hector St. John de Crevecoeur immigrated from France to the American colonies in the mid-1700s, he marveled at how settlers from many countries— "a mixture of English, Scotch, Irish, French, Dutch, Germans, and Swedes"— blended together to form a new breed: the Americans. This new breed, according to de Crevecoeur, left "behind him all his ancient prejudices and manners, and received new ones from the new mode of life he's embraced, the new government he obeys, and the new rank he holds. . . . Here individuals of all nations are melted into a new race of men."

Such romantic visions of melting pots drive minority citizens of Disia into rage. The "mixture" of which de Crevecoeur wrote was all white. Instead of wanting to "melt," people of color want to restore their own dignity and ethnic identity. Disians want public schools to protect and enhance children's awareness of their ethnic origins and differences. Critics of Disia call this attitude "separatism," condemn "multiculturalism," and defend the "Eurocentric" school curriculum.[16] But these critics forget where the "separatism" started, Disians respond. It started with Americans who were white and European.

Although blacks, Latinos, and Asians[17] all have their own unique version of the Disian belief system, they unquestionably have one thing in common: their numbers are growing. According to Louis Farrakhan, the leader of the Nation of Islam, who is (outside Disia) notorious for his bigotry and (inside Disia) revered for his moral leadership:

> If the plummeting birth rate of white people in America continues, in a few years it will reach zero population growth. As for blacks, Hispanics, and Native Americans, if their present birth rate continues, by the year 2050, demographers say, blacks, Hispanics, and Native Americans will conceivably be 50 percent or more of the United States population. . . . If things continue just birthwise, we could control the Congress, we could control the Supreme Court, we could control state legislatures; and then it will be "Run, Jesse, run," or "Run, Jesse Junior, run," or "Run, Jesse the Third, run."

Whether or not this futuristic Disian fantasy of an America dominated by dark-colored minorities becomes reality, Farrakhan's demographics are sound: this country in the twenty-first century will no longer be a white nation.[18]

Exploitation |
"MR. HOPE IS GONE."

The other America, the America of poverty, is hidden today in a way that it never was before. Its millions are socially invisible to the rest of us. . . . The poor are increasingly slipping out of the very experience and consciousness of the nation.[19]

MICHAEL HARRINGTON,
The Other America

What do Brownsville, Texas; College Station, Texas; Monroe, Louisiana; Laredo, Texas; and Camden, New Jersey, have in common? They are the five poorest cities in America, with over 35 percent of their citizens below the poverty line.

Among major metropolises, Detroit (32 percent) and Chicago (with 21 percent) rank poorest.[20] But every large city in America, from Tallahassee to Tucson to Tacoma, has a "subcity" where the poor live. In some places, it is called the "inner city"; in other places, the "ghetto." At other times it is called the "poor part of town," or, more neutrally, something like "South Central" (as in Los Angeles) or the "South Side" (as in Chicago). Whatever the term, everyone in town knows what it means. It is the area where crime is high and drugs are sold; where housing is substandard, food markets are scarce, and liquor stores are abundant; where check-cashing stores are common and the checks come from the welfare department; where racial minorities are clustered and gunfire echoes in the night. These areas are, in other words, the hometowns of the underclass.

"Underclass" is lower than lower class. The lower class has jobs. The underclass is unemployed. The lower class is poor, the underclass trapped in poverty. As black sociologist William Julius Wilson has pointed out, the role models in poor communities have moved away. Those who are left are isolated from any positive connections to mainstream society and trapped in poverty. Or, as the young black journalist Omar Tyree puts it: "Mr. Hope is gone to the suburbs, leaving behind Mr. Hopeless—the typical customer for the drug trade."[21]

According to Disians, racism and poverty reduce opportunity to the point where it no longer exists. How can a woman like Sharif Abdullah's mother break out of poverty? Disians ask. Even abandoning her sick child, the only ways for her to earn money without jeopardizing her welfare payments are illegal. As a result she and other similar workers are severely underpaid. The average child care worker working full-time in the home was earning $154 a week compared to $191 for a cleaning person, $219 for a cashier, $222 for a waiter/waitress.[22] In other words, they were paid less than in any other form of employment in America.

Some Disians live below the poverty line, others above it; but the world in which they live doesn't permit them the luxury of saying that money doesn't matter. The poverty line, after all, is nothing more than an arbitrary income level devised by a statistician in the Social Security Administration named Mollie Orhsanky. To her dismay, the Johnson administration turned her statistical model into an official poverty line, which determines who is eligible for government assistance and who is not. By manipulating the figures, the government can—and, Disians believe, often does—make millions of poor people "disappear."[23]

In terms of the quality of their lives, Disians know that things are getting worse for their children, not better—and they have the evidence about poverty to prove it. Data on income distribution also support Disians' argument that things are getting worse. In a society in which (to use the figures of Harvard professor Cornel West) 10 percent of Americans own 86 percent of the wealth, "equality" is a myth. According to the "women's budget," prepared by the Women's International League for Peace and Freedom, "the average after-tax income of the richest 1 percent of American households rose 122 percent (adjusted for inflation) from 1977 to 1988. For the poorest fifth of households, the average after-tax income fell 10 percent." In other words, the haves have more, and the have-nots have less.[24]

Just as Corporatians use numbers to prove that their beliefs are correct, Disians provide numbers to show the reality of oppression. According to the Disian view, chronic poverty proves that radical change in the system itself is necessary. As Columbia University professor Manning Marable puts it: "Capitalism is still responsible for the perpetuation of institutional racism and ethnic violence . . . power, privilege and the ownership of productive resources and property has always been unequally allocated in a social hierarchy stratified by class, gender, and race." Or, as the black poet Audre Lord put it more succinctly: "The master's tools will never dismantle the master's house."[25]

The Plight of Ghetto Schools Proves That Opportunity Is Unequal.

If America was one nation where all children had an equal opportunity, children from disadvantaged backgrounds would have a fair chance to compete. Unfortunately, as Disians see it, America is not one nation. In every major metropolitan area, there are rich school districts and poor ones. In the city of Camden, New Jersey, where Sharif Abdullah grew up, nearly a quarter of its families earned less than $5,000 annually as of 1985. More than half lived on public assistance, and Camden's children had the highest rate of poverty in the entire country. "We have children coming to kindergarten or to first grade who are starting out three years delayed in their development," says the principal of Camden High, Ruthie Green-Brown, who despairs of repairing the damage with the meager resources available.

To those children who have less, less is given; and to those who have more, more is given. In the city of New York, per pupil expenditures in 1990 were $5,500. In the highest spending suburbs of New York City (Great Neck or Manhasset, for example) funding levels rose to $11,000, with the highest districts in the state at $15,000 per pupil. Thus some children are having three times as much spent on their education as others in the "land of the free."[26]

San Antonio, for example, is divided into more than a dozen school districts. Some of these, like Alamo Heights School District on the north side, are primarily white and affluent. Other school districts, on the west side of town, are primarily poor and Latino. Because of the school funding structure in the state of Texas, the children in Alamo Heights are the beneficiaries of more tax dollars than the children in the poor communities. The United States Supreme Court has ruled this school funding structure unconstitutional and has ordered the state of Texas to change it. But to date, nothing has been done.

Disians feel that instead of confronting this kind of fundamental injustice honestly, American society brushes it under the rug. With their children tucked away in elite private academies or comfortable suburban school systems, affluent conservatives contend that "throwing money at the problem" isn't a solution. Editorial writers in the *Wall Street Journal* advance precisely this argument when they conclude that "money doesn't buy better education . . . the evidence can scarcely be clearer."[27] But if it does not matter, Disians ask, why are the affluent school districts guarding their budgets so vigilantly? If money is not a vital ingredient in education, then why don't they share it?

From the Banks to the Schools to the Supermarket,
Every Institution Victimizes the Poor.

If race is the lock on the door preventing the children of Disia from achieving, then poverty is the dead bolt. A poor child grows up in a family that makes less than others; goes to a school which has less money than others; and, to make matters worse, has to pay more for everything he or she buys. Whether it's food from a store, or services from a bank, the poor pay more in America's cities for virtually all products and services than families in middle-class neighborhoods.

This is not rhetoric, Disians argue, but hard fact. A study conducted by the West Coast Regional Office of Consumers Union systematically analyzed and compared middle-class neighborhoods and poor neighborhoods in Los Angeles and Oakland and concluded that virtually everything costs more in the poor neighborhoods. For the same piece of meat or the same loaf of bread, the poor paid more than suburban shoppers a few miles away. And since supermarkets and other stores with necessary goods and services are rarely available in poor neighborhoods, the economically disadvantaged also had to travel more to make their purchases. For every $100 that low-income consumers spent on food, only a third was spent in their own neighborhoods. In middle income neighborhoods, by contrast, more than four out of five food dollars were spent in the same neighborhood. Consumers Union found that the same inequality applied to virtually every sphere of life.[28]

With the lack of resources and education, unemployment is almost inevitable, Disians argue. In their State, the percentage of joblessness is always in double digits. Unemployment among New York City's teenagers rose to 40 percent in the first three months of 1993, nearly double the rate of two years before and the worst in the twenty-five years that records have been kept. According to the executive director of the Manhattan Valley Youth Program, a nonprofit group that helps teenagers find work: "Our young people used to be on the bottom of the list; now they're not even on the list."[29]

And so the cycle of poverty continues. Economists may debate the causes of wealth and poverty, but Disians know the consequences. They are sicker than the wealthy, and are dying at a rate more than three times that of people with incomes of $25,000 or more.[30] This is not an accident, not an arbitrary twist of fate, not an "act of God" like a hurricane or earthquake, and not—Disians insist—their fault. The inner cities of Disia are "programmed to be the poorhouses," writes David Rusk, the former mayor of Albuquerque, New Mexico. According to Rusk, two out of five of America's central cities are "programmed to fail." According to his data, Bridgeport, Newark, Hartford, Cleveland, and Detroit are "on life support systems"; Baltimore, Chicago, St. Louis, and Philadelphia are "sinking"; Boston, Minneapolis, and Atlanta are "infected." The social disease which is killing these cities is poverty—*programmed* poverty. When an urban family succeed, they leave the cities for the suburbs. Consequently, the inner cities are "steadily and inexorably being converted into the equivalent of giant public housing projects."[31]

The hundreds of organizations that belong to the Poverty and Race Research Action Council (PRRAC) network confront these realities every day. From the Southern Justice Institute in Durham, North Carolina, to the Women's Economic Agenda Project in Oakland, California, Disian organizations struggle against a structure of inequality keeping millions of people from ever achieving the American dream. The entire institution of public housing, from a Disian perspective, is bricks-and-mortar evidence of economic apartheid. Entire tracts of land are turned into poverty city-states. In Chicago, for example, the Henry Horner Homes occupy thirty-four acres. The Robert Taylor Homes house 15,000 impoverished residents. One of the most violent is Cabrini Green, an area which became famous when in less than two months eleven people were killed and thirty-seven wounded. To dramatize the problem, then-mayor Jane Byrne moved into the project for three weeks. But her heavily policed effort to bridge the gap between rich and poor, in the view of one journalist, only "highlighted the isolation of these poor, mostly black, inner-city islands. It was as if the mayor, with her entourage of police, advisers, and reporters, had decided to visit some distant and perilous Third World country—except that Cabrini Green was barely seven blocks from the mayor's posh Gold Coast apartment."[32]

That any reporters were present, however, was an unusual event in Disia. As the *Wall Street Journal*'s Alex Kotlowitz points out, very few newspapers have bureaus within inner city neighborhoods. "One of the most logical moves to take would be to place a bureau where the action is," observes Kotlowitz, one of the few reporters who have intimately chronicled the lives of Disian families. "We have foreign bureaus located in other countries, but not in our own inner cities. Our bureaus here are usually in safer, more comfortable neighborhoods."[33]

As a result, the only news coming from Disia neighborhoods is crime news. Drug busts, homicides, arson, riots, or reports of other mayhem appear in the newspapers; but the ceaseless struggle by men and women to survive against the odds is rarely reported.

Disians believe that the media regularly and systematically distort the reality of their state. A powerful story about a ghetto family, Alex Kotlowitz's book *There Are No Children Here,* was turned into a made-for-TV movie. It chronicled the story of two boys, Pharaoh and Lafayette, and their mother LaJoe, who lived in a Chicago housing project. With poignant detail, Kotlowitz's book showed how the boys tried desperately to have some semblance of childhood in a violent, oppressive world that made that virtually impossible. But when their story came to prime time TV, the family's real life was too much for the show's producers. Casting Oprah Winfrey in LaJoe's role, they gave the story an ending that is more upbeat than anything Kotlowitz wrote: Pharaoh is rescued from the gangs; Lafayette gives a graduation speech; their father confronts the drug dealers; and LaJoe is honored at a school event for being an outstanding mother. Although this family is not quite like Ozzie's and Harriet's, or even the Huxtables on the Bill Cosby show, the implication is that in a few years they will be doing just fine.

These lies are tools, Disians argue, to keep the oppressed in their place. Mired in ignorance, blinded by lies, and distracted by the myth of progress, the citizens of this long-suffering State have not made the revolution happen. But even when they try, Disians argue, the Establishment still has its ultimate form of social control: violence.

The security forces of the Establishment, usually called "law enforcement agencies" or the "criminal justice system," are viewed by most Disians as the true criminals of our society. They are paid billions of dollars to put millions of young Disians behind bars, and to control millions more through parole and other legal forms of intimidation. While others complain that Disia is a violent State, Disians themselves believe that they are the victims of the violence of an oppressive, exploitive system. That one out of five boys polled at inner-city high schools admit that they own guns, and more than one out of ten say they carry their weapons regularly, does not make most Disians blame these boys. Even when citizens of their State are violent, true Disians still blame the system that has forced them to live in fear and to protect themselves.[34]

Crime and Drugs Are Used by the Establishment To Weaken and Undermine the Underclass.

From a Disian perspective, criminals are themselves victims—victims of a system that has stunted their moral development and turned them into savages, blindly and helplessly striking out at random targets. As racism is defined by leading Disian scholars, such as Columbia's Marable, it is the "systematic exploitation of people of color in the process of production and labor, the attempt to subordinate our [African-American] cultural, social, educational, and political life."[35] According to this argument, young thugs are not personally responsible for what they have done; rather, their violence is evidence that they have been destroyed as human beings. While what they do to their victims is obviously wrong, they can be punished fairly, Disians believe, only if we understand that they are victims too. Similarly, blacks' views of the Los Angeles riots were substantially different from whites': two out of three African-Americans called them a "rebellion" against a judicial and social system that is unjust.[36]

While crime is a problem in Disia, it is often considered by Disians to be the consequence of prior crimes—namely, oppression and exploitation by the system. From this perspective, crimes committed by minorities are not the real problem, but rather the social conditions that produced the criminality. To prove their point, Disians cite crime statistics that show that, despite an increase in incarcerations far exceeding that of other nations, crime in the United States has not been reduced. Since 1973, imprisonment has increased more than fourfold, and violent crimes are up 24 percent. While the amount of time served by those who have committed violent crimes has tripled since the mid-seventies, it has had "apparently very little" impact on the crime rate, according to the National Research Council of the National Academy of Sciences. A quick glance at the state of New York shows why: more than two out of three prisoners in the state come from eight neighborhoods of New York City, and those neighborhoods consist heavily of minorities living in poverty. Crime cannot be prevented by more prisons or more police, Disians argue, but only by changing the social conditions that make crime inevitable.[37]

When Disian drug-dealers and criminals are put on trial, they argue that society itself should be put on trial. When Kevin F. Williams-Davis was sentenced to life in prison for his involvement in two drug-related murders in D.C., he did not walk silently away after the judge pronounced the verdict. Although he had been found guilty of racketeering and being part of a continuing criminal enterprise, namely a drug-dealing gang called R Street Crew, he did not feel ashamed. On the contrary, he spoke for seventy-five minutes in court about how the criminal justice system should be ashamed. With a brilliance and eloquence that left many in the courtroom spellbound, he addressed the injustices being committed against young black men like him. "This war on drugs is truly a war on young black men," he said. "Why is it that when young black males come into this courthouse they are made out to be mobsters or villains? Even when I was a child, drugs were on Lincoln Road and R, and when this trial was going on, drugs were at Lincoln Road and R, and when I'm gone, there will still be drugs at Lincoln Road and R." He expressed no remorse or regret, and claimed that he was being sentenced so that prosecutors could show the public that they were making progress and advance their own careers. "We didn't have a fighting chance in this courtroom, really. We felt that we were sitting through a Nuremberg trial."[38]

If you ask a cab driver to take you to the corner of Lincoln and R, he hesitates. He fears for his life. And yet, when you are standing at the corner, the dome of the Capitol looms on the horizon. Within a few blocks of each other are the power elite who run America and young Disians like Williams-Davis who believe that he is a citizen in a colony called Disia and the elite are guilty of war crimes against his people.

Sexism |
THE "WAR AGAINST WOMEN"

According to Disians, particularly those who call themselves feminists, the decision of the Founding Fathers to make women as well as slaves second-class citizens was no oversight. It was an intentional act to subjugate women, an act which even now, two hundred years later, has not been repudiated by most men. While the majority of American men today may approve of women's right to vote, they nevertheless do not want women to be their equals.

Yes, there are a handful of women in Congress, Disians argue, but that is not enough. In the summer of 1995, on the eve of the seventy-fifth anniversary of women getting the vote, six congresswomen draped themselves in purple, gold, and white, the historic colors worn a century earlier by the suffragettes, and announced in the Capitol that the conservative-dominated Congress was waging a "war against women." In every legislative action (with the sole exception of stronger child support enforcement), these women lawmakers argued that Congress is trying to turn back the clock. The Republican majority in Congress, argued these women, gained power because of the votes of "angry white men" determined to put women back in their place. Pat Robertson and the Christian Coalition, alleged Representative Nita Lowey (D-N.Y.), are "calling the shots." Decrying the assault on women's rights, Representative Lynn Woolsey (D-Calif.) said: "This Congress put women and children first . . . first on the chopping block."[39]

Whatever Gains Women Make,
Men Immediately Try To Take Away.

Women in Disia are not fooled by the media-promoted myth that the "second sex" has gained an equal footing with their male counterparts. Despite four movements for women's rights in America—in the mid-nineteenth century, the early twentieth century, the 1940s, and most recently the 1970s—the male Establishment has conspired to undo any progress women have achieved. As Susan Faludi's 1991 best-seller, *Backlash*, made clear, each women's movement has been followed by retrenchment. Disian feminists believe we are in the middle of precisely such a backlash now.[40]

Unlike the early 1970s, when such books as Robin Morgan's *Sisterhood Is Powerful* and Kate Millett's *Sexual Politics* rocked the nation, many Disian women today, particularly those who are poor, are fighting just to stay where they are. They feel oppressed not only by the white ruling class, they feel oppressed by the men of their *own* race and class.[41] Hemmed in on all sides by what appears to be institutional racism, and faced with economic opportunities that are virtually invisible, life in Disia shapes the most private and personal choices which young men and women make. Sexuality becomes unhinged from familial, white, middle-class society. As the cycle of poverty grows tighter, teenage girls born into it have children who then grow up in poverty too.

Unlike most middle-class teenagers, who postpone pregnancy in order to protect their future, adolescents in poverty "see no future to derail—no hope for a tomorrow much different from today—hence they see little to lose by having a child out of wedlock," concludes Elijah Anderson, a black sociologist at the University of Pennsylvania. After studying closely the beliefs about sex that shape behavior among young people in the inner city, Anderson found that, for a "variety of reasons tied to the socioeconomic situation," sex becomes a "contest" between men and women. Anderson finds women tangibly the losers. The young man can walk away from the responsibilities of parenthood, but the young mother cannot. She must bear the responsibility for raising her children and supporting them as well, a dual role which even women of privilege find overwhelming.[42]

The consequences of this sexual warfare are reflected in the family structure of Disia. In America as a whole, only 13 percent of families are headed by a single mother; but in Disia, 70 percent of the families have that structure. As the nineties began, more than half of the children who live with single mothers were poor, compared to 22 percent of children in single-fathered families and 10 percent in two-parent families. According to the Children's Defense Fund's report *State of America's Children 1991*, the median family income of single-mother families with adolescent children was less than $14,000 in the late eighties, compared to $42,000 for two-parent families. From 1960 to 1989 the percentage of white women age 15 to 34 who had their first child outside of marriage rose from 9 percent to 22 percent. For black women in the same period the rate rose from 42 percent to 70 percent.[43]

These women believe they are victims of "the system." Anna, a young black single mother, has tried to get off welfare many times, but the cards are stacked against her. "I don't think this system's here to help me," she laments. "It's just to keep you right where you're at—to be poor—to make you psychologically dependent." Working forty hours a week in a department store at $5 an hour, she earned enough to lose her eligibility for food stamps and Medicaid, but not enough to survive. So she quit working full-time and went back on welfare. "I hate being on ADC [Aid to Dependent Children]; they make you feel so belittled and I hate that. . . . Sometimes they make you think that they're the ones giving you this money, and they're not—it's the government." Sara, another young mother, agrees. "Obviously the system doesn't really want you to succeed," she says, but she refuses to be victimized. "I can become what statistics have designed me to be, a nothing, or I can make statistics a lie." "To be not only poor and black but also female," as one Disian writer concluded, "is to live at the intersecting points of a gendered and racist welfare system."[44]

Any Person Born a Woman is Oppressed by the Patriarchy.

But there are many women in the state of Disia who are neither poor nor uneducated, but who feel that they, too, are victims. Among feminists in Disia, many are affluent, white, and college educated. Many have high-paying jobs and live in suburbia. Yet they feel victimized by the "patriarchy," a concept that stands for the male-dominated world in which they, like poor minority women, are victims of oppression and exploitation. Discrimination against women is often more subtle than against minorities and the poor, but its impact can be just as devastating. The Federal Glass Ceiling Commission, a 1994 government study about gender biases in the workplace, found that only 5 percent of the senior managers in Fortune 1000 companies were women. According to the commission: "At the highest level of business, there is indeed a barrier that is rarely penetrated by women or persons of color."[45]

Disian feminists believe that the sexism of American society oppresses *all* women at *every* economic level. That is why, as of the beginning of this decade:

- The average female high school graduate earns less than a male high school dropout.

- The average female college graduate earns less than a man with only a high school diploma.

- The gap between the average working woman's salary and her male counterpart's is as large as it was a generation ago.

- Less than one out of a hundred corporate officers and directors are women.

- More than half the boards of directors of major corporations include not even a single woman.[46]

This is why feminists who are affluent, white, college educated, have high-paying jobs and live in suburbia still feel victimized.

In *The Feminine Mystique,* Betty Friedan suggested that the suburban housewife is in a position similar to that of an inmate in a Nazi concentration camp. Isn't the suburban house, Friedan asks, "in reality a comfortable concentration camp? Have not women who live in the image of the feminine mystique trapped themselves within the narrow walls of their homes? They have learned to 'adjust' to their biological role. They have become dependent, passive, childlike; they have given up their adult frame of reference to live at the lower human level of food and things. The work they do does not require adult capabilities; it is endless, monotonous, unrewarding."

Of course Betty Friedan acknowledges that American women are not, in fact, being "readied for mass extermination." Nevertheless, she feels her metaphor is warranted because "they are suffering a slow death of mind and spirit. Just as with the prisoners in the concentration camps, there are American women who have resisted that death, who have managed to retain a core of self, who have not lost touch with the outside world, and who use their abilities to some creative purpose." Seeking language strong enough to describe the dehumanization of women, she concludes that the subordination of women has "succeeded in burying millions of women alive."[47]

Although women in other Divided States consider this inflammatory exaggeration, many other feminists consider Betty Friedan's views to be far too moderate. Many "radical feminists" consider the National Organization of Women (NOW), which Friedan founded, to be "conservative" because it concentrates only on "the more superficial symptoms of sexism," such as employment discrimination and legal inequalities. According to these radicals, the economic class system originates in the "sexual class system," which is "the tapeworm that must be eliminated first by any true revolution."[48]

According to Disian feminists, exploitation is present at home in the bed-room and the kitchen; at work, in the office and the factory; in the media, in en-tertainment and advertising; in child-rearing, at schools and on the sports field; in writing, from fiction to school textbooks; in politics, from health care to job policies. Every major social institution plays its part in the subjugation of women—including the church. Every major denomination in Western religion has discriminated against women. Thus women of all faiths leapt to the defense of Sonia Johnson when she was excommunicated from the Mormon Church because of her feminist views. In her writing and lecturing, Johnson dared to expose the church's hypocrisy. "As long as God is male," Johnson preaches, "the male is God."[49]

Even the Bible, if interpreted literally as the word of God, lends support to women's oppression. Disian feminists can point to centuries of theology ("Man is the beginning of woman and her end," wrote Thomas Aquinas, "just as God is the beginning and end of every creature") that induced women to submit to the patriarchy. Because of this patriarchal religious doctrine, many women through-out the ages have been denigrated by the church. Indeed, according to the Disian view, throughout history hundreds of thousands of women have been raped and killed because religion considered them less than fully human.[50]

Perhaps nothing captures the essence of the feminist contribution to the Disian belief system more than the reality and metaphor of rape. What the sys-tem does metaphorically to the poor and to minorities, it does physically to women. It subjugates them, uses them, and exploits them for their own profit and pleasure. "Violent, rapist, and sadistic"—these are the adjectives another feminist, Miriam Miedzian, uses to describe our culture, in which the violence of men toward women is inculcated through every communications medium. Like her feminist sisters cited above, Miedzian cannot overstate the brutality that is inflicted on the second sex. To explain why American culture has to be radically transformed, she refers to Hannah Arendt's study of Eichmann and other cultures in which torture and sadistic authoritarianism ruled the day.[51]

Similarly, when Helen Caldicott, the anti-nuclear activist, focuses on cor-porate culture, she refers to its "rapacious quest for more and more money." And in the writings of "eco-feminists," the rape metaphor appears so fre-quently whenever the relationship of mankind to the earth is discussed that it has become almost a cliché.[52]

For those who think these attacks on our society are overstated, Disian femi-nists point to the daily barrage of sexism. The abuse of women by politicians (such as Senator Robert Packwood), psychiatrists (whose sexual abuse of their patients is widespread), and media moguls (whose profits depend on T&A, industry shorthand for "tits and ass") is well documented. Any close-up look at the male power elite reveals, again and again, the prevalence of the patriarchal, power-driven mentality. Dennis Levine, the multimillionaire Lehman Brothers financier convicted of insider trading, enjoyed telling his friends how he had enough money that he could have "any babe" he wanted. "Fuck it if you can't buy it," he would say, and his male colleagues on Wall Street would laugh.[53]

So absurdly chauvinistic is our society, Disians point out, that even institutions designed exclusively to serve women are often dominated by men. For example, Simmons College in Boston has always been an all-women institution of higher education run, until recently, by men. With the selection of Jean Dowdall in 1993 as the first woman to be president of the school, change finally came to Simmons. "It took them long enough," said Kristen Heineman, who was editor of the campus newspaper at the time. "Most students think having a man as president of a women's college is ridiculous."[54]

Sexism Victimizes Not Only Women
But Also Men Who Deviate from the Norm.

Just as religion can be used to justify the subjugation of women, so can it be used to discriminate against gays and lesbians. Homosexuals feel excluded by most denominations and have consequently formed their own churches and synagogues. Anti-gay stereotypes, like racial or sexual stereotypes, persist despite overwhelming evidence contradicting them. They persist in the armed forces, despite the fact that gays were decorated for bravery in Vietnam and continue to serve with distinction in every branch of the military. Gays are considered a security threat in government, despite the fact that their ranks include distinguished government representatives at every level. They are considered antireligious, even though they include many devout believers of all faiths and many homosexuals are nuns, priests, or ministers. They are considered unfit to care for children or young people, even though many gays and lesbians are among the most caring teachers, coaches, therapists, and counselors. Obviously, Disians say, homosexuality should not be grounds for discrimination at all. But because the system is so corrupt, these invidious stereotypes continue to take their toll.[55]

Gary Phelps was born and raised a Catholic, was an altar boy, and wanted to grow up to be a priest and a missionary. He wanted to be a good, God-fearing Catholic. In high school, when he had decided to go to seminary, he finally faced the truth that he was gay. At Boy Scout camp that summer, he decided to confess his sins to Father Leo, a wonderful man who worked at the camp and who had always treated him kindly. "I asked for penance," Gary recalls, "but Father Leo said I couldn't have it; I wasn't forgiven because I chose to be a sinner. He said, 'You served at my Mass earlier this week.' He started yelling, saying that I was the devil incarnate and that because of me Christ was never on the altar . . . that whenever I was present, Christ was never there—that everything I did was null and void."

Gary ran into the woods that night and did not return until the following morning. He believed that he was a horrible person and was destined to damnation. He repressed any awareness of his own homosexuality, became an athlete, and did everything he could to pretend that he was normal. The turning point came a few years later in college, however, when a friend named Allen gathered his courage and confided anxiously in Gary that he was gay.

"Why aren't you yelling at me?" asked Allen, terrified that his friend would turn against him as every one else had.

"Because I am, too!" Gary replied.

Their friendship helped Gary accept himself more, and ultimately was the catalyst for his becoming a gay activist. He received a telephone call at college informing him that Allen had tried to commit suicide. Gary knew what had driven Allen to despair. Despite all of Allen's good works—volunteering at nursing homes, fund-raising to support a home for retired nuns, devoting himself to helping others—Allen still believed what the church had told him. Allen still believed he was a sinner.

"Then I got very angry at the Church," Gary says, "because I realized that Allen was dying because he, as a Catholic, believed that he could never be good. I got angry and said, 'I've got to do something. The Church is wrong.' It was a revelation that I could make moral decisions on my own, that I didn't have to listen to the Church, because I knew they were wrong. That was hard to say, that the Church is wrong and that I am right. And it still is."

His friend's attempted suicide spurred Gary to a life of gay activism. He went on to become student body president at his college, a lobbyist in the New York State Legislature, a board member of the Boston Lesbian and Gay Political Alliance, and an outreach coordinator for the Dignity for Today Catholic Church.

"We meet together every Sunday and have a service that's well attended," says Gary, who still retains a deep, committed faith. "It's full of love and caring. We raise money for people with AIDS. We run a soup kitchen every Friday. We raise the money to do that, and we run it as volunteers. You know, gay people helping the homeless, which is great. Reaching out, I think, is a sign of maturity . . . our community reaching out to help those who are more oppressed than us, or at least feel the same oppression. "When Allen's church makes donations to Catholic charities, their donations are returned. The Catholic Church does not recognize them."[56]

Homosexuals like Gary are citizens of Disia because they, too, are victims of oppression. To them, it is obvious that whether one makes love with the same sex or the opposite sex should be a "nonissue," as two lesbian writers put it, "of no more importance than a person's preference for Swiss or American cheese." When other citizens make it an issue, gay Disians are convinced that is further evidence that the social system is based on oppression and exploitation.[57]

Oppression |
"WE DIDN'T HAVE A FIGHTING CHANCE."

From the Old Left of the thirties to the New Left of the sixties to the current crop of radicals on campus, every generation includes its own version of Disians. As evidenced by the reminiscences of Tom Hayden, the sixties radical who became a California state senator, and a host of other sixties memoirs, youthful idealism turns quickly to Disian outrage when confronted with the realities of "the system." Since the privileged Disians like Hayden are likely to be white and middle-class, they are outraged on behalf of others, not themselves. But like the poor and minority citizens, they too feel victimized. They argue that the system has "dehumanized and atomized us all," as Hayden puts it when explaining the demise of his first marriage. They have been robbed, not economically but spiritually; they have been deprived, not of money but of meaning. They walk in solidarity with the powerless because they, too, want a revolution.

Not only minorities, the poor, and feminists believe that oppression is real. So do many nonpoor, nonminority students and workers. These Disians, who are associated with a wide variety of organizations supporting fundamental change, were a huge presence in the sixties and early seventies; were a smaller presence in the eighties; and are showing signs of resurgence in the nineties. But whether their numbers are small or large, the fact that they exist shows that the Disian belief system is not limited to society's most impoverished victims.

Even Some Children of Privilege
Join the Fight Against Injustice.

Anger about oppression and exploitation is present among even the most priv-ileged and best educated. Indeed, Disian views are most prevalent among stu-dents and campus activists at the nation's elite colleges and universities. There are hundreds of thousands of white Americans who identify themselves as citi-zens of Disia. For reasons of their own, they have turned their backs on the privilege and power available to them. In universities throughout the country, affluent young men and women—who have spent their childhood in privilege and have access to life-styles that afford them citizenship in almost any State they want—choose to align themselves with the dispossessed. Even though they may not have been directly victimized by "the system," they believe that it is oppressive and exploitive and must be changed. Consequently, they reject citizenship in Corporatia or other, more comfortable States and commit them-selves to the Disian cause.

Disian attitudes also flourish in the factories and union halls of America. Listening to an automotive worker complain about management, one detects many of the Disian attitudes about exploitation and oppression. Whether in an account of life on an automobile assembly line or in the sardonic portrait of top management in the film *Roger and Me,* workers often express their own cynical brand of Disian beliefs. The conflict between union and management often gives rise to the Disian battle cry: "Whose side are you on?" For Disians in the working class, the answer is unambiguous: the side of the "working man" against the "top brass."[58]

Just as Disians believe that the Establishment oppresses "the people" at home, so do they believe that the Establishment oppresses the powerless abroad. This view was common not only during the revolutionary era of the sixties, but resurfaces to varying degrees whenever the American government takes mili-tary action. Whether in Panama or Grenada, Iraq or Somalia, Disian critics can always be heard arguing forcefully that the true motivation behind military action is not protecting democracy, but exploiting and oppressing the weak. Indeed, when Disians explain almost any event, domestic or foreign, America is usually the villain.

Caught in an impoverished world where trustworthy knowledge is scarce, citizens of the state of Disia are susceptible to untruth, rumor, and conspiracy theories of all kinds. They lose the ability to distinguish facts from factoids, truths from half-truths. Much of their information flow is controlled by other States. They are caught in a veil of lies which blinds them to their own self-interest and destroys whatever confidence they may have in public institutions.

Disians point out, for example, how deeply a single lie has affected America. A *New York Times*/CBS poll found that three out of four Americans believe that John F. Kennedy's assassination was the result of a conspiracy. Only one murder and one lie, Disians point out, deeply shook the faith that millions of Americans have in their government and the press.[59] Disians feel they have been lied to again and again.

Consequently, they believe politics is a con game rigged to keep the down-trodden down and the powerful in power. Like slaves on a plantation, they view the quarrels between owners with a jaundiced eye. They feel they can see through the charade of electoral politics. Disians are resigned to the fact that those who represent their interests rarely reach the highest echelons of power; and when one of their own does become powerful, he often betrays them and is "bought off" or "co-opted" by the Establishment. If he refuses to compromise, he is often blackmailed, libeled, or even killed.

Conventional partisan politics, which is so captivating to the affluent, is painfully irrelevant in Disia. While the Republicans are in power, Democrats blame them for the plight of the dispossessed; when the Democrats are in power, the Republicans blame the Democrats. Instead of serious debate about real injustices, Disians witness well-dressed, well-fed folks arguing about who gets to hold the reins of power, while their dark-skinned nannies do all the work.[60]

The Major Media Are Nothing But a Tool of Oppression.

In contrast to the Corporatian public relations machine, which extols the public benefits generated by the private sector ("Progress is our most important product"), big companies are one of the principal targets of Disian rage. Disian leaders know that one of the tactics used to keep their people oppressed is the steady barrage of misinformation and hype that persuades consumers, including some Disians, that they too can have the good life if they join "the system." But thoughtful Disians know better. Like Cornel West, author of *Race Matters*, they know that corporations are not a symbol of value creation, but of value destruction. "Corporate market institutions," according to West, "which have profit as their primary motivation, have contributed greatly to the collapse of black cultural institutions." While the private sector has been "sacralized," the public sector has been "gutted." Citizens of Corporatia may reap great benefits from the economic system; but to say that Disians benefit from such progress is a lie.[61]

The job of the entertainment media, citizens of the Disempowered State believe, is to compound the lie. For years, the poor have been fed a steady diet of television shows that make it appear that everyone, even minorities, lives in comfort. When a black family finally reaches prime time TV, it is a two-parent family named the Huxtables, consisting of an obstetrician father and a lawyer mother. Such a family is about as representative of black America as Donald Trump is of white America. But it becomes an all-time hit, Disians argue, because it supports the myth that anyone can find affluence in America.

Through the eyes of radical critics of the media, almost everything is part of a systematic disenfranchisement of the "other America." To cite but two examples, one historic and the other current: Frank Capra's well-known film *It's a Wonderful Life* (1946), starring Jimmy Stewart (which non-Disians consider to be uplifting family storytelling) is seen by many Disians as propaganda that capitalism itself is not the problem, just unscrupulous bankers. Potter, the monopolist banker in the film, is a bad man because he operates under the imperative to "accumulate, accumulate, accumulate"; but George Bailey, played by Stewart, is a good man who helps ordinary folks. Thus the film subtly makes the point that there is nothing wrong with the bank itself. Similarly, *Down and Out in Beverly Hills,* the comedy about a homeless man, is seen by Disian critics of the media as supporting the "Reaganite mythology" because it suggests that the homeless *choose* street poverty as a "preferred life-style," rather than being victims of oppression.

These lies, say Disian critics of the media like Michael Parenti, are not accidental artistic "blind spots" but rather part of the architecture of oppression that systematically distorts reality. The news media, like entertainment, directly support the status quo. Parenti argues that the priorities in news coverage are not determined by the news-gathering process or by journalistic values but rather by the "underlying structure of political and economic interest." Disians say that journalism is biased because it is owned and operated by a capitalist elite. As Parenti puts it: "We don't have a free and independent press in the U.S., but one that is tied by purchase and persuasion to wealthy elites and their government counterparts."[62]

For Disians, then, American-style oppression is a formidable adversary. The American society not only exploits racial minorities, the poor, and women;

it then systematically lies and intimidates in order to camouflage the exploitation. "White males continue to dominate every institution—business, government, the media, the church. White males are one-third of the American population, yet they are 80 percent of professors, 80 percent of Congress, 92 percent of the Fortune 500, the owners of all the major publishing houses, 100 percent of U.S. presidents."[63] Despite this overwhelming dominance, affluent white males lament on talk shows, in news columns, and even in Congress that they are somehow victims. They complain about "feminazis," about welfare queens, and about affirmative action.

Disians, however, are not fooled. They know who the real oppressors and victims are. The facts are clear: America is based on exploitation and oppression. The leaders in Washington may say that the Cold War is over, but for Disians it continues as before. Their enemy is not some foreign power, but the power elite within America.

Disians want other Americans to resist. They want citizens of the other Divided States to recognize that, as the Black Panthers used to say, "You are either part of the solution—or part of the problem." They want us to take sides, *their* side, and reject the oppressive structure of our society. If we do, they will call us "brother" and "sister." If we do not, then we are part of the Establishment they hate.

MEDIA

The Superstate

Core belief:	Society is liberated from ignorance and parochialism through freedom of communication.
Defining events:	Invention of television, computers, and the information superhighway.
Sacred text:	The First Amendment.
Primary organization:	Electronic and print media.
Spokespersons:	Entertainment superstars such as Madonna, Michael Jackson; media moguls such as Ted Turner, Michael Ovitz, and Jack Valenti; TV and print journalists.
Electronic media:	Television, computer networks, radio.
Periodicals:	*TV Guide, Columbia Journalism Review, Time, Newsweek, Entertainment Weekly, Rolling Stone, Wired, RTNDA Communicator.*
Educational institutions:	Columbia School of Journalism, film schools, American Film Institute.
Advocacy groups:	The guilds in both journalism and entertainment, Radio and Television News Directors Association (RTNDA), People for the American Way, American Civil Liberties Union, Association of Talk Radio.
Ultimate authority:	Best-seller lists, *New York Times, Washington Post,* Nielsen ratings, box office receipts.
Quote:	*"There will be a high-tech box on your television. I want to feed that box."* —MICHAEL OVITZ, FORMER CHAIRMAN *Creative Artists Agency*

MEDIA, THE SUPERSTATE, through sound waves and air waves and through silicon chips and fiber optics, flows above us and below us, around us and through us. It touches everyone; it covers everything. A homemaker in Dubuque who clicks the remote control to find a TV channel, a ten-year-old girl in Memphis who dons a Walkman headset, a young couple in Provo who go into a movie theater, an office worker in Manhattan who buys a tabloid—all of them are entering the State of Media, the kingdom of words, sounds, and images.[1]

From the Median perspective, America is not just a political entity or a geographic region. It is a never-ending stream of news reports, talk shows, made-for-TV movies, books, computer programs, song lyrics—all transmitted by a web of electronic networks, cable channels, newspapers, periodicals, films, and videos. Once a mere trickle, this flow of information, entertainment, and hybridized "infotainment" is now a torrent, rushing through all the Divided States. However divided we are as Americans, we are connected to the media.

This state is so powerful and so ubiquitous that no major belief system can avoid it. Televangelists use the media to maximize their influence and to extend their pulpits into the political arena. Corporations use it to reach their markets and sell their wares. Activists use it to promote their causes. New Agers rely on audiotapes, videocassettes, books, and a host of new media to promote their higher consciousness. Political leaders seek media coverage to gain citizen support for their programs and to keep themselves in office. And the Superstate uses itself to promote itself, through books about film stars, TV commercials about films, films based on news stories, news stories about authors.

On one level, mass media is business and is controlled by Corporatia. When one media conglomerate buys another or when there is a bidding war for a film studio or a merger between two newspapers, the business decisions are made by corporate executives. Although selling words and images is different from selling breakfast cereals or minivans, the business of communications is still business. To varying degrees, the belief system of media executives, like their Corporatian cousins, is about growth, innovation, competition, and profits.

But the Superstate is more than business. A part of the corporate conglomerates, yet distinct from them, the State of Media has its own belief system, based more on words and images than on dollars and cents; more on communication than on commerce; more on professional standards than profits. As we shall see, some parts of Media (usually referred to as the news companies) carefully maintain some distance from the ordinary marketplace, while other segments of the Superstate (called the entertainment business) mingle with it freely. But despite these differences, most citizens of Media share a belief system which is as powerful as it is camouflaged.

Economically and Politically, the Media Keep America Strong and Healthy.

Messages from the Superstate are, on the one hand, more ubiquitous than those of any other State; yet in certain ways they are almost invisible. This apparent paradox is rooted in Marshall McLuhan's famous line: "The medium is the message." The other Divided States are continually trying to get their messages out. The Superstate itself is its own message. What matters most to the State of Media is not what people are watching on TV but the fact that they are watching. If someone spends most of their nonworking, waking hours consuming words and images from the mass media, then the Superstate triumphs, regardless of what words and images are being transmitted.

There are times when more people are involved with the State of Media—for example, when they are seeing Oprah Winfrey interview Michael Jackson or watching Ted Danson and his colleagues in the closing episode of "Cheers"—than inhabit most countries represented in the United Nations. There are events—such as the Super Bowl games on TV or the Academy Awards telecasts—that are witnessed by more people than have ever heard a minister preach or a politician make a speech. There are songs which almost overnight make more eardrums vibrate than music in previous eras could have reached in centuries. And there are images—of cowboys riding against a blood-red sunset, or a naked-chested, well-muscled man carrying a machine gun, or a blonde dancing with metal cones covering her breasts—that have been seen by almost all adult inhabitants of every State at some time in their lives.

This is the unique power of the Superstate, a power which its citizens believe is well deserved and well used. By Median accounts, it is the oil that lubricates the economy; the electronic stimulus that extends culture beyond the elite to the masses; the information flow that combats ignorance and parochialism; the key to America's economic progress and political stability; and the glue that holds together our increasingly diverse democracy. It accomplishes these vital tasks because its belief system, like its technology, is uniquely suited to the modern era. Because of their State's powerful role, Medians rarely speak about their private beliefs. They don't feel they can foist their views on the public, because they have a responsibility to be neutral, fair, and objective. After all, if Medians imposed their values on their viewers, the media would not be free.

This is Media's primary belief: *freedom*. Those Medians who are journalists believe that freedom should be tempered with *objectivity*. Those who are in entertainment believe that their freedom is limited only by *ratings*. But all are enthusiastic believers in the expanding power of media *technology*.

Let us examine these four Median beliefs more closely.

Freedom |
"PUSHING AT THE EDGE"

The sacred philosophy of Media derives from the fundamental precepts of the Founding Fathers. Even when America was in its infancy, the press was accused of being unfair, unbalanced, and sometimes libelous. But James Madison, in opposing the Alien and Sedition Acts, argued eloquently that "some degree of abuse is inseparable from the proper use of anything; and in no instance is this more true than in that of the press." For a democratic nation, Madison felt the choice was clear. It is far better, he concluded "to leave a few of its noxious branches to their luxuriant growth, than, by pruning them away, to injure the vigor of those yielding the proper fruits."[2]

The other Divided States, failing to heed Madison's warning, are determined to limit Media's freedom. Although citizens of other states shop, spend, learn, worship, and relax with programming from Media, many are becoming increasingly uncomfortable with the power the Superstate has over their lives. Christians, for example, often fear Media because it not only questions authority, but often ridicules it: Christian believers feel helpless as they struggle desperately to defend their world against movies like *Footloose* or *Pulp Fiction* or television programs like "Melrose Place" and "Roseanne." Medians, however, aren't intimidated by their wrath and know that they must hold their ground. While free media may occasionally make mistakes, they are far, far better, in the Medians' view, than a communication system controlled by the state or the church.

From the Median perspective, freedom of speech is what makes America flourish. Medians believe that communications frees us all to make our own choices. Were it not for their efforts, Medians believe, the Union might have splintered apart long ago. Their communications provide a common culture for the millions of new citizens, and provide a forum for the several Divided

States to confront each other and themselves. By providing a forum where all the States can express their concerns and be entertained, Media serves as "the commons"—a place where citizens can encounter each other and participate vicariously in each other's lives.

The Artist's Freedom of Speech Is More Important Than the Community's "Morality."

"My mother caught me," says George (Jason Alexander) in "Seinfeld" on TV, as he sits down in a booth in a Manhattan diner with his three friends: Jerry Seinfeld (playing himself), Elaine (Julia Louis-Dreyfus), and Kramer (Michael Richards), the tall, wavy-haired goofball who has rapidly become a cultural icon.

"Doing what?" asks Jerry Seinfeld.

"You know," he replies evasively. "I was alone."

Pause.

"Ohhhh," Kramer murmurs knowingly.

"Ohhhh," echoes Elaine.

Without ever using the word *masturbation*—which would have triggered alarms in Standards and Practices, the network censors—the conversation unfolds. What makes their conversation so special is that tens of millions are watching it. It had a 10.5 rating (each point represents almost one million homes) and a 29 share (signifying the percentage of homes with televisions in use at the time).

The four characters proceed to place bets as to which of them can hold out the longest against the overwhelming urge to pleasure themselves. To heighten the dramatic tension, each of the four is exposed to provocative, irresistible sexual turn-ons.

George visits his ailing mother in the hospital, assuming that this outing will involve no sexual temptations that might test his will power. Unfortunately, just as he sits down to listen to his mother, the big-breasted woman in the bed beside her is being readied for a sponge bath. The nurse handling the sponge pulls the thin cotton curtain between them and the next bed and begins bathing her patient. Like the television viewers at home, George witnesses these two voluptuous silhouettes through the curtain. The scene is structured so that the viewer cannot help but feel sympathy for poor George, doing the best he can to keep his eyes from being riveted on this titillating drama unfolding only an arm's reach away from him.

Meanwhile, Elaine is undergoing an equally tantalizing ordeal in her after-work aerobics class, surrounded by other women trying to get in shape. But, as she later recounts to her friends, she finds herself doing her workout directly behind John F. Kennedy, Jr. Overwhelmed by his cute body, she too finds herself nearly overcome by the urge to give herself some sexual release.

In the next scene, Jerry, too, is being sorely tested while "making out" with his date on the couch in his living room. Although she kisses, hugs, and fondles him, she refuses to complete the act of lovemaking because she's a Catholic virgin. Her loyalty to chastity combined with her passion for heated foreplay leaves Jerry sexually aroused but entirely unsatisfied. For virtually the entire program, these three forlorn souls squirm sleeplessly as the bet forces them to discontinue their habitual method of giving themselves orgasms.

Producer Larry David wrote the script for this episode and titled it "The Contest." A veteran of television, David developed the show to give his friend Seinfeld a forum for the humor that had made his stand-up comedy act one of the hottest in the nation. "The Contest," David said in an interview shortly after the show was broadcast, "gave me more pleasure than any show I've ever done." It allowed him to transcend one of television's remaining taboos. It earned him the respect of his peers in television because the program showcased his extraordinary skill. Writing and producing an entire show about masturbation without ever actually mentioning the word evaded the "censors" in Standards and Practices, who allowed the show to air without any cuts because they could find nothing objectionable. From the Median perspective, it was an artistic tour de force.[3]

The Median belief system doesn't require agreement with Larry David's high evaluation of this program, but it does require sharing his abiding belief in his right to broadcast whatever he wants. Medians who feel uncomfortable about this episode believe nonetheless that it is his unquestioned right to broadcast it into millions of homes. If people don't like it, Medians say, they can turn off the TV.

Any Attack on Media Freedom Is Unfair and Antidemocratic.

Adversaries of the Superstate portray its citizens as suffering from an obsession with sexual titillation, and consider episodes like "The Contest" further evidence of it. But Medians deflect such criticism by arguing that the issue isn't masturbation but freedom of speech, and they are determined to defend it. Citizens of Media have always been in the forefront of defending democracy from what they consider demagogues. Thanks to their vigilance, their state is so strong that its enemies tread cautiously. Unlike the fifties, when Senator Joseph McCarthy could intimidate the entertainment industry, Media today is too powerful to be blackmailed. With their power greater than ever before and their technological reach expanding rapidly, leaders of the State of Media are determined to continue playing their unique role in defense of freedom.

As they view themselves, their State is neither Christian nor anti-Christian; neither liberal nor conservative; neither consciousness-raising nor consciousness-lowering; neither pro-this nor anti-that. Their belief system, they believe, is a paragon of flexibility and open-mindedness. Simultaneously, one cable channel may be broadcasting fundamentalist preachers exhorting believers to join their denominations, while on the next channel, a talk show host may be interviewing a coven of pagan witches. Similarly, a political commercial defending a candidate may appear one moment, and another attacking the candidate the next moment.

According to Median leaders, the Superstate does not interfere with viewers' choices: it merely expands their range. The state of Media has succeeded in providing viewers and readers with a seemingly infinite array of choices, a menu so vast that virtually all the citizens of every State freely decide almost every day to ignore their own real-life surroundings in order to focus their attention on the media.

Because Medians dare to use the freedom guaranteed by the Constitution, they upset citizens of other States who do not want to be exposed to new ideas. But the heroes of the Superstate are not daunted by the public's timidity. Forty years ago, TV could not show two people in bed together. Thirty years ago the word *pregnant* could not be uttered. Twenty years ago, it was a breakthrough when Mary Tyler Moore, who was single, referred to having sex, or when Archie Bunker's son-in-law Michael (Rob Reiner) confided that he was impotent. Since then, the march of freedom has quickened: on "Charlie's Angels" (1976–81), the three women detectives didn't wear bras; on "Maude" (1972), the heroine (Beatrice Arthur) had an abortion when her diaphragm failed. "Bay City Blues" (1983) showed men naked from the back: the miniseries "Lonesome Dove" (1989) contained a split-second frontal shot of a naked cowboy. Emboldened by these breakthroughs, producers pushed forward with compelling gay characters (Billy Crystal on "Soap" and gay lovers in bed on "thirtysomething"), single women having babies ("Molly Dodd" in 1991 and

"Murphy Brown" in 1992), and teenagers having sex (with "Doogie Howser, M.D." loving it and "Beverly Hills 90210" 's Brenda regretting it).

Today, the struggle to defend—and extend—freedom of speech continues. Stephen Bochco, creator of top shows such as "L.A. Law" and "N.Y.P.D. Blue," is seen as a leader in Media because he is committed to breaking new ground. He has been on the front lines in the fight for freedom and intends to stay there. "Pushing at the edge of broadcast standards," he says, "is something I've always done." He is part of a tradition that he is proud of: expanding the frontiers of freedom.

When gay performance artist Tim Miller struts on stage in the Lower East Side of Manhattan, he strips off his jeans, shirt, and shoes and begins denouncing Senator Jesse Helms. Former artistic director at Highways, a Santa Monica, California, theater that stages shows with titles like "The Bible Belt and Other Accessories," Miller has received grants from the National Endowment for the Arts—and considerable free publicity—for his outspokenly pro–gay rights, anti-homophobia performances. His show called "My Queer Body" includes passionate monologues in defense of gay life-styles and attacks what they see as the hate tactics of Helms and other heterosexual hypocrites. He would probably not have been the focus of national news stories except for the fact that, for most of the time he is on stage, he is utterly naked.[4]

"Sexuality has always been a taboo subject," says Madonna, who articulates what many other Medians also believe. "I'm trying to change that." When asked whether she's trying to change people's attitudes with her book *Sex* and her album "Erotica," she replies bluntly that she sees herself "as a revolutionary . . . I think it will open some people's minds for the good and that's enough as far as I'm concerned." Insulted by people who think she published this book and album to make money or indulge her exhibitionism, Madonna says that her motivation is to help people "enjoy their bodies." *Sex*, priced at $49.95, was packaged in a Mylar bag, dutifully marked with the warning "Adults Only," and sold 150,000 copies on its first day. A total of half a million copies were destined for America's bookstores, and millions more watched her on MTV and on the major networks during prime time.[5]

At the 1995 MTV music awards in New York City, Madonna stated the belief system of the media succinctly. Before giving the award for best rap song to Dr. Dre for "Keep Their Heads Ringin'," she ridiculed Republican Presidential candidate Bob Dole, who had dared speak out against rap music. "Rap has proven itself a force to be reckoned with," Madonna said, "either listen up or get the fuck out of the way."

According to Medians, the argument that the media have too much free-dom is silly. Citizens of the Superstate believe they have too little freedom—and that what little they have is in danger of being further eroded. Unless Medians defend their State, the media marketplace won't be based on what people want to watch, but on what censors let them watch. Many organiza-tions—from the Media Institute to the Motion Picture Association of Amer-ica—are dedicated to fighting any encroachment on First Amendment rights. Highly trained and dedicated lawyers work vigilantly to ensure that neither government censorship nor industry self-censorship will ever undermine our freedom. The freedom to be unfair and offensive, concludes Radio-Television News Directors Association counsel J. Laurent Scharff in *Television Quarterly,* goes hand in hand with the "courage and ability to bring the public the infor-mation and opinion it needs in a democracy." If we want a democracy, we must have free media.[6]

Once this core belief is acknowledged, citizens of the State of Media, par-ticularly those in the news business, will agree that freedom requires responsi-bility. Perhaps the greatest responsibility rests with journalists who, unlike entertainers, must exercise sound judgment. For these Medians, freedom also requires professional objectivity.

Objectivity |
"TO LET THINGS BE WHAT THEY MAY BE"

When Geneva Overholser, once named the nation's top newspaper editor by the *Washington Journalism Review,* resigned from her post at the *Des Moines Register,* it was news. When David Westphal, Overholser's forty-six-year-old managing editor, simultaneously resigned after a lifetime with the paper (he had even delivered the paper as a teenager), it was bigger news. And when word spread that their resignations were due to meddling by the owners in edi-torial matters, the story became front page news across the country.

"I've always been honest in saying that newspapering in America is in-evitably driven by business pressures," Overholser said. "I've said it to the board of Gannett [which owns the *Register*]. I wish we were more open about the profit pressures."[7]

Although both Overholser and Westphal were careful not to blame the corporate powers for their joint departure, the message was clear: defending journalistic objectivity against corporate interference had worn them down.

They had lost their "passion and zest" (to use Westphal's words) because the number crunchers had undermined them. In the war between journalistic professionalism and corporate capitalism, journalism had just lost a battle—and two of its best officers.

"Sometimes I feel like a Rorschach test," says Geneva about her much publicized resignation. "When I resigned, everybody interpreted it in a way that supported what they wanted to believe." Geneva stresses that what led to her resignation were long-standing disappointments and concerns about the news business. "I care a lot about this profession, and I was distressed to see how much of it today is driven by profit pressures which can only be met by catering to advertisers. It's dangerous for a democracy."

When she entered journalism twenty-five years ago, advertising only brought in half or less of a newspaper's revenue. The other half came from subscriptions. Now, she says, advertising constitutes three-quarters or more of the revenue and its proportion is steadily increasing. "The subscriber is not nearly as important as he or she thinks. Editors meanwhile are much more like business executives than we used to be. For six and a half years [as editor of the *Register*], I tried to raise in a very collegial way my concerns about what the relentless quarter-by-quarter pressure for profits was doing to us. But my concerns were not very welcome in the corporate environment. Newspaper companies are very private about their business—ironically, because they hound everybody else to be so open about theirs."

"There is no question that big corporations which happen to be in the news business are more concerned about keeping up corporate profit margins than about covering the news," says Howard Kurtz, the veteran media critic for the *Washington Post* who covered the story of Overholser's resignation and whose paper subsequently hired her to become their ombudsman. "Most journalists are sort of independent spirits who don't even think about the profits of the corporations they work for. In most cases, they are able to go about their business without corporate interference. But where the two worlds intersect is on the question of what sort of financial resources are going to be needed to cover the news. The editors of most papers, including the *Post,* have to wrestle with this every day."

Kurtz says reporters are seldom pulled off news stories because it will ruffle corporate feathers. Journalistic objectivity is undermined by more subtle means. "It goes beyond dollars," says Kurtz, "to the question of risk-taking. The best news organizations take an aggressive approach to digging out the news and take certain risks. The corporate mind-set, however, is averse to taking risks, which leads to shying away from controversial stories and the muting of the reportorial instinct."[8]

Objectivity Means Respecting the Facts
More Than Your Self-Interest.

True Medians believe they must resist corporate pressures to cover stories which bring higher ratings and ignore other news which does not. Their titles say it all: *Read All About It! The Corporate Takeover of America's Newspapers* and *When MBAs Rule the Newsroom* (coauthored by James D. Squires, former editor of the *Chicago Tribune*). They are warning newspaper readers that the content of their news is based less and less on journalistic standards and more and more on corporate concerns. So intense is the pressure to make profits that many Medians fear their reputation with the public is being undermined.

For years, "being objective" has been the phrase with which journalists describe their unique responsibility. According to this standard, facts ("the news") are transmitted by neutral messengers and delivered, still fresh, to consumers (TV viewers, newspaper buyers, and so on). "The public's right to know of events of public importance and interest is the overriding mission of the mass media," reads the code of ethics of the Society of Professional Journalists, Sigma Delta Chi. "The purpose of distributing news and enlightened opinion is to serve the general welfare. . . . Journalists must be free of obligation to any interest other than the public's right to know." Or, as Walter Lippmann put it more elegantly, the ideal journalist "has conquered his desire to have the world justify his prejudices."[9]

Objectivity is the ideal, and while no news editor or reporter can maintain pure objectivity, it is a goal for which a free press is obliged to strive. If that ideal is lost, Medians argue, liberty too will be lost.

Clear Violations of Journalistic Integrity
Are Recognized and Punished.

"I went to bed Monday night and tossed and turned," Michael Gartner, then president of NBC News, told the press in mid-1993, "and I came in the next morning and said, 'I want to go on the air tonight and apologize to the viewers.' " And apologize he did.

In a medium where thirty seconds are worth hundreds of thousands of dollars, anchors Jane Pauley and Stone Phillips read a three-and-a-half minute apology on "Dateline NBC." They were apologizing for a segment that had been broadcast a few weeks earlier portraying a simulated crash in which a gas tank on a GM truck exploded into flames. The show's producers failed to reveal that they had used "incendiary devices" purposely placed near the gas tank to ignite an explosion. By using this technique to create visual impact and failing to inform the TV audience of it, the segment implied that the viewer was watching the natural consequence of a crash rather than the result of a careful setup.

The apology, however, was not enough. Gartner resigned, as did the segment's producer Robert Read, senior producer David Rummel, and executive producer Jeff Diamond. The network's top executives wanted to leave no doubt about the journalistic standards they intended to follow. If people broke the rules of objectivity, they would lose their jobs.

What caused this breach of Median beliefs? Citizens of the Superstate believe that the problem comes from Corporatia. "It's so disheartening to see what's happened to a first-rank news organization," said Lawrence Grossman, the former president of NBC News. "By saying that NBC will no longer use unscientific demonstrations, they're saying that NBC will no longer cheat and fake the news. I think this is what happens when you confuse show business with news. It's the climate of the whole place that's responsible."[10] When 44 percent of the public believes news reports are "often inaccurate" and 68 percent believe the news media "tend to favor one side," it's clear that those fears are warranted.[11]

Citizens of Media are proud of their integrity. As a matter of principle, editors and reporters forego rights that citizens of other states take for granted. Other citizens are entitled to express their opinions, to march in demonstrations, to join any organization they see fit. A journalist, however, is suspect if he or she marches in a demonstration about issues that they themselves may cover. When a gay rights march was organized in Washington, news organizations forbade their staff members from participating. To be identified as an advocate for one point of view in a controversial cause, argued news executives, would undermine the public's confidence in journalistic objectivity.

"Those who cover and report on these issues shouldn't march," said Peggy Hubbel, a spokeswoman for NBC News. Similarly, the Associated Press's executive editor, William Ahearn, issued an electronic memorandum to his staff saying that they "should not participate in activities, be it a gay rights parade, anti-abortion or pro-abortion protest, anti-war demonstration, etc., that are partisan and compromise, or give the appearance of compromising, their ability to be objective."

Thus the National Lesbian and Gay Journalists Association had no choice but to forego participation in a gay rights march. If they participated as an organization, they would be Disians, not Medians. Although some of their members participated "as individuals," the organization did not, for fear of losing its standing in the Superstate.[12]

Journalists Hold Themselves to High Ethical Standards.

Journalists must sacrifice certain rights in order to gain others. They must sacrifice their opportunity to participate in political events the way an ordinary citizen does, and in return they are given special access to influencing the opinions of the public at large. But giving up their rights to speak out as private citizens in order to report as journalists is not easy. Many reporters don't even think the two should be connected. Ahearn's memorandum, for example, was greeted with irate responses by AP reporters who felt that it was infringing on the freedom of journalists to participate in political parties or religious groups. The president of the union representing AP reporters, the Wire Service Guild, concurred, saying that the policy conflicted with employee rights. The Guild warned that, if the AP tried to enforce the memorandum, the union would take legal action.

Despite these obstacles, news executives hold fast to their beliefs. Leonard Downie, Jr., the executive editor of the *Washington Post*, defends his organization's decision to curtail reporters' rights even though he knows the *Post*'s policy is stricter than that of many other newspapers, because he subscribes to the Median belief in objectivity. "We feel it's important to our credibility and our relationship to our readers," he says.

Women and minority journalists face the day-to-day dilemma of deciding how to respond to what white male editors and reporters consider "objective" reporting, but which they find anti-female or anti-black. There is such a wide gap between black and nonblack journalists in the newsroom, according to Dorothy Gilliam, vice-president of the National Association of Black Journalists (NABJ) and a columnist for the *Washington Post*, that one-third of NABJ members said they were "afraid to speak up about race issues pertaining either to the content of the news or to issues that simply pertain to staffing. We learned from this survey that many of our members are operating in an atmosphere and environment of frustration and fear."[13]

So committed are Medians to their own belief in objectivity that even such criticism is dutifully reported in the press. The NABJ's desire for wider black participation in journalism and greater sensitivity to minority viewpoints was reported by the Associated Press, and appeared in newspapers throughout the country. Such self-criticism is part of the tradition of a free press, and even the best journalists know that they, too, must constantly deepen their understanding of how to practice what they preach.

The Violations of Privacy Involved in Exposing the Truth Are a Necessary Part of Democracy.

It is much easier for a reporter to write a generous, glowing portrait of his subject than to do a trenchant, multidimensional analysis. But flattery is not objectivity. The reporter's job, Medians insist, is to challenge, to confront, to dig.

Citizens in every one of the Divided States have been exposed by reporters. Televangelists have been exposed for associating with prostitutes and stealing money. Gurus have been exposed for sexually abusing their followers, cheating on their taxes, and violating basic codes of common decency. Corporate leaders, self-styled revolutionaries, and government bureaucrats have been exposed for lying, corruption, and fraud.

Obviously, these investigations involve risks. They violate privacy. They have resulted in lost businesses, broken marriages, failed political campaigns, and even suicides. But incredible benefits accrue from objective, intrepid investigations by the press. Without them, Medians believe, democracy would sooner or later be destroyed.

According to Medians, their State's responsibility is to expose the truth. In 1994, NBC explored how four powerful legislators used their elected offices for personal gain. First, they took on the former chairman of the House Ways and Means Committee, Representative Dan Rostenkowski, accusing him of a "lavish life-style" underwritten by the taxpayers. Next they investigated Texas Congressman Craig Washington's shady real estate transactions. Then they turned the spotlight on powerful Republican Senator Orrin Hatch, who had proposed and passed a bill in the Senate directly benefiting a company in which he owned 71,000 shares. Finally, the show examined special treatment that enabled former House Speaker Tom Foley to make a large amount of money in the stock market.[14]

Rostenkowski, Washington, Hatch, Foley—none of whom accepted NBC's requests for interviews—were kingpins in the Democratic and Republican power structures. It is the journalist's duty to ask tough questions, to ruffle feathers, to ask the unaskable and think the unthinkable. For if they do not dare to challenge the powerful, Medians ask, who will?

Journalists Are Open-Minded, Unbiased, and Nonpartisan.

Medians take pleasure in noting that two of the most common challenges to their objectivity are (1) that they are too liberal and (2) that they are too conservative. As long as they're being condemned by both sides, most Medians feel reassured that they must be doing *something* right.

The Left is outraged by the news media's conservative bias and the corporate influence on news coverage. "Remember," warns Jeff Cohen, executive director of FAIR (Fairness and Accuracy in Reporting), "when you're watching NBC, you're watching the network owned by GE. Remember that the other broadcast networks are owned by big business. And remember who *doesn't* own or sponsor the news. . . . No unions own any daily papers or TV stations." Put bluntly, the Left believes the media are biased in favor of the rich and powerful.[15]

Nothing could be further from the truth, respond media critics from the Right. As William A. Rusher, the conservative publisher and activist, writes in *The Coming Battle for the Media,* the "media elite" is overwhelmingly and undeniably liberal. Concludes Rusher: "It lies within their power to present a more balanced picture of the 'news'; but they don't because they prefer to paint the world in the primary colors of the liberal superstory."[16]

Fairly consistently, polls of journalists provide evidence that supports Rusher's view that Medians are much more liberal—and secular—than their viewing and reading public. One of the most thorough polls, conducted in 1985 by the *Los Angeles Times,* confirmed that journalists are on the progressive side of almost every major controversial cultural issue. Of the three thousand newspaper reporters and editors polled randomly in the survey, 82 percent were pro-choice on abortion, 89 percent favored homosexual rights, and only 24 percent voted for Ronald Reagan in 1984. Consistently, in poll after poll through the

1970s and 1980s, at least twice as many journalists described themselves as liberal as conservative. And when asked about religion, according to another independent survey of over 200 journalists in the media elite, half checked "none." Less than 10 percent go to church or synagogue regularly.[17]

But Medians respond that these polls are irrelevant because their personal beliefs don't interfere with their professional objectivity. They remove their biases from their reporting. When right-wing extremist Patrick Buchanan makes a speech, for example, Medians must cover it whether they agree with him or not. "Our culture is superior because our religion is Christianity and that is the truth that makes men free," Buchanan said, to 2,000 members of the Christian Coalition in Washington, D.C. Although the majority of reporters and editors detest such moralistic politics, they nevertheless provide all this information about the Religious State (and other States with which they fervently disagree) to tens of millions of Americans who open their newspapers the next morning or who turn on their television sets that night. They provide this service not only for the Right but also for the Left, and for a host of other movements and causes with which they disagree. They do so because they believe that their devotion to a free and uncensored press is the cornerstone of liberty.

Ratings |
"THINGS THAT TOUCH THE HEART"

The rules change when one crosses the border from news to entertainment. Now the priority is popularity, not objectivity. The question Medians in entertainment ask themselves is not "Is it true?" but "Will it sell?"

When it comes to mass appeal, Media is king. Anyone who wants to reach the masses must work with the Superstate. A minister who wants a congregation numbering in the millions? He must turn to TV. A corporation that wants to reach a mass market? It must advertise in the media. A New Age guru who wants to get her message out to the public? She must market her books, tapes, and workshops on the air waves. Politicians who want name recognition? They must buy commercial time on radio and TV. Activists who want social change? They must stage events and hold press conferences that attract reporters.

But no matter how savvy outsiders are about using the communications media, no one reaches audiences as large as does the State of Media itself. Trained for decades in the art of reaching maximum market share, Medians have mastered the art of mass appeal. While others place their highest priority on the content of their belief systems—whether it is Christianity or capitalism or revolution—the first priority of Medians who are wise in the ways of entertainment is ratings.

Ratings mean something more to Medians than just cash. They make them feel that they are meeting a public need. Some Medians in entertainment even take pride in producing shows that violate their own tastes and values. When they produce highly successful shows that don't reflect their own values, they feel like true professionals. After all, their huge market share proves that they are meeting a public need, not just promoting their own belief systems.

Talk shows hosted by Jerry Springer, Ricki Lake, and Jenny Jones are a case in point. They have come under intense criticism for ever sleazier subject matter and increasingly ugly treatment of their guests. But the networks and advertisers that back these shows justify them because of their ratings. Even those who find such programming repugnant defend it.

- Robert C. Wright, the president of NBC, which broadcasts Jerry Springer, admits that the show is "not my best moment of the day." But he quickly justifies broadcasting it by adding: "It's obvious the audience is out there."

- "Some people are certainly questioning what we're putting in households all across the country," says Bill Croasdale of Western International Media, who buys advertising on such programs, "except the viewers are sopping it up."

- "These shows make huge amounts of money," says Dennis McAlpine, a media analyst with Josephthal, Lyon, and Ross. "They're doing so well, I can't imagine any of these companies deciding to tone them down."[18]

From the Median perspective, broadcasting such shows means honoring the right of the audience to choose what it wants to see without interference.

Popularity Is the Best Principle for Deciding What Is Broadcast.

A high school student (played by actor Kevin Bacon) moves with his mother to a small midwestern town dominated by a hellfire-and-brimstone minister. The repressed young people in the town, including the minister's daughter, have been prevented from dancing, by a town ordinance. Spurred on by music written by Kenny Loggins, the young people rise up and dance their way to freedom.

Footloose was a movie with a nationwide publicity campaign; countless TV appearances by the stars; a record album, cassette, compact disc; a hit single that still plays on radio stations across the country; and finally a best-selling videocassette—this, in microcosm, is the state of Media in action. On one level, it was just a set of ordinary business transactions in which intellectual properties were bought and sold, produced and distributed, and finally "consumed." But on another level, it was an effective and eloquent campaign by Media on behalf of its belief system. By portraying the young, dynamic, fun-loving high school student as the hero and the stodgy, old-fashioned, hypocritical minister as the villain, Medians feel that they are advancing a set of values that serve society. And the proof that they are doing so is in the popularity of what they produce. *Footloose* was a huge commercial success: it became one of the six top-selling sound tracks of all time. And the values it promoted—sexual freedom, rebellion against tradition, etc.—were also exemplified in the other five: *Grease, The Bodyguard, Saturday Night Fever, Purple Rain,* and *Dirty Dancing.*[19]

When Amy Fisher, the "Long Island Lolita," shot her alleged lover's wife, no less than three networks rushed to cover the story and turn it into a television movie. Media critics claim that commercial greed, pure and simple, drove the media into their feeding frenzy. When John Matoian, CBS's senior vice president for movies and miniseries, reflects on the upsurge of Amy Fisher-type movies, he finds positive social value. "I suppose these are as hard and difficult times as ever," he suggests, "and people are looking for windows into behavior. Hopefully from these kinds of stories they'll gain insight, and I hope—and this will sound naive—that these movies will explain events that could have been prevented had someone stopped them before they went too far. In every one of them, the perpetrator is found, sentenced, and not let go. That's the basis of classic drama. I'm not saying that we're doing Shakespeare here, but these stories do have similar themes running through them."

Across town at ABC, Judd Parkin, vice president for movies and miniseries, found his analogy in Greek drama. "Domestic violence stories in which someone acts on their darkest impulses have a catharsis. How can a man murder his family? How can a man molest his child? How do people act on their darkest impulses? These are questions that go beyond everyday experience. This may sound pretentious, but these are the questions the Greeks were dealing with."[20]

Although Medians admit a ratings-based mass communications system has flaws, they believe such a system is far superior to its alternatives. An entertainment system based on ticket sales, Nielsen ratings, advertising revenues, and other market measures is, in their view, a positive force. What the public wants to see, argue TV producers, is what they have the right to see. And although the viewing public's tastes don't always please the ministers, gurus, or public officials, Medians argue that the public's choices are superior to corporate or governmental control.

The Media Must Protect Itself Against Government Censorship.

Medians are ever vigilant against intrusions by government into the communications field. They fume when they hear Federal Communications Commission Chairman Alfred Sikes argue that, since broadcasting plays such a "central role . . . in forming our nation's culture, absolute freedom is denied." According to Mr. Sikes, government officials should decide how "national values" can be "reflected" in the choice of programming. Of course Sikes promises that outright government intrusion will be kept at a minimum through self-regulation by the industry itself. But Medians believe that once the door is opened to political censorship, it will never be closed.

Consequently, citizens of the state of Media stand fully behind the First Amendment. In their defense, they cite such legal precedents as the flag-burning case of *Texas* v. *Johnson,* in which the United States Supreme Court stated clearly that government "may not prohibit the expression of an idea simply because society finds the idea itself offensive." This principle holds, declared the Court, even if the offensive material has an impact on "things that touch the heart of the existing order."[21]

Those Who Condemn Immorality in the Media Are Religious Fanatics.

Screenwriter Joe Eszterhas was paid three million dollars for his script for *Basic Instinct,* which opens with a scene of sex and murder. A woman is making love with a man who feels an orgasm welling within him. He thrusts his head back in ecstasy. At precisely the moment of his orgasm she pulls out a razor-sharp knife and cuts his throat. As the novelization of the movie put it: "Again and again her arm plunged to his throat, his chest, his lungs. The cream sheets turned red. He died, blowing body and soul into her." In short, it had everything that works at the box office: sex and violence, compelling characters, a fast-moving plot, and a tag line that was a surefire winner: "Sex was the foreplay . . . death was the climax."

What made the project hot in the State of Media, however, was precisely what made it so objectionable in Patria. The year after the film was released, a full-page ad (financed by Reverend Donald Wildmon's American Family Association) appeared in the *New York Times* under the headline: "We are Outraged! And We're Not Going to Put Up With It Any Longer!" The ad excoriated the movie and television industry for undermining the morals of American young people.

> Shame on the boards of directors of music companies for letting singers encourage sex. Shame on those in charge of Hollywood for an endless stream of films filled with profanity, nudity, sex, violence and killings. For example, the giant hit *Basic Instinct* features murders during orgasms, setting a new standard of perversion even for today's movies.

And so the issue is sharply drawn. In the State of Media, *Basic Instinct* is considered a triumph, but in the State of Patria, a travesty.

Most Medians consider Wildmon to be a dangerous zealot, whose boycotts of advertisers they find dangerous. Recently, Wildmon aimed his organizational guns on a new TV program by veteran producer Stephen Bochco, "N.Y.P.D. Blue." It was predicted that the campaign by Reverend Wildmon to boycott Bochco's show would fail. "The Reverend Wildmon is as overrated as the New York Mets," said Paul Schulman, who defended Bochco by saying: "This is a brilliantly creative guy who doesn't want to repeat himself." Bochco argued that "N.Y.P.D. Blue" broke new ground because it "goes a little farther than anything that's gone before."[22]

When faced with the decision whether to air "N.Y.P.D. Blue" or respect their own communities' values, some network affiliates opted to cut Bochco's show from their schedules. "You're not going to find much representation of America's greatest heroes among affiliates," Bochco replied bluntly. "I find it regrettable that there are station managers out there who are acting as community censors."[23]

From Bochco's perspective, the State of Media demands courage. American life is violent; it is sexual; and artists with integrity must be free to explore that violence and eroticism without outside interference. It is even worse, according to Bochco, when creative writers and directors put limits on their own work. "One of the worst things we do in TV is to precensor ourselves," Bochco warns. "It's cowardly."[24]

Violence Is Not Caused by the Media, But Merely Reflects a Violent Society.

After years of defending themselves against repeated attacks on their integrity and incessant infringement on their freedom of speech, representatives of Media feel they are being scapegoated. "What is needed more than anything is parental responsibility," said Jack Valenti, the president of the Motion Picture Association of America. Valenti believes that filmmakers can and should make whatever films they want and it is the responsibility of filmgoers to choose the films they see. It is not the filmmakers' responsibility to censor themselves in order to appease public tastes.

Geraldine Laybourne, president of the youth-oriented Nickelodeon channel on TV, took the trouble to spend time with children to talk about television violence. "Even kids know that TV is not the problem," she told a government-industry summit meeting in Hollywood. The kids, she said, "just wondered how come it's so easy for people to get guns in this country." Her comment was greeted with ringing applause by the Median audience, who agreed with her that the availability of guns, not the media's glorification of violence, was the real problem.[25]

And why, ask Medians, focus on television? Aren't other forms of communication and entertainment even more violent? After all, any child can walk into a video game store and buy a game like "Mortal Kombat" in which they control a martial arts character who rips out the spines of his adversaries, cuts off their heads, or tosses them onto a bed of spikes littered with other corpses. Made by Acclaim Entertainment, Inc., of Oyster Bay, New York, this top-seller has been popular for years in arcades but is now available for any child's private use (price: $80). Once government censors begin wielding their ax on network programs, won't they also go after video games? And then board games and other toys? And then comic books? If we don't draw the line in defense of the

First Amendment to protect all communications, say leaders of Media, soon it will protect none.[26]

While other states attempt to scapegoat Medians for all the problems in society, network executives are erecting their defense. Some, like Capital Cities-ABC, Inc., chairman Thomas Murphy, who recently co-engineered the Disney-ABC merger with Michael Eisner, try to stave off government regulations by promising that "we can handle our own problems responsibly." Executive vice president of Fox Broadcasting George Vradenberg said his network believes its shows "America's Most Wanted" and "Cops," which critics cite as part of the increasing violence on TV, are in fact engaged in effective violence *prevention*. Vradenberg is proud of the fact that "America's Most Wanted" has led to the apprehension of 250 criminals. "Far from glamorizing violence," he said, "it is dedicated to the prevention of violent crime." Said Howard Stringer, former president of the CBS Broadcast Group, "There are 200 million guns, 66 million handguns in America. That has a lot to do with violence. The frustration in this society only takes it out on us. That is not going to solve violence in America."[27]

In 1993, government officials, led by Senator Paul Simon (D-Ill.), told the networks that if they didn't police themselves to limit depictions of violence, federal regulations would follow. Representative Ed Markey (D-Mass.) went further, sponsoring a bill which would require new TV sets to contain a device to allow parents to electronically block children from gaining access to certain shows. In the end, the major networks agreed to a combined effort to prelabel shows with a parental advisory warning of violence, hoping this would forestall further government regulations.

But those Medians on the front lines in defense of their State were unhappy with the compromise, fearing it was another erosion of the First Amendment. "This is the thought police," said Don Ohlmeyer, NBC West Coast president, after hearing a host of academic researchers try to link TV violence with real violence. "I have no intention of altering the elements [in my shows] in regard to the hue and cry over violence," said "L.A. Law" 's William Finkelstein. "I've heard all this stuff before," complained a frustrated Stephen J. Cannell, action series producer. For those Medians, what counts is what's popular. If it sells, it has value. If people want it, they deserve it. If it can capture a market share, then it belongs in America.

Technology |
"WE CREATED LIFE."

Freedom, tempered in newsrooms by objectivity and in entertainment by popularity, is the core of the Median world view. But the most profound impact of the State of Media in the future will be rooted in yet another core belief which underlies the most far-reaching revolution of all: faith in media technology.

In the early days of film, the act of watching a moving picture on a screen was cause for wonder. In the 1950s, having a choice between three television networks was considered significant consumer choice. Now, almost a half century later, the number of television channels has increased more than a hundredfold. Events from all over the world can be experienced as they happen. Human senses now are extended beyond the body so that virtually any sight or sound (and soon smell and taste) can now be experienced by almost anyone anywhere.

But all these changes, and all these choices, did not change one basic limitation: the passivity of the viewer. No matter how exciting the programming, now matter how arresting the visual images or how realistic the sound track, the viewer has remained inactive. He or she could switch the channel, but could not enter the drama. Consequently, leaders of the Superstate have begun searching for ways to make the next media revolution. Their goal is as simple as it is unprecedented: to enable the viewer not just to witness, but to participate.

The More Deeply Audiences Are Involved in the Media,
the Better It Is for Them, and for America.

Citizens are now participating in electronic town meetings (ETMs) in metropolitan areas throughout the country. Technologies are on-line which will allow shoppers to browse through catalogues and make purchases without ever leaving their homes. Voters in some areas will soon be able to track candidates' positions on the issues, and to cross-check their positions against a data bank of factual information. Newspapers will be available on home computers. Through computers, hooked up via modems to telephone lines and using e-mail and a portion of the Internet called the World Wide Web, anyone can join the more than 30 million users who communicate through cyberspace. (This number is expected to reach 100 million by the end of the decade.) Computer clubs with hundreds of thousands of members exist for a wide variety of special interests. Singles have located and met their mates through computer courtships.

Having chafed at criticisms that consumers are becoming increasingly passive, Medians are ecstatic about these new interactive possibilities. Terms like "couch potato" grated on their nerves. The communications media were supposed to awaken and enliven culture, not deaden it. So the new technologies seem like a dream come true. Medians are so enthusiastic about the emerging technologies they are publicizing them before they're available for the consumer. "Welcome to the information highway," exhorts *Newsweek*, for example. "Just punch up what you want and it appears when you want it."[28]

Today the electronic superhighway already enables plugged-in Medians to go almost anywhere in the world. But unlike ordinary travelers, they "arrive" at their destination as fast as the electronic impulses can travel through the circuitry. A citizen who lives in the most remote part of the country can, with a push of a button, be in touch with climbers in Nepal, surfers in Hawaii, or commodity traders in Chicago.

"What are they going to play on those 500 channels?" asks Michael Ovitz, former chairman of Creative Artists Agency (CAA). "There will be a high-tech box on your television that enables you to access a cornucopia of choices. I want to feed that box." Now, as president of the newly expanded Disney empire, he can "feed" television and movie screens all over the world.

At CAA, he represented a vast number of the major stars, directors, and producers, and was extremely influential in arranging major financing for a number of studios. On his telephone in his corner office at the CAA headquarters, designed by I. M. Pei, was a single-word admonition: *Communicate!*

"This place is beginning to feel just like the White House," says Anna Perez, who is now CAA's chief spokeswoman after four years as Barbara Bush's press secretary. And no wonder: CAA has been the White House of the entertainment industry.[29]

The "Information Superhighway" Is a Revolution Allowing Ordinary Mortals To Transcend Time and Space.

Media's next goal is to transcend time. Unlike the early television viewer, who could watch any of three programs being broadcast in "real time," first-class travelers to Media within the near future will be able to watch any visual scene ever recorded on film or videotape, and any sound ever recorded in any medium at any time.

There are still millions of miles of fiber optics cable to be laid before Media can offer these attractions to potential visitors.[30] But just as today's freeway system is taken for granted by the younger generations, so will the information superhighway be taken for granted by coming generations. Moving a viewer's consciousness backward and forward in real time and real space is already becoming standard operating procedure. What challenges creative citizens of the Superstate today is the creation of *other* realities. The greatest breakthrough is not to move around within ordinary reality, but to invite human beings into alternative realities which exist only in Media. Rather than merely reporting stories from the real world, Media is on the verge of creating its own world. While Disneyland attracts millions, the new cyberworld will ultimately attract billions—because people will not have to leave their own homes in order to be there.

Excited by the "dawn of the interactive age," cutting-edge filmmaker George Lucas calls the information superhighway "one of the great technological developments of the twentieth century." From his base at Skywalker Ranch, one of the most technologically sophisticated facilities in the film industry, Lucas talks about bits and bytes as easily as about movies. He loves the new technology because it allows him "to tell stories that I couldn't even dream of at the time of the first *Star Wars.*" Lucas thinks that within his lifetime, not only dinosaurs (as in *Jurassic Park*) but people will be created in his shop. The electronic film lot might be a simple blue room in which computers provide everything, including the actors, and moviegoers will witness on the screen a reality which existed at no time, at no place, except in the imagination of the Medians who produced it. It will be a computer-generated reality entirely under the control of its creators.

From the Median perspective, this power is almost divine. Although the millions of moviegoers who watched the dinosaurs in the movie *Jurassic Park*—which were created at Lucas's Industrial Light and Magic (ILM)—may not have known it, the terrifying *Tyrannosaurus rex* spent only six and a half minutes on the screen. But it took fifty ILM employees a year and a half, using $15 million worth of equipment, to make those few minutes of time travel possible. "We created life on a deadline and a budget," said Steve Williams, a twenty-nine-year-old ILM computer animator. "Nobody gave God those limitations."[31]

This young Median's hyperbole reflects the Superstate's enthusiasm for the godlike powers technology has given them to create human "life." While less tangible than the life created in the book of Genesis or by the cosmic unfolding of evolution, it is much more responsive to human will. In the actual world, what happens is not under our control. In this "virtual" world, however, Medians will control everything.

***

"Virtual Reality" Is Becoming
a Better Place To Live Than Reality Itself.

***

In MIT's Draper Laboratories, at the NASA/Ames Human Factors Research Division, and at Silicon Graphics, "virtual reality" was born.[32] Initially one could enter virtual reality only in special labs or military flight-simulation rooms. Now one can do so in malls and arcades across the country where participants play "VR" games wearing special headsets linked to hand controls. The revolution now under way will bring this new dimension of reality into every living room that has a television set, into every office that has a computer, and to every person holding a telephone. When this breakthrough occurs—and scores of Medians are working on it today—citizens of any State will be able to choose their reality.

For those who are at the edge of the "VR trade," a new language has by necessity emerged to describe this new reality. The entire techno-electronic system is called a "reality engine." The three-dimensional world, which is stored in the computer's memory, is called "cyberspace." Those who enter that dimension are called "cybernauts." And the total experience of virtual reality is, in Howard Rheingold's cyber-hip lingo, "a cooperative production of the microchip-based reality engine sitting on the floor of the laboratory and the neural reality engine riding in my cranium." In other words, human senses and computer circuits become one interacting organism. Medians are elated by their potential control over the internal psychosensory environment we call the "mind." The potential impact is so revolutionary that, according to Medians in the VR trade, "we are on the brink of having the power of creating any experience we desire."[33]

Virtual reality has enormous appeal, Medians realize, because of mounting fears about living in the "real world." Violence makes the streets unsafe; AIDS makes sexual experimentation more risky; environmental pollutants erode the beauty of nature; overcrowding makes travel ever more congested; and so on. Consequently, the new generation is living less and less in natural time, and increasingly in electronic time; not in natural space, but in cyberspace. Regardless of the State into which they were born, more and more young people are becoming citizens of Media. In this media-generated new frontier, citizens can find what reality no longer offers. Community, natural beauty, safety, excitement—you name it, Media has it. Since the "pursuit of happiness" has become so much tougher in real life, the Superstate is increasingly providing a virtual alternative.

What could be better for America, Medians ask, than a new territory of unlimited size that can reach throughout the world and be largely controlled from our country? It is a blessing beyond belief, a gift beyond value. Medians want all Americans to cherish the fantastic benefits that the media bring. They want our homes, cars, and offices to be filled with the sights and sounds of their productions. They want all good citizens to cry with their televised tragedies, laugh with their situation comedies, be informed by their news and reality-based programming. In short, they want us to become citizens of their State. By doing so, Medians believe, we will enrich our lives and strengthen our nation.

GAIA

The Transformation State

Core belief:	Social action based on higher consciousness will save the world.
Defining events:	Earth Day 1970, the Age of Aquarius, sixties counterculture.
Sacred text:	*Silent Spring, The Whole Earth Catalog, The Perennial Philosophy, The Aquarian Conspiracy.*
Spokespersons:	Ram Dass, David Brower, Stewart Brand, Willis Harmon, Barbara Marx Hubbard, Fritjof Capra, Deepak Chopra, Lester Brown, Hazel Henderson, Matthew Fox, Sam Keen, Marianne Williamson, Theo-dore Roszak.
Electronic media:	New Dimensions radio, EcoNet, local cable programming, personal growth audio tapes.
Periodicals:	*New Age, Yoga Journal,* environmental periodicals, alternative health newsletters, *Natural Health, Common Boundary, World Watch, Creation Spirituality, Parabola, Science of Mind.*
Educational institutions:	Esalen Institute, Naropa Institute, Omega Institute, New York Open Center.
Advocacy groups:	Greenpeace, Natural Resources Defense Council, New Age Publishers and Retailers Association, Earth Day USA, World Wildlife Fund, National Audubon Society, Foundation for Conscious Evolution, Institute of Noetic Sciences, ZPG (Zero Population Growth), Cousteau Society, Wilderness Society, Association of Humanistic Psychology, Windstar Foundation, Seva Foundation.
Ultimate authority:	Tao, Great Spirit, Life Force, Creator, Mother Earth.
Quote:	*"The main obstacle we face as a species is found in the present evolutionary level of our consciousness. That is the primary cause of the senseless plundering of natural resources, the pollution of our water, air, and soil."*[1] —Dr. Stanislav Grof

I T IS 1966. Outside the main gate of Columbia University is a tall, skinny twenty-seven-year-old wearing a sandwich board and hawking lapel buttons, both of which bear the same message: "Why Haven't We Seen a Photograph of the Whole Earth Yet?"

That was how Stewart Brand, founder of the *Whole Earth Catalog*, called attention a quarter of a century ago both to the planet and to human consciousness, which he felt were intimately connected. Because of the recent space flights, Brand knew NASA had pictures of the dazzling blue-green ball framed against a black universe. But he suspected that they hadn't released it yet for a simple reason: the image would transform human consciousness.

And it has, according to citizens of Gaia.

Thirty years later, the motto for much of the younger generation is: "Think globally, act locally." Generation after generation have committed themselves to one kind of consciousness-raising or the other. Earth Day is a national institution with more citizen involvement than many traditional holidays. Half the best-seller list is comprised of books involving New Age ideas. Concepts once unknown to most Americans—ecosystem, self-actualization, alternative medicine, meditation—are now part of everyday life. As Stewart Brand wrote in his introduction to the most recent edition of the *Whole Earth Catalog*: "Here are the tools to make your life go better. And to make the world go better. That they're the same tools is our theory of civilization."[2]

Welcome to Gaia, a State whose citizens believe that during the second half of the twentieth century a new paradigm of thinking has emerged which is transforming every aspect of society. Rooted in the new physics, new psychotherapies, new organizational theories, and new religions, the power of this "rising culture" cannot be measured in votes or dollars. It is grounded in consciousness rather than power, and reflected in networks rather than hierarchies. It manifests itself in a web of interlocking Gaian movements—an "Aquarian conspiracy," as Marilyn Ferguson put it—which includes "the ecology movement, the peace movement, the women's movement, the holistic health and human-potential movements, various spiritual movements, numerous citizens' movements and initiatives," etc.[3]

For astronaut Russell Schweickart, a change in his consciousness happened as a result of his being in space. "When you go around the earth in an hour and a half," Schweickart said, "you begin to recognize that your identity is with the whole thing." For Gaians who are earthbound, however, a change in their consciousness must be inspired in other ways—from therapy to affirmations, from meditation to mind-altering drugs, from returning to nature ("vision quests") to embracing high technology ("biofeedback"). Whatever method Gaians choose, their motivation is to expand their consciousness to ever higher levels and to live in harmony with the earth. Consequently, these citizens care as much about the god within each of us as Patrians care about their God in heaven. They care as much about the sacredness of nature as Corporatians care about exploiting natural resources. Citizens of the Transformation State believe that raising human consciousness, grounded in a profound reverence for our shared planet, is the way to bring peace on earth. As the Gaian monthly *Science of Mind* puts it: "Change Your Thinking, Change Your Life." Or as the sign in a New Age bookstore on the island of Maui reads: "Specializing in Self-Discovery."

"There will never be a better world until there are better people in it," concludes John White in his book *The Meeting of Science and Spirit: Guidelines for a New Age,* "and the place to start building better people is within yourself." To that end, White offers a new "pledge of allegiance" from a Gaian perspective:

> I pledge allegiance to Humanity
> And the planet on which we live,
> One world, under God, indivisible,
> With peace and enlightenment for all.

Precisely how many people would take this Gaian pledge is impossible to determine. Certain values-based demographic studies suggest a range of 8 percent to 12 percent of the American public. One out of twelve Americans say they have "participated in New Age practices." One out of five say they are "nonreligious," i.e., do not subscribe to any of the traditional Judeo-Christian religions. And an even larger percentage say they are very concerned about the environment and "think globally." But since Gaians value their independence, individuality, *and* privacy, it is impossible to assign an accurate figure to the population of this State.[4]

The major difference between the New Age pledge of allegiance and the more traditional one are three words: *planet, peace,* and *enlightenment.* These terms are key entry points into the Gaian belief system. Citizens of this State pride themselves on thinking more globally than nationally; raising consciousness to a level higher than ordinary reality; and working for social change in a harmonious, collaborative style.

But these three features of the belief system of Gaia will be incomprehensible to citizens of other States unless we first examine the Gaian interpretation of the word "God." Although spelled and pronounced the same way in Gaia as in Patria, its meaning is radically different. That difference is a fitting starting point for our journey through the Transformation State.

God |
"THE MOTHER OF US ALL, INCLUDING JESUS"

"This is where Mary and I got married," Jeffrey says, pointing to their prayer tree, a big gnarled old spruce twice the size of any of the other trees in the area. Mary spreads her arms halfway around the tree's trunk. "Every other tree this size in the valley has been felled," Jeffrey continues. "This is the lone survivor. The old guy has been around a long time. Everything we do affects him; everything he does affects us. So it seemed like the right place to have our marriage ceremony."

Jeffrey and Mary live in a 500-square-foot cabin in a small village nestled in a Rocky Mountain valley at an altitude of almost two miles. Jeffrey is a massage therapist who also leads men's workshops and vision quests. Mary is a former director of the summer program at the Naropa Institute, a private, Buddhist-oriented college frequented by Tibetan monks and home-grown mystics like Allen Ginsberg, and a teacher of singing and dance.

Walking a little farther, the couple come to the nearly frozen creek that winds its way through the floor of this secluded alpine valley and stop to listen to the water rushing beneath the layer of snow-covered ice.

"The ski resort up over that ridge wants to buy some of this water to make artificial snow," says Jeffrey, his eyes wandering toward the pine-covered mountains framing the valley to the south. "They want to expand their business—extend the ski season into late fall and early spring. It makes perfect sense to them. But I think they're crazy. I mean, it's like the folks from the city who come driving through to go skiing. They drive through this village as if they're still on the freeway. They don't even see this village. They just want to get on the slopes. I've almost been hit head-on a couple of times by people who don't even see local traffic. Just like the resort developers, the only thing that matters to them is where they're headed. The land, the trees, the water, even us locals—all that doesn't figure in their vacation plans. So they don't even see it. They just don't see."

"That's why we like taking folks on solo fasts in the wilderness," says

Mary. "By the third day, they slow down. They *see* where they are. They *feel* the sacredness. A tree stops being just a tree. A rock stops being just a rock. They connect. It's a beautiful process to watch."

Jeffrey finds a pine tree with a split trunk, with resin oozing down its bark. He slides his forefinger through the ochre glue, brings it to his nose, and sniffs. The scent brings a wide grin to his face.

Jeffrey was raised in a small city outside Detroit and Mary lived for several years in Manhattan. No strangers to civilization, they have strong feelings about how disconnected Americans are from the sacredness of nature. "It's just how we're raised," says Jeffrey. "We're raised on food that comes in plastic packages and water from a faucet. We're raised thinking that nature is something to study in biology class—if we happen to be interested. We're raised thinking that human civilization is complex, but nature is simple. We're taught that nature is just stuff that's sitting around, waiting for human beings to find a good use for it."

For Humanity to Survive,
the Earth Must Become Sacred Once Again.

The developers who exploit the land for corporate profits, and the skiers who use nature but do not respect it, worry Jeffrey and Mary. They do not fear for themselves because if life in their Rocky Mountain wilderness loses its purity, they can always move farther up into the mountains or north to Montana or Idaho. They fear for the earth itself, which they feel is being wounded by those human beings who do not hold it in reverence. Jeffrey and Mary don't think of God as a heavenly father, passing judgment on mortals down below. For them, the divine is the tree beneath whose branches they were married; the divine is the rocks, which they call the "stone people" and which warm their sweat lodge; the divine is the animals, the four-leggeds and the creepy-crawlies, with whom they share creation. The divine is the natural world with which they are one. Walking with pine needles beneath their feet and listening to a rushing mountain stream nearby, they know this valley is their sanctuary. If God is to be found anywhere, He is here, and He—more than in any of the other Divided States—is *She!*

The Patriarchy Is Dying;
the 'Feminine Principle' Is Awakening.

The state of Gaia, after all, is named after a Greek goddess. Its official philosophy, often called eco-spirituality, was catalyzed in a conversation between British scientist James Lovelock and novelist William Golding, walking through the woods in England. Lovelock was about to announce a controversial theory which, in Lovelock's words, challenged "the conventional wisdom that sees the earth as a dead planet made of inanimate rocks, ocean, and atmosphere, and merely inhabited by life." Golding immediately suggested that Lovelock name his theory "Gaia." Lovelock recalls feeling "glad and grateful" for his neighbor's suggestion, because it was a "simple four-letter word and not an acronym . . . so beloved of my fellow scientists." What it stood for was complex indeed, namely, the hypothetical "chemico-bio-geo-cybernetic . . . system which regulates this planet." So was born the Gaia Hypothesis, a grand synthesis which considers the earth one vital, living organism.[5]

Small and white-haired, Lovelock is as modest as his theory is ambitious. When asked how "Gaian thinking" would fare in competition against other world views, from fundamentalist to corporate, he pauses. "This is a difficult question," he responds. "I am just one isolated man. I live in the country. I see people only when I am out speaking, so it is hard for me to judge. But I would say if Gaian thinking is of value to our society, it is because of its ecumenism. It reduces the fragmentation of science and other special interests. It emphasizes the whole."[6]

This "whole" is not created by a (masculine) God who sits apart from and above His natural creation. In the Gaian world view, the "whole" of creation is masculine *and* feminine and includes everything—not just nature, but human beings and our gods. Some Gaians, such as Lovelock himself, refer directly and specifically to his efforts to prove "her" (God's) existence. Other Gaians, when evoking the sacred force within all life, may refer to an androgynous Tao, Great Spirit, Life Force, or Creator. But whatever their terminology, Gaians do not see the divine as a masculine entity *above* nature but rather a more feminine (or "gender-neutral") being which is *part* of nature.

Although Lovelock proposed Gaia as a scientific concept, it is a spiritual hypothesis as well, opening up the possibility that "God," whatever he or she is, is synonymous with creation, not separate from it; is innate or immanent, not abstract; is natural, not supernatural. It also implies that nature itself is sacred, as are we, *Homo sapiens.* "The one-sided emphasis on deity as a loving father simply can't hold any longer," says Peter Caddy, the cofounder of a spiritual community in Scotland called Findhorn, which is a popular Gaian retreat center. "As our God concept becomes more androgynous, we'll relate to the source of life as both God and Goddess."[7]

Male as well as female citizens of the Transformation State believe that their embrace of the "feminine principle" is part of a profound new awareness of the planet and of the imminence of its evolution—or its destruction. From a Gaian perspective, we are destroying creation. As Thomas Berry, whom *Newsweek* called one of the "new breed of eco-theologians," puts it, we human beings are the "peril of the planet."

Through human presence, argue Gaians, the forests of the earth are being destroyed. Fertile soils become toxic and then wash away in the rain or blow away in the wind. Mountains of human-derived waste grow ever higher. Wetlands are filled in. Each year approximately ten thousand species disappear forever. The ozone layer above the earth is being depleted. To reverse this ecocidal trend, which Gaians consider to be the ultimate sacrilege, requires more than accelerated enforcement of environmental safeguards. The recycling of garbage, reductions in carbon emissions, or the elimination of chlorofluorocarbons (CFCs)—these are of course necessary technical and political steps. But they alone are not sufficient.

What is needed, according to Gaian leaders, is a fundamental shift in our view of the sacred. We must bring it down from heaven and back to the earth. From a Gaian perspective, for example, water is not just two atoms of hydrogen and one atom of oxygen, a "fortuitous combination" of elements, writes Kirkpatrick Sale in *Annals of Earth*. In the Judeo-Christian tradition, Sale explains, water lost the divine status it held in virtually every other culture. In Persian myth and in ancient Babylonia, among Native Americans from the Aztecs to the tribes in California, water was "a benign and powerful and often a central deity—and most often, because of its fertility and fecundity, a goddess." But all this changed when science, "that mechanistic process to which the Judeo-Christian heritage has given rise," secularized water and, as Sale puts it, turned it into "one more element to be manipulated at the whim of the one true God."[8]

Transforming human consciousness and our concept of spirituality is Gaians' primary mission for their State. It's a task they undertake, not out of a desire for power, but out of devotion to the planet. When they wax most prophetic, citizens of this State speak of Gaia in terms almost identical to those Patrians use when speaking of God. "Gaia is immortal," says Lovelock. "She is the eternal source of life. She is surely a virgin. She does not need to reproduce herself, as she is immortal. She is certainly the mother of us all, including Jesus."[9]

As Gaians shift from worshiping a God in heaven to God as earth—what renegade Catholic theologian Matthew Fox calls "creation spirituality"—many devout Christians are outraged. The biblical commandment "Thou shalt have no other gods before me" is being violated, argue many followers of Jesus Christ. "New Agers who had rejected God," writes Tal Brooke in a scathing fundamentalist critique of Lovelock's Gaian thinking, "were only too eager to become Gaia's children in servitude to Mother Earth. . . . Those who stand before the altar to venerate Gaia illustrate a principle corollary to goddess worship—spiritual degeneration."[10]

Gaians understand that traditional, rigid mind sets are bound to be threatened by the new paradigm. Eco-spirituality is called "paganism" by various fundamentalists, Gaians believe, because that is the way closed, security-driven minds work. Unorthodox thinkers—which Gaians, naturally, consider themselves to be—must threaten the orthodox. "Great spirits," as Albert Einstein once said (and as Gaians frequently repeat), "have always encountered violent opposition from mediocre minds."

By taking care of themselves, Gaians believe they are also taking care of the sky and the earth. "It takes a broad vision," writes former priest Thomas Moore in *Care of the Soul,* "to know that a piece of the sky and a chunk of the earth lie lodged in the heart of every human being." Embracing this "broad vision," which in some ancient traditions was called enlightenment, is the spiritual goal to which Gaians strive.

Enlightenment |
"GOOD TO HAVE YOU, MR. BUDDHA!"

The northeast coast of the United States, which futurist Herman Kahn called the "BosWash corridor," is one of the most urbanized areas of the world. But nearby are some of the world's largest and most unspoiled tracts of protected wilderness. Deep in the heart of one of these pristine natural habitats, the upper gorge of the Hudson River high in the central Adirondacks, is the small town of Jonesboro, where Bill McKibben receives his mail. He lives out of town, however, as close to "nature" as he can get. He lives in Gaia.

As he wrote in *The End of Nature,* published first as an essay in the *New Yorker,* McKibben knows that what he sees outside his small, wood-heated home is no longer the real thing. It has been altered by human beings. We—humankind—"are ending nature," he warns. Even in his magnificent realm, "the meaning of the wind, the sun, the rain—of nature—has already changed." After analyzing the data about the damage to the ozone layer and about the notorious "greenhouse effect," McKibben concludes starkly: "We have built a greenhouse, a human creation, where once there bloomed a sweet and wild garden."[11]

"I come at this as an environmentalist," McKibben says, almost like a fundamentalist might say "as a Christian." "Because I am trained as a reporter, I hesitate to call my views a 'belief system.' I began with data, not with my own convictions. But it's true that from that data grew certain beliefs. Five hundred years ago, it would hardly be necessary to think in Gaian terms. But today we have to. I believe you're a better journalist when you care. When I wrote *The End of Nature,* nobody had written a book about the greenhouse effect. I thought it was really important that I not pretend"—he pauses, and then his voice rises with passionate intensity—"that I not pretend *anything.* It's a faithful reporting of what I felt. That may not be right for the front page of the *New York Times,* but it is my truth."

On a recent book tour, he was asked by one autograph seeker how, if he lives in such a remote area, he manages to travel so much to promote his books? "It's not a big hassle," McKibben replied. "We're only two hours from the Albany airport."

"That's not far at all," his fan commented.

"Not far enough," McKibben replied.

Indeed, those three words—"not far enough"—is a lament heard frequently throughout the state of Gaia. Wherever Gaians look, civilization has encroached on nature and, in McKibben's phrase, ended it. As Western civilization struggles to adapt to the enormous changes in consciousness and life-styles required to "save the planet," Gaians like McKibben fear that the grudging, bureaucratic, piecemeal environmentalism practiced by government and corporations is simply not going far enough, not happening fast enough, and not cutting deep enough in human consciousness.

High-Tech Civilization Is Self-Destructive;
Only Nature Can Teach Us How To Save Ourselves.

McKibben happens to be on a book tour on the day following the broadcast of the final episode of the TV comedy "Cheers," a TV show which, McKibben says, "half of the American population watched." He asks the audience how many of them saw the show. Sheepishly, several hands go up.

"Don't be ashamed," he reassures them. "It's okay. It's a fun show. It was the most popular show of the Reagan-Bush era. One reason why is that it provided a sense of community. In that Boston bar, as the theme song clearly spelled out, 'Everybody always knows your name, and everybody's glad you came.' It fed our desperate craving for that kind of connection and that kind of contact. It was the exact opposite experience of sitting alone on your couch watching it!

"There was no doubt in my mind that they had become a real community, and that they really cared about each other. But they didn't know *our* names, did they? While they were having an intimate, *actual* experience, we were all sitting at home having an isolated, *vicarious* experience. Never before in any culture at any time in history have so many people spent so much time substituting vicarious experience for actual experience.

"I'm really depressed that virtual reality will be the next wave. We'll soon be buying these helmets manufactured by some corporation, and inserting some kind of software. And for what? We have the most fascinating, diverse, exquisitely beautiful realities on this planet—and we ignore them. Yet soon folks will be paying top dollar for some manufactured, 'virtual' realities. It makes no sense! Think about it. The reason virtual reality is virtual is that someone has already figured out what's going to happen. You can always push 'reset' and start over again. It's arriving as a gift from the people who brought us TV. Instead of taking responsibility for what they've done to us in that medium, they are trying to get us to buy into *another*. This leads to ignorance about the environment—an ignorance for which we are paying a very high price."[12]

McKibben suspects this wall of ignorance is more impenetrable than the Berlin wall ever was. "I was going on the 'Today' show," he recalls, "and I was worried about what I was going to say. But afterward, I realized that it really didn't matter. After a quick commercial, Tom Cruise came on. A few minutes later there was a psychologist talking about what to do if your pet dies. You could go on that program and say the most profound, the most enlightened things and it wouldn't matter." McKibben laughs. "If the Buddha himself appeared on the show and said something absolutely earth-shaking, the interview would end with the host saying: 'Good to have you, Mr. Buddha. We look forward to seeing you again on your next tour.' "

The Mass Media Undermine Human Values
and Obscure the Sacredness of Creation.

The trivialization of Media, the commercialism of Corporatia, or the self-righteousness of Patrians—Gaians expect such behavior from those who have not yet made the paradigm shift into the New Age. Consequently, a host of Gaian prophets continue to initiate campaigns to "save the earth," launch organizations designed to "raise ecological awareness," and issue books which, in the tradition of Rachel Carson's *Silent Spring*, will awaken the people before it is too late. Father Thomas Berry's *The Dream of the Earth*, for example, has rapidly become a primary Gaian bible. It is a sermon about the urgency of replacing the old above-the-earth religion with an earth-centered enlightenment.

We are just emerging, Berry believes, from a prolonged period of "technological entrancement," during which the human mind occupied "the narrowest confines it has experienced since consciousness emerged from its Paleolithic phase." Like most Gaians, Berry thinks that the indigenous peoples of the earth, these so-called primitive tribes, had a wisdom that we've lost. They had "a larger vision of the universe, of our place and functioning within it, a vision that extends to celestial regions of space and to interior depths of the human in a manner far exceeding the parameters of our own world of technological confinement."

In ways that parallel the Patrian belief in the "second coming" of Jesus Christ, Gaians believe that a profound shift is now occurring in human consciousness. Humanity is starting to break out of the narrow technological consciousness that has become its prison. "The excessive analytical phase of science is over," pronounces Berry, and a "countermovement toward integration and interior subjective process is taking place within a more comprehensive vision of the entire universe." This shift in human beings' relationship to the planet Berry considers the beginning of the "Ecological Age."[13]

Lower Consciousness Is the Problem;
Higher Consciousness Is the Solution.

Citizens of the Transformation State believe that something is going wrong with the planet because something has gone wrong with us. "The ecological crisis that threatens our planet derives from a dysfunctional notion of the self," says

Joanna Macy, a Buddhist scholar and "deep ecologist" well known throughout the State of Gaia. The problem is that the other Divided States, which Gaians often refer to as "mainstream" or "straight" culture, have separated us from nature. Cut off from creation, children are raised to identify with what Alan Watts called the "skin-encapsulated ego," a self separate and distinct from the web of life. Based on this pathological individualism, we exploit nature, overconsume nonrenewable resources, and degrade the biosphere. Thanks to Gaian consciousness-raising efforts, many citizens have adopted a new belief system— "greening of the self," as Macy calls it—which she calls a prerequisite for far-reaching ecological action. Until we raise our consciousness and view ourselves as another strand in nature's complex web, we will continue to destroy ourselves. What Gaians are working toward is a higher, earth-based consciousness that honors rather than destroys our planetary home.[14]

Gaians are saddened by the way the broader culture denigrates them and dismisses them as nothing more than tofu and gurus. In fact, they argue, their movement has traveled far beyond its roots a century ago, when British intellectuals in turn-of-the-century England clustered around a dozen vegetarian restaurants, pontificating about Hindu philosophy and rejecting "the roast beef of old England."[15] Gaians blame Corporatia and Media for corrupting many aspects of the New Age, leading to an emphasis on the trappings of enlightenment rather than the deeper reality. This has led to an eco-chic life-style in which, as Gaian author David Spangler points out, "one can acquire New Age shoes, wear New Age clothes, use New Age toothpaste, shop at New Age businesses, and eat at New Age restaurants where New Age music is played softly in the background." The genuine Gaian movement is not a spiritual supermarket, but rather "the birth of a new consciousness . . . humanity becoming more fully integrated with the being of Gaia, more fully at one with the presence of God." Spangler interchanges the words "Gaia" and "God" freely, because at the center of his faith is not a separate being, as in the Christian view, "but rather a presence made up of the collective spirit of humanity and the spirit of our world, of Gaia."[16]

The Earth, Called Gaia, Is the True God,
the True Source of Wisdom and Salvation.

Because Gaians believe that we must take an evolutionary step from an "old paradigm" to a new, ecocentric, holistic paradigm, they refer often to a "higher" consciousness they are trying to achieve and spread to the other states. Gaians read their favorite psychologists or philosophers (such as Abraham Maslow, Stanislav Grof, Fritjof Capra, or Ken Wilber) in order to "raise" their own consciousness. Although they are wary of referring to "lower" states of consciousness, Gaians have developed a sophisticated vocabulary to describe the residents of the other Divided States who don't share their views. They portray ordinary (or "mass") consciousness as driven by basic needs such as "belongingness" and "self-esteem" rather than higher needs such as "self-actualization" and "self-transcendence" (Maslow). The citizens of the less developed consciousness have a "self-sense" that is "self-protective" or "conformist" rather than "conscientious," "autonomous," or "integrated" (Loevinger). Gaians view the citizens of the other States, furthermore, as acting out "conventional" or, worse yet, "preconventional" morality (Kohlberg).

Despite their sophisticated terminology, Gaians are perceived by citizens of the other Divided States as naive and self-righteous at best, or at worst condescending and dangerous. When Marilyn Ferguson spread New Age thinking to a mainstream readership through her best-selling *The Aquarian Conspiracy,* for example, it was seen by Gaians as a masterful weaving together of the various emerging schools of thought and a popular invitation to the wider public to adopt the new paradigm. To non-Gaians, however, it was a vague, utopian manifesto by flaky consciousness-raisers out of touch with the real world.

Those With Higher Consciousness Must Provide
the Leadership to Save America.

Just as the Claritas Corporation's forty-level hierarchy of ZIP codes reflected the Corporatian belief system, so does the Stanford Research Institute's VALS ("Values and Life-styles") Program mirror Gaia's. Arnold Mitchell, for many years VALS's director, used the full range of demographic data and analytical tools available in 1969 to write, with his colleague Mary Baird, a scholarly demographic study called *American Values.* Using psychologist Abraham Maslow's well-known hierarchy of needs, Mitchell drew a psychological profile of the American public using five ascending categories based on their dominant psychological need: (1) survival, (2) security, (3) belonging, (4) esteem, and (5) self-actualization.

This portrait of America (which, as Mitchell reported, "received an enthusiastic reception as a pioneering effort") pleased Gaians immensely. Citizens of

Patria, Disia, Corporatia, and Media were obviously in the first four categories. The final and highest category captured perfectly the Gaian self-image: seeking to develop the full potentials of the self as part of the healing of the planet. To Mitchell's dismay, however, his book produced a backlash among the elite because it suggested the existence of a hierarchy. As Mitchell put it: "If I'm at Level Three and you're at Level Four (and I know it), it's hard for me not to despise you for your superiority. And you, of course, have a marvelous put-down weapon at your disposal!"

In an attempt to rectify this error, Mitchell issued a series of books which became increasingly subtle and complex in their portrayal of the "values and life-styles" of the American citizenry. But the fundamental Gaian premise remained unchanged: those at the top (whom he now called "integrated" rather than "self-actualized") had a higher, more evolved consciousness than those at the bottom.

At famous "growth centers" nestled in rural beauty, like Esalen in Big Sur, California, and the Omega Institute in Rhinebeck, New York, as well as urban-based centers like the California Institute of Integral Studies in San Francisco and the New York Open Center in Manhattan, Gaians participate in workshops, seminars, retreats, vision quests, and a wide range of consciousness-raising activities. Since they too are children of the old paradigm, they know that to enter the promised land of the New Age they must continually work to raise their own consciousness. If they succeed, they will be more effective at lifting the citizens of the other Divided States out of darkness and toward enlightenment and peace.

Peace |
"TOTAL FREEDOM AND PERFECT BLISS"

A quarter-century ago, an extremely popular book entitled *The Greening of America* concluded with a call for a "revolution in consciousness." Written by a professor at Yale University Law School, Charles Reich, the best-seller concluded that the Establishment—corporate, governmental, military, academic— "cannot be fought by the legal, political, or power methods that are the only means ever used up to now by revolutionists or proponents of social change." Instead, Reich asserted, "the only plan that will succeed is one that will be greeted by most social activists with disbelief and disparagement, yet it is entirely realistic . . . *revolution by consciousness.* "[17]

Unlike Marxist dialectics or New Left confrontations, Reich's proposed revolution was peaceful. It was green, like the earth, not red, like blood. In his Gaian view, consciousness was like an elixir which would gradually transform the institutions of the Divided States. Reich argued that the government, the corporations, the legal and financial institutions essentially *have no mind.* On the contrary, "they administer whatever values there are to be administered." Changing the values and consciousness of individuals, Reich argues, will lead to a profound transformation in the way these institutions operate—the "greening of America."

The Source of Social Progress Is the Evolution of Human Consciousness.

Gaian thinking has since grown more sophisticated and complex, but it continues to subscribe to Reich's core belief: social change is driven by changes in consciousness. Thus philosopher-physicist Fritjof Capra, a leading Gaian theorist, describes the shift in the meaning of power. In the old paradigm, power meant "domination over others," and is reflected in the top-down, boss-employee, man-woman hierarchies so common in political, military, and corporate structures. Power in the new paradigm, however, is power as "influence of others." So powerful are these new Gaian values, Capra believes, that they were the driving force behind Mikhail Gorbachev's perestroika and the end of the Cold War. "The use or threat of force can no longer and must no longer be an instrument of foreign policy," Gorbachev said in a major speech delivered at the United Nations. "This is the first and most important component of a non-violent world as an ideal. . . . We are speaking of cooperation, which could be more accurately termed co-creation and co-development. . . . We must build a new world—and we must do it together."[18]

Gaians apply their values and ideals to virtually every social institution. Education, economics, energy, politics, even corporate management—in these and many other areas, Gaians are seeking to influence the way society works.

- In *education,* Gaians call their approach by many different names: student-centered, holistic, transpersonal, affective, intuitive, and so on. Their core educational beliefs are that education is a process, not a product; that the inner life of the student ("emotional literacy") is as important as his or her outer performance; that unorthodox learning modes ("right-brain") are as important as linear ("left-brain") learning styles; and that guided meditation, "centering," and "relaxation" exercises, are all vital educational tools.[19]

- In *economics,* Gaians advocate greater recognition for nonlinear as opposed to linear models; for viewing change as fundamental (rather than as "disequilibrium"); for including of "noneconomic" and nonmonetarized variables (rather than regarding them as "externalities"); for more qualitative rather than quantitative forecasts; for a long-term focus that includes intergenerational costs rather than short-term, bottom-line approaches; and, finally, for recognizing the human variable, not as a reactive and mechanical response, but as proactive—that is, emphasizing human choice and responsibility.[20]

- In *politics,* the new Gaian paradigm is based on viewing change as emerging from consensus, not imposed by authority; on de-emphasizing Left vs. Right thinking in favor of a new synthesis; on moving away from external, imposed reform by recognizing "transformation in individuals as essential to successful reform"; and a reduction of centralized and compartmentalized bureaucracy in favor of decentralized, interdisciplinary structures.[21]

- In *business,* visionary corporate leaders are embracing such Gaian values as recognizing the social responsibility of the corporation to the public and to the environment, not just to its stockholders; emphasizing corporate mission and values, not just products and profits; making room for employees' creativity, not just their productivity; and a fundamental rebalancing of priorities away from competition toward collaboration.[22]

As Gaian beliefs penetrate these and other institutions, residents of this State grow bolder and more optimistic. For instance, when Gaians peel away the business jargon surrounding Total Quality Management (TQM), the management theory that swept through corporate suites during the past decade, they are pleased to find their own beliefs at its core. Consider, for example, the following paragraph:

The first step is transformation of the individual. This transformation . . . comes from understanding the system of profound knowledge. The individual, transformed, will perceive new meaning to his life, to events, to numbers, to interactions among people. Once the individual understands the system of profound knowledge, he will apply its principles in every kind of relationship with other people. He will have a basis for judgment of his own decisions and for transformations of the organizations he belongs to. The individual, once transformed, will be able to . . . pull away from their current practice and beliefs and move into the new philosophy . . .

Such a paragraph would not be unusual if it were from one of the early Gaian texts of philosophy and metaphysics; what makes it striking is that it is from *The New Economics for Industry, Government, Education,* written by one of TQM's fathers, the late W. Edwards Deming. "W. Edwards Deming is to management," says Secretary of Labor Robert Reich, "what Benjamin Franklin was to the republican conscience—a guide, a prophet, an instigator."

"Quality," writes Deming's student Mary Walton, author of *The Deming Management Method* and *Deming Management at Work,* "must become the new religion." Examine Deming's writings and one realizes that her word is accurate: his management theory resembles the work of a missionary. The corporation is a system, Deming argues, in the first of a three-step logical chain. Second, the "system must have an aim. Third, the aim must include plans for the future," which is in fact " a value judgment." Thus the basis of the corporation is not profit, but values, and Deming is adamant about the meaning of those values. "We cannot afford the destructive effects of competition," Deming argues. He asks executives to "throw overboard the idea that competition is a necessary way of life. In place of competition, we need cooperation."

*Old Paradigm Thinking Requires Enemies;
in the New Paradigm, Everyone Wins.*

Deming's final point—the emphasis on "win-win" solutions—is the cornerstone of Gaian political and economic beliefs. For citizens of the Transformation State, relentless opposition between economic classes is part of the old paradigm. Gaians believe in "whole systems" thinking, according to which society is not based on a struggle between classes, but on synergy; not on conflict, but on cooperation.

For old-fashioned Leftists as well as neoconservatives, this sounds like "econo-psycho-babble" (as Leon Wieseltier put it in the *New Republic*). It is as if Gaians think that by waving their rhetorical wands, they can magically bring consensus out of conflict and unity out of polarity.

Once again, Gaians greet such hostile misinterpretation as just further resistance from minds still snared in the old paradigms. Because the Gaian theory of social change is on a different plane, they know that it will inevitably be met with suspicion, sarcasm, and derision. Citizens of the other States who still see the world through anachronistic, one-dimensional mind-sets (Left vs. Right, right vs. wrong, good vs. evil) just do not understand. Gaian thinking "is neither Left nor Right, reactionary nor avant-garde, but all of those at once," writes William Irwin Thompson in his introduction to *Gaia: A Way of Knowing*. Just as one cannot say "that the ocean is right and the continent is wrong in a Gaian view of planetary process, so one cannot say that management is right and labor is wrong." From Thompson's perspective, "the movement from archaic modes of thought into a new planetary culture is characterized by a movement from ideology to an ecology of consciousness."[23]

Fundamentalism Is an Anachronism;
All Religions Are Part of the Same Design.

The Parliament of the World's Religions, held in Chicago in September 1993, was an extraordinary, multihued ecumenical gathering which translated this Gaian belief into action. Virtually every religious group or sect in the world was part of the 6,000-person gathering. Alongside Hindu swamis and Muslim imams were goddess worshipers and Roman Catholic archbishops. The opening session began with five Native American elders blessing the Four Directions and concluded with the reading of the "Our Mother Prayer." In the same workshop time slot, "Zoroastrianism: History and Modern Relevance" coexisted with "Eco-feminism and the Return of the Female Principle"; and "The Westernization of Buddhism" was across the hall from "What is Wicca?" a workshop about "the beliefs and practices of neo-pagan witchcraft." The Dalai Lama, one of the international heroes of Gaia, articulated the underlying philosophy when he called humanity the "Rainbow Tribe."[24]

"Why can't there be one religion for the whole world?" the Dalai Lama asked. "This is a question many people have asked over the years. Of course, they always want it to be like their own. . . . Every tradition present in this room, like every color of the rainbow, holds an honorable place in the parade of faiths. Imagine a restaurant that served only one dish. It would soon go out of business. So we need to practice compassion, learning how to honor the truth that is every faith, not just our own."[25]

For eight days the Palmer House, a landmark Chicago hotel, contained thousands of religious emissaries in every conceivable religious garb, carrying instruments, blankets, and icons. It was a microcosm of human faith, with one major exception: fundamentalist Christians.

"They had the most to lose," says Barbara Bernstein, the Parliament's program director. "In a gathering whose official mandate was dialogue, the fundamentalist religions are based on the opposite. When the fundamentalists of any faith hear the word 'dialogue,' they react with fear. They immediately assume they are being asked to reject their own past and adopt a world religion. That was not our purpose—we weren't trying to rob anyone of their religious faith. We were simply trying to bring the spiritual diversity of this planet together."

Being the target for anyone who wanted to complain about the event, Bernstein was told by Christians that she was doing the work of the Devil. One fundamentalist even said he was putting the "armor of Christ" on her because she was associating with so many heathen religions. "The fundamentalists' premise is that there is only one God, only one scripture, only one faith," says Bernstein. "So they feel they are polluting themselves by being part of this. They are angry and defensive, but I know they are just afraid. I feel compassion for that because I cannot imagine living for a lifetime with that kind of terror in my soul."

Going even further than the Parliament, one of the most popular and successful Gaian consciousness-raising training courses, called "Avatar," deliberately sets out to free trainees from their belief systems. Avatar, whose name is derived from Hindu mythology and means "a being who voluntarily assumes physical form to participate in creation," has helped tens of thousands of initiates in over thirty countries complete the nine-day, $2,000 course and learn to consciously choose their own beliefs. As founder Harry Palmer explains it, the world is dominated by—and on the verge of destruction because of—belief systems. Palmer thinks in terms of a hierarchy of consciousness: Type One belief systems, which "depend upon an emotional appeal to fear, sympathy, distrust, or hatred" and consider nonbelievers to be evil; Type Two belief systems, which appeal to the "needs and insecurities" of people; and Type Three belief systems, which prefer to call themselves "sciences" or "technologies" and claim to be based on "hard, objective fact" and whose adherents "are frequently addicted to thinking or arguing."

The purpose of the Avatar training parallels the purpose of Gaia itself: to enable individuals to move beyond the less developed levels of consciousness to embrace a Type Four belief system—and "experience a remission of his or her insistence on rightness and, from a new perspective, begin to see that certain 'facts' are only a greater degree of conviction in some transparent belief. It is a moment of transformation," which leads to the awareness that one can choose one's reality simply by choosing one's beliefs. Since, according to Palmer, whatever beliefs you hold "will cause you to create or attract the experiences which will support those beliefs, why not choose beliefs that bring you the experiences you truly want? We may believe anything we please, and if we believe it without reservation, it will determine our experience."

Avatar Masters understand that the uninitiated (that is, those with Type Three belief systems or lower) will challenge such statements. But grateful graduates of the Avatar training know personally how liberating and enlightening the training is. "Avatar brought me very quickly and very easily to a place where I could step in or out of the whole complex web of my own creation," says Katie Baier of Miami, Florida, "and the relief . . . is incredible." Dr. Gerald Epstein of New York agrees: "Avatar opened a door to my being the observer of my own process and no longer getting trapped in it." The first issue of *Avatar Magazine* is filled with doctors, lawyers, corporate executives, psychologists, and others from virtually every profession providing heartfelt testimony about how the training changed their lives. Since Avatar courses are now being offered in virtually every state, as well as almost forty countries (from Germany to the Republic of Gabon), the goal of the enterprise—to create "an enlightened planetary civilization"—seems to Avatar Masters to be a realistic and achievable mission.[26]

Avatar, of course, is only part of the Gaian wave entering American culture. At about the same time as *Avatar Magazine* appeared, the *New York Times* bestseller list was filled with Gaian books that echo many similar beliefs. The list was headed by *Embraced by the Light,* a profoundly spiritual account of a woman's near-death experience. The list also includes *Women Who Run with the Wolves,* which encourages women to reconnect with their instinctive natures; *Care of the Soul,* a psychotherapist's discussion of spirituality in everyday life; *Healing and the Mind,* which explores the connection between illness and our thoughts and emotions; and *Ageless Body, Timeless Mind,* a book by Dr. Deepak Chopra which applies Eastern philosophical beliefs to issues of aging.[27]

This avalanche of Gaian reading is accompanied by tape cassettes and videos which are streaming across this State's borders and into the homes of citizens of many other States, all with the common theme that, in the words of Dr.

Deepak Chopra, "You are your own reality." This bold phrase opens his "personal letter," which accompanies the mailing that Nightingale-Conant, the Chicago-based audiocassette company, sent out to thousands of potential buyers of his new audio series, *The Higher Self.* Dr. Chopra's letter continues:

> You create it [reality]; you carry it around with you; and, most importantly, you project it onto everyone else and everything else you encounter. But the traditional Western notion of reality is much too limiting for a true realization of life. If you are to understand yourself and the world around you properly, you need to expand your boundaries of reality—of time, space and matter.

Armed with the belief that we create reality, it follows naturally that fulfillment is now attainable. "Come!" exhorts the letter from Vic Conant, president of Nightingale-Conant (a multimillion dollar company). "Free yourself from earthly constrictions and reach for the light of total freedom and perfect bliss with a glorious new audiocassette program." Mr. Conant quotes Dr. Chopra as saying, "The highest spiritual goal one can possibly reach is to know reality totally, because with that knowledge we can transform reality."[28]

To assist you in "knowing reality totally," Gaian techno-wizards are developing a range of new tools to awaken your as yet unrealized potentials. For example, you can order from the *Superlife* catalog ("Amazing Tools to Enhance Your Life") your own Power Pyramid, which is guaranteed to "transport your soul into twelve amazing universes." Using a "totally new technology for sound generation," the Power Pyramid permits you to listen to the sounds of the Amazon rain forest as you fall asleep and awaken to the sounds of birds singing on a spring day. Guaranteed to help you "to relax, focus and escape the stresses of the outer world," the publisher of *Superlife,* Dave Spotts, promises that his product is "the most powerful sleep seducer/dream machine ever invented." (Cost: $179.95.)[29]

Planet |
"TURNING GLOBAL CONSCIOUSNESS INTO ACTION"

ECONOMICS IS A FORM OF BRAIN DAMAGE, screamed the headline of an advertisement on page five of the *New York Times*. Under a photograph of the earth appeared the subhead: "An urgent message . . . to President Bill Clinton from environmental elder David Brower." The article detailed the credentials which make Brower a leader in Gaia. Largely unknown outside this State, he was the head of the Sierra Club for many years; he helped found Friends of the Earth (now in fifty countries), the League of Conservation Voters, and the Earth Island Institute; and he has been at the center of virtually every major environmental initiative during the past quarter-century. The white-haired, eighty-year-old environmental activist is also a hero to many younger Gaians who revere him as "the [Henry David] Thoreau or the [John] Muir of our time," says Amory Lovins of the Rocky Mountain Institute. Brower is the "greatest living conservationist," says Lovins. "He has done more than anyone to build the modern environmental movement."[30]

After carefully itemizing the destruction of the earth's soil, water, air, and animal and plant life, Brower quotes Thoreau: "What's the use of a house if you haven't got a tolerable planet to put it on?" Brower then hammers the point home, asking what's the use "of a nation, or economy, or jobs" without the earth? Warning of the apocalypse to come, Brower thunders: "There will be no universities, churches, media, customers, or even love, on a dead planet. It is time to realize that we are killing it with apathy, carelessness, and wanton development."

Brower's advertisement was mobilizing political support and raising funds to found a Global Restoration and Conservation Service, which "can help the world pull together in the Green Century." Brower determined its agenda and began recruitment. (Two-thirds of the 300,000 people he has "addressed lately on four continents" have committed one year during the next decade to enlist.) He has also picked its headquarters: the Presidio, the former Army base in San Francisco that has been turned into a national park.

"Let President Clinton know," Brower exhorts his readers "that there will be wide support for the bold leader who pilots human society and its associates into the Era of Restoration that will keep the island Earth and its passengers alive."[31]

*Commerical Values Are Leading Rapidly
to the Destruction of the Natural World.*

The week the advertisement appeared, Brower was asked to explain its anti-business tone; in his answer, he was even more outspoken. The problem, he said, is "greedlock." Corporations have become so mesmerized by profit that the survival of the planet simply doesn't figure in their thinking. Economics is like "brain damage," he said, borrowing from the ad headline, because it "leaves out the cost to the Earth. If you don't put that in the calculations, the result is worthless." The legal entity of the corporation is inherently responsible, Brower explained, because it has the "rights of a person but they didn't put a conscience in that person."[32]

Within the borders of Gaia, Brower's argument sounds compelling and coherent and has wide support. Many Gaians consider their arch enemy to be the hallowed institution of the marketplace: the corporation. According to Gaians, this institution is inherently amoral, exploitative, dehumanizing, and destructive to the earth. Father Thomas Berry, whose book *The Dream of the Earth* was published by the Sierra Club, calls the corporation a "destructive manifestation of patriarchy" which is creating a "geological, biological, and ultimately, human disaster."[33] As another respected Gaian, Jerry Mander, puts it: "In dominating other cultures, in digging up the earth, corporations blindly follow the codes that have been built into them as if they were genes. Like any out-of-control demonic force, Corporatia will grow larger and larger, devouring everything in its path and excreting profit for its citizens."[34]

So concerned are some environmentalists about the threat of overpopulation that they speak out publicly and proudly in favor of birth control and abortion as ways of limiting our numbers. For them, the individual fetus is not as sacred as creation itself, and limiting population is as necessary as pruning a tree. Some Gaians, like National Park Service biologist David Graber, even "hope for the right virus to come along" in order to cut down the numbers of *Homo sapiens* despoiling the earth.[35]

Gaians believe that fighting to defend the planet requires courage and sacrifice. Across the country—from East Liverpool, Ohio, where they are battling a toxic waste incinerator; to Portland, Oregon, where they are fighting to save the northern spotted owl; to northern New York state, where they are protecting the Adirondack Park against those who would violate this unique wilderness area—Gaians are turning their words into deeds.[36]

Nonetheless, they dispute among themselves the right tactics for making human civilization more earth-friendly. Some organizations, like Earth First!, Greenpeace, and Sea Shepherd Conservation Society, employ confrontational strategies such as sinking whaling ships, sabotaging logging equipment, or trespassing on oil company property. At the other pole, organizations such as Ram Dass's Seva Foundation, John Denver's Windstar Foundation in Snowmass, Colorado, and the Institute of Noetic Sciences in Sausalito, California, take a more meditative, long-term, consciousness-raising approach to change. Occupying the Gaian middle ground are organizations which have adopted a legal or communications strategy, such as Ted Turner's Better World Society, the Nature Conservancy, the Environmental Defense Fund, and the Natural Resources Defense Council (which instigated McDonald's fast-food franchises' switch to recyclable containers).

*Saving the Planet Requires That
We Adopt Alternative Life-Styles.*

Squeezed into Folsom Field, the University of Colorado's football stadium, 38,000 new and old Beatles fans stomped and danced as Paul McCartney and his "New World Tour," which included his wife Linda, rock 'n' rolled in the Rockies. But it was more than a concert, it was a consciousness-raising event.

The lyrics of the songs, and the various groups distributing literature outside the arena, were preaching the gospel of a new, more peaceful world. Although the causes were varied, the theme was clear: we must change our way of living and thinking to save the world. "I have faith the day will come," says a serious-looking Linda McCartney in the glossy concert souvenir book, "when the world looks back and says, How *could* we have eaten animals."

Paul and Linda don't just talk about their values; they act on them. People for the Ethical Treatment of Animals (PETA), with Friends of the Earth (FOE) and Greenpeace, each took a full-page spread in the back of the book, and constructed a booth where concert-goers were joining and paying their membership fees. The three organizations differ in focus: PETA's is preventing animal abuse, FOE's is networking global environmental organizations, and Greenpeace's is engaging in direct action campaigns. But all of them share the same eco-philosophy which, like the Greenpeace ad copy, pleads: "Join us and help save the natural world."

"Remember [former president George] Bush at the Earth Summit?" McCartney says. "Wouldn't sign! Because stopping the manufacture of CFCs, which damage the ozone layer, would lose jobs. But keep on manufacturing CFCs and you lose the planet. Where are jobs without a planet to have jobs on?"

While Paul takes on the bigger environmental issues, Linda has focused specifically on animals. And both McCartneys took a stand in their own neighborhood by purchasing eighty-seven acres of woodland in order to protect deer against stag hunters. "The hunters say that if they don't cull the deer—which means 'kill' them," Linda explains, "then we'll be taken over by them. Now when was the last time you were mugged by a deer?"

The McCartneys crusade for the planet because, for them and for many citizens of Gaia, it is not enough to live right and think right. They also want to engage in *right action* on behalf of the planet.

Such spiritually aware, ecologically grounded action is needed, Gaians believe, in every aspect of our lives. The contents of the *New Age Sourcebook*, published annually by the editors of *New Age* magazine, reflect some of the most common areas of Gaian concern. The *Sourcebook* contains sections on food and fitness ("It is OK to eat meat?"), parent/child ("building multicultural awareness"), good health ("Homeopathic travel kits"), adventure ("pilgrimages and sacred journeys"), spirituality ("Turning rush hour into a sacred journey"), and so on. The final section, titled "Activism," informs readers on "How to stand up and make a difference in the world." By translating their consciousness into action, Gaians believe the world can be saved.

6

OFFICIA

The Governing State

Core belief:	Government represents the people and should have ultimate authority.
Defining events:	The New Deal, The New Frontier, The Great Society.
Sacred text:	The U.S. Constitution.
Primary organizations:	U.S. Congress, local and state government.
Spokespersons:	The President, Cabinet officers, Speakers of the House, governors.
Electronic media:	C-Span.
Periodicals:	*Federal Times, National Journal, Congressional Record, Governing, Government Executive, Campaigns and Elections.*
Educational institutions:	Graduate schools of public administration.
Advocacy groups:	Senior Executives Association of the Federal Government, American Federation of State, County and Municipal Employees (AFSCME), liberal Democrats
Ultimate authority:	The electoral process.
Quote:	*"I grew up with a sense that the absence of a strong federal government did not necessarily mean that people had more freedom and opportunity. In fact, the national government had to affirmatively step in to make sure everybody had a fair chance."*[1]
	—WILLIAM JEFFERSON CLINTON

THE CITIZENS OF Officia believe in the role of government. They are committed to their conviction that the government, whatever its flaws, serves the American people. Officia is the glue that holds the Union together, the loom that weaves the diverse threads of this sprawling democracy into one fabric. The country needs the Governing State more than ever, Officials believe, because without it there would be no country.

While Officials acknowledge that each of the Divided States is part of the Union, they believe that the Governing State should have—indeed *does* have—the ultimate right to control the nation's destiny. While Corporatia contributes to the GNP and Media contributes to the flow of information, neither they nor the other Divided States can perform the crucial role of governing. The other States can promote their particular agendas; Officia must promote the public interest.

For citizens of the Governing State, Abraham Lincoln and Franklin Delano Roosevelt are heroes because they used the power of government to save the Union from disintegration. Although today citizens in many of the other Divided States want to turn their backs on the New Deal and are clamoring for less government, Officials strongly disagree. Those who believe in the legitimate, growing role of government believe that the Divided States which we have just visited provide eloquent testimony of Officia's vital role.

Take a look back for a moment at the divergent lenses through which the other five Divided States see America:

PATRIA: *family, education, media, morality*

CORPORATIA: *growth, innovation, profits, liberty*

DISIA: *racism, poverty, sexism, oppression*

MEDIA: *freedom, objectivity, ratings, technology*

GAIA: *spirituality, enlightenment, planet, peace*

The agendas of all the States are strongly at odds. Their language, values, and priorities vary enormously. Each of the Divided States has a constituency that participates (to varying degrees) in the political process and expresses its views. It is the responsibility of government, according to Officials, to weigh the competing interests and forge them into a unified nation.

When Officials confront the evidence of the public's distrust of politicians (only one American of every four approves of the performance of the U.S. Congress, and four out of five think Congress serves "special interests"[2]) they do not blame government. On the contrary, they blame citizens for not being more involved in public affairs. Officials do not interpret such statistics to mean that government has turned against the people, but that the people—cynical, apathetic, and angry—have turned against the government.

Today, unlike a generation ago, many government leaders are anti-Officia. They enter government service not because they believe its role should grow, but because they believe it should shrink. They seek to dismantle significant departments of the government, decimate the federal work force, eliminate vast areas of regulation, and reduce overall the presence and power of government in our lives. Although citizens of the Governing State recognize that their critics have a right to attack government, they resent the anti-government vigilantes for undermining the very institutions which, Officials believe, made this country great. It is just not right to enter public service in order to undermine it.

Some citizens of Officia are elected officials; others are government bureaucrats. But the vast majority of those who subscribe to the Official belief system are ordinary citizens who see the government as the ultimate guarantor of their security, and regard those who work for the government as public servants.

The More Divided the Public,
the More Vital the Role of Government Becomes.

Again and again, the word "service" appears in the speeches of virtually all governmental leaders, both Republican and Democratic. In his 1992 inaugural address, President Clinton acknowledged his predecessor, George Bush, for his "half-century of service to America." Again, when President Clinton concluded his address, he challenged the younger generation of Americans to a "season of service," and expressed his hope that millions of others would "answer the call." And when Bob Dole announced his candidacy for president, he too used the word, because public service is at the heart of the Governing State. From the Official perspective, no other force in the country speaks for the people. No other organization is mandated to act in the "public interest." No other institution is designed to respond to the public will.

But, as we have seen, the public lives in different States, and the States are divided against each other. As senior White House advisor David Gergen put it, "We're walking through minefields."[3] The Clinton administration, like those before it, found itself in conflict with the Divided States because among them there is not one public but many. Public Service is, indeed, a minefield because Government has increasingly become the war zone among the Divided States. As the conflicts both intensify and proliferate, Officials believe that the role of government only becomes more vital.

Not surprisingly, this belief system is widely held by those Americans who actually work for one of the 83,000 governmental entities in the United States, including state governments, municipal or county governments, school boards, water and transportation districts, and many others. The majority of our public services are delivered by local governments—cities, counties, towns, and districts. In fact, four times as many people—12 million of the 15 million full-time civilian public employees—work for state or local government. Together, these government officials control a third of the nation's land area, 1.4 billion acres of ocean floor, 12,000 miles of waterways, and 400,000 buildings, equal to all the office towers in America's ten largest cities.[4]

But many other citizens who share the Official belief system have never worked for government, and never will. Traditionally, most citizens of this State call themselves "liberal," but the old political categories do not do justice to their beliefs. According to the Times Mirror Study of the American Electorate "the conventional labels of 'liberal' and 'conservative' are about as relevant as the words 'Whig' and 'Federalist.' While Americans may respond to the *terms* 'liberal' and 'conservative,' these expressions have not only lost much of their traditional meaning, they do not even remotely come close to defining the nature of American public opinion."[5]

Not surprisingly, one of the groups which the pollsters found subscribe most heartily to the Official belief system were called the "New Dealers."

Government, Though Imperfect, Is Vitally Necessary to Maintain and Improve Society.

The Great Crash, 1929. Stock prices plummeted. Fortunes were lost overnight. Depositors lined up helplessly outside bank doors, unable to reclaim life savings. Bankruptcies decimated the economy. Families were torn apart, marriages and friendships were destroyed, and suicides were common. Not only the economy, but society itself, was in critical condition. Action was required.

From the perspective of Officia, it was natural that all eyes turned to Washington, because government, and government alone, can rescue the nation from economic depression and social disaster. The Great Depression, Officials believe, taught America the vital lesson that government regulation is not a problem, as Corporatians always insist: on the contrary, it is a *solution* to a problem.

Officials do not consider themselves to be ideologues of either the Left or the Right, but rather "progressive pragmatists," determined to find ways of fostering social progress. Their primary faith is civic rather than religious. Although they may regard "growth" as a social goal, they (unlike Corporatians) speak of it as "growth with fairness"—a goal, they believe, which only the government can and will ensure. They follow FDR's New Deal motto: "Take a method and try it; if it fails, admit it frankly and try another. But above all, *try something.*"[6]

FDR recognized that government could, and did, make mistakes. But, like citizens of Officia today, he believed that some government action is almost always better than no government action. An active government may make errors, but at least it is trying to defend the true interests of the nation.

If the New Deal's triumph over the Depression was not proof enough to Officials, World War II provided the final piece of evidence. Enormous planning was required to turn our peace economy into a war economy, and the architect of those plans was the United States government. And for citizens of the State of Officia, this aggressive, activist approach was compelling proof that faith in government can keep America strong, free, and prosperous.

In addition to the "New Dealers," the other group which the Times Mirror Study of the Electorate found highly supportive of the role of government were those whose attitudes were shaped in the sixties by the civil rights movement. After all, it was marshals from the federal government in Washington who forced George Wallace, then governor of Alabama, to step aside and allow African-American students to enter the state university. It was the White House under President Lyndon Baines Johnson who built the Great Society programs and supported the Voting Rights Act. The imagery of the era was built around the notion of an enlightened federal government in Washington and benighted local governments in the South. At the time, it was not surprising that people who believed in the American dream of "liberty and justice for all" would believe in the expanded role of the national government.

Whether shaped by the New Deal or by the civil rights movement, whether employed by government or just supportive of it, citizens of Officia share the belief that government can solve all kinds of complex social problems. Robert N.

Bellah and his co-authors of *The Good Society* believe that government can be the solution to problems in almost every area of life.

> The government provides or guarantees medical coverage and income in old age, unemployment insurance, and protection against job discrimination; it subsidizes college education for the middle class, guarantees home loans for veterans, and underwrites much of the research and technical innovation that fuels the national economy. . . . We expect government to protect children against abusive parents, wives against battering husbands, and employees against sexual harassment by their bosses. More and more we think of problems that government cannot, will not solve—infant mortality in poor communities, the AIDS epidemic, rising drug use—as public problems for which government is responsible.[7]

Since solving America's problems is a big job, according to citizens of the Governing State, it requires a big government. It requires an expanding public sector responsible for economic policy, military policy, justice policy, social policy, regulatory policy, environmental policy, and others. In areas where public policies are lacking, the Official perspective is that the people are not being protected.[8] The goal of Officials is not big government per se, but rather a strong government role to protect the public interest and ensure social progress. While others both inside and outside the Beltway are raising a battle cry for less government, Officials know that the size of government is increasing and will inevitably continue to do so.

Nothing illustrates this better than the bombing of the Murrah Federal Building in Oklahoma City. It was an act in total defiance of the federal government, and utter contempt for it. Those persons responsible for the act, and the thousands more who sympathized with it, detest the "feds" and want to bring them to their knees. Yet the consequence of that terrorist attack was precisely the opposite. It will toughen federal law enforcement, intensify government security measures, expand the power of Washington, enlarge its budgets, and increase its authority. While citizens of Officia abhor the bombing, they nevertheless endorse its consequences. For they believe that an ever more fragmented society requires an ever stronger government.

Specifically, Officials believe in four interlocking functions that are critical to progress: *representation, regulation, administration,* and finally *leadership.* We now turn to these four elements of the Official belief system.

Representation |
"ORDINARY PEOPLE ARE COUNTING ON ME."

One day during the early years of the Reagan administration, U.S. Representative Claudine Schneider, a liberal Republican, was sitting in her Rhode Island office when one of her aides brought into her office a very troubled seventy-two-year-old woman, Mrs. Flannery.

"I've never been to talk to a politician before," Mrs. Flannery said to Representative Schneider. "But since you're a woman, I thought maybe you'd understand."

"Understand what?" Schneider asked.

"My husband and I always planned that if he died, I would live on his pension. Now I find out that I'm not going to get one dime. I don't know how I'm going to survive. I don't want to go on welfare. I need your help."

Moved by the woman's plight, Schneider tried at first to comfort her. "I told her she must have gotten bad information," Schneider recalls. "But I checked into it and found out that there was, indeed, a loophole in the pension law. She had fallen between the cracks."

The pension law did not enable spouses to claim their deceased husband's pension if he had recently changed jobs. There was only one solution: elected representatives, such as Claudine Schneider, would have to take up these spouses' cause (representation), change the law to remove the loophole (regulation), and make sure it was enforced (administration).

---

*The People's Representatives Are Motivated by
the Public Interest, Not Narrow Self-Interest.*

Schneider had been in Congress long enough to lose her naiveté. She knew that some members of Congress were "scoundrels," as she put it, "with their hands in the till." Many others, she felt, "had no core belief system, no agenda, except their own reelection." But, during her five terms in Congress from 1980 to 1990, she modeled herself after the congresspeople she most respected, the true public servants, with the "primary goal of doing what is in the best interest of the public."

"When I moved from being Claudine Schneider, private person," she says, "to Representative Schneider, congresswoman, my first challenge was to develop selflessness. I don't mean trying to be a saint. I was raised a Catholic, so I knew that wasn't possible! I just mean trying to do my very best for the ordinary people who are counting on me to represent their interests. If someone calls in the middle of the night with a problem, as their representative I have to show compassion. I have to help them identify who can be of assistance to them. I can't be resentful that my personal time has been interrupted. During my term of office, I was, in a way, public property. I was at the beck and call of my constituents. As long as they kept me in office, I was determined to be an honest problem-solver for them."

This belief in the power of representation, Officials passionately believe, is the key to democracy. Scores of men and women at every level of government have dedicated their lives to serving the public. They do so not because it will make them rich or famous, but because they believe it creates a better society for themselves and their children. Representative Schneider decided to take on Mrs. Flannery's cause, and as a result, legislation was passed which ensures that widows like Mrs. Flannery will be protected.

The People's Representatives Are Increasingly Diverse and More Reflective of Their Constituencies Than Ever.

Those who are elected to represent the public today represent a broader-than-ever cross section of the American people. A generation ago, the overwhelming majority of political candidates and civil service employees were "affluent white males." So flawed was the system that, as recently as the early 1970s, even the Civil Service Commission—the organization responsible for ensuring minority hiring—was underhiring African-Americans and other minorities.[9]

Today, however, Officials proudly note that the WASP male stereotype fits far fewer members of Congress. In 1992, twenty-four newly elected women joined an equal number of women returning to the House; seventeen new black members, including Senator-elect Carol Moseley-Braun, joined twenty-three returning black members; and nine newly elected Hispanic members joined thirteen returning Hispanics. "If you add two or three caucuses together, you've got a hell of a voting bloc," says Representative Louise Slaughter (D-N.Y.).

And as more minorities were being elected, more were being hired to work in the federal government. The Clinton administration made an unprecedented effort at appointments that demonstrated the president's commitment "to casting the net wider than in the past and getting a diversity in terms of race and geography and background."[10]

No matter what critics of government may say, Officials point out that the "system" has proved that it can change as America changes. For example, women candidates used to be turned aside because they couldn't attract funding. But, according to Ellen R. Malcolm, president of Emily's List, a fundraising network that helps Democratic women running for office, female Senate candidates in 1992 were better fund raisers than their male opponents. "The victories of many of these candidates will help change public perceptions and help future candidates fight negative stereotypes," says Malcolm. "And we will begin to see enough women in high office that our representative democracy actually begins to represent all the people."[11]

Government Representatives Must Adhere
to a Higher Moral Standard Than Citizens of Other States.

To ensure that the representatives of the people are not only diverse in terms of gender and race but also of the highest character, both elected and appointed officials are subjected to the most rigorous scrutiny imaginable. When President Clinton, for example, named Zoe Baird to become attorney general, the fact that illegal aliens had worked in her home killed her nomination. Despite Baird's apologies, the press and public opinion demanded she withdraw her nomination.[12]

Whether the appointee is from the Left or the Right, male or female, black or white, he or she is destined to be scrutinized for every possible character flaw. At one end of the political spectrum, Roberta Achtenberg, a lesbian activist, was subjected to a brutal review when nominated to become assistant secretary of the Department of Housing and Urban Development. Although liberals leapt to her defense ("Bigotry should not disqualify her," Senator Edward M. Kennedy said), her private life was ruthlessly dissected and analyzed. At the other end of the spectrum, self-made millionaire and Miami real-estate executive Stanley Tate, a Republican picked by President Clinton to clean up the savings and loan scandal, was so offended by the scrutiny that he withdrew his nomination to head the Resolution Trust Corporation. He called Washington a "vicious city of rumors, allegations, accusations, and hidden agendas."[13]

No one enters public administration—not even the president's closest allies—without being scrutinized and called to a high standard of ethical conduct. This applies to appointed as well as elected government officials. President Clinton's choice for commerce secretary, Ronald H. Brown, had to cancel a lavish inauguration party planned in his honor by several large corporations, including some of his former Japanese clients. Organized by a group called Friends of Ron Brown, held at the John F. Kennedy Center for the Performing Arts, and arranged before he was chosen as commerce secretary, the event was originally designed to highlight his distinguished work as the chairman of the Democratic National Committee. But what was appropriate for Ron Brown, private citizen, was no longer appropriate for Ron Brown, government official. "There's a big difference between being chairman of a political party . . . and having a Commerce job where you actually make decisions," Clinton said.[14]

Although Officials believe this kind of scrutiny sometimes goes too far, they recognize it to be a vital part of the democratic system of representation. The people's elected representatives, and those whom they ask to work closely with them, should be asked to live up to a higher standard. Candidate Clinton pledged to stop the exodus "from public service to private enrichment" that has characterized most administrations, because he felt it was wrong that high-level government executives should leave the public sector to take high-paying corporate jobs that exploited their government experience. While citizens in other States, such as Corporatia, feel entitled to "cash in" on their experience, knowledge, and contacts, citizens of Officia are discouraged from doing so and often publicly criticized if they do. Thus when the Clinton administration's chief congressional liaison, Roy M. Neel, resigned to become chairman of the public relations firm Hill and Knowlton, the propriety of his behavior was immediately and fully questioned in the press.[15]

This higher moral standard, Officials believe, justifies the higher authority of government. Such ultimate authority requires a higher ethical responsibility and a more demanding code of conduct. This is what gives Officials the right to make—and remake—the nation's laws, with which citizens of *all* the states must comply.

Regulation |
"THE FEDS HAVE TO DEFINE CONDUCT."

According to the Official belief system, regulation of society by government is vital. *How* government should regulate is disputed by both liberals and conservatives, but Officials on the Right as well as the Left concur that government has the right to regulate—and in some cases, the duty to do so.

Nowhere is the case for regulation clearer, Officials believe, than in economic matters. Ever since FDR rescued the country from the Great Depression, citizens of the Governing State have been convinced that the ultimate authority in economic matters should rest with the federal government. While Officials concede that the free market is a useful instrument for generating wealth, they consider the market to be a primitive mechanism requiring careful regulation by government. "A market system, however inventive, is not self-regulating," writes liberal economist Robert Kuttner in *The End of Laissez-Faire.* Left to its own devices, the market can cause cycles of boom and bust that are as devastating as they are unnecessary. The market doesn't distribute wealth fairly. It doesn't allocate funds efficiently for scientific research, or roads, or education, or other "social goods." The market does not prevent the production of toxic substances. It does not defend the integrity of the securities markets or monitor financial institutions. Markets may "punish innocent bystanders and reward unproductive speculators." Even worse, the values of the market "tend to crowd out social values."[16]

In short, the market, like an unruly child, cannot be trusted, and the government, like a mature parent, must regulate it by setting limits on its behavior, guiding it through crises, and teaching it positive social values. This applies to scores of institutions in the private sector, from banks to TV networks to pharmaceutical companies.

Consequently, Official publications such as the *National Journal,* "The Weekly of Politicians and Government," have no trouble filling their pages every week with reports on countless public policy matters: welfare reform, the abortion controversy, telecommunications legislation, strategies to combat homelessness, health care reform. All these were the subjects of major stories in just one recent issue.

Citizens Must Support the Government With Their Taxes Because the Government Supports Them.

All this public policy-making and implementation requires a coordinated effort on the part of federal, state, and local governments, and sustaining this structure requires taxation. But it is worth the cost, Officials believe, because otherwise life would not be safe, fair, free, healthy, or, ultimately, productive. We need the departments of Defense and of State to protect us from external threats, and the Department of Justice to protect us internally. To have a productive economy, Officials argue, we need the Department of the Treasury, the Office of Management and Budget, and the Federal Reserve Board. To have a healthy citizenry, we need the departments of Housing and Urban Development (HUD), Health and Human Services (HSS), and Education, as well as the Food and Drug Administration, the Consumer Product Safety Commission, the Environmental Protection Agency, and many others.

Ralph Nader is no cheerleader for government. On the contrary, he is one of its strongest critics. Yet the work which he and his "Nader's Raiders" have undertaken over the last twenty years has led to scores of new government regulations. Perhaps no story more dramatically illustrates the Official belief system than Ralph Nader's exposé of the auto industry's irresponsible attitudes toward car safety. With what Officials view as his courage in the face of corporate harassment and his devotion to the public good, Ralph Nader saved lives, and established that the role of government regulations is fundamentally a positive force.

Legislators Override Special Interests and Reach Fair Solutions to Conflicts.

One of the Governing State's most important jobs is to make the laws that resolve, or prevent, disputes between competing interest groups. A quick look at the economic package, presented by President Clinton during his first year in office, shows how this process works.

The economic plan involved an energy tax, which was based, in part, on the heat content of fuels as measured in BTUs, or British thermal units. It faced enormous opposition because it affected almost every individual and industry in the country. Just look at some of those who wanted a tax break:

INTEREST GROUP	BENEFIT
Grain growers and grain companies	Tax break for ethanol
Farmers	Tax break for farm diesel fuel
Northeastern states	Tax break for home heating oil
Coal states	Tax break for coal
Chemicals, glass, other heavy energy users	Tax on competing imports
Aluminum	Tax break on electricity
Barges	Lowered tax on fuel
Natural gas industry	Tax consumer, not industry

Acting in their self-interest, everybody wanted the tax to be imposed on anyone but them.

"The $22 billion tax would take money from the productive private sector and waste it on the new pork programs Clinton is pushing," complained the Odessa (Texas) *American,* speaking for natural gas interests. "This plan will not be passed as recommended to us by the president," said Nebraska senator Jim Exon, voicing the concerns of his farming constituency. Echoed Representative Doug Bereuter, a Nebraska Republican: "It seems tax-heavy and light on spending cuts." An anti-tax alliance—financed primarily by the National Manufacturers Association, the United States Chamber of Commerce, and the American Petroleum Institute—unified the opposition to the new tax by spending $1 million to $2 million in about twenty states in order to undermine the new tax.[17]

This is the democratic process, Officials maintain. If a new law does not truly serve the public, the people's representatives will not pass it. The legislative process reflects the people's will and is designed to challenge everyone to serve the higher interests of America. Democratic government remains the best instrument designed by humankind to govern itself for the greatest good of the greatest number.

Since there is no shortage of conflicts between Divided States, Officials are busier than ever. Consider three recent examples:

PRO-LIFE PROTESTS. How can Officials resolve the conflict between the rights of patients at abortion clinics and the rights of anti-abortion protesters? The protesters have the constitutional right to assemble and speak freely; but patients also have the right to medical care. Can anti-abortion protesters shout abuse at clinic employees as they walk along the sidewalk to work? If so, how near? Can they block their path? Can they print posters with an abortion doctor's photograph and with the word "Wanted" at the top, and post them in public places around town (as they did with a photograph of Dr. David Gunn, the Pensacola doctor who was later murdered)? At what point does freedom of expression become harassment?

State Senator Jim Boczar from Sarasota and Representative Elaine Gordon of North Miami were confronted by the executive director of Operation Rescue, Keith Tucci, who was angry over the handling of anti-abortionists' demonstrations outside Florida abortion clinics and worried about pending legislation that would further curtail protests. Senator Boczar and Representative Gordon didn't agree with his views, and he became furious. "Your bill is a hate-mongering bill that is whipping people into a frenzy and painting pro-life demonstrators as gun-toting crazies!" he shouted at Representative Gordon. Tempers later became so hot in Senator Boczar's office that the lawmaker called the Capitol police to escort Mr. Tucci from the premises.[18]

Without leadership by the federal government, conflicts like this could be repeated all over the nation for years to come. But as Officials point out proudly, "the system" took action: the U.S. Senate voted 69 to 30 in favor of a law to prohibit bombings, arson, and blockades at abortion clinics. They did this, Officials argue, in the public interest. Not only pro-choice senators but also pro-life ones supported the bill. In fact, twenty-eight senators who a few weeks earlier had voted *against* federal financing of abortions voted *for* the measure because, in their view, the real issue wasn't abortion: it was maintaining public order. Most senators knew that it was their responsibility, and theirs alone, to enforce basic rules of civilized behavior.[19]

GAYS IN THE MILITARY. The thorny question of whether and when those in the armed forces can show affection to others has recently required a reexamination of the codes of conduct applying to public displays of affection (PDAs) between men and women. A debate arose as to whether the same code should apply to male-male kissing, hand-holding, and the like. Although all four branches of the armed services have discouraged PDAs while in uniform, these rules have generally been unwritten and loosely enforced when applied to heterosexuals. But the recent controversy compelled government to consider regulating the behavior of homosexuals in the military. "At the officers' club, my wife and I could be hugging and kissing, and because that's a social forum it wouldn't be inappropriate," said Captain Buckner, an army public affairs officer. "Would it be inappropriate for homosexuals? That's why they [the feds] have to define conduct."[20]

As mores about homosexuality change, the government finds itself struggling with thorny issues: what is acceptable to one constituency but offensive to another? Modern-day legislators are compelled to march into this thicket, because it is indeed Official responsibility to make policy.

FUNDING FOR THE ARTS. John E. Frohnmayer, the former chairman of the National Endowment for the Arts (NEA), charged that the White House staff under President George Bush worked steadily "to cripple the NEA internally by putting in political operatives." In his book, *Leaving Town Alive,* Frohnmayer says a White House staff member told him that he should try to be "a little right of center" and that he shouldn't provide financial support to artists who were controversial. Mr. Frohnmayer said he regarded such an approach as "illegal, unethical, and stupid," and he informed the president that the courts—and not the arts endowment—should decide issues of obscenity. As a result, he was continually "undercut by the staff of the White House," in particular John Sununu and William Kristol, vice president Dan Quayle's chief of staff.[21]

Clearly seeking the sympathy of his readers, the question Mr. Frohnmayer skirts is whether the NEA should, in fact, be free to do whatever it wants with taxpayer money. Why, ask NEA critics, should they pay taxes to support grants to artists whose sole creative purpose seems to be to trash traditional values?

This dilemma, like so many others, falls squarely into the lap of legislators. In 1990, Congress decided against banning the depiction of certain body parts and erotic activities from NEA-sponsored art. Instead, they called for guidelines that respect a "general standard of decency." Pro-arts groups objected to those constraints, prompting a Clinton administrator official to restate the view that "publicly funded art should strive to respect community values."[22]

As the fight about the small NEA budget ($176 million for fiscal 1993) continues, lawmakers will remain at the epicenter of the conflict because only elected representatives of the people can be held accountable for making decisions in the public interest. Artists can be expected to defend their freedom no matter what the consequences; and fundamentalists will want to limit NEA funding to artists who don't offend their particular religious sensibilities. The government, Officials believe, will weigh these competing interests and develop a reasonable solution through wise regulation. That is their job.

Administration |
"I WAS SERVING THE PUBLIC."

Someone who dives into a freezing river and saves the life of a drowning person is a hero, and becomes front page news. But when the federal government saves two million lives, this goes virtually unnoticed, and in fact, those in the government responsible for heroic deeds can sometimes find themselves embroiled in controversy.

According to the Surgeon General's office, at least two million Americans are alive today who would otherwise have died of lung cancer. The reason: government warnings that smoking causes cancer. First issued by Dr. Luther Terry on January 11, 1964, the warnings appear on every cigarette package and have helped to reduce the number of smokers from approximately 40 percent of adult Americans thirty years ago to 25 percent today. According to the last seven U.S. Surgeons General, America could become smoke-free were it not for the "stranglehold" that the tobacco industry holds over federal policy. In a recent joint statement, these seven officials advocated even more stringent regulations in order to further reduce the number of smokers in America.[23]

The stranglehold to which the Surgeons General refer is an organized, well-funded lobby, based securely across the border in Corporatia. Citizens of the Governing State firmly believe that these lobbyists, along with tobacco industry executives, are denying the overwhelming evidence that cigarettes kill; or even worse, trying to pretend that such evidence does not exist.[24]

When the chairman of one of the major cigarette conglomerates was asked if it was correct that he had never read a Surgeon General's report dealing with the issue of smoking and health, he replied that it was indeed correct. Outraged at this kind of intransigence, Officials cannot understand why so many people continue to question the role of government. To them, it is clear that no force in our society other than the government is powerful enough and responsible enough to develop laws that defend the people's interest.

Instead, Officia hears the scorn and hostile humor continually directed at "the feds." ("Q. Why is the Pentagon's new weapon called the Civil Servant? A. Because it won't work and it can't be fired." Or: "Did you hear about the clerk who needed an entire week to fill out the forms required by the new Paperwork Reduction Act?") But without Officia, nothing gets done.

When Ellen Baer first started in government service in her mid-twenties, her idealism and enthusiasm was rooted in her desire to make her hometown of New York City a better place to live. She knew that some government bureaucrats are so eager for job security that, as Ellen says, they "keep their heads down and their mouths shut." They figure that they will survive that way, and usually they do. But Ellen decided to take the other, more idealistic route, which she calls "public administration."

After several years in city administration, she took on a key position trying to attract more companies to set up operations in New York City. Because Ellen worked in economic development, she was often sitting across the table from corporate hotshots and big real estate developers. "I would get this feeling of civic responsibility," Ellen recalls. "These guys were at the table representing their bottom line and I was there representing the city of New York. I would often find myself saying to these guys, 'That's not in the best interest of the city'—and I meant it! That, after all, was my job: representing *all* the people.

"Unlike most jobs," she says, "I found myself at a relatively young age accomplishing things that had a positive impact in the lives of your friends, your family, and your community. I had an impact and found a satisfaction that, I think, is hard to find anywhere else. I stayed in government because of the charge I got, the thrill I felt in doing good. I remember thinking: I'm just a kid. But I am making decisions that will affect the entire city. I felt a genuine devotion. There I was, working for less money, putting in long hours. It may sound corny, but I had a sense of civic honor because I was serving the public."

"Civic honor" may sound odd to many citizens of other Divided States. But to administrators like Ellen Baer it is the heart of democracy.

The Goal of Government Is To Ensure That Life in America Is Fair and Equitable for All.

Citizens of the Governing State don't trust the market to determine the distribution of wealth. They feel that the government is entitled to redistribute income in order to keep the rich from becoming too rich and the poor from becoming too poor. They believe that Officia must act, and can act, to make America a fairer, more humane society.

Thus the Clinton administration, shortly after taking office, made good on its campaign promises to limit tax deductions for companies that pay any individual more than $1 million in a year. According to Officials, the public was angry about the exorbitant salaries that corporate chiefs were being paid even when the companies they ran were failing. Is it right, Officials ask, that CEOs like Toys 'R'

Us chief Charles Lazarus make about $3,400 an hour, compared to a minimum wage worker who earns $4.50 an hour? Why should CEOs in 1990 make 100 times the pay of an average worker, as compared with 43 times as much three decades earlier? What rules should govern the pay of CEOs who in most cases have sufficient control over the boards to virtually determine their own compensation? Most Officials maintain that skyrocketing CEO pay has nothing to do with the rational economic choices of the "free market," and should be limited by government regulations.[25]

Officials know that taxes are unpopular, but they believe that the more money people have, the more they should contribute to society. Whether the taxpayer is Richard Gelb, CEO of drug firm Bristol-Myers Squibb (estimated 1991 income: $12.7 million), or rapper M. C. Hammer (estimated 1992 income: $16 million), Officials believe that it is the government's right to levy significant taxes on significant wealth. According to the Clinton tax plan, for example, Gelb would owe the government $1.3 million more per year than previously, and Hammer $1.6 million more.[26]

*In a Society Scarred by Injustice and Inequality,
the Government Should Be a Force for Fairness.*

At the other end of the economic spectrum, Officials also believe that government has a unique responsibility to ensure that the very poor are not abused. When a forty-three-year-old homeless woman, Yetta M. Adams, died a few weeks before Christmas at a bus stop across the street from the Department of Housing and Urban Development, not only did the government pay for the funeral, but one of the highest government officials, HUD Secretary Henry Cisneros, devoted much of his workday to delivering the eulogy. "You see," Cisneros told the hundred assembled mourners and (through the media) hundreds of thousands of Americans, "a homeless person was what Jesus was. Mary and Joseph were looking for a place to spend the night, and they were turned away." Cisneros's point cuts to the very heart of the belief system of the Governing State. Citizens of other States may settle for the rhetoric of justice and decency, but it is the government, Officials assert, that ensures that we practice what we preach.[27]

As the controversies over wealth and poverty suggest, Officials believe there is a higher law than that of the marketplace. Like the first U.S. marshals who patrolled the frontier towns of the Wild West, Officials believe that they are calling Americans to a higher standard of behavior. No one, no matter how poor, should be left to die on the street; no one, no matter how rich, should be above the law.

The Private Sector Worships Profit;
the Public Sector Serves the Public.

Government administrators are committed by law to serving the public's interest, not their own, and are specifically prohibited from making a profit. Nevertheless, executives in Corporatia routinely ridicule the Official belief system by saying: "If I ran my business the way they run the government, I'd be in Chapter Eleven by the weekend." They act as if government should be measured by the standards of private industry, although it is a different world.[28]

The word "profit" is as alien to the public sector as it is integral to the private sector. Consider two examples:

- A government employee in Rhode Island began marketing an innovative state software program to the private sector, and he made more than a quarter of a million dollars a year for the state. He was neither supported nor encouraged in his efforts, because "making money" was not the purpose. So he quit his government job and started a private company—and the state disbanded its marketing effort.

- The Minnesota Department of Administration InterTechnology Group negotiated a deal with IBM to develop six "expert systems" which they had invented. The state attorney general ruled that the Department had to limit its royalties, because it was a nonprofit organization.[29]

Personal profit is so anathema to the belief system in Officia that even the smallest earnings in the marketplace by a government officer become a cause for alarm.

While First Lady Hillary Clinton was developing health care policy during the first year of the Clinton administration, it was discovered that she owned a 0.9 percent share in a fund managed by Capital Management, Inc., of Little Rock, Arkansas. Mrs. Clinton had earned less than $2,500 in 1991 from this investment, and less than $15,000 in 1992. But it made headlines across the country because critics of government corruption, such as Charles Lewis of the Center of Public Integrity, believed that Ms. Clinton should have distanced herself from the investment.

The Clintons, of course, were expected to place their investments in a blind trust as soon as they took office, a ritual rite of cleansing which symbolized their passage into the State of Officia. Not to do so immediately sends a warning signal that their loyalty may not be to their new State, but to their old one. Like a priest with a *Playboy* magazine under his bed, a high government official with large stock holdings, particularly in areas where he or she is involved in policy-making, is suspect.

From the historical perspective of the Governing State, the sacrifices required of government servants are part of the code of conduct that has emerged over generations to ensure that those who have authority do not abuse their power. From this Official perspective, bureaucracy is not a problem to be solved, but rather the solution to a problem. Compared to feudalism, under which individuals were stratified by birth—from the all-powerful monarchs to the powerless serfs—bureaucracy was progress. Compared to corrupt back room politics, in which bullies like Boss Tweed wielded Mafia-like control over the machinery of local government, bureaucracy was a breakthrough. Using words that today would astonish Ross Perot and his government-bashing followers, sociologist Max Weber called bureaucracy "superior to any other organization," particularly because of its "precision, speed [and] unambiguity." Bureaucracy was designed to govern impersonally, impartially, and impeccably. It was based on respect for rules and regulations, rather than on the whims of royalty or the blackmail of roughnecks.

To prevent politicians' families, friends, and supporters from getting all the posh government jobs, more than 100,000 pages of personnel rules and regulations spell out who can be hired—and fired. To prevent federal employees from awarding contracts to their friends and getting rich in the process, elaborate procurement processes that require mounds of paperwork have been instituted. To ensure that tax dollars are spent only for what was intended, every expenditure is predefined and tightly monitored.

The labyrinth of bureaucracy was constructed in order to create a system that was rational, efficient, and public-spirited. But since public officials are, after all, only human, they must be regulated to prevent them from acting in typically human ways. As a result, roughly 700,000 federal employees are engaged in managing, controlling, and checking up on somebody else. Although most bureaucratic rules were originally laid down with the best of intentions, their cumulative effect is gridlock.[30] Because of such gridlock, government is held in low esteem, and presidents are reduced to pleading for support.

"I need your support and your contribution," President Clinton told about 200 business executives and their Washington lobbyists, whom he had invited to the White House. "Everyone will have to pay their fair share. But if you do, we will all be better off, and the business community will be stronger in the years ahead." Needless to say, the higher taxes the president was proposing did not please his business audience. "We are very, very disturbed with this initiative with regard to corporate rates," Dirk Van Dongen, president of the National Association of Wholesaler Distributors, told reporters later. Mocking Clinton's Kennedy-like call for "sacrifice" on behalf of the national interest, Republican presidential hopeful Jack Kemp scoffed: "Sacrifice is not an economic policy. . . . It's not the people who need to sacrifice; it's the bloated government."[31]

The same selfish response comes whenever government asks the rich to pay higher taxes for the benefit of the overall economy. When President Clinton suggested that taxes should be raised on the "people who did well in the last decade," former president Ronald Reagan argued that Clinton was confusing the public by calling for "political courage" to vote for his "bold" plan when, in fact, doing so was an act of political cowardice and economic stupidity. The "simple truth," Reagan concluded, was that "this plan is bad for America."[32]

Government Agencies Are a Reliable Source of Accurate, Unbiased Information.

The Congressional Budget Office, the General Services Administration, and scores of other unheralded government agencies have the vital task of providing the people with facts. Even the smallest statistical error can have overwhelming consequences for thousands, sometimes millions, of American citizens.

When the Labor Department acknowledged that a flaw in its survey techniques had significantly underestimated unemployment, it was a detail virtually ignored by most citizens. But Officials knew that the statistic mattered; the lives of millions of women hinged on it. The Labor Department had been determining the official level of joblessness in America according to a formula that had not been revised for a quarter of a century, although clearly American society had changed in many ways, including the position of women in the work force. Not surprisingly, the survey was counting hundreds of thousands of women as "homemakers" when in fact they were seeking work but unable to find it. This minor error had quite an impact. Instead of 6.0 percent of women being unemployed during the period August 1992 to August 1993, the correct figure was 6.8 percent.[33]

The difference is considerable. It affects who receives unemployment compensation; it affects how the public perceives the economy; it may even affect who is elected to office. Accurate information is essential to democratic governance. Unlike corporations, which run image campaigns; unlike movie stars, who hire public relations firms; and unlike tabloid newspapers, which print outright lies to boost their sales, the government is obliged to tell the truth. It must provide the best possible information on which to base public policy decisions.

Are there 600,000 homeless Americans on any given night? Or are there 7,000,000? Are the homeless mostly drug addicts, mentally ill patients, and people who prefer a street "life-style"? Or are they mostly decent, hardworking Americans who have been victimized by a tightening economy or plain old bad luck? Conflicting statistics and stereotypes, some preferred by Republicans and some by Democrats, are subjected to systematic inquiry by officials. Without such fair-minded assessment, divisiveness and slipshod policymaking are inevitable. It is the government's job to undertake such inquiries and provide the information to the voters.[34]

Leadership |
"LET US NOT BE WEARY IN WELL-DOING."

Before his White House appointment returned him to government power, David Gergen was a political commentator and journalist appearing on ABC's "Nightline" who judged Clinton's leadership to be deeply flawed. Clinton's performance "has gone from poor to perilous," he told Ted Koppel and millions of American viewers. "He's not only gone off track; he's going around in circles."

Within a few weeks of joining the Clinton administration, Gergen, by then a presidential counselor, was very positive about leadership in the White House. He now appeared on the same TV talk shows defending the administration against its detractors. "I don't think he needs to save his presidency," Gergen said of his new boss, on the David Brinkley show. "This president's got a lot going for him. He's accomplished a lot. He's had good, strong leadership here."[35]

Although Gergen's former colleagues in the media tried to tar him with charges of hypocrisy and opportunism, another explanation is that he had simply switched from being a citizen of Media to being a citizen of Officia: his job was not to attack the government, but to defend it; not to expose it, but to protect it; not to stress its weaknesses, but to highlight its strengths.

In short, Gergen had become an Official.

Government Leaders Focus on
the Long-Term Well-Being of the Nation.

One quality of leadership that Officials admire passionately is devotion to nurturing the nation's children—*all* its children. Officials believe that many children enter American life facing a stacked deck: unequal access to health care, to education, to job opportunities, to income and loans, and ultimately to political power. These disadvantaged children need a special boost. From the Carnegie Council on Children in the 1970s (which employed Hillary Rodham Clinton) to the Children's Defense Fund in the 1980s and 1990s (where Ms. Clinton served as chairman of the board), countless liberal organizations, foundations, and activist groups support the notion that it is the government's job to help these kids succeed by escaping the underclass and entering the mainstream.[36] Taking care of our nation's children as defined by the Governing State is not only good ethics, but sound economics. It enriches not just a privileged elite, but a whole civilization.

According to longitudinal studies begun in the 1960s, investment in preschool programs for disadvantaged children yields social dividends so extraordinary that, if it were a company on the New York Stock Exchange, everybody would buy shares. Comparing children in preschool programs to similar children without them, the studies showed that an initial investment of only $5,000 per child per year would result in the following savings:

- $3,000 less spent on delinquency and crime.
- $5,000 saved on remedial programs later in public schools.
- $16,000 saved on welfare and other public assistance programs.
- At least $5,000 more in taxes collected from higher earnings.

And all these savings were yielded by the time the child reached the age of nineteen. Spread over a lifetime, the savings on this modest public investment of $5,000 would be astronomical![37]

But to realize these savings, Officials argue, action is required—*government* action. This willingness to take action—to "above all, try something," in FDR's memorable phrase—is called leadership. While others may instinctively look for guidance and inspiration from church leaders or corporate leaders or media leaders, Officials turn to political leaders.

Instead of looking at the quarterly reports or the latest Nielsen ratings, true leaders must look to the future. These committed, visionary men and women stand up for the role of government and commit its resources to long-term investment—not just in children, but in countless public causes that require far-sighted concern for the common good. Thus Officials approved of President Clinton's intentions to expand the Women, Infants, and Children (WIC) nutrition program so that "every expectant mother who needs our help receives it," and also expand the Head Start program so that it "will cover every eligible child." To justify these additional expenditures at a time of tightening budgets, President Clinton used the argument that investing in these programs is not only "the right thing, it's the smart thing. For every dollar we invest today, we save three tomorrow." The Clinton administration's childhood immunization program, according to the president, was an even better investment. The country will "save ten dollars for every one we'll spend," he argued, "by preventing childhood disease."

Disians would say the effort was too small; Corporatians would say it was more "big government." Because President Clinton knew that his economic policies would be attacked from all sides, he closed his economic address to a joint session of Congress by warning that "the special interests will be out in force, trying to stop the changes we seek."[38]

Despite his attempt to forestall attacks from the other Divided States, his plan was savaged. But Officials defended it, because Clinton had touched on the Governing State's core belief: good government works for the public interest; everyone else represents just their self-interest.

Instead of Honor and Respect, Public Servants Get Harassed and Maligned.

At first glance, Tim Honey does not seem to be a likely target of government-bashers. He is a white, affluent, educated, middle-aged male who lives in a comfortable, primarily white neighborhood in Boulder, Colorado, a safe and seemingly tolerant college town nestled at the foothills of the Rocky Mountains.

But if you sit with him in his office, you quickly realize that appearances can be deceiving. In fact, Tim Honey is one of those who bear the brunt of America's decline in civility. His job, city manager of Boulder, makes him a member of a much maligned and stereotyped minority—the "government official."

Tim Honey has committed no crime. He has not broken any promises or deceived anyone. But because of what he calls "the increasing negativity towards government," doing his job has put him on the receiving end of insults, innuendo, and outright venom.

"When I am attacked personally, I always wonder why the person didn't write me a letter and tell me what was on their mind. There are always some individuals who, for whatever psychological reasons, like to blast away. I know they engage in uncivil behavior when they feel they have no control over what is happening to them. They are angry at the institutions, which I understand. But then they insist on making it personal. It's simply not acceptable for people to come into a city council meeting and have stickers or placards that say 'SO-AND-SO-SUCKS.' We were debating open space [undeveloped land surrounding the city], and some of our council members were viciously attacked by name. The small percentage of brick throwers set a tone of incivility, and the media rewards them. If you sit down and have a discussion with the city council, you won't get your name in the paper. But if you engage in the most uncivil, outrageous behavior and insult me or my colleagues, you'll be on the front page of the paper tomorrow."

As the person who manages the city government's entire work force, Honey witnesses firsthand the toll that this treatment takes on them. "The stress on our employees," he says sadly, "is excruciating. When people stand up in the audience and attack my employees personally and viciously, some of them react by saying: 'It's just not worth it.' In city management, it is getting increasingly difficult to be effective. Managers are getting more and more cautious, not taking risks, and becoming less effective. If they take risks, they get the shit kicked out of them by an increasingly hostile public."

"I've never seen anything like it—the viciousness, the personal attacks," concurred Boulder mayor Leslie Durgin. "It used to be that good and caring citizens who had different perspectives worked together. What we are hearing from citizens today is that if you disagree with me, you are evil. It's very wearing. It's not a healthy part of our community right now."[39]

"If entering the city management profession means that you and your family will be crucified in the public arena and your professional reputation destroyed," Honey concludes, "not many people will enter the profession. The quality of people who aspire to government service will decline. When I graduated from school, to work in government was one of the highest aspirations you could have. My fear is that this allergy to federal service will infect state and local government too. If the quality of public servants erodes further, our problems will get worse."

As city manager, Tim Honey does not expect blind support for government. On the contrary, he is one of the toughest critics of public bureaucracies. He has seen firsthand how arrogant government officials can be, as if they were the only force in our society that could bring progress. And he has seen how defensive government officials can be when criticized. "We are always complaining that the citizens don't trust government enough," he says, "but why should they? Why shouldn't they have a healthy skepticism about us, just like they do about big business, big union, and all the other giants?" He knows all the new catch phrases—from "customer-driven" government to "collaborative decision-making"; from "reinventing government" to managing in a "new team environment." And he has seen it all from close enough to know that there is no panacea for what ails democracy. "There is no perfect system out there just waiting to be discovered," Honey concludes. "Democracy is messy, and while we government and citizens try to make it work, the question is: how will we treat each other?"

The Cynicism and Hostility of the Electorate Undermines Government.

Campaign financing illustrates the double bind in which politicians are caught. They are being held to higher ethical standards than in previous eras. Their every move, and even those of their families, is scrutinized. Yet at the same time, campaigning is more expensive than ever. A candidate for Senate must raise an estimated $13,000 a week for an entire six-year term in order to mount a serious campaign. (For candidates for president, it is $77,000 a week.) In the words of former Senator David Boren (D-Okla.), they are forced to become "part-time senators and full-time fund raisers"; but when they do so, the public—and of course the self-righteous media—portray them as money-grubbing animals. "Their relentless, almost druglike appetite for money," says former White House official Jack Valenti, "is like flesh-eating bacteria attacking our national soul."[40]

Officials complain that, even when government tries to reform itself, the other Divided States seek to undermine it. Within months of becoming elected, President Clinton ordered his cabinet to cut the federal work force over the next four years by 100,000 jobs. He also announced that he would cut his own White House employment rolls by 25 percent. If all the reductions were carried out, Mr. Clinton said, they would save $9 billion over four years. A few months later, Vice President Gore, who spearheaded the "reinventing government" task force, announced that 250,000 federal jobs would ultimately be eliminated (an amount equal to the jobs in ten average Fortune 500 companies).[41] After a half-year of intensive study formally called the National Performance Review (NPR), the administration issued an agency-by-agency review of how government could become more efficient and began the process of trimming waste and streamlining the structure of government. It was, most Officials believed, what every cost-conscious American had been waiting for: a complete overhaul of government.

Officials were dismayed by the public response. In every media forum, liberal or conservative, from the *New York Times* to the major networks, the report was greeted with jeers. The public has "good reason to be cynical," said the *Times* on its op ed page.[42] Using virtually identical wording and strategy, every major outlet challenged, belittled, or scorned the Clinton administration's commitment to reaching its stated goals.[43]

No wonder public service as a career has lost its prestige. The author of *Opportunities in Federal Government Careers* concluded: "a doctor in private practice has more prestige than one who works for the government, . . . a lawyer with a private firm outranks one with the government, and . . . accountants with private corporations are better thought of than ones who work for the government. Government jobs, except for those at the very top, are low in prestige."[44]

Such attacks worry citizens of Officia because they undermine the very basis of governance. Both Republican and Democratic leaders have begun to feel the effects of the system's poisoning. Senator Howell Heflin (D-Ala.), who chaired the Senate ethics committee for thirteen years, says proudly: "We are probably today the most ethical Congress . . . that has ever existed." Yet he adds: "You can't convince the media of that." Senator Trent Lott (R-Miss.) says ethics is often in the eye of the beholder. Even as Congress improves, the media and public are so critical of politicians, he says, that "they've made criminals of all of us."

Politicians are forced to defend themselves again and again against accusations which are sometimes politically inspired. In the process, they can amass legal bills of $300,000 to $500,000, effectively crippling them financially. "In my opinion, legislatures and legislators generally, like members of Congress, are being unfairly accused," Alan Rosenthal, a Rutgers University authority on ethics in state governments, told Congress recently.[45]

Reputable men and women who could bring great talents to government are so repelled by the harassment and character assassination that government service doesn't seem worth the effort. What makes this kill-the-leader attitude outside the State of Officia so dangerous, argue those inside it, is that strong leadership is vital. If we are to confront our growing challenges, America must have vision: inclusive, civic-centered, fair-minded, and farsighted vision. This can only come, Officials argue, from respecting public leadership, not undermining it.

Against Enormous Odds, Our Government Is Holding Our Nation Together.

For the best interests of all Americans to be served, Officials believe that the Governing State must play the central role in our society. After all, what other group is capable of it? Ordinary citizens inevitably bring parochial, limited, and usually local perspectives to complex problems. The critical issues affecting the nation are simply too complex for most ordinary citizens to understand, argue most citizens of Officia. When voters left the polling booths following the 1992 election, the exit polls listed nine issues, two of which the voters could choose as "important" in deciding their vote. Voters listed the economy and jobs as the most important issue (at 42 percent); and the deficit was second (at 21 percent). But other polls demonstrated that voters' understanding of the economy and the deficit was extremely weak. If even the two issues about which voters cared most deeply were so complex as to be almost incomprehensible, imagine how little they understood about the other seven (which included issues such as health care and foreign policy).[46] The only rational conclusion is that the federal government and its elected representatives must have the power to decide what is in the best interests of the country, and to make and enforce laws that protect these national interests.

The citizens of the Governing State believe in democracy. But they know that with the public divided into warring camps and ignorant of many of the intricacies of public policy-making, strong leadership is needed to steer the ship of state. Politicians who want to reduce the government's budget and limit its power, Officials believe, are weakening our government precisely when it needs to be strengthened.

Officials want their fellow citizens to stop blindly criticizing the government and recognize that it deserves their support. They want us to stop hypocritically taking from the government and then refusing to give back. In the words of John F. Kennedy, they want us to "ask not what our country can do for us, but what we can do for our country." They want us to be willing to sacrifice for the public good; to pay our taxes with pride; to submit private enterprise to public oversight; and, ultimately, to stand up for our public institutions and the public servants who run them.

This is not just a belief system, citizens of the Governing State argue. This is the American way.

II

The

UNITED
STATES

of

AMERICA

We shall nobly save, or meanly lose,
the last best hope on earth.

ABRAHAM LINCOLN,
Second annual message to Congress,
December 1, 1862

C AN THE DIVIDED STATES of America be reconnected, to form a new *United* States?

Now that we have reached the midpoint of our journey, the challenge we face is clearer. As individual citizens, our challenge is to retrace our path through the ideological minefields we have just visited and to decide what we stand for—and against. As a nation, our challenge is to deepen our commitment to the ideals on which our democracy is based.

I recognize that I may overestimate the dangers that these "wars between the States" pose to the union. But as someone whose relatives were incinerated in Nazi concentration camps while good Germans said their prayers and polished their silverware, I prefer to be safe rather than sorry. Probably because my own existence once hung in the balance, I have always been interested in the conflict between belief systems. If Nazis had killed my father, a coroner's report would have cited the cause of death as gunshot wounds, but in fact, as a European Jew, he would have been a victim of organized beliefs.

While one belief system almost snuffed out my life before it began, another saved it. Because of America's and its allies' defense of freedom, my father survived the war. He married my mother, found a new home in New York, and started a family. After the war, they could have settled anywhere from South Africa to Latin America, to Europe. But they became citizens of this country because its belief in freedom and equality—"life, liberty and the pursuit of happiness"—drew them here. In this cradle of democracy, I was born, grew up, and raised a family of my own, and have remained grateful to this home ever since.

Given this background, my interest in what people believe, and how those beliefs affect their behavior, is in my blood. In one way or another, almost everything I have ever written or done has reflected my desire to explore and understand the often invisible architecture of beliefs that leads human beings to treat each other with compassion or cruelty.

My life has taught me that beliefs can make a person either loving or bitter. They can either open our hearts or close them; make a nation either strong or weak; and either nurture life or destroy it. The remainder of this book is about what makes the difference.

In my own beliefs, I will no doubt part ways with some readers, and some readers will part ways with each other. This is inevitable, because beliefs are intensely personal. Some of you may feel at home in one of the Divided States; others may identify with several of them; and still others may be uncomfortable in all of them. Being citizens in a democracy means making choices, and our choices can differ. What is crucial now is how we will treat those with whose choices we disagree.

Again and again, as I have worked in conflicted communities, I have met people who were neighbors but were treating each other like aliens. They were shouting hate-filled epithets at each other—treating their opponents as if they did not deserve to be called Americans. The level of frustration, bitterness, and anger is steadily mounting in all the Divided States. It seems as though people feel they are not getting what they want or achieving their objectives. They are no longer confident that America is becoming what they want it to be.

As I traveled through the Divided States, interviewing their citizens and studying their views, I concluded that, when they were at their worst, they resembled one another in several ways:

- FEW PEOPLE ACTUALLY LISTEN. Either the combatants shout, or wait for their turn to shout. Conversation is reduced to aggressive "sound bites." Facial expressions often reveal anger and contempt for others.

- EVERYONE FEELS MISUNDERSTOOD. Everyone in an argument feels stereotyped, or dehumanized, by their opponents. Both sides leave an encounter complaining of being misquoted, misheard, misused, or otherwise disrespected.

- LANGUAGE BREAKS DOWN. Attempts at discourse are futile because words are used as weapons, and talking makes things worse. The same charges and countercharges are repeated again and again. "There you go again" is a common refrain.

- PERSON-TO-PERSON COMMUNICATION FAILS. In an atmosphere of fear and tension, antagonists speak in generalities and slogans. Rarely do they address one another as flesh-and-blood human beings.

- THE MEDIA EMPHASIZE AND REINFORCE EXTREME POSITIONS. The loudest and most obnoxious voices capture the most attention in the media. People with moderate views, who recognize the complexity of an issue and who speak quietly and respectfully, are ignored.

With behavior of this kind on the part of the citizenry, America is paralyzed. People are pitted *against* each other, rather than working *with* each other. While the nation is not about to be plunged into a civil war, it does face a future of chronic gridlock. As a people, we are likely to be increasingly cut off from each other, separated by fear and suspicion. As a consequence of the many impasses, our society faces a slowdown. The United States can become less competitive in world markets, and less able to inspire other nations around the globe. America's famous "can-do" energy can give way to a "can't-do" bitterness.

This bleak scenario is not inevitable. There are alternatives. I invite you to come with me now to communities across the country where I have witnessed citizens successfully counteracting the politics of hate and fragmentation and managing their civic affairs with mutual respect and collaboration.

In my work for the Rockefeller Foundation and in the research for this book, I have studied closely the combatants in America's culture wars and probed deeply into their beliefs. I would go to one group in a controversy and ask such questions as:

- What are the beliefs that support your position?
- How did you arrive at those beliefs?
- Why do think your beliefs are good for the country?
- Who do you consider to be your enemies?
- What do you think *they* believe?

I would then go to the opposing group and ask similar questions. I went back and forth in this "shuttle diplomacy," each time digging deeper and deeper into the competing belief systems.

I began my research as a sixties liberal, with a predictable set of built-in biases. Encountering caring, decent people who had views diametrically opposed to mine, I began to reexamine my own assumptions. Sometimes the inquiry confirmed my original opinions; and at other times my opinions changed. But always, my personal view of what was "right" and "wrong" was deepened so that my adversaries were humanized and became fellow citizens.

After spending several years traveling through the Divided States, I no longer view Patria, Corporatia, Disia, Media, Gaia, and Officia as monolithic forces. Many of the citizens in every one of these Divided States love their country. Deep concern for "my country" is both widespread and deep. A population approaching 300 million people, scattered across a vast continent, separated by ethnicity and ideology and economics, surprisingly often make day-to-day decisions based on what they believe is "good for America." *Isn't there some way to build upon this genuine patriotism and restore our faith in America?*

I believe this is possible, but only if we recognize that these six States are part of the Union *for a reason*. At their best, they all have a gift to give America—and, at their worst, they all pose a danger. As I see it:

Patria's gift is its *faith;* **the danger of the Religious State is its** *dogmatism.* Some Americans express their love for their country from a religious or moral vantage point. Their religious faith is the root that nurtures their patriotism. They seek to provide a moral cornerstone for American life that calls all of us to devote ourselves more fully to what is sacred. They give America the gift of their personal faith. But while believing in God is our inalienable right, Patrians at their worst allow one faith to become exclusive and intolerant of other faiths. Faith then turns into dogma. Instead of nourishing the deeper roots of democracy, dogma weakens them. Instead of deepening the dialogue between citizens, dogma poisons it. Instead of morally uplifting America, Patrians' dogma can divide, stigmatize, and polarize.

Corporatia's gift is its *ingenuity;* **the danger of the Capitalist State is its** *materialism.* Americans with business experience naturally focus their attention on economic strategies for strengthening America. They speak in terms of dollars and cents, jobs and opportunity. Their goal is to turn political dreams into practical realities. They express their patriotism through civic entrepreneurship. However, when generating profits becomes the only goal in Corporatia, material values crowd our civic ones. Communities are used and abandoned; ecosystems are scarred; public institutions are undermined. Wealth is generated for a few at the expense of the many. The very essence of America, "liberty and justice for all," is betrayed.

Disia's gift is its *conscience;* **the danger of the Disempowered State is its** *defeatism.* Some Americans are called to express their patriotism through criticism. Demanding progress in our society, which is deeply flawed, is vital to democracy. Expressing love for America by focusing on our nation's flaws is a critical ingredient in making our nation fulfill its destiny. Disians are determined to provide America with a constant challenge to the status quo by urging their fellow citizens to live up to their nation's lofty ideals. Their gift is persistent, creative, principled dissent. But when Disians manipulate their victim status, the cause of justice is not served. When they begin to stereotype and dehumanize their alleged oppressors and succumb to self-serving conspiracy theories, they undercut their own cause. Such hostility and self-pity then only serve to strengthen oppression, not overcome it. By allowing resentment and vengeance to shape their worldview, they become part of the problem rather than part of the solution. Embittered or vengeful, passive or hostile, they help defeat themselves.

Media's gift is *communication;* the danger of the Superstate is *sensationalism.* Some Americans, blessed with communication skills, express their patriotism through the storytelling power of words and images. Aware of the competing belief systems, they seek to serve as translators between the Real States. They seek to provide a common language and meeting ground for America. Their media has the power to connect 280 million citizens in a network of constructive, civic interaction. Their challenge is to bear witness to all of America. But when the media is used to exploit rather than to inform, crass sensationalism replaces civic communication. Our culture is debased, not elevated; numbed, rather than awakened. When popularity is pursued at all costs, and profits overwhelm purpose in programming decisions, readers and viewers are subjected to a media diet that sickens rather than heals. Hatred, rather than connection, is fostered, and voyeurism, rather than engagement, is encouraged. In less than a generation, the fabric of society can be torn apart.

Gaia's gift is *vision;* the danger of the Transformation State is its *elitism.* These Americans' patriotism is expressed through their concern for America's ecological and spiritual crisis. Their worldview, often grounded in the work of great thinkers and expressed in planetary terms, informs their globally oriented form of patriotism. They seek to provide an integrative vision for America. But when Gaians contend that every American "creates his own reality" and when they show more compassion for endangered animals than for endangered families, their New Age spiritualism verges on indifference. Just as Corporatians reduce everything to material terms, Gaians attempt to reduce everything to a metaphysical level—and thereby oversimplify and distort reality. Under the guise of higher consciousness, they can become arrogantly smug and callously condescending. They believe they are exploring enlightenment when they are regressing toward blame and taking refuge in isolation and elitism.

Officia's gift is its *leadership;* the danger of the Governing State is its *divisiveness.* These Americans express patriotism by their emphasis on governance. Their primary focus of attention is on how public institutions work. They seek to provide America with a new kind of leadership that will enable government and citizens to be partners who bring out the best in each other through public service. Instead of seeking private profit or promoting their own self-interest, they genuinely seek to serve the welfare of the whole society. But citizens of Officia have let government run amok. Many bureaucracies have ended up serving their own needs, not the public's. Government employees have lost sight of their role as servants and expect instead to be treated like bosses. Candidates use elections to manipulate voters, not educate them. Instead of self-governance, we are left with gridlock. Instead of striving for the public interest, we are held hostage by special interests and ordinary citizens are withdrawing from public life.

Each State, in other words, is part of a larger whole—the Union. What turns conflicts into wars—that is, what turns fellow citizens with different beliefs into warring armies with different belief systems—is a refusal to acknowledge this complexity. Each belief system exaggerates its gifts and denies its dangers and does precisely the opposite to their adversaries. Armed with their own belief system, Americans now are doing to each other what the United States and the Soviet Union used to do during the Cold War—dehumanize each other into enemies, put on ideological uniforms, and join the wars between the States.

Most Americans do have a common bedrock of beliefs, but it is buried under layers of conflicts and confusion, misunderstandings and mistakes. America's shared values will not surface on "Crossfire," or during televised debates between sparring candidates, or at sidewalk demonstrations outside abortion clinics. "Drive-by debates," as Sheldon Hackney, director of the National Endowment for the Humanities, calls them, only exacerbate conflict. To rediscover our common ground as Americans, we have to ask more of each other, and of ourselves.

Listening closely to Americans talk about our country—both the powerful and the powerless—I realized that citizens of all the Divided States felt threatened by change they could not understand or control, and were afraid that some terrifying "other" was trying to dominate them. Fragmentation had reached the point that there was no culture to be a "sub" of or a "counter" to. In different ways, everybody felt marginal or peripheral, because the center no longer existed. Everyone felt isolated.

In San Antonio, for example, my colleagues brought together representatives from seven high schools which reflected the city's diversity: the rich, white, north side high school; the poor, heavily Latino west side school; the widely criticized, mostly black east side school; and four others. Many of the student representatives had never set foot in each other's neighborhoods; it was too dangerous. They knew each other only from media reports and from taunting each other from bleachers on opposite sides of the football field. They assumed they had nothing in common. But when they began talking with each other in small groups, they discovered they all shared the same powerful feeling: they *all* felt isolated. It was not just the minorities who didn't like being segregated: nobody did. They quickly banded together to form a citywide student coalition and are now working side by side in several projects to help their city.

The yearning these young people felt to transcend the different States in which they were trapped and to reconnect with the rest of their generation inspired us. We realized that although our nation is deeply wounded, it has the capacity to heal.

To understand how such healing happens, we sought out the healers. We studied the work of those who were caught in conflicts that seemed intractable, who had tackled problems that seemed insoluble, who had worked with adversaries that seemed incompatible, and who had nevertheless achieved goals that seemed impossible. We talked with Baptist ministers and MIT organizational consultants, New Age facilitators and street-wise community organizers, multimillionaire developers and ghetto activists. We identified community leaders who were strengthening and revitalizing their communities in countless ways. As different as these Americans were, they shared a common quality: a willingness to confront their adversaries, face their differences, and work things through.

In Tucson, Arizona, for example, a city wounded by a series of conflicts about the public schools, my colleagues brought together citizens who represented the primary competing points of view. Among them were affluent whites who wanted higher academic standards, Latinos angered about the high dropout rate among Hispanic students, Native Americans bitter about the way their traditions were being ignored; fundamentalist Christian parents who wanted stronger religious values in the curriculum; home-schoolers who disliked the entire system. For weeks they met together to explore their differences and to see if they could find ways that they could work together to improve the schools.

At one pivotal meeting, the participants in the dialogue had developed enough trust so that they were all speaking candidly. From their wildly different perspectives, each took the floor and chastised the school district for letting down their kids. One wanted more multicultural instruction; another wanted less. One wanted more religion; another wanted none at all. One wanted more money spent per child; another wanted a freeze on school spending. At first glance, the conversation seemed to be leading nowhere. They seemed to have nothing in common but bashing the school system.

Listening to their divergent and often contradictory complaints was a high school teacher. Clearly agitated, she finally could stand it no longer. "You all are entitled to your own views," she said, her face flushed with frustration. "But we have *all* your children in our classes. What are *we* supposed to do?"

Her outburst awakened everyone. Finally, one of participants said: "Let's talk: *we* have a problem." Out of a splintered and fractured set of "they's," they formed a diverse and dynamic "we" that proceeded to bring healing dialogue and much-needed renewal to their local school district. If public education was to continue, they knew they had to seek common ground—and they are now doing so.

Fortunately, scores of citizens in communities all across America are refusing to join the war between the Divided States and instead are building bridges. As different as they may be—private citizens or government officials, corporate executives or religious leaders, famous spokespersons or unknown community leaders—they have clearly pledged their allegiance, not to one of the Divided States, but to the United States. They are America's *new patriots.*

"To restore the Union," wrote Abraham Lincoln in his final letter before he was assassinated, Americans must work together "to make it . . . a Union of hearts and hands as well as States."[1] Today, on the eve of a new millennium, we face this challenge again. If, as President Lincoln said at Gettysburg, "government of the people, by the people and for the people, shall not perish from the earth," it will be because we learned how to use the differences between ourselves to deepen our common bond as Americans.

In the following three chapters, we explore this new patriotism: specifically, how the competing belief systems of the Divided States all can be part of one democracy. Discerning areas of common ground, we chronicle how our neighbors are redefining democracy and taking responsibility for re-creating it in their daily lives. Because their story cannot be written in any single voice, I tell the story in the words of scores of Americans who are on the front lines of struggle for America's soul. That story, ultimately, is larger than those of the individuals whom I have interviewed. It will be written by you, by your family, your friends, and your neighbors. It will be written in the hundreds of decisions and choices that we make every day. On the eve of the millennium, America has to be rediscovered by us. Each of *us* has to be its founders. We cannot be connected to each other only by our glorious past; we must find a living bond that means something to each of us today. The patriotism of old must be reborn—and transformed.

BEYOND
THE
DIVIDED
STATES

*Do unto others as
you would have others
do unto you.*

CHRISTIANITY

*What is hateful to you,
do not do to your fellow man.*

JUDAISM

*No one is a believer until
he desires for his brother
that which he desires for himself.*

ISLAM

*Do not do unto others
what would cause you pain
if done unto you.*

HINDUISM

*Hurt not others in ways
that you yourself would find hurtful.*

BUDDHISM

*Regard your neighbor's gain
as your own gain,
and your neighbor's loss
as your own loss.*

TAOISM

I pledge allegiance to the flag of my State,
and to the belief system for which it stands,
one State, invincible,
with liberty and justice for us.

THIS IS OBVIOUSLY not the Pledge of Allegiance we recited as children. It does not reflect the original patriotism of the founders of this country. On the contrary, it reflects the narrow and short-sighted patriotism of the Divided States that has taken root in America. Many of us have either forgotten the words to the original pledge, or forgotten what it means—if, in fact, we ever knew.

The founders of this nation knew that loyalty to a state, rather than to the Union of all states, would set us on a dangerous course. Indeed, when states seceded from the Union during the Civil War, the following bloodbath left wounds in our national psyche yet unhealed. Just as we don't give our ultimate loyalty to Pennsylvania or Georgia, so we cannot give our ultimate loyalty to Patria or Gaia. California may be where we live, and Corporatia may reflect what we believe, but to neither of them can we, as Americans, pledge our final allegiance.

The actual Pledge of Allegiance says this:

I pledge allegiance to the flag of the United *States of America,*
and to the republic for which it stands,
one nation, indivisible,
under God,
with liberty and justice for all. [1]

If we compare the actual Pledge of Allegiance to the distorted one, we witness the challenge America faces. The six belief systems described in this book are pitting citizen against citizen, dividing us. It isn't a question of whether one of the Divided States is right, and the others is wrong. They are *all* right—and *all* wrong. In almost all public policy controversies, the antagonists represent different aspects of the real truth. To split serious, committed citizens into opposing groups—using knee-jerk, meat-cleaver rhetoric of right versus wrong or Right vs. Left—is a travesty of democratic dialogue. For new patriots, the challenge is to defend the complexity of the truth. Unlike *partisans*, who stand up for only *part* of the truth, new patriots strive to represent the whole.

The questions is: how do these competing belief systems, and the scores of variations and combinations of them, coexist in a democracy?

Patriotism Must Be a Living Force,
Growing and Changing Like the Country Itself.

The answer, in a word, is patriotism. But the new patriotism which America so urgently needs is not the old-fashioned, I'm-right, you're-wrong, love-it-or-leave-it kind of patriotism that caused so much turmoil during this century. Catalyzing the gifts of all of the States, and restraining the dangers they pose, will be the challenge of the twenty-first-century patriotism. But before we can meet that challenge, we must understand the old patriotism—and break free.

Twentieth-Century Patriotism |
"LOVE IT OR LEAVE IT"

The second half of the twentieth century has witnessed a growing awareness of the paradoxes buried deep within the old patriotism. The paradoxes turned vicious in the fifties with McCarthyism, and exploded in the headlines again during the sixties in the struggles over civil rights and the Vietnam war. During the years of war in Vietnam, the old patriotism was wielded like a club to force people into conformity. To tell a young person that he or she should be "more patriotic" often meant supporting, rather than questioning, the war effort. Because challenging the legitimacy of the war was considered by many to be unpatriotic, they drew a line in the sand: from their perspective, hawks were patriotic, doves weren't.

Patriotism, alas, was frequently reduced to partisanship. It became synonymous, not with love of one's country, but with support for a specific war. Those who did not agree with the controversial government policy toward Vietnam were subjected to epithets that implied they were somehow un-American. Slogans such as "My country, right or wrong" and "America: Love it or leave it" were used to imply that those who opposed the war were no longer entitled to American citizenship. Meanwhile, dissenters sometimes called their fellow citizens who supported the war "pigs," "fascists," and worse. They spit on the flag and equated patriotism with mindless, Nazi-like obedience.

Vietnam was not the only influence that undermined the old patriotism. Government deceit, fraud, and corruption, combined with the Watergate lawlessness, also fueled cynicism and distrust. In addition, the civil rights movement under the leadership of Reverend Martin Luther King, Jr., catalyzed

Americans' awareness of the gap between democratic ideals and racist realities. All these combined during the Vietnam era to undermine the old patriotism.

The old concept of patriotism fell into disrepute and was used less frequently. But it didn't disappear: it splintered. Its underlying belief is inherent in each of the Divided States. In essence, its message is: If you don't share my belief system, then you aren't a patriot.

The Old Patriotism Preached Freedom
But Practiced Conformity.

The old patriots expected uniformity, that is, one relatively narrow set of identities. Senators could not be African-American; Miss Americas could not be deaf; sports heroes could not be gay. Limited diversity was accepted only if it could be adapted to the traditional way of life. Despite our rhetoric about freedom and equality, those who didn't fit fell outside the definition of patriotic Americans.

The old patriotism's demand for uniformity all too frequently led to a kind of hypocrisy, even in the Declaration of Independence. "As a nation we began by declaring that 'all men are created equal,' " wrote Abraham Lincoln to his friend Joshua F. Speed almost a century after the Declaration was written. "We now practically read it 'All men are created equal except Negroes.' " In terms of the right to vote, for example, it took another century—and the deaths of hundreds of thousands of Americans in the Civil War—before dark-skinned men were given the same rights as white-skinned men. It took another half-century before women of any color were allowed to enter the voting booth. So deep was this hypocrisy that, at the ceremony unveiling the Lincoln Memorial in Washington, D.C., more than a half-century after Lincoln's death, African-Americans in the audience were segregated from whites. In other words, there was—and still is—a significant gap between what the Declaration of Independence preached and what we, the people, have practiced.

Built into the old patriotism, then, was a split between those Americans who were included and those who were not. Over generations the boundary shifted, but it never disappeared. As a result, exclusion has always been part of our history. Those who did not fit were by definition "un-American" (commies, troublemakers, rabble-rousers, secret agents, agitators, nigger-lovers, traitors) and had to be shunned, exiled, imprisoned, or killed. Patriotic Americans would avoid association with these unpatriotic, dangerous elements in our society.

Consequently, the basic attitudes of this conformity-based old patriotism were intolerance and disrespect toward those different from us. Both the McCarthyism of the fifties and the die-hard racial segregationism of the sixties are recent examples of the old patriotism in action. Incredible pressure was put on Americans to conform to a set of attitudes. Intolerance was turned into a virtue. At its worst, the old patriotism considered it heroic to destroy the reputations of those whose political attitudes were deemed "un-American."

To confirm that the old patriotism is still with us, simply open your newspaper or watch the evening news on television. Public discourse today reflects the corrosive impact of the old patriotism. The prevalent debating style is characterized by increasing hostility. Shouting is common; blame is everywhere. Wherever one turns—from the talk show on the car radio to prime-time TV, from the political speech to the televangelist's sermon, from the high-profile court case to the city council meeting—the level of public discourse seems to be deteriorating. The more vicious the talk show host, the larger his audience. The more angrily someone trashes another, the longer the sound bite. The uglier the campaign, the more air time the candidates receive. None of the Divided States are raising the level of discourse in America, yet all complain loudly that it is falling into the gutter.

The Blind Obedience of the Old Patriotism Has Corroded into Cynicism.

While once the old patriotism led to faith in America, today it has eroded into cynicism. Citizens of the Divided States, who care more about their belief systems than about their country, become painfully cynical about their fellow citizens. And cynicism, in its most extreme form, is the opposite of patriotism.

"Cynical" means: "Marked by or displaying contemptuous mockery of the motives or virtues of others: a cynical attitude toward society."[2] Being cynical implies that we expect to be treated badly by each other, and cynicism leads us to confirm those expectations. We expect anyone who is not a citizen of our Divided State to "rip us off." We expect politicians to be liars, the advertiser to mislead us, the salesman to be disreputable, the policeman to be corrupt or brutal, the lawyer to be unscrupulous, the government worker to be lazy, the teacher to be ineffective, the doctor to overcharge, the news reporter to sensationalize, the New Age guru to be a fraud, and the televangelist to embezzle.

This is far from what cynicism originally meant. Founded by a student of Socrates in the fifth century B.C., the school of philosophy called cynicism established an austere, independent way of thinking that would not be corrupted by social conventions or material pursuits. Even today, cynicism can be a life-saving antidote to naiveté, gullibility, and ignorance. Instead of blindly believing in unworthy leaders, unjust policies, or hand-me-down ideologies, postwar generations adopted the attitude summarized by the bumper sticker: QUESTION AUTHORITY. Such cynicism helped expose many ills, embarrass demagogues, expose widely believed untruths, and improve many of our institutions.

But too much cynicism, like too much salt, can spoil what it was supposed to enhance. That is precisely what has happened to citizenship in America in the closing third of this century. When the Gallup poll in 1990 asked voters in what institutions they had "a great deal" or "quite a lot" of confidence, their replies revealed how far cynicism had diminished our faith in each other and in our institutions. Only 13 percent had confidence in political parties, 18 percent in business, 18 percent in the federal government, 20 percent in state government, and 23 percent in local (municipal) government. In 1994, just four years later, when the Daniel Yankelovich Group (DYG, Inc.) asked the same questions, cynicism had corroded citizenship even more deeply. Confidence had dropped even further: confidence in political parties was 11 percent; in national business leaders, 15 percent; in the federal government, 16 percent; and in state government, 19 percent. Even the trust in institutions that have traditionally inspired faith, such as the churches, dropped precipitously during this decade.[3]

In a democracy, such cynicism is extremely dangerous. Self-government depends on the involvement of citizens and on their confidence in public institutions. When that confidence erodes, eaten away by resentment, bitterness, and apathy, democracy becomes an empty shell. Democracy is "vulnerable to the erosion of meaning in its institutions," observed Peter Berger and Richard John Neuhaus. "Cynicism threatens it; wholesale cynicism can destroy it."[4]

As mistrust rises, the bonds of citizenship fray. When these bonds are overly weakened, society breaks down. Almost two out of three Americans in 1994 believed that their communities were unhealthy because of a lack of public accountability and a lack of shared values and vision, and because "everyone is looking out for themselves."[5] Or as the Iowan farmer Jim Rohlfsen said: "We're all looking at what's good for us, not the country. . . . Everybody is their own lobby."

The Old Patriotism, Now an Anachronism,
Breeds a Politics of Polarization.

Since the old patriotism requires conformity and excludes those who do not conform, politics has become increasingly polarized. Based on competing ideologies which separate all issues into pro or con, left or right, and patriotic or unpatriotic, it has become increasingly out of touch with the complexity of modern life. This breeds division among citizens, pitting partisans on both extremes against each other. Repelled by the political game, the majority of citizens have become merely spectators. The result is low voter turnout and widespread despair about the political process and America's future.

In Hawkins County, Tennessee, a fundamentalist Christian mother objected to her sixth-grade daughter's reading a science fiction story in school in which astronauts encounter Martians who communicate telepathically. Offended by what she perceived to be a New Age, anti-Christian story line, this offended parent helped catalyze a conflict between conservative Christians, on the one hand, and liberal defenders of free speech on the other. After four years of litigation and more than $1.5 million in lawyers' fees, the involvement of national organizations like Concerned Women of America and People for the American Way, intensified hostility and divisiveness in the community, and an increasingly polarized educational system, nothing was gained. Trust had eroded; money had been wasted.

"The conclusion I draw," says lawyer Stephen Bates, who studied the case in detail, "is that *everyone* lost . . ." [6]

In hundreds of school districts, parents, teachers and school administrators are spending precious dollars and even more precious time and energy in battles that do little to strengthen their children's education. Everyone loses—except, of course, the legal profession. "Does America really need 70 percent of the world's lawyers?" former vice president Dan Quayle asked. Most Americans clearly don't think so. In a *National Law Journal* poll, three out of four Americans said there are too many lawyers for our own good. From the Right to the Left, concerned citizens sense that the old patriotism needs to be overhauled. Our combative ways of solving our civic problems must change. [7]

Hypocrisy, hostility, cynicism, division, blame—the result of these ugly features of the old patriotism is gridlock. Moderate lawmakers of both parties have been thrown out of office, and political experts across the political spectrum predict several years of stalemates. Dan Mitchell, a political analyst at the conservative Heritage Institution, foresees "gridlock in the true sense of the word. . . . Neither side will have the power to get anything all the way through."[8] "People are as discouraged about politics as they have ever been," observed a front-page *New York Times* article based on scores of interviews across the country. The condition of the country was captured in the headline: "Anger and Cynicism Well Up in Voters as Hope Gives Way."[9]

A few days before the 1994 elections, the Associated Press asked Americans whether they would rather see the Republicans take control of Congress or see the Democrats keep control. The people split evenly, one out of four wanting Republicans at the helm and the same percentage wanting the Democrats. The surprising news was that 42 percent said that, no matter who won, it wouldn't make much difference.[10]

In poll after poll, most Americans preferred that Republicans and Democrats work together for the good of the country; and said they were tired of petty bickering and polarized political maneuvering, were angry with Congress, and wanted real leadership. But the same polls showed that people were pessimistic and cynical, afraid nothing would change; and that polarizing, self-serving "politics as usual" would continue.

Twenty-First Century Patriotism |
"A UNION OF HEARTS AND HANDS"

As we contrast the old and the new patriotism, let us not be confused. Just as the past and the present are both within us, so are the old and the new patriotism. On the edge of the next millennium, they are struggling for our souls.

Before we reject the old patriotism, let us remind ourselves of its virtues. Behind its rigid and sometimes cruel conformity, for example, was cohesion, which held the nation together. The old patriotism, it is true, suffered from hypocrisy, but that was a result of the Founding Fathers' idealism, a vision of equality and justice so perfect that no nation on earth has yet achieved it. And yes, the old patriotism led to gridlock, but it also provided stability: a century since the Civil War with far less internal strife than in many other nations.

The old patriotism has clearly played a vital role in the experiment called America. But now our generation is called to reinvent democracy, as Jefferson predicted each generation would be. We can't just substitute one set of attitudes for another. We can't just follow a new leader, or join a new political party. The change required is deeper.

If the Divided States are struggling for America's soul, then the struggle is also happening within each of us—that is, at the deepest level of our beings, where what we hold sacred resides.

Although today it is easy to forget, patriotism is about love. It means loving one's country—the whole, complex, beautiful and ugly, amazing kaleidoscope of human beings who call themselves Americans. And as we all know from our own lives, there is more than one way to love—and there is more than one way to be a patriot.

A "pledge" is more than just a statement of belief. To pledge means to "promise solemnly," and to "stake one's life, honor, word"; or, as another dictionary phrases it, it means "a formal promise to do something."[11] And what we do, if it is truly patriotic, must be done out of love, not out of hate. As Martin Luther King, Jr., said when he accepted the Nobel Peace Prize: "Man must evolve for all human conflict a method which rejects revenge, aggression, and retaliation. The foundation of such a method is love." And this is the common denominator of the new patriotism: to promise to do something out of love for the whole country.

The New Patriotism Is Rooted In Love, Not Hate.

Just doing something is easy; the citizens of the Divided States "do something" every day. But doing something out of love for the whole country is hard. It involves our souls. It is so hard to do that even the wisest, most enlightened, and most compassionate men and women of our times find it challenging, and sometimes impossible.

One of the people who has described what loving one's whole country requires is Thich Nhat Hahn, a Vietnamese priest who during the Vietnam war was part of a Buddhist fellowship that tried to minister to the needs of both sides. Because they tried to care for the souls of both pro-communist and anti-communist forces alike, many priests were killed. His work, for which Martin Luther King, Jr., nominated him for the Nobel Peace Prize, was based on the following philosophy:

> To reconcile conflicting parties, we must have the ability to understand the suffering of both sides. If we take sides, it is impossible to do the work of reconciliation. And humans want to take sides. That

is why the situation gets worse and worse. Are there people who are still available to both sides? They need not do much. They need do only one thing: go to one side and tell all about the suffering endured by the other side, and go to the other side and tell all about the suffering endured by this side. That is our chance for peace. That can change the situation. But how many of us are able to do that?

This philosophy, which would be utterly alien to the old patriotism, is the cornerstone of the new. It is a new standard of citizenship that requires that, if we love our country, we must at least respect its citizens—even if we disagree fundamentally with them. As Lincoln advised us:

> Let us neither express nor cherish any hard feelings toward any citizen who . . . has differed with us. Let us at all times remember that all American citizens are brothers of a common country, and should dwell together in the bonds of fraternal feeling.[12]

Such "fraternal feeling"—which Lincoln elsewhere called "a Union of hearts and hands"—is a kind of love. It is rooted not just in the mind or even the heart, but also in the soul. It requires the deepest and most profound commitment of which we are capable. Fortunately, unlike pioneers such as Reverend King and Thich Nhat Hanh, most of us do not have to risk our lives. But we do have to take risks. We have to stretch ourselves to embrace the sacred dimension of citizenship. The Golden Rule that appears in every major religion is also the Golden Rule of patriotism: treating others the way we ourselves want to be treated.

Like the earlier pioneers who spread America westward, the new patriots who are developing this faith are spiritual pioneers.[13] They are committed to learning, not dogmatism. One of the reasons the Founding Fathers placed such an emphasis on publicly funded education was that they knew a democracy depended on continued learning. Thomas Jefferson underscored its importance when he wrote:

> I know of no safe repository of the ultimate powers of the society but the people themselves; and if we think them not enlightened enough to exercise control with a wholesome discretion, the remedy is not to take it from them, but to inform their discretion by education.[14]

Applied to patriotism, learning is critical. If we listen to many conflicting opinions, as Thich Nhat Hahn advises us to do, learning is inevitable. The premise of the new patriotism is that in virtually all conflicts the opposing parties each hold a piece of the truth. Helping the different sides find common ground requires bringing those pieces together into a coherent whole—and that requires a willingness to learn.

From the outset, diversity is at the heart of the new patriotism. It assumes that there is no single way to be an American. "It is a common belief," says Mayor Frederic Peralta of Taos, New Mexico, "that 'all-American' means baseball, hot dogs, the Fourth of July, and apple pie. We now understand that these beliefs aren't entirely correct. It also means enchiladas, sopapillas, powwows, fiestas, and more."[15]

To incorporate this growing diversity, we must learn as citizens—politically, psychologically, culturally, intellectually, and spiritually. Our generation, and those that follow, must let go of the notion of racial, ethnic, or religious purity; let go of the comfortable image of a "melting pot" (in which "others" melt down into a homogeneous "us"); and let go of other static metaphors (like "mosaic" or "salad bowl"). Instead, we must view America with the humility and wonder with which a child looks through a kaleidoscope. What we behold is constantly changing, with an infinite number of combinations.[16]

This magnificent diversity, though hard to encompass in our fixed ideologies, may turn out in the end to be the key to our survival. Just as the history of the planet shows that biodiversity is the key to evolutionary survival, so may social diversity be a key to human progress, if—repeat *if*—we will let it.

In opposing California's Proposition 187, the so-called "anti-immigrant" ballot initiative, Republican leader Jack Kemp spoke of the Statue of Liberty and its welcome to the world's refugees. He advised his fellow Republicans to make their party "the party of immigrants . . . the party of men and women who seek civil and legal and voting and equal rights." It was good advice, not just for his party, but for his country. It is not just the challenge of Republicans or Democrats to become "inclusionary, not exclusionary," to use Kemp's phrase, but a challenge for every one of us who call ourselves Americans.[17]

Honoring diversity can lead to a wide range of views about policy issues such as immigration, affirmative action, bilingual education, and a host of other thorny issues. But what it requires of all of us is a personal integrity—an acknowledgment of our own imperfections, the willingness to see situations as a whole, and a recognition of our adversaries' positions as well as our own.

Universal though the Golden Rule may be, it is rarely practiced. This is the challenge which the new patriotism must meet. If we believe that "all men [and women] are created equal," then we must practice what we preach. We cannot exclude vast numbers of American citizens, and regard them as enemies. Instead of excluding others, the new patriots are reaching out to work with them. As citizens, we must act in accordance with the ideals on which our country is founded, whatever the views we may hold on particular policies. To do this requires tolerance and respect for others who differ from us, however difficult this may sometimes seem.

The nation in which we live is far, far different from the one the Founding Fathers began more than 200 years ago. When the nation was founded, the overwhelmingly white and European population considered itself homogeneous. Three-fifths were English, one-tenth German, and the remainder a European potpourri. The indigenous peoples and the black slaves were not counted. The nation's early leaders felt confident that American citizens would continue to be white Protestants primarily of British origin.[18]

By the 1800 census, however, the population of just over five million was already one-fifth African-American. One hundred years later, the population of over seventy-five million included Chinese, Japanese, and the now recognized "Indians." In the period between 1819 to 1955 over forty million aliens entered the United States, a migration of truly epic proportions. As diverse as the immigrants were, however, still more than three out of four had originated in Europe.

Today, this is no longer true. By the mid-eighties, the flow of immigrants from England, which once represented the vast majority of newcomers, had dwindled. Mexicans, Filipinos, Koreans, Cubans, Indians, Chinese, Dominicans, Vietnamese, Jamaicans, Haitians, Iranians—all contributed more new citizens than the English. With new immigrants arriving during the 1990s at a projected average of nearly 900,000 a year, demographers foresee that by the year 2000 the proportion of whites among America's children will shrink to less than two-thirds. It is already half or less in three states: Texas, California, and New Mexico. By the middle of the next century, no ethnic or racial group will constitute a majority. The number of Hispanics will surpass the number of blacks within two decades.[19] By the middle of the twenty-first century the once predominant ethic group—white Europeans—will become a minority.

America's kaleidoscope of ethnic, racial, and ideological diversity has unfortunately been accompanied by hostility, disrespect, prejudice, and violence.

The New Patriotism Embraces, Rather Than Denies, America's Exploding Diversity.

The alternative to hostility is civility. Civility doesn't just mean keeping our mouths shut. It does not mean lying about our true feelings, or even "settling for half." Civility implies cultivating personal humility rather than indulging in self-righteousness, and valuing tolerance rather than force. Whether a conflict is between Koreans and blacks in South Central Los Angeles, or between pro-life and pro-choice advocates outside an abortion clinic in Tallahassee, or between irate townspeople and the city council, the new patriots facing such conflicts remain civil. They do not abandon their beliefs; they can still get angry at their adversaries. But they know that Americans are connected to each other by this cord of courtesy. Once the cord is broken, it is hard to repair.

Nan Aron, director of the liberal advocacy group Alliance for Justice, put it bluntly when she said that groups like hers profit from "being able to point to a monster."[20] But the problem is: the monster is *us*, including our neighbors—our fellow Americans. Unlike the old patriots who took sides, joined their respective armies, picked up their weapons, and started firing at the "enemy," the new patriots face a tougher task. For them, ostracizing their fellow Americans is not an acceptable option. Whether they vote for one party or another, whether they are pro-this or anti-that, their country comes first. They know that America's strength depends on finding legitimate common ground among adversaries.

This cannot be accomplished through the conventional hit-and-run, punch-and-counterpunch style of public discourse that is so prevalent in political campaigning and media-sponsored debate. New patriots do not engage in shouting matches with their adversaries, but listen to them with the same attention that they expect from their own listeners. If there's an impasse, they try to analyze what each party has contributed to it and to find a common solution.

These virtues are easy to preach, but extremely difficult to practice. Genuine patriotism has never been easy—not for the revolutionaries of 1776, not for the men and women who defended America against aggression in the 1940s, and not today, as the new patriots attempt to protect America against subtle threats from within. Instead of being cynical, which provides an excuse for doing nothing, the new patriots attempt to involve themselves in the affairs of their communities. In the following chapter, we will turn to some of their stories, showing what an impact genuine citizenship can have.

The New Patriotism Inspires
Collaboration and Partnership.

To understand how vital the new patriots are to our future, allow yourself to imagine for a moment that you are a patient on an operating table. You overhear that three out of four members of the surgical team agree on how your operation should be performed, but the fourth vehemently disagrees. Do you feel comforted—or afraid? Or imagine that you are a resident in a burning building. You see the firemen discussing outside how to put out the fire and hear that over half of them agree to cooperate. Do you feel relieved—or angry?

Some tasks, and some occasions, require a high degree of partnership. Most of the challenges we face today simply cannot be achieved with 51 percent support. They require of us all a capacity to oppose or to challenge each other while at the same time working with and respecting each other. The new patriots put the country first—the *whole* country—and their citizenship is sacred to them.

Precisely what they believe, however, varies enormously. The new patriots do not have unanimous opinions. The increasingly heterogeneous human beings who call themselves Americans cannot fit the white, Anglo-Saxon, Protestant stereotype of yesteryear. Today, the "national conversation" includes people of many languages, not just English; people of various colors, not just white and black; people of many educational levels, not just the literati; and of many income groups, not just the affluent; not just the "old boys network," but women and gays as well; and, as we have seen, people with many competing belief systems.

Consequently, our future must be based on partnership, not polarization. Just as a healthy dose of skepticism about our political adversaries is necessary to the political process, there always will be a place for partisanship in democracy. In a democracy, interests are often pitted against each other. Our system of checks and balances is designed to mediate these conflicts and yield acceptable compromises. To be partisan—that is, to argue strongly on behalf of your interests as against someone else's—is a vital part of citizenship.

Obviously the new patriotism will not resolve all our domestic conflicts. Of course, in a complex world, individuals will inevitably become polarized in their response to issues, as they seek to define their positions. Of course, in a two-party system, partisans will clash as they seek legislative solutions to pressing problems. But the emerging twenty-first–century patriotism will keep us focused on the larger challenge of rebuilding the bonds that connect us to each other and to our country.

Transforming partisan polarization into patriotic partnership is clearly a challenge to every State, every belief system, and every American. The easy way out—to call one's adversaries dirty names and walk away—is dragging America down. The challenge is to join the new patriots who are turning enemies into allies. Anyone who thinks the process of enabling enemies to become partners is quick or easy has never witnessed the process. It is long and difficult and fraught with danger. It is not a magical transformation, but an act of the deepest will, compassion, and civic courage.

When we stop trying to destroy our adversaries and acknowledge that they too are part of American life, they then become merely competitors, as athletes are; and we find ourselves competing against worthy opponents who actually share our goals. Ultimately, our rivals may even become our partners, when they recognize that, despite appearances, we need them and depend on them. To evolve from enemies to adversaries, from adversaries to rivals, and from rivals to partners—this is part of the challenge of the new patriotism.[21]

The New Patriotism in Action |
UNITING THE STATES

The contrast between the old and new patriotism should now be clear; at least in theory: learning, instead of conformity; diversity, instead of uniformity; integrity, not hypocrisy; partnership, not partisanship. But words are not enough.

What makes these concepts of a new patriotism meaningful are the ordinary citizens who turn them into action. The new patriots step out of the narrow confines of their comfort zones—their belief systems, their race, their religion, in other words, their Divided States—and explore their interconnection with their fellow Americans. Some do so out of principle; but many others do so out of sheer necessity—simply because it has to be done. Whether children of slaves or of Ku Klux Klan members, whether victims of U.S.-trained assassination squads or children of wealth, they have not hidden behind barricades of anger or ivy-covered walls of privilege but have engaged as citizens in the healing of America.

The new patriots whom we will meet in the following chapter are as different from each other as America itself. They include devout Christians, Jews,

Baptists and committed secular humanists; liberals and conservatives; blacks, whites, and Latinos; multimillionaires and impoverished immigrants; bank presidents, corporate executives, and inner city activists; policemen and "criminals." But as different as these Americans are, they have one thing in common. Like Patrick Henry, who declared that he was "not a Virginian but an American," the new patriots are transcending their loyalty to whichever Divided State they may once have belonged.

Notice, however, that these new patriots do not turn their backs on the Divided States to which they have previously belonged. On the contrary, they recognize the gifts of their respective States. Whether or not they believe in God, they recognize that they do believe in something higher than themselves—a vision of diversity joined into a greater whole. They pledge their allegiance to this vision—the United States of America—which beckons us to serve together a purpose higher than any of us could ever imagine, much less achieve, alone.

MEETING THE NEW PATRIOTS

❧

Patriotism alone is not enough. There has to be citizenship as well. Citizenship is the willingness to contribute to one's country. It means the willingness to live, rather than to die, for one's country.[1]

PETER DRUCKER

N
EW PATRIOTS have emerged from every one of the Divided States. They live in every city and neighborhood. They are among your friends and neighbors. Of the tens of thousands of new patriots already hard at work in America today, only a few will be introduced in this chapter. For every one you are about to meet, there are legions more.

Patria's Gift: Faith |
"WALKING BETWEEN THE WORLDS"

Some say the earth doesn't have a prayer;
50,000 congregations have a chance to prove them wrong.

On Earth Day 1994, fifty thousand churches and synagogues received a packet emblazoned with the above message sent by a new interfaith organization called the National Religious Partnership for the Environment. The packet included materials on the sacredness of the environment and how to protect it. The message was clear: it is time for those who love the Creator, and those who love His creation, to work together.

But even before the packets were received, they had already come under attack. The *Wall Street Journal* lent its pages to Reverend Robert A. Sirico, president of a conservative Michigan think tank, who charged that the system of beliefs called environmentalism "pose[s] a threat to orthodox faiths." After warning about the danger of those beliefs' becoming "a religion itself," Sirico accused committed ecologists of breaking one of God's commandments. "There is no commandment against littering, but there is a very straightforward one about worshipping false gods." Using the old hellfire-and-brimstone warnings, Sirico concluded: "It is God, not Gaia, whom we will face on Judgment Day."[2]

But new patriots like Paul Gorman, the executive director of this new interfaith effort to awaken ecological concerns within the religious community, challenge this narrow vision. Gorman is impatient both with Christians who refuse to face the ecological crisis honestly and with Gaians who are hostile to Christianity. "Both sides love the land," he says. "I see that in both the fundamentalists and the environmentalists. But they don't seem to be able to see that love in each other. Beneath their conflicts, they have that love in common. I can work with both New Agers and evangelicals. Because I have the security of my own beliefs, I can walk between the worlds, treating both sides with respect."

The New Patriots Seek Collaboration
Toward a Common Goal.

One of Paul Gorman's most powerful experiences as a bridge-builder between Gaia and Patria took place at a meeting about Christianity and the environment convened by *Christianity Today,* a magazine founded by Billy Graham. Twelve serious evangelical Christian scholars were given the daunting assignment of drafting a statement which has since been sent to twenty thousand evangelical churches. "It was one of the happiest experiences of my life," Paul recalls. "When they reached dissent and confusion, they would stop and pray. When a paragraph would not come together, they would stop and say: 'Dear Lord, please give us guidance. Help us find our way to serving you.' Seeing my fellow evangelical citizens of the United States was exciting for me because I could see how their theology and prayer was enabling them to make a contribution to the fate of the earth. I felt I was part of a process that was holding together the United States."

Paul was moved by how both sides truly practiced what they preached. The Christians treated the environmentalists with the love and compassion their Lord symbolized; and the environmentalists treated the Christians with the same respect and care they believe should be given to the earth. Inspired by the collaboration, Paul found himself even more impatient with what he calls the "tyranny of territoriality" that keeps both sides from learning about each other. "There is a deep ignorance about one another," he observes. "Some Christians believe environmentalists are theologically heretical, culturally alien, politically offensive. They are old adversaries in a new green cloak. The thing that distresses evangelicals the most is heresy. For them, believers in Gaia lack the knowledge of Christ. And both sides use the scriptures to defend their own views."

Paul remains a committed Christian. "Religiously, I'm more akin to the evangelicals than to most Greens, more at home religiously with evangelicals than with New Agers. I am a Christian who wants God to be put first. I need to take two or three spiritual retreats a year in order to have the seriousness, depth, and vigor to be a useful instrument for God's work. By virtue of my Christian belief, I have trouble with those who do not put Christian faith and practice first. I know that one can hear a rigidity in what I am saying, but I can't help it. I believe it is important. It may be a crude stereotype, but I think Gaians can be oversimplifying and provincial in their own way. They worship creation, not the Creator. Gaians might say it is the same thing, but I don't think it is. I have problems with the spiritual perspectives and practices of Gaia. For a worldview that supposedly reveres the soil, its beliefs seem very shallowly rooted."

Paul believes that invocations of neither God nor Gaia will settle our environmental policy differences. We must find a civil way to resolve them, citizen to citizen. We must assume that creation is unfolding, and that the Creator, whoever we believe He or She may be, is asking us to participate in the unfolding, not the undoing, of his design.

*Protecting Young People Is a Vital
Part of the New Patriotism.*

Throughout America, citizens are fed up with the way the media are handling their responsibilities. "I hate 'em so much they make my teeth hurt," said one participant in a focus group in Plano, Texas, run by James Kunde, executive director of the Coalition to Improve Management in State and Local Government. "People have always criticized the media," Kunde says. "But this was at least ten times as strong as I have ever heard it. There seems to be a very strong consensus that you can't depend on the media. Most people say they don't trust any of it."[3]

Million of Americans who distrust the media are among the congregation to which Christian media activist Robert DeMoss preaches. Now almost forty years old, Robert made his first movie in tenth grade. A high school disc jockey and rock and roll musician, he is deeply aware of the power of sound and image. His career led him to Colorado Springs's Focus on the Family, where he serves as a youth culture specialist for the organization's three million members.

Robert advises parents how to protect their children from the excesses of the mass media by preparing them to live in a media world using the media's tools—the video camera, video cassettes, VCRs, and television itself—to warn parents and children about the media's disregard for their physical, emotional, and spiritual health. In his video *Learn to Discern,* Robert documents how advertising exploits the insecurities of young people, and how filmmakers and songwriters profit from teenagers' fears.[4] "When I use these communication devices, my desire is to elevate the human spirit. There are many people who have more skill and money and time than I do. But I bring my heart to my work. When I see that something is desperately wrong in the media, I'll take a swing at it."

His current crusade is against bands like Nine Inch Nails and against MTV, which promotes this group and its suicidal song "Downward Spiral" ("He couldn't believe how easy it was/He put the gun into his face/Bang"). Day in and day out, Robert monitors the cascade of words and images that engulfs young people and sends them powerful messages about life and death. He believes young people need support, encouragement, and guidance from adults who care about them and their development. He does not believe the emotional fragility of young people should be exploited by mega-corporations using the most sophisticated multimedia marketing strategies at their disposal. "Anything that fuels those feelings of despair and self-destruction in the heart of a young person," Robert says, "I will do everything in my power to confront."

Because Robert believes young people are vulnerable, impressionable human beings seeking guidance from their elders, his mission is to help them learn to defend themselves and their own values. Although they have grown up in a society that has bombarded them with commercial sounds and images, Robert believes they are media illiterates. "The speed and power with which the media assault the brains of young people weakens their cognitive capacities, as we are discovering in schools. At the same time, the education system is shying away from teaching them about the media—and right and wrong."

Robert DeMoss doesn't advocate censorship or advise parents to throw out their children's record collections. Instead, he tells parents to go nose-to-nose with their own children, to quit sticking their heads in the sand, ostrichlike. Religious faith does not immunize children against the corrosive effect of commercial media exploitation, Robert argues in his cover story about MTV in *Focus on the Family* magazine. In fact, kids in Christian families are more likely to have watched MTV in the past week (42 percent) than their non-Christian counterparts (33 percent). It's not just sex and violence to which Robert objects; it is the anti-family, anti-social context in which they are so sensationally portrayed.

On the road speaking to audiences almost half of his work life, Robert is a hero to many parents for waging his crusade to protect children. In all his travels, he feels nothing has captured the endangered status of children in America more poignantly than what happened when he testified at a Tennessee senate hearing. The senators were considering a statute that would require warning labels on all records containing obscene language. In his testimony, Robert mentioned the song "Find 'Em, Fuck 'Em, and Flee," recorded by NWA (Niggers with Attitude). Before he could finish his sentence, Robert was interrupted by a senator who was offended by the foul language.

"He asked me to apologize," Robert says. "He made me apologize for using language that any young person can buy at the record store. There's something wrong about a society which says that you can sell it to an eight-year-old but you can't discuss it among adults."

The Faith of the New Patriots Transcends Race, Class, and Religion.

Citizens who quietly form partnerships that bring progress do not "get much ink," as journalists put it. Even if they risk their lives, it is not news. Unfortunately, the headlines still go to those who preach hatred, not to those who practice love.

Off and on for years, newspaper headlines have reported (and often misreported) every rhetorical excess of Reverend Louis Farrakhan, the charismatic leader of the Nation of Islam. Although sometimes he temporarily loses his place in the limelight of national media, all he and his various followers had to do to be assured of headlines and TV coverage was to derogate the Jews. Even minor scholars, speaking at otherwise un-newsworthy gatherings, could work their way into the *New York Times* and onto CBS News simply by lacing their speeches with anti-Semitism. The more outrageous their racism, the bigger the story. But in communities across the country that never see the camera crews and big-city journalists, a different story is unfolding: African-Americans and Jewish-Americans are working together in ways never reported in the morning paper or the evening news.

In Milwaukee, a town with a history of racial and ethnic tensions, one may enter the synagogue of Congregation Sinai on a Friday evening and find a black Baptist minister preaching to the attentive Jewish worshipers in the pews. The following Sunday, at the Bethesda Church of God, one may find a rabbi delivering a sermon to the all-black congregation. The exchange would never have happened if Liller Bates (or "Mother Bates," as church members call her) hadn't noticed how many hungry-looking kids were hanging around their church on a Sunday morning. Located in a poor neighborhood where many families are on welfare, Bethesda Church of God was like a magnet for the poor. "They'd had nothing to eat—I could just tell," Liller recalls. "They weren't part of our church, but they were part of our community."

So, twelve years ago, Bethesda Church of God began what they now call their "food pantry." At first it was just a handful of hungry kids. But soon, as Liller recalls, "they got to be more and more and more, and then the grown-ups started coming. People would tell their story. We realized Sunday morning wasn't enough. So we started doing it on Wednesdays; then we added Tuesdays, and then Thursdays."

As the program grew in size, it also grew in cost. Rabbi Terry Bookman heard from one of his Congregation Sinai members about the food program and about the struggle Bethesda Church of God was having to meet its burgeoning size. The rabbi then visited Bethesda, met with Reverend Rudolph Bates and his wife Liller, and saw how many people they were feeding. Congregation Sinai responded by creating a "Tzedakah" fund (translation: "righteous action") to help support the Bates's church food pantry. "We added a three percent tax on every program here in the synagogue," says Rabbi Bookman. "That, plus straight contributions, went to start the Tzedakah fund."

After a while, Bookman was visiting Bates's church so often that it started to feel like a second home. The idea of a pulpit exchange just came naturally. Now the two clergymen switch places at least once a year. Many members of both congregations attend both services, not just their own. "The exchange has been beautiful," Mother Bates says. "Our congregation enjoys going to the synagogue. We take the senior choir up there. They sing with such jubilation that everybody joins in."

After a while, as the bonds between the two communities grew stronger, they decided to deepen their relationship. Instead of just exchanging preachers, they decided to exchange their children. The Bethesda kids participated in Congregation Sinai's children's program, and the Jewish kids went to Bethesda's Sunday School. "A lot of the kids in that day-long exchange said it was too short," Rabbi Bookman says. "They wanted to get to know each other better. So we created a weekend where we took all the kids to camp."

"Our kids just love going to camp," Mother Bates reports. "It's fun. But I think it's important because they have a chance to look at other people and to understand their culture. Our young people begin to know how to get along with other people and accept them as they are. They see people are different—that God *made* us different. It's good for us to become more unified here on earth because otherwise we'll miss out when we go to heaven.

"I don't see why we can't all hold onto the same banner before this world comes to an end," Bates continues. "I believe that God loves us all, and that he had a son named Jesus. But if someone doesn't believe that, I'm not going to fall out with them. Everybody has feelings. I believe we should love everybody. If we could learn more about each other's beliefs, we'd see things differently. Even if we don't see eye to eye by the time we get to heaven, we'll have some good fellowship here on earth."

The exchange, now in its fifth year, has received little publicity—certainly far less than the media-saturated story of Reverend Louis Farrakhan's anti-Semitism. Rabbi Bookman isn't interested in publicity. "We don't feel it is right to make something out of doing what is the right thing in the first place," he says. "My personal feeling about creating these kinds of bridges is that they are done one step at a time. Some people who are political activists or Washington organizers might believe in top-down kinds of changes. But I don't. America has all this wonderful civil rights legislation that was passed thirty years ago. You have all the busing programs. But so what? The kids go and sit by themselves and eat lunch by themselves, and then they go home. I feel if we want to do something about racism in the country—and, believe me, it *is* a problem in the Jewish community—individual Jews must create relationships with people different from ourselves. I believe that this kind of citizen-to-citizen change is lasting and real."

For this rabbi, Judaism leads naturally and directly to the new patriotism. "For me, as a Jew, there is the notion of 'mitzvah,' or commandment, which is a divine imperative worked out over three thousand years of Jewish history. It means that God has expectations for us. One of them is take care of the poor. It is a clear mandate in the Torah. It says it is our challenge to make sure their needs are met. There is also the tradition of being an advocate for those who have no advocate: the widow, the orphan, the homeless. So from the notion of mitzvah, we then become God's hands and feet in making the world a better place."

Working Together As Partners, New Patriots Accomplish What Is Otherwise Impossible.

In Spartanburg, South Carolina, meanwhile, two other ministers have been building a unique bridge between their communities. Mount Moriah Baptist Church, which sits at the corner of South Church Street and Marion Avenue in Spartanburg, has the city's largest African-American congregation. It has never included a white member, says the Reverend Benjamin Snoddy. Sunday morning, he says, is the most segregated time in the United States.

Several blocks to the north of Reverend Snoddy's neighborhood, among tree-lined streets and the sprawling lawns of homes belonging to affluent white families, stands the Church of the Advent. The 1,400-member church, led by Reverend Clay Turner, is virtually all white. Although one can drive from one church to the other in only a few minutes, the two institutions have for years been worlds apart. "God is color-blind," Reverend Snoddy maintains, but the churches in Spartanburg aren't.

But in early 1990, Reverend Turner had an idea. "When I first came to Spartanburg," he recalls, "I recognized that my congregation was ready to do something. They were searching for a mission. I started asking questions about the community, and was reminded of my experience in Roanoke [Virginia] where I served on the board of a community clinic. I started checking around about the Spartanburg area and learned that, according to a Duke University study, sixteen percent of area residents had no medical insurance—thirty thousand people. I learned that the emergency room was overloaded. I learned that people couldn't get prescriptions filled. Simple bronchitis would turn into pneumonia. Small problems would often become life-threatening. It was clear that preventive care was needed, at little or no cost."

After Reverend Turner took his ideas for a community health clinic to his church's outreach committee, the Church of the Advent invited members of the community into the discussion. "People started getting excited," Turner says. "Our parish had forty doctors, and a great group of volunteers. But the challenge was to learn how to reach out beyond ourselves. Locating the clinic in the old, rich Episcopal church didn't seem right. It would be too laden with patronage and that old paternalistic imagery. We wanted to locate it on the south side of town, where there is a lot of public housing."

Although the south side of town was indeed the best location, it was outside the Church of the Advent's territory. So Reverend Turner reached out directly, person-to-person, to Reverend Snoddy, a fellow minister whom he trusted. The Mount Moriah church community didn't have money or physicians. But Reverend Snoddy and his congregation had something that all the money or clout could never buy: the trust of their neighbors. "If it hadn't been for Ben and his church," Turner says, "we'd still just be talking about it.

"Reverend Snoddy agreed to cooperate," he says. "Our church, like many others, is becoming more conscious of what our real mission is. People who make up churches are taking more seriously what it means to be a Christian, what it means to be a part of a community of faith. Such a community does not think about race or socioeconomic levels. You think about people standing before God. We saw a need to focus on the needs of the people rather than what we think they ought to be. The needs of the community dictated the response of the church. There are thousands of people who don't have medical care. They have problems that can be taken care of with a pill. If they don't get it, before long they need surgery."

Such inequality isn't fair, Reverend Snoddy believes, and fairness should matter to Christians. "Don't say you 'Love me' or 'Jesus loves me' and then not be fair to me. That's not how Christ would love me. Until we are willing to be fair across the board, some blacks are just not going to be that excited to sit down and worship with whites."

As much as he dislikes segregation in churches, Reverend Snoddy doesn't think that's what's bothering God. "What really concerns God," Reverend Snoddy believes, "is not whether we worship together in an integrated fashion. Culturally, after all, there are differences. He is concerned about how we live together day by day. If a black man works side by side with a white man, doing the same job, with the same credentials, starting at the same time, but the two men are not earning the same, then that is our challenge, a *spiritual* challenge. Or, when you look at the executive staff of a corporation and it's primarily white, but the janitorial staff is primarily black, that is also a spiritual challenge. The nitty-gritty of the Christian faith is being fair with each other—fair on *all* levels of life. Church, work, school, community, housing, banks, government, health care—it *all* matters to God."

As Reverends Snoddy and Turner began working together, they quickly realized they had more assets than they had ever imagined. Mount Moriah owned a building right next door to the church, and the congregation included many talented bricklayers, masons, carpenters, and other skilled builders. In addition, the two ministers contacted the First Presbyterian Church, which responded with enthusiasm, committing $15,000 a year to the project for three years as well as the energies of the many physicians in their congregation. "We were not only becoming ecumenical," Turner says, "but were drawing on the best skills of the entire community."

Turner draws a careful distinction between serving and proselytizing. "When we offer ourselves to meet the community's needs, we aren't there to change anyone's beliefs. We are there to respond to their needs. This is service, not conversion. We follow Albert Schweitzer's approach. In Africa, he said, his first responsibility was to meet the needs of people's health. Then, *if asked*, he would explain his faith. We didn't want it to be just another social service agency, but to have a quality of care that ministers to the whole person."

When the St. Luke's Community Clinic opened, it served thirty-three people the first night, fifty the next night. Now it's filled to capacity each and every night. (It is open only in the evenings.) Its board—interracial and ecumenical—includes Seventh Day Adventists and Jews, blacks and whites. In addition to the medical staff, eight to ten volunteers from thirty churches or civic groups are also employed there. To supply the pharmacy, the clinic received surplus supplies from pharmaceutical companies, samples from doctors, and finally a donation from the Junior League. The clinic now has a patient load of over 5,000 and is an integral part of the community. As a labor of love, it has become a catalyst for other even more ambitious collaborations.[5]

"The doctors tell me how gratifying it is," Turner says, "because they feel genuinely thanked. They say it really rejuvenates them. It brings out the best in all of us, I think, because the clinic always was greater than any of us. It is truly a community effort. We have not had those internal struggles that come from pride. Our pride was in the overall effort, not in personal recognition. We knew we needed each other's help and could not do it alone."

When New Patriots Stand Up for Their Faith, They Strengthen America.

Bob and Marla Boulter did not intend to risk their lives. It happened because they took their faith seriously.

Only ten minutes north of the White House is a Washington, D.C., neighborhood called Adams-Morgan. Anyone who tries to explain why this neighborhood didn't become a segregated, impoverished, crime-ridden neighborhood like much of the city must give some of the credit to Jubilee Housing, Inc. And no one who explores Jubilee's success fails to recognize the role of Bob Boulter, who has worked in the community since 1978.

For more than two decades, Jubilee has been buying decaying buildings and turning them into low-income, cooperatively-managed housing, ultimately placing them under tenant control. "The work itself involves working with the residents to meet a whole range of practical needs, not just a roof over their heads," Bob explains. "You can do that in a for-profit setting, of course, or even in the government. But Jubilee allowed me to put my faith to work in an open way because the company itself was an expression of faith."

Jubilee Housing was started by the minister of a local church, called the Church of the Saviour, and several members of their congregation, including James Rouse, the renowned developer whose company is responsible for some of the most innovative urban projects in the country. Bob heard about the church's work and decided that Jubilee might offer him the chance to put his career in property management together with his Christian faith. "When Jim and Patty Rouse asked me to get involved in Jubilee," Bob recalls, "it was an answer to a prayer."

He had always wanted a sense of mission at the heart of his professional life, rather than at the edges. By allowing him to put his spiritual values into practice every day, Jubilee did just that. Bob still remembers the day he received a several-page memorandum from one of the regional offices of the U.S. Department of Housing and Urban Development (HUD) saying that any housing program that received federal money could have no connection to any spiritual values or religious institutions. Bob had no problem with HUD's insistence that employees not be discriminated against on the basis of religion and that no preference be given on the basis of religion. But he was outraged to read that housing providers could "exert no other religious influence in the provision of such public services."

"I was appalled," Bob says. "I was then, and I am now, absolutely persuaded that we cannot deal with the problems of society if we don't bring our spiritual selves to meet the challenge."

Because many of Jubilee's projects involved HUD, Jubilee had to decide whether it would meet the government's anti-religious regulations or not. Bob decided to fight it, contacted Jubilee's lawyer (who happened to be Jewish), and got his support. "I'll go with you all the way to the Supreme Court," the lawyer said. In the end, HUD backed down and accepted a deletion of the offensive paragraph. It was a victory not only for Jubilee, in Bob's view, but for Americans of all faiths.

Soon afterward, Bob's faith was seriously challenged when his wife Marla was mugged and robbed. Profoundly shaken, the couple considered moving elsewhere. But after much soul-searching and Bible-reading, they decided to stay.

One night only a few months later, Bob noticed that some of their donors' cars were being vandalized. He went out to investigate and followed the thieves around the corner and was attacked by several men. As he lay on the sidewalk in a pool of blood, one of the muggers continued to stomp on his head. Finally, another resident intervened and told him to stop before he committed murder.

When Bob came to consciousness in the hospital, his head was swollen and many of the bones in his face were broken. He had been so badly beaten that the surgeons had to wait several days for the swelling to subside before they could begin surgery. Bob was in tremendous pain and knew that were it not for the intervention of the resident, he would certainly be dead.

As he lay there in agony, he reflected again on his life choices. "I realized that I had been foolish in exposing myself to a lot of danger unnecessarily. I realized that, to do this work, I had to be more prudent about where I went and how I handled myself. It would have been easy to leave the community—and believe me, Marla and I thought about it—but instead we stayed and dealt with the reality of the threats that we have to live with. We realized that even when we are obedient, even when we are faithful disciples to our faith, we are not exempt from suffering."

What makes Bob and Marla Boulter new patriots is their devotion to what Bob calls "the expression of faith that transcends the framework of the church." They are unquestionably Christians, both in their faith and their lives. Some would call them fundamentalists. ("There is a pure body of Christ that is maturing in our world now," he says.) But their commitment as new patriots transcends their church and their faith and encompasses their entire community. They remain, as ever, determined to be devout Christians and to let their faith fuel their service to the world.

"On the religious Left," Bob observes, "church activists focus on corporate sin. On the religious Right, they focus on personal sin. I know very few people who balance the two. Even the Church of the Saviour is biased towards the Left. This imbalance is common. Those that care about social sin are very lenient toward individual sin, and vice versa." Bob doesn't think this makes one side wrong and the other right. It's simply further evidence that faith in a higher power, a greater intelligence, and a deeper integrity is as vital a part of the new patriotism as ever.

While he is ready and willing to cooperate with those of other faiths, Bob remains committed to working as a Christian. When several synagogues wanted to get involved in the work of Jubilee and donate some money, the rabbis asked if Jubilee would become an interfaith agency. But Boulter and his colleagues declined. "We must be true to the faith-based nature of our ministry. We motivate our own people much more to give money and time if [we strike] a chord with their personal faith. To reduce our faith to whatever we hold in common [with other faiths] would be to lop it off at our commonality. The ultimate result of that commingling would lead to a global religion, a world church that claims to make a place for all but will not leave room for the true faith of individual believers." To Bob's great pleasure, his Jewish colleague began a similar program for those of his own faith.

Bob applies this same philosophy to society at large, including such contentious issues as prayer in the schools. "To me, the solution lies in allowing space for our diversity to continue. The image I have is, if our public institutions are to survive, they have to allow for the 'subsets' of belief to flourish. Rather than saying no prayer in schools, we should encourage *all* prayer. Pluralism only works when you allow each of us to be true to ourselves."

The Boulters have much in common with Robert DeMoss, Paul Gorman, and the other ministers and rabbis we have just met. They have all been true to themselves, and true to their faith. There are hundreds of thousands of other citizens whose faiths are the wellspring of their love for America. It is time that all spiritual beliefs—Christian, Jewish, Muslim, and more—be welcomed back into the public square. There is room for them all in the new patriotism. They are how we safeguard and celebrate America's soul.

Corporatia's Gift: Ingenuity |
"A CEO AND A CITIZEN"

The vital connection between profits and purpose is the crucial link being forged by today's new patriots in business. "Isn't this precisely what the democratic ideal means in business?" asks Marjorie Kelley, founder and editor of the popular Minneapolis-based magazine *Business Ethics*. "Business's first purpose is to make a profit: that makes sense," she says. "The profits-are-evil world view leads nowhere. Cooperatives all too often end up living hand-to-mouth. We have to generate value."

But Marjorie believes that profits are only the beginning, not the end. While the goal of an individual business may be making money, the business community fits in a larger human context, which, as Majorie puts it, "is to meet human needs." Forging this partnership between business and society is the purpose of Majorie's magazine—and her life. "The old belief system focused entirely on profit—with profit going to shareholders—is giving way to a broader vision. I have committed my life to aligning myself with this new vision that is emerging in business today."[6]

The passion these new business patriots bring to solving social problems is a powerful antidote to the poisonous cynicism weakening America: their new "eco-nomics" requires looking at the whole social fabric, not just the few elements that appear on the accountant's calculator.[7] Whether the challenge is revitalizing the inner city or safeguarding the environment, people's talents and skills in the marketplace are essential. "Social entrepreneurs," "merchants of vision," "virtuosi of the market"—they are a vital element in the nationwide partnership that can meet the monumental challenges of a twenty-first–century democracy.[8]

New Patriots Collaborate Across
the Boundaries of the Divided States.

William Edgerly, for many years chairman of Boston's prestigious State Street Bank and part of the financial power elite, believed so strongly in such partnerships that he put his own money on the table to create the Foundation for Partnerships. After a lifetime of working in a variety of public-private partnerships, he named his foundation after what he believed was the key ingredient in making our democracy work. Says Bill, "My definition of partnership is 'people who are different working together voluntarily to achieve a common objective.' " Fostering scores of innovative partnerships across the social landscape is what Bill believes can revitalize America. "I never considered myself just a bank president," Bill says. "I am also a citizen of Boston."

Like his hero James Rouse, Bill is a firm believer in the free enterprise system. But precisely because he believes in it, he feels that he and others like him must take responsibility for the system's weaknesses, particularly chronic and persistent poverty. Bill saw during the late 1970s how financial institutions, while paying lip service to the issue of poverty, had turned away from the real challenges of inequality. Recalling the first meeting of the community development committee of the American Bankers Association, Bill says: "Our first meeting was the last. There was a consensus that we shouldn't do more. Frankly, I was disappointed. I understood my colleague's pragmatism, but I didn't agree with it. They felt poverty wasn't their responsibility. They felt that making their banks successful was challenge enough. I felt we had to do more. I felt we had to focus on our larger social responsibility."

As a highly successful CEO (under his leadership State Street's stock price increased seventeen-fold and had the highest return to investors of any of the top 100 banks), Bill held the respect of Boston's business community. He wanted to do something that dealt with what he calls society's "intractable needs"—issues such as housing, education, jobs, and poverty—but he was unsure where to get involved until a 1982 meeting in which a black leader from an inner-city community organization got fed up with the discussion about low-income housing and shouted: "You people just don't want us in this city. You'd like it if we disappeared!"

Bill traces the birth of the Metropolitan Boston Housing Partnership (MBHP) to that very moment. "I didn't believe that any of us had behaved in a way that could cause him to think that. I told him it wasn't true," says Bill. "But I didn't feel that *saying* it was enough. I felt we had to *do* something about it." He decided he wanted to put his energy, and some of the State Street Bank's credibility, into convincing that man—and the scores of other residents of Boston who felt shut out—that Boston was their home too. But the bank couldn't accomplish this alone; a new partnership was essential. "We couldn't mandate this new housing. We had to collaborate to make it happen. We needed the resources from *outside* the community and the energy and commitment of people *inside* the community to make it happen. Our belief was that the only way to turn around the neighborhoods was to do it through their own organizations."

The board of MBHP included Boston-based CEOs (who provided financial resources, building materials, bank loans, and other technical assistance); government officials (who helped MBHP "thread our first project through seventeen different government departments," as Edgerly puts it); and community leaders. This three-way partnership over the years enabled MBHP to play a crucial role in creating low-income housing that enabled thousands of families to stay in the city.

"I don't believe that the only social responsibility of business is to make a profit and that just doing that will help everybody," Bill says. From his perspective, the bottom line must be widened enough to include civic responsibility. All too often, big business does not act as a partner with the country, but takes advantage of it. As a result, the kind of radical language one expects from campus socialists has begun to appear in the prose of mainstream economic analysts. "America is not doing very well, but its corporations are doing fine," announced the *New York Times* Market Watch column in 1992. *Business Week* lamented, "Corporate America is surviving at the expense of Household America." An economic columnist in *U. S. News & World Report* was the bluntest of them all when he wrote scathingly that "corporate America has been maximizing shareholder value on the backs of the working stiff."[9]

But new patriots like Bill Edgerly are determined to turn the tide. "It is possible to be successful as CEO *and* as citizen," Bill says. "It's easier to be just one or the other, but the challenge is to do both. It was our business success that enabled me to make a public contribution."

With Visionary Leadership,
Private Enterprise Can Work for the Public Good.

John Mutz, the former Republican lieutenant governor of Indiana and president of the Lilly Endowment, is now vice president of PSI Energy, Inc., one of the Midwest's largest utilities. Now in his fifties, he could, if he wished, live a quiet life in his comfortable home on Indianapolis's affluent north side. Instead he turned his position at the utilities company into a bully pulpit for the new patriotism, translating his faith into a dedication to public service. "Many small towns do not have strong local leadership," John says. "Sometimes the utility is the largest institution in the area. When we can, we try to convene the community to deal with issues which concern them. Don't get me wrong: it is in our company's interest, because as the community grows, so do we. But it's the kind of leadership one does not expect from business."

John is most concerned about education. Although his children are grown, he feels a loyalty to the young that transcends family. "As the number of people directly involved in education declines," John asks, "how do we involve the rest of the community in education? We must make education one of the central values of the community. I travel to many small Indiana towns and everywhere the people who run small businesses say to me, 'I can't find enough qualified people.' The reason they can't find them is that education is not doing its job. We haven't made the case for it, and now we have to."

When he headed the Lilly Endowment, the largest philanthropy in Indiana and one of the largest in the nation, he tried to put money behind his vision. His goal was to create scores of chapters of "Hoosiers for Kids" all across the state. Consisting of organizations from Boy Scouts to 4-H to local businesses, these chapters would work together to build support for education and other programs benefiting youth. Hoosiers for Kids would ultimately, John hoped, inspire everyone to recognize that all of Indiana's children mattered, and that it was in everybody's self-interest to see that every child got a fair start in life.

"Why does anybody care about anybody else?" John asks. "Seriously, what stops us all from just saying, 'I'm in this world for me. I only care about what I want. Everybody else can fend for themselves'?"

As a corporate executive, John knows corporations can be self-centered and profit-based. But the answer to his question, John believes, is where corporate values and spiritual values intersect. "The undergirding reason why we care about each other—you can call it the 'collective unconscious,' if you want—is the Judeo-Christian tradition. Whether we are believers or not, it's in our bones. It tells us that we have to care about other people. It's not a matter of choice, or of opinion. It's our faith. It is what counterbalances the natural human tendency to care only about oneself."

But John doesn't think passive avowals of religious conviction translate into action by magic. It takes work. "Once awareness is raised, the strongest motivation is first-hand experience with the real problem. Don't just *tell* somebody that kids in the inner city aren't getting the education they need. Take them there. Let them *meet* the kids. It's the face-to-face encounter that catalyzes action. When I talk to people who have worked in Big Brothers or Big Sisters, they always tell me how it has changed their lives. But I firmly believe that what makes them get involved in the first place are the spiritual values that are part of who we are as a culture."

The gift of private sector ingenuity, which John Mutz symbolizes, can turn these values into civic action. Unlike believers, whose passion goes entirely into their prayers, John's passion also goes into his work. He is helping his company become a leader in making private resources catalyze efforts for the public good.

By Honestly Facing Their Adversaries, New Patriots Heal Our Nation's Wounds.

Who would want to buy an increasingly unprofitable steel mill plagued by internal conflict? The answer was: no one. Like much of the United States steel industry, the G S Technologies steel plant in Kansas City was losing ground to foreign competition, and failing to compete in a global marketplace which included many other steel producers. As a result, ARMCO, its multinational parent company, was considering cutting its losses by either closing the whole plant or selling it. Both union and management recognized that the only way to keep the G S Technologies plant alive would be to inspire someone to invest new capital in it, and the only way that could happen was if union and management learned to work together. But how could generations of mistrust be turned around? How could two polarized groups—who wouldn't even sit on the same side of the room, much less the same side of the bargaining table— become partners?

"I felt like a pawn in a long-established union-management battle," says Rob Cushman, the CEO of G S Technologies. When he accepted his job in 1990, the company's Kansas City plant had a terrible safety record, almost 500 unresolved grievances, and chronic conflict between the top and the bottom of the work force. Recalls Rob: "I was receiving hate mail every day."

John Cottrell, then president of United Steelworkers Local 13, represented the workers at the Kansas City plant. "In twenty-four years, I'd seen good and bad management," he says. "But I'd never seen management willing to treat us as an equal and listen to us."

With the help of a team of facilitators led by William Isaacs, director of the Dialogue Project, based at MIT's Organizational Learning Center, the two sides set up a new framework for discourse. Their first challenge was to create what the Dialogue Project calls a "container," an atmosphere where a new and deeper kind of dialogue between the adversaries could take place.

Joe Tuttle, the company's "director of organizational effectiveness," recalls how the ivory tower concept of the "container" was transformed by the steelworkers. The folks from Cambridge arrived thinking of a container as something "like a mixing bowl for cookies," Joe recalls. But after taking a tour of the steel plant, their idea changed. One of the things Joe made sure they witnessed was the mammoth ladle in the smelt shop, called a "cauldron." Molten metals are poured into it at about 3,000 degrees Fahrenheit. Sparks fly, and the heat can burn bare skin halfway across the room. Even though the steelworkers wear skin-protecting clothing and safety gear, their lives are on the line every time they are on the shop floor. For them, the "container" was not a concept; it was a vital tool: it kept the heat from burning them alive. "We ended up renaming the container a cauldron," says Conrad Fisher, the former vice president of Local 13.

Applying the term "container" to the new framework for labor-management talks met its first test when representatives of the two sides finally came together. With each side mistrusting the other, conversation was more like a boxing match than a dialogue. B. C. Huselton, vice president for human resources and business systems, conceded: "Some managers argued that the more business decision-making we gave the union, the more it could hold us hostage later." Meanwhile, union members thought the worst of anyone in a coat and tie. "I had the idea that management doesn't care about the workers," Conrad Fisher says. "They work in air-conditioned offices and make big money; they take it easy; they aren't sympathetic toward us at all. They just use us."

Slowly, over months of dialogue, this began to change. A team consisting of both management and union representatives met twice a month to deal with the fate of their company. "Moving into dialogue was an experiment to see if we could reach a place where we talk to each other anew," says Joe. "We realized that we could move beyond the past. We developed a commitment to talking through the issues without breaking apart. We got to the point where it stopped being them and us, and we started really focusing on the issues together."

"I had a lot of preconceived ideas of what management was," Conrad admits. As an officer of the local union representing the steelworkers, he had felt almost honor-bound to be suspicious of management's every move. "But during the dialogues, I found out that they weren't anything I thought they were. When you just jump to your own conclusions, they are about as far from being right as you can imagine. Your imagination sure can do some strange things to you!"

Through the dialogue process, which continued for more than two years, they all saw that they'd be better off working *with* each other rather than against each other. In large part as a result of the partnership that emerged, new investors were found that began modernizing the company. Productivity increased, and so far, at least, the company has survived. Two small fragments of our society, a local union and the management of a company, learned to see themselves as part of a larger whole.

"Sure, we all have our own separate interests and our likes and dislikes," Conrad concedes. "But our common interest is the steel industry and making this company work. Without the dialogue, we wouldn't have a company. Enough time has gone by that you can look at other sites and see what would have happened to us if we hadn't joined together."

From the management perspective, Joe Tuttle agrees. "When people ask me what the impact of all the talking was on the bottom line, I say to them: 'Without it, we wouldn't even *have* a bottom line.' "

---

*New Patriots Use Their Entrepreneurial Spirit
To Rebuild Their Communities.*

In the inner city of Baltimore, Maryland, a seventy-two square block area known as Sandtown-Winchester is evidence of what partnership between profits and purpose can accomplish. Sixty percent of the area's residents are African-American, and the remainder includes scores of other ethnic groups, including whites. Just a few years ago, more than half of the area's residents lived in poverty; buildings stood abandoned, their windows boarded up; crime and drugs were rampant. According to the Urban Institute, there are a thousand other communities just like Sandtown-Winchester spread across the country. It is an archipelago of Disia—the disempowered, dislocated, disheartened, and disrespected "underclass."

While ideologues of the Divided States blame others for this persistent poverty, the new patriots have stopped blaming and started building. They know the problems in the thousands of Sandtown-Winchesters are too intractable for any single institution to solve. The only way out is through pulling together: not just the poor pulling themselves up, but the entire community, including business, pulling with them.

This is what happened in Sandtown-Winchester in the early nineties. Mayor Curt Schmoke, representing the city government; the Enterprise Foundation, which mobilized corporate and philanthropic interests; and the residents, representing the community itself, formed a three-way alliance to revitalize the area. Together they created Community-Building in Partnership (CBP), a nonprofit organization that is slowly bringing Sandtown-Winchester back to life. The partnership has already had enormous practical results: 1,000 units of housing have been renovated; 400 middle school students have received alternative career training; job training or job placement has been provided for 500 youths and a mentoring program for teenagers has been launched; twelve community gardens have been created; and 1,700 voters (more than 10 percent of the area's population) have been registered to vote.

None of this happened from the top down. It was all decided by the partners. With residents constituting a majority of the board of directors, CBP mobilized and united residents to work together to decide what their community needed. So, for example, when they learned how low were the test scores of elementary school students in the area, they formed a compact to develop a strategy so that within five years a majority of the childrens' test scores would meet state standards. To combat drug-related crime, CBP developed a partnership linking local, state, and federal law enforcement personnel with 120 block captains, resulting in a 15 percent decrease in violent crime from the previous year. After only four years in operation, says the Enterprise Foundation's Pat Costigan, "there is a new sense of hope."[10]

There is only one fundamental obstacle to revitalizing communities like Sandtown-Winchester, says James Rouse, the spark behind the Enterprise Foundation: "That obstacle is disbelief." Sitting with his wife Patty in their home in Columbia, Maryland, a "new city" which the Rouse Company created and built, James believes that this "can't-do" attitude is our greatest adversary. "There is a pervasive state of mind that the problems of the inner city are not solvable. It's despair; it's depression. It's denial. Once we break through that disbelief, as we have in Baltimore, transformation *is* possible."[11]

All across the nation, there are scores of stories just like Sandtown-Winchester's. From the work of the Urban Strategies Council in Oakland to the Dudley Street Initiative in Boston; from the Atlanta Project spearheaded by former President Jimmy Carter to the TACOLCY project (Taking Care of Liberty City Youth) in Miami; from the New Community Corporation in Newark to the South Shore Bank in Chicago—communities are reclaiming their capacity for self-governance. In each of these efforts, the key is partnership. Government alone can't fix what is wrong. Private enterprise alone can't solve the problems. The community can't revitalize all by itself. All three forces—public sector, private sector, and the crucial "citizen's sector"—must work together.

Disia's Gift: Conscience |
"MOVING BEYOND THAT HATRED"

When outsiders came into Baltimore's decaying Sandtown-Winchester neighborhood claiming that they would "revitalize" it, the people who lived there were suspicious. They had heard it all before. They were used to rich white folks with fancy ideas coming in to announce this program or that plan, and then going home to their big houses in the suburbs. Nothing ever changed.

"The residents thought from the start it was a hoax," recalls Loretta Smith, an African-American mother of two children who has lived in the area most of her life. " 'Community Action' agencies came in the sixties—that folded. Then 'Model Cities' came in—that folded too. So then these Enterprise Foundation folks came in here, and we knew it wouldn't work. We figured their plan would fold, too, like everything else had."

But it hasn't. If you ask Loretta today how residents feel about the revitalization of their community, she reports an enormous shift in attitude. "A lot of our fears have gone away. The whole thinking behind the partnership here in Sandtown is that the community will run it. Community residents have a big voice. It's not top-down anymore, like the earlier projects were. City government officials sit in on our meetings. We set policy. If we don't like what's happening, we can go back to the drawing board and change it."

Loretta was so impressed with how the foundations, business, and city government officials approached the residents that she overcame her suspicions and decided to work with them. Today she is a family advocate with Community-Building in Partnership, acting as a "red tape person" who assists families in dealing with the social services. "You know, those government agencies don't talk to people," Loretta explains. "They just talk to numbers. My job is to empower people to become more able to cope with the system so that they can go back to their neighborhoods and teach their neighbors."

As an advocate for families in the neighborhood, Loretta knows things are getting better—but are still not good enough. With two kids in the local schools, she is painfully aware that education experts with their "sixteen-letter words" still think they can come in and tell parents what is best for their kids. Regarding drugs, she believes that abuse is more widespread today than it was before the Partnership began its work five years ago. And as far as employment is concerned, there are still too many people in Sandtown-Winchester without jobs and without hope. But despite the challenges ahead, Loretta believes they are making progress. "We are taking ownership of this project," she says proudly. "We are working to change the system. We're not there yet—but we're moving!"

New Patriots Transform Disrespect into a Genuine Regard for Diversity.

Ibrahim Munim is an attorney who works as a program officer for the Committee to Reduce Chronic Poverty in Washington, D.C. He was the first Muslim ever to head a chapter of an organization called (until recently) the National Council of Christians and Jews. But as a black boy growing up in Columbus, Georgia, it was his Christian neighbors who made him sit in the back of the bus. "Being a Christian didn't get me a seat at the front," he says. "My faith didn't matter. All that mattered in the South then was the color of my skin."

Growing up with the reality of discrimination, Ibrahim has more reason to be angry with American government than most whites. But his story bears witness to the power of the new patriotism.

"Throughout my life I have been an activist," Ibrahim says. "It was always important to me that I live according to what I profess to believe. I was arrested as a young man for trying to get into an all-white library. I was a Christian then, heavily influenced by Dr. Martin Luther King. But the people who called themselves Christians supported segregation. I simply could not be part of that kind of a religion."

Drawn to Islam, Ibrahim began studying his new faith and recognized for the first time how deeply racism had entered his own mind. The prophet Jesus, whom he had worshiped as a child, was always portrayed with blue eyes and blond hair. "Everybody knows that people in Palestine two thousand years ago did not look like that," Ibrahim says, "but the white European Christians weren't willing to change their image of Jesus. They could only imagine their savior looking just like them." In 1973, at the age of twenty-five, and very angry, he became a Muslim. At first, Ibrahim (his newly chosen Muslim name) hated whites and considered them the devil. As a follower of the Nation of Islam, he was surrounded with support for his view that whites were evil, a point of view he held for years.

"God blessed me and helped me move beyond that kind of hatred. But I admit it. I face it. If we don't face it, we develop a personality like that of a person who is addicted to drugs. That kind of personality is based on denial. Until you acknowledge your own racism and admit that it is wrong, you are just like that addict."

Today, Ibrahim is committed to fighting racism in himself as in others. Not long ago he spent one day a month for almost a year in a program called Leadership Washington in which residents of diverse backgrounds worked together to improve the quality of life in the city. "I made a joke about someone being an Indian giver, and didn't think twice about it. How I grew up, if you gave somebody something and then took it back, you were an Indian giver. Well, it turned out that what I said was offensive to one of my classmates, who was a Native American."

The encounter forced Ibrahim to come to terms with his own ignorance about the people to whom this land originally belonged. He learned that in most of the Native American cultures things weren't owned by individuals. "It was a concept that was difficult for me to understand," Ibrahim admits. "I had been influenced by my culture. But I consider it my responsibility—and everyone's—to learn to reach out beyond our limitations and find our common bond. As Jesus said, 'Ye shall know the truth, and the truth shall make ye free.'"

Although it surprises some, Ibrahim often quotes scriptures from all faiths. "I recognize that there are people of other faiths who share my commitment to justice. If you read the writings of Mohammed and Moses and Jesus, there are very few things about which they differ. It's not the differences between them that really matter, it's the differences between us, their followers. Many people erroneously think that Muslims and Jews should be enemies. I suppose it's because of the conflict in the Middle East. But if you look at the holy Koran, there is nothing that would cause a Muslim to hate a Jew. There's no theological basis for it at all. What Moses taught and Mohammed taught is very close. People exploit the differences for their own purposes."

When Ibrahim heard that the National Council of Christians and Jews was doing good work in the fight against drugs, an issue in which he was deeply involved, he contacted the Council's executive director to explore possible collaboration. Ibrahim informed him that he was concerned about the Council's name. Originally intended to communicate inclusiveness when the organization was founded in 1927, its name now connoted exclusiveness. Ibrahim also learned that the organization itself was also worried about its name. In recognition of Islam, one of the nation's fastest-growing faiths, as well as Buddhism and Hinduism and numerous smaller faiths, the Council also soon realized the importance of bringing into its leadership someone of a non–Judeo-Christian faith.

So it was that Ibrahim Munim in 1993 became the head of the Washington chapter of the organization, which has been renamed the National Conference. Thrust into a leadership role, Ibrahim now speaks out in forums around the country about issues of race, poverty, and diversity. He recognizes that, historically speaking, Mississippi Governor Fordice, who called America a "Christian nation," was correct. "The people who ran this place were Christians," Ibrahim says. "The slave-owners were Christians too. So when people say that they want to go back to the spirit of the Founding Fathers, that is also the spirit of slavery. If we want to be honest with ourselves, we have to tell the good, the bad, and the ugly. The Founding Fathers were outstanding leaders, but they had their weaknesses."

Ibrahim doesn't become lost in self-righteous outrage, however. "I don't keep my moral spotlight on the white slave-owner," he says. "I hurt people, too, like my Native American colleague. We all do. The biggest challenge of living in a country with a diverse set of faiths is mutual respect. If God had wanted us all to be the same, he would have created us that way. What I try to do is do unto others as I would have them do unto me. If my colleagues set meetings at twelve or one o'clock on Friday, I can't attend. That's when Muslims go to prayer. Well, I want my colleagues to respect that. Similarly, if a Jewish colleague wants to be exempted from anything happening on Friday evening, I need to respect my colleague's beliefs. That's just part of being an American."

Instead of Cynically Polarizing a Community,
New Patriots Reconnect Its Fragmented Parts.

The Massachusetts Association of Community Development Corporations (MACD) devoted much of its annual meeting a few years ago to reflecting on its mission. But executive director Pat Libby had no idea that she would also fall in love there.

"Our organization was doing some necessary soul-searching," Pat Libby recalls, "because we had started to forget that the heart of our work—the calling of the CDCs—is to be community-run and community-based." Pat was worried that some of the fifty member organizations were getting too professional and too removed from the communities which they served. Chapter 40-F of the General Statutes of the state of Massachusetts specified that CDCs must (a) be located in low-income neighborhoods, (b) serve a minimum population of 10,000 and (c) have boards of directors with a majority of members who live and work in the community. Nevertheless, during Pat's eight years as executive director, she had become concerned that the CDC movement was becoming less and less grounded in the communities it served.

To help the CDCs reflect on whether they were truly serving their communities, she invited Mike Eichler as keynote speaker.

When Mike had begun working as a community organizer a decade earlier in Pennsylvania's Monongahela Valley, hostility and bitterness pervaded the valley. Scores of big steel mills had shut down many of their unprofitable plants. Communities throughout the valley were thrown into crisis. Steelworkers were losing their jobs. The economic emergency was compounded by the social fragmentation. "The communities didn't know how to get together," Mike says. "Each group only knew how to press for their own self-interest. Nobody was holding the whole community in their heart."

The steel companies felt they weren't responsible for what happened to the communities after they moved. David Roderick, then head of U. S. Steel (now renamed USX Corporation), was quoted as saying that unemployed workers' towns like Homestead, Pennsylvania, should just move somewhere else. Once the steel plants were gone, he said, the town was no longer needed.

Before Mike arrived, community organizers were staging predictable protests. "Everybody pointed their finger at somebody else: somebody else was at fault; somebody else had to fix it. Organizers for unemployed steelworkers considered their people to have been screwed. They had to demonstrate how their people were shafted. So they went to disgruntled steelworkers and exploited their resentment. They told the steelworkers that they had no responsibility and all they had to do was bitch and moan about the banks and the steel company executives and make them look bad. Their strategy was to get media to paint the executives and bankers as cruel, heartless bastards. They even harassed the families of company executives when they were leaving church."

The entire strategy, Mike believes, was "a carryover from the sixties." These community organizers assumed that they had to humiliate and belittle the other side so they would give in. Any other approach was considered a sellout, or "con job," and those who cooperated with it were stooges. The protests succeeded in attracting some attention. "60 Minutes," for example, showed demonstrating steelworkers being carried out of a bank with blood running down their faces.

"But what did this all accomplish?" Mike asks. "It shamed the power brokers, true. But did it solve the problem? Did it make the mills more efficient? Did it promote investment in the region? No! It did just the opposite!"

The only way to change the situation, reasoned Mike, was "to turn things on their head." Business was avoiding the valley because it felt its residents were only willing to whine, complain, strike, and cause trouble. The first goal, Mike reasoned, had to be to prove this premise wrong. As a new patriot, Mike was determined to mobilize people not by making the power brokers look bad, but by making *everybody* look good.

"The buzzword used to be that to develop power in people, they had to bring the powerful to their knees," Mike says. "But I don't believe that is the best motivator for community change. That kind of power is like crack cocaine: it gives you a few minutes of pleasure, but then it's gone. It boosts the movement for a day, but then enthusiasm fades away. Treating others with respect, and being treated with respect, makes everybody feel good. It's not a one-day thrill, but a permanent change in our community."

Mike helped catalyze seventeen community development corporations along the valley, each with grass-roots leadership and with its own specific projects to improve life in their area. Each CDC involved positive collaboration between people of all walks of life. In addition, spokespeople from all seventeen groups formed an area-wide organization that represented the region in negotiations to bring new investment into the area. The CDCs were run by neighborhood volunteers. Ordinary citizens become the experts and the driving force in the community.

Since then, Mike has catalyzed similar movements in other American cities. With variations, his approach has worked on a wide range of different issues— health care and school reform, low-income housing, and community economic development. To train others in this inclusive style of community building, he founded the Consensus Organizing Institute, based on this philosophy of civic partnership.

In terms of religion and class, Pat could not have been more different from the man standing behind the podium. She was the daughter of a Jewish family who had become wealthy from a profitable plumbing supply business which they owned; Mike was the son of poor German Catholic parents who were both unskilled laborers. But within two years after they met, Pat and Mike were married. Religion and class meant little to them because they shared something much more important: their purpose in life.

"It's hard to put into words," Pat says. "We both felt that people have a right to have a voice in the decisions that affect them. That means respect. We both feel people should be treated with respect regardless of where they come from or what they have or what they do." Libby saw in Mike a man who not only shared her philosophy, but was a pioneer. "I think Mike will have an enormous impact on community organizing. He is changing it from the ground up."

New Patriots Move Beyond Blame and Take Responsibility for Their Own Future.

Like most Americans, Ken Earl thought the men's movement consisted of a bunch of middle-class white men complaining about women. He never imagined that it was a place where he would confront the racism of this nation—and his own.

"I had no interest in the men's movement whatsoever," he says. "It was the usual white mentality: you know, 'We'll create something for ourselves and then, as an afterthought, we'll get some black guys.' " But when he saw how valuable the "New Warrior" training was for one of his friends, he decided to take the risk and enroll.

Because he found the training deeply healing, Ken volunteered to staff many weekends around the country and became increasingly dedicated to the training. The training promises to provide men of all ages with a "rite of passage," a way of coming into their own power as men. Unfortunately, Ken was almost always the only black man present. But at a recent training session in Memphis, Tennessee, for the first time, half of those present were men of color. Although hundreds of "trainings" had taken place in cities across the country, this had never happened before.

The Memphis training site was actually located in nearby northern Mississippi. As Ken crossed the border into the state which had been the site of so much racial violence, he couldn't keep images of the Ku Klux Klan out of his head. The thought that somebody might be lynched flickered across his consciousness. As the car filled with black men from up north passed through small southern towns, scenes from the movie *Mississippi Burning* flashed through his mind. "Instead of thinking about the positive meaning of this black-and-white training," Ken says, "I was terrified."

As the staff gathered on their first night together, they drummed. But this time, it felt different. "Drumming at a normal weekend is just a beat. But that night I heard tribal rhythms from Africa. If I closed my eyes, I could almost see elephants walking across the savanna." Another difference Ken noticed was the way the black men clustered together. He was used to walking up to a man, hugging him, and introducing himself. "But this time, when one man in a cluster stood up, the whole cluster stood up. It was like tribes. It was like back in Africa, man. I have never been there, but it felt like a meeting of the tribes—coming together for a common good." One of the Memphis men had brought along the lyrics of "Soul to Soul," and the men stood in a circle singing or humming. "Black men and white men, in the circle, singing like a men's choir," Ken remembers.

One white participant in the training, the son of a Ku Klux Klan member, made Ken feel rage. "I wanted to kill the son of a bitch. I felt he was carrying all the injustices that had ever been done to blacks. But then I looked in his face and saw the pain of what he and his ancestors had done. His face was filled with shame. He hated his male line. When I saw that, I felt sorry for him. I identified with him. When Martin Luther King died, I was throwing bricks at white guys riding by on their bikes. I felt hostility toward any white person. 'How dare you drive through my neighborhood after you killed Martin?'—that's how we felt. So who was I to judge this man? I started thinking about 'He who is without sin cast the first stone.' "

One black participant, a gang leader, had brought his .45 Magnum. To help break down the wall this man had built around himself, the staff used a technique called a "trust fall," in which the man falls backward with his eyes closed into the arms of several men. When the man landed, Ken whispered in his ear.

"What color do you see?" Ken asked the gang leader.

"The color of love," he replied, and began crying.

But the most vivid image Ken took away from the weekend took place when a white man who, as Ken put it, "looked like he had just taken off his Klan mask," walked over to the darkest-skinned black guy and hugged him. Both of them were so filled with love they were crying. "It was like watching one of the yin and yang symbols come alive right there in front of me. At the beginning of the training, everything was black or white. But before long everything went gray. It wasn't black or white, it wasn't Chinese or Portuguese—it was just men. Everybody there had experienced pain and was seeking their own truth. When we got into the deep work—which was what we were there to do—color vanished."

Since that weekend many other interracial trainings have taken place. Many of the New Warrior "brothers" in the 4,000-plus national network are working with juvenile offenders, at-risk high school students, and other young men in trouble at home or with the law. These men have stopped conforming to the unwritten code of racial segregation and have found the courage to confront the deeper complexity of racial differences. They have stopped labeling their fellow Americans by the color of their skins and recognized that they can learn something about being an American from another race that their own could never teach them.

In America today, metaphors about kaleidoscopes and evocations of the Statue of Liberty often run into a stone wall of pessimism. The stones in this wall are racist attitudes that have emerged from the experiences between African-Americans, the descendants of slaves, and white Americans, many of whom are descendants of slaveholders. That experience, unfortunately, has been so bleak and painful for many of our citizens that it can make us skeptical, if not downright despairing, about the possibility of interracial understanding. The new patriots, however, refuse to surrender to despair. In myriad ways, in thousands of communities, blacks and whites are rejecting these very labels and looking beneath the color of a person's skin to (in Martin Luther King's phrase) "the content of our characters." What they are finding is, whenever a stone in the wall of racism is dislodged, our view of each other widens. A black man or white man becomes a fellow citizen and, if we are fortunate, even a brother.

New Patriots Overcome Exclusion and Intolerance,
and Renew the American Dream.

Ricardo Olivares Carranza was once a student radical in El Salvador, part of the liberation movement seeking to overthrow the U.S.-backed government. Ricardo and his comrades participated in so many demonstrations and were so frequently attacked by government troops that they had to defend themselves. While continuing his studies at the National School of Commerce, Ricardo became an active member of the Popular Liberation Front militia, and received his military training in the secluded jungles at the foot of the Guazapa volcano. In January 1980, as Ronald Reagan was running for president, Ricardo took part in his first attack against the Air Force installations in Ilopango.

Less than a year after his first military action, Ricardo was walking with his girlfriend and another friend down the street when they noticed they were being followed by a slow-moving car. Before they could run, the men in the car opened fire. His two friends were killed. Ricardo was left bleeding to death from multiple bullet wounds in his chest and legs. He was taken to a hospital and survived.

"Death squad," he says, in his choppy English, when asked who the assassins were. "Military officers with high rank. They are paid to kill, but don't wear uniforms. Trained by United States government."

Because his mother was so afraid assassins would succeed in killing him, eventually Ricardo left El Salvador. From Mexico, Ricardo illegally crossed the border to Texas (EWI, it is officially called—"entry without inspection") and found his way to Houston. He took a job as a janitor, cleaning buildings for $3.25 an hour, until he was hired by a painting company. Assigned to jobs in the border area, Ricardo had to quit: it was simply too dangerous for an illegal alien to work there.

"It was scary," he says, when asked about the stress of being an illegal. "But I'd seen worse. I felt unsure about my life. I had to make up my own social security number. I had to invent myself. It wasn't easy—but at least I was alive. I was still having nightmares—still having flashes from the back. But I didn't have time to feel sorry for myself. I had to survive."

Scarred by bullet wounds and frightened of the authorities, Ricardo was an unemployed illegal alien unable to speak English, living in the country that had trained the assassins who almost killed him. It would have been easy to hate America. But although he and his comrades despised American military policy, he respected the American people. Ricardo is familiar with the stereotype of Latinos lazily feeding at the trough of the American welfare system; he doesn't let it bother him. His faith in America is so deep, and his character is so resilient, that he forgives America's racism just as he forgives the U.S.-financed assassins. Despite it all, Ricardo Olivares Carranza wanted to be an American—and today he is our fellow citizen.

Ricardo had two priceless qualities that so many immigrants to America before him have shared: a vision of the future and the willingness to work. Building on his skills as a janitor, he became the caretaker for an apartment building in College Station, near Texas A & M, where he quickly earned the respect of the tenants. After a few years, he was able to buy a ramshackle little house, fix it up, and rent it out. Using this income as a base, he fixed up another house and another. Finally, he qualified for a bank loan of $46,000, enabling him to buy a run-down four-unit apartment building which he is currently remodeling and preparing to rent.

With his income, Ricardo has put two sisters through high school back home in El Salvador and bought a four-wheel-drive Toyota truck for himself. Like waves of immigrants before him, Ricardo is determined to make the most of what he has. "The whole problem is that some of the American people take for granted so many things," Ricardo says slowly. "They don't do anything to change things. They want everything to just fall out of the sky. What they call poor here, we call rich back home. You have opportunity here. I know, because back where I come from, we didn't have it."

Like Loretta Smith and her colleagues in Sandtown-Winchester; like Pat Libby and Mike Eichler; and like Ibrahim Munim and Ken Earl, Ricardo believes in the American dream, and is helping to make it come true. These people are asking America, and those of us who love it, to renew it constantly with our lives. They are reminding us that loving America does not mean loving it as it is, but for what it can become.

Media's Gift: Communication |
"INSPIRING A RETURN TO PUBLIC LIFE"

A working journalist for forty-two years of his fifty-seven years, Davis "Buzz" Merritt, Jr., started as a fifteen-year-old sports editor at a daily newspaper in his hometown of Hickory, North Carolina. He has since worked at papers throughout the South, served as news editor of Knight-Ridder's Washington bureau, and for the past several years he has held the title of executive editor of the *Wichita Eagle*. In 1988, he stepped forward and called upon his fellow media professionals to join him in developing a new, more public-spirited and civic-minded brand of journalism.

What catalyzed his call to arms was the 1988 elections—"totally an image campaign," Buzz recalls in disgust. "There was so little flesh-and-blood on the issues. I had been editor here for fifteen years, and had covered a lot of elections. I had watched the campaigns during that time deteriorate. Politicians had decided that there were easier ways of getting elected than dealing with the issues."

Buzz was angry with the candidates, but he was even angrier with his own profession, which he felt was letting the public down. He was not alone. Many successful journalists acknowledge that their craft, as currently practiced, is in terminal condition. In the view of Carl Bernstein, the *Washington Post* reporter who helped break the Watergate story, "the lowest form of popular culture— lack of information, misinformation, disinformation, and contempt for the truth—has overrun real journalism." Outraged that "ordinary Americans are being stuffed with garbage by the great information companies of America," Bernstein denies that media exploitation of the public is practiced only by marginal publications like the *National Enquirer*. The biggest and most prestigious companies in the country, Bernstein argues, "are now in the trash business. . . . And the garbage that they are hauling is helping poison the American environment." In words more damning than anything Patrians like Jerry Falwell or Donald Wildmon have ever uttered, Bernstein charges that "there is hardly a major media company in America that has not dipped its toe into the social and political equivalent of the porn business in the last fifteen years."[12]

By Listening to Citizen Voices, New Patriots
in the Media Catalyze Citizen Participation.

One week after what he calls "that awful election," Buzz issued his manifesto in the form of an op ed article in his own paper. Under the headline MUST RE- STORE MEANING TO ELECTIONS, he announced his determination to find a new way for the *Eagle* to cover the next election.

"Telling the news isn't enough," Buzz says. "Providing people with information is not sufficient. If it was, we wouldn't be in the fix we're in. If the world was going well, if the nation was all right, if our communities were safe, then maybe journalism could continue business as usual. But providing endless information about crime is not going to reduce it. We need to give people a handle on it, and some hope, so that they can *use* the information to make their world better. We used to view ourselves as people who gather information and send it out to people. Now, increasingly, we send it out to customers. We need to shift from seeing our readers as customers to seeing them for what they are—citizens."

In addition to changing the way it covered other local issues, the *Eagle* decided to develop a new approach to election coverage, putting less emphasis on the glitz and competition of the campaign, and more on the issues. "The old belief on election coverage," Buzz says, "was that my job as a journalist was to cover the campaign. Whatever the campaign was, that's what I'd cover. If George Bush goes to a flag factory, or Michael Dukakis rides a tank, my job is to write about that. The new belief is that citizens have the right to know what the candidates are going to do if elected. They have the right to have the candidates address what matters to them."

Buzz used his op ed page as a bully pulpit in the 1990 gubernatorial elections, telling the state of Kansas that his paper "has a strong bias: we believe the voters are entitled to have the candidates talk about the issues in depth." He made it clear that the paper's coverage would be tough and insistent, refusing to be lured into photo opportunities and joy rides and sticking to the issues facing their community. After calling the readers' attention to "slick, no-brainer, packaged candidates" and to TV commercials that leave "gaping loopholes that make postelection accountability impossible," Buzz vowed that the *Eagle* would be fierce in its devotion to the issues. "What the eventual winner intends to do with the great gift that voters will bestow," Buzz concluded, "is a straightforward question that deserves a clear answer."[13]

The people of Kansas responded. The *Eagle*'s campaign generated increased requests for voter registration material, and voter turnout in the *Eagle*'s circulation area showed a marked increase. Managing editor Steve Smith felt the response validated the paper's new approach of listening to their readers as citizens and reporting their views. "We're adopting the community's agenda," Smith explained. "We're asking *them* to tell us what is most important to them."[14]

By 1992, other papers reported similar results. Some, like the *Charlotte Observer* or the *Tallahassee Democrat*, focused their political coverage on issues defined by citizens rather than on the competitive maneuvering of the candidates. Others, such as the *Portland Press Herald* and the *Minneapolis Star Tribune*, inspired citizens to become involved in neighborhood round tables and living room discussions. Across the country, word began passing through the newsrooms that a movement was building within the profession. "Over time," Buzz concludes, "if we do public journalism right, we will inspire a lot of people to return to public life who have abandoned it, or to enter it for the first time."

The movement started by Buzz and his colleagues doesn't have a name yet. Whether it is called "public journalism," "community journalism," "civic journalism," or simply the "new journalism," what matters is that the movement is leaving its mark. Just as a corporation is responsible for the effect its hiring practices or environmental codes have on the community, so does journalism have a larger responsibility to the community. Journalists are, in the words of Ed Fouhy of the Pew Center for Civic Journalism, "creating the public space where citizens can discuss their concerns." Just as corporations can no longer say that their sole job is making profits for their shareholders, so newspapers can no longer say their sole job is to report the news.

Working in Partnership with the Community,
the Media Can Connect Rather Than Polarize.

Most people have heard of CBS, NBC, CNN, and ESPN, but few know about MTN, TVCA, ACTV, or CTN. These are some of the scores of community-level media ventures that are, in Tamara Blaschko's words, "rewiring community to talk to itself."

An administrator who has worked for the past decade with the Minneapolis Telecommunications Network (MTN), Tamara Blaschko was drawn to MTN because she was interested in community access. "Freedom of speech may be a right," she says, "but having an outlet for what you say is not a right. I wanted people to be aware of how important that access is, whether or not they choose to use it, because it could disappear. As all of the technologies converge, people could be left out in the cold. Most of the citizenry is not up to speed on a tech level. A large majority of the population have never used a computer. They can't be disenfranchised. We can't let ordinary citizens be left out of the communications loop. We must preserve freedom of speech *and voice.*"

The mission of MTN is to give voice to the community. Unlike traditional media, which operate on the basis that they as professionals will tell the consumers what is happening in the community, Tamara and her colleagues see their role as enabling citizens to speak for themselves. For $30 a year, the 500 volunteers of MTN give each member access to quality cameras and basic training. Together they have produced 22,000 hours of programming, which has aired on MTN's eighteen channels, "We lend eight-thousand-dollar cameras for people to take out on their word," Tamara says, "and we never had any trouble. We found that when you put out trust, you usually get trust back. We're giving people the skills and tools to use their voice—and the mechanism and the channels to broadcast it."

"I don't like the superhighway analogy that is now so popular," says Tony Riddle, MTN's executive director. "I see the new media as a nervous system for the body. A highway goes some places, but bypasses others. The nervous system has to go everywhere. If the nerves down to your big toe don't work, the whole organism is going to feel it." When the whole organism is connected, Tony believes there will be an evolutionary leap. "Every major change in the complexity of the organisms of life has been preceded by changes in the communication between the various parts of the organism. I believe we are now at the advent of such a shift."

Tony is also national chairman of the 1,200-member Alliance for Community Media, which connects more than 3,000 government education and public access centers. Its members produce more than 20,000 hours per week of community-based programming. "It's a different world from when I grew up," says Tony. "Then there were three or four or five channels. Channel time was scarce. It would have been absurd to talk about a channel just for citizens to talk to each other. But what would have been unthinkable then is happening now."

As an African-American, Tony participates every year in the celebration of "Juneteenth," a holiday commemorating the day (June 19, 1865) when the slaves in Texas were granted freedom. "It took two and a half long years," Tony explained, "before the news of the Emancipation Proclamation reached the slaves in many parts of Texas. During all that time, they gave the fruit of their labor without knowing that it was being stolen from them. They had been freed, but they didn't know it."

While watching news coverage of the event, Riddle heard someone say that those slaves were "at the bottom of the information chain." When he heard that phrase, he recalls, "something clicked. I realized that our work was turning that upside down. You're just as much a slave if you don't have information as if you have a chain around your neck. If all the common people in the world have some access to means of communication, there is only so far any tyrant can go."

From Seattle to Taos, from North Carolina to San Francisco Bay, from Austin, Texas, to Portland, Oregon, Americans are harnessing the new technology to strengthen their sense of community.[15] "Minneapolis is just one of scores of cities doing the same thing," says Richard Civille, executive director of the Center for Civic Networking, a Charlestown, Massachusetts, nonprofit organization that promotes the public benefits of the converging media industries. The Center for Civic Networking serves as a clearing house where a variety of groups—community initiatives, city-run operations, and emerging efforts at the federal level—can refine their craft. "Today, we can safely say dozens of cities are involved in this movement," Richard says. "In a year, I'll be able to say it's one of hundreds. It's a gargantuan change."

All the new patriots in the media—not just Richard Civille, Tony Riddle, Tamara Blaschko, and Buzz Merritt, but the thousands of men and women who are using communications to heal the splits between the Divided States—are making this change happen. They will never relinquish their right to use words and images as they see fit, but they are also shouldering their responsibility to use their power to communicate, in order to reconnect Americans to the communities, large and small, in which they live.

What the communication media all too often do now is just the opposite: they *dis*connect. "The media in public affairs are overwhelmingly adversarial," observes John Marks, the founder of Search for Common Ground, a Washington, D.C.-based nonprofit conflict resolution organization. It's all about "good guys and bad guys, white hats and black hats. . . . Most journalists seem to work within the framework that conflict is interesting and agreement is dull; they tend to reward discordant behavior with air time and column inches, and they penalize—by ignoring—action aimed at building consensus and solving problems." As John told National Public Radio's Susan Stamberg a few days after a doctor at an abortion clinic in Florida was murdered: "That shooting in Pensacola could be a wake-up call for the rest of us."[16]

Once an award-winning investigative reporter himself, John knows that the adversarial confrontations cannot be replaced with kisses and hugs. His goal is simply to create an alternative that would "drain some of the poison from the national political debate" and "change the dynamics" of the conflict. "My vision is that we could *also* have media that are nonadversarial, that could promote ways to move the society forward in a positive way, and that could contribute to our overall capacity for problem solving. By all means, let's report on conflict; but let's also report on the *resolution* of conflict."

Gaia's Gift: Vision |
"THIS DIALOGUE HAS TRANSFORMED ME."

In 1989, Search for Common Ground launched a public television series which put adversaries on a variety of public issues through what John Marks called mediated conversations. "Ted Koppel and Phil Donahue like to sharpen the differences, and exaggerate them in order to exacerbate conflict," John explains. "Instead, we saw our job as trying to find areas of agreement. If you ask a different set of questions, you get a different set of answers. If you ask the adversaries where they agree, you will get a different answer than if you ask them why they disagree."

In a program dealing with abortion, John featured Dr. John Willke, then president of the National Right to Life Committee, and his adversary, Kate Michelman of the National Abortion Rights Action League. As moderator, John structured the debate so that these polarized, publicly visible opponents could discover whether there might be some common ground between their well-known positions. In less than thirty minutes, both Willke and Michelman agreed that unwanted pregnancies should be minimized as much as possible, and that promoting adoption and reducing infant mortality were efforts on which they could agree.

The program aired on over a hundred PBS stations as part of the "Search for Common Ground" series and was well received throughout the country. Encouraged by the positive response, John returned to the foundation which had funded the program and asked for follow-up funding. But the foundation was committed to a pro-choice position and declined further funding. "They did not want to jeopardize their credibility with the pro-choice community," John observes matter-of-factly.

Without funding, "Search for Common Ground"'s efforts to build bridges between the pro-life and pro-choice communities might have ended there. But in the spring of 1992, a phone call came from Buffalo, New York—a city polarized following a series of protests at abortion clinics. The Council of Churches of Buffalo asked John to help the two sides in the abortion debate to find "cooperative alternative approaches." In response, Marks searched for other new patriots who were willing to take on this daunting challenge and found Adrienne Kaufman, a Benedictine nun, and Mary Jacksteit, a sixties activist and labor lawyer. Together these two women became codirectors of the Common Ground Coalition for Life and Choice.

*Loving Our Country Means Treating Our
Adversaries with Civility and Respect.*

"A girl either got married, went to the convent, became a secretary, or entered nursing school," says Adrienne, recalling her girlhood in rural South Dakota. In 1956, Adrienne entered a Benedictine monastery. Part of an order founded in A.D. 480, the Benedictine sisters have a mission specific to their order: to be community-builders. "Our job is to bear witness to community. As a Benedictine, it is really important to me that pro-life and pro-choice people experience themselves as part of the same community. Our calling is to create the experience of the body of community wherever our lives may take us."

In addition to attending college, majoring in chemistry, and eventually teaching, Adrienne's calling led her to become a founder of the South Dakota Peace and Justice Center, a liberal social action group that was united around issues such as Central America, the death penalty, and Native American rights. When it came to the issue of abortion, the center's membership split down the middle. Half were opposed, while the other half felt it was a woman's right to decide for herself. Adrienne tried unsuccessfully to bridge the gap.

Mary, meanwhile, had taken a different route toward becoming a mediator. As a labor lawyer, she had grown accustomed to the incessant warfare between management and unions. But after several years, she says, "it became more and more obvious to me as a lawyer that pitting two sides against each other as adversaries was incredibly ineffective. I wanted to develop a third-party approach, so I started working with a labor arbitrator." She soon realized that she needed a different kind of training than law school, and ended up in George Mason University's conflict resolution program, where she and Adrienne met.

The Common Ground Coalition for Life and Choice is a bridge between the two sides. Starting in Buffalo and then spreading to cities across the country, Mary and Adrienne have been convening small groups of advocates from both sides to join in dialogue. Their goal is twofold: to ensure that both sides become humanized in each other's eyes, and to explore the possibility that the sides will find a common agenda. Using a variety of team-building techniques, the two women bring adversaries together in workshops that often yield agreement on areas where they can all work together.

When asked by cynics which side they are really on—as if taking sides is inevitable—both Mary and Adrienne explain they are mediators and no more.

"I am not in Congress," says Adrienne. "I don't have to cast a vote. I don't have to be on one side in every battle. That's not my job. On some issues, I do that. But on abortion, I play a different role. My role is strictly bringing people together. Perhaps—just perhaps—we can make some difference in defusing this conflict. Perhaps we can take some steps toward developing a model that can be applied to other social conflicts. When we can help people find some way of dealing with conflicts less violently, that would mean a lot to me. If people could learn not to hate their adversaries in this kind of conflict, it would make a world of difference."

It is a source of great joy to these two women when people in their workshops begin to loosen up and to come alive. They remember the response of one pro-choice woman who worked full-time in an abortion clinic and who was astonished by the fact that, after spending time with the other side, she found herself hugging them. "If anybody had told me that I would be reaching across the table and touching some of those folks, I would never have believed it," she wrote. "This dialogue has been transforming to me."

After Dr. David Gunn was murdered by anti-abortion crusaders in Pensacola, Florida, in February 1993, the nation was stunned. Headlines covered the murder and the trial of the murderer. But the news media missed the other story. The city of Pensacola hired Adrienne and Mary to work with the pro-life and pro-choice forces in town. Slowly but surely, the two women brought both sides together into a dialogue. For the first time, the enemies met. The shouting stopped; the listening—and learning—began.

New Patriots Dedicate Themselves
to Turning Their Visions into Reality.

Instead of complaining about an educational curriculum that failed to teach ecology, Cheryl Charles decided to change it. Her goal was simple: to break down the wall between the classroom and nature.

Since the mid-seventies, Cheryl has been a pioneer in bringing the natural environment into the schools. Two projects which she shepherded—Project Learning Tree, which brought plants into the classroom, and Project Wild, which focused on the animal world—have over the years became the most widely used environmental curricula in the country. "What we did differently was enable teachers to put plants and animals in context," she says. "Textbooks before then didn't do that. There was no way for kids to get a grounding of how the whole works. Our curriculum got across that the environment is bigger than its parts, and that each of us takes actions every day that are part of that whole system."

Cheryl seldom used the word "sacred" in describing these environmental curricula, because she knew it would be a red flag to school administrators afraid of controversial issues. But when asked to reflect on her two decades of work devoted to breaking down the walls separating schoolchildren from the earth, the word comes up often. "We are all a part of the fabric of the living world," she says. "We must learn how to be responsible contributors to our environment to keep it healthy for the long term. We have a sacred trust to be responsible members of the larger environment that we are a part of. We are one species of a larger whole.

"Our high-tech society has created a yearning in all of us to be reconnected," she says. "In schooling, we can learn enough to keep the life support systems intact. But we can't do it just out of fear. That emotion may wake us up; it may ignite our self-interest. But today, we need generations who feel something more. Just having humans survive is not enough. It's a sacred commitment to life itself. It is a sacred responsibility."

Cheryl not only had a vision; she turned the vision into reality. As a result, millions of schoolchildren encounter the natural world of plants and animals and begin to learn about the earth on which their lives depend.

Instead of Taking Refuge in Conformity,
New Patriots Engage with Diversity.

"We must practice and test our ideas about transformation in *all* the institutions of society," says Michael Murphy, author and co-founder of the Esalen Institute, the pioneering institute nestled on the Big Sur, California, cliffs. Just how serious Michael is about this is evidenced in the way he lives. Now in his mid-sixties, he has been a leader in fields often lumped under the heading "New Age" for more than a quarter of a century. When he and his partner Dick Price founded Esalen in the early 1960s, it was not long before the giants of Gaia each wanted this renowned institute to reflect their particular perspective: Fritz Perls promoting gestalt therapy; Ida Rolf championing body work; Will Schutz advocating encounter groups; and so on. For Michael, the challenge was to ensure that the Esalen Institute would remain a home for all these ways of thought—and more.

For decades now, Michael has been pushing beyond the borders of Gaia. That's why not long ago he consulted for a public utilities company struggling with the pressures of deregulation and downsizing and the challenge of managing a 7,000-person work force spread across an entire state. The company was doing well, but its top management realized that they had to help each employee raise his or her level of performance to the highest possible level if the company was to stay profitable. Michael was invited to speak at a company gathering on the subject of "extraordinary human performance": the subject of his latest book, *The Future of the Body*.

"The rationale for inviting me," Michael explains, "was that people can expand their human skills beyond what anyone thought was possible." The CEO of the company, seated in the audience, was skeptical that this Esalen consciousness-raiser would have much of value to say to his team. But to his astonishment, Michael received a standing ovation from the employees, for his lecture on meditation, visualization, and affirmation.

From Michael's perspective, the workplace has been too slow to adopt supportive rituals. Consequently, for most people, the workplace is "a place of stress, not a place of flow." Employees feel alienated, not connected; this not only limits the development of their personal abilities, but also undercuts the potential effectiveness of the enterprise. Michael's message is simple: by enabling individuals to reach higher levels of performance, the company too will do better.

Invited by the CEO to return, Michael finds that his message has taken hold at the company. "Employees have started using my material," Michael recounts, "and they now have lists of hundreds of specific applications to improve their performance. The linemen, for example, have dangerous jobs; and the company wanted to reduce the number of accidents on the high power lines. Now, before the linemen go out on the job, they are using some of the concentration and focusing techniques I have taught them. Most of them had heard about such things but nobody had a chance to practice them—certainly not on the job."

The extraordinary diversity among the company's employees forces Michael continually to translate his thinking in new ways. "I deal with a lot of fundamentalists down there," Michael says. "My workshops there are at most fifty percent WASP Americans; the rest are black, Hispanic, Hindu, Muslim. A lot of the committed fundamentalists have responded extremely positively."

One of Michael's themes concerns what scientific research has revealed about human consciousness. "The nation's founders appealed to reason and to universal principles," he says. "When I speak at the company, I encourage them to draw upon the riches of all the cultures that bring complementary perspectives to bear. Hinduism and Buddhism are good at talking about the impersonal nature of the divine. Judaism and Christianity are good at talking about the personal God. When it comes to the human body, the yogis are far advanced over the West. But the West is far advanced in the technical and scientific sphere. Every tradition has its own unique riches, and once you have been exposed to them, you can never forget them. The Enlightenment's faith in reason is what informed the Founding Fathers. 'We hold these truths to be self-evident . . .' they wrote. Well, now we have to find deeper truths."

Michael's vision for this country springs from his faith in the spiritual riches of America. "Remember that half of the Founding Fathers were Masons. For them, patriotism was not just political; it was deeply spiritual as well. Until we as a people fully develop our relationship to the divinity around us—until we make it real in our civic life—all the half-measures are doomed. We have to get married to this spirited dimension of life." (This is the theme of his perennial best-seller, *Golf in the Kingdom,* his novel about the supernatural dimensions of the sport which he irreverently calls a "mystery school for Republicans.") Public utilities, scientific research, even golf—these interests are iconoclastic for a lifelong Buddhist mystic who is associated with hot tubs, LSD, and encounter groups. But for Michael, New Age thinking can become a mental straitjacket. To practice what he preaches about the possibilities of human transformation, he knows that his life must reflect his beliefs. The many theories of human transformation that abound in New Age circles are all "grist for the mill," he says. "Theory can guide us, but putting these ideas into practice will refine the theory. There must be constant feedback between the two. This is what keeps us honest, and keeps us growing."

Officia's Gift: Public Service |
"LEADERSHIP MUST BE ABOUT STEWARDSHIP."

A lieutenant with the Boston Police Department, William (Bill) Johnstone has practiced what America preaches. Behind his desk hangs an award from the Anti-Defamation League, a certificate of appreciation from the gay community of Boston, and other symbols of gratitude from many other minority groups. First, as a decoy on the street, and later as an officer with the Community Disorders Unit, Bill has risked his life to ensure that "liberty and justice for all" is more than a slogan.

"The decoy operation was unique," Bill says. "It was our job as police offi-cers to go out and become victims of crime." With his partners waiting nearby, Bill would make himself a target for assault or robbery by appearing to be a de-fenseless drunk or a vulnerable gay. Then, hopefully before he was seriously hurt, his partners would intervene and arrest the criminals.

Bill's worst injuries occurred while playing the role of a gay man. Emerging as a decoy from a straight bar acting drunk, he would often be robbed. But almost every time he exited a gay bar, he would be robbed *and* beaten. As his fellow offi-cers put the criminals under arrest, the criminals seemed shocked that straight policemen were collaring them for roughing up homosexuals. "I remember hav-ing my guts going into my throat," says Bill about the beatings he received before his buddies stepped in. "I didn't have to call nine-one-one—the cops were right there. But it still didn't stop the fear."

Bill later became a lieutenant detective on the Community Disorders Unit. If a hate crime happened in Boston, he and his colleagues were the first to know. "Hate crimes are so dangerous because they aren't just crimes of indi-viduals against individuals. Whole sections of the cities and the country pay the price. When one person commits a hate crime, we all get tainted. Unless we stop hate crimes, it's all going to fall apart. There's is an ugliness now in this country that's horrible. America is heading toward the place where it'll be okay to hate. Everybody is taking care of their own group."

New Patriots Seek the Integrity
To Live According to Their Ideals.

Bill Johnstone had arrived at the Community Disorders Unit in 1980 thinking that civil rights was what was happening down south and that the hate crimes in Boston were "lightweight by comparison." He and his colleagues considered name calling and broken windows "Mickey Mouse crimes." After all, nobody got hurt, and with a new pane of glass everything was fixed, right?

Bill realized how wrong he was one cold February night when he showed up in a white neighborhood where a black family of four, recently arrived, just had their windows smashed by a bunch of rock throwers. "The father was cry-ing," Bill recalls. "Big, strong guy—and he's crying. The family thought they had bought their dream house. But it turned out to be a nightmare. Eighteen windows had been shattered within a few seconds. One of his kids was in the bath, the other was in the living room watching TV, and his wife was washing dishes in the kitchen. When the glass started shattering, all three screamed at once. His wife shouted to him, 'In the name of Christ do something.' He tried to explain to her that if he had gone outside he would have killed somebody or been killed. Frozen in his tracks, the guy felt absolutely castrated by that act of violence. He told me that he made a man's vow to his family to protect them. But that night, he realized he couldn't keep his promise.

"I looked into that father's eyes," Bill recalls, "and I felt not just his pain but my own. At the time, my wife was dying of cancer. We had five children. When I saw the look in that guy's eyes it reminded me of how I felt every morning. It was the look of helplessness. There was nothing I could do to help her. I felt the same fear—the same desperation.

"Today's victim of a hate crime is tomorrow's perpetrator," Bill continues. "I couldn't see any physical scars on that family. But the emotional scars will be carried for the rest of their lives. The haters are not stupid. They know the pain they cause. They attack what is sacred. They attack the places we live, the places we worship, and the places we bury our dead. As police officers, our job is finding and punishing the perpetrators. But that is not enough. That will not help this family. The only thing that will help the family is making sure it never happens in the first place.

"It's a major crime if you steal a hundred thousand dollars," Bill says. "But what price do you put on someone's dignity?" Bill and his colleagues arrested the rock throwers, who turned out to be young men between the ages of seventeen and twenty from nearby Irish and Italian neighborhoods. What he once naively called "Mickey Mouse crimes" had put an entire neighborhood on edge.

Today people still come up to Bill and ask him why he's so involved in this issue of human rights. They tell him that he's a white guy, so why bother? For many years, Johnstone didn't know exactly how to reply. But after the Los Angeles riots, he knew why. "If all the Billy Johnstones out there in Los Angeles had the courage to stand up and say that this will not be tolerated, the beating of Rodney King would not have happened. If you're committed to equality, you're going to make enemies. I look to see who my enemies are. If my enemies are the haters and the cowards, we'll win the prize. The prize is civil rights. The prize belongs to all of us. It's ours. It's our humanity. It enriches *all* of us."

*New Patriots in Government
Work in Partnership with Citizens.*

Four out of five Americans do not believe that government serves them, but rather that it is "run for the benefit of the few and special interests."[17] Any candidate who wants to go *to* Washington now runs *against* Washington. But the new patriots in government refuse to engage in this self-hatred. Because they believe in self-governance, they are entering public service in order to create a new kind of partnership with the citizenry.

One of these new patriots, Camille Cates Barnett, served as city manager of Austin, Texas, from 1989 to 1994. She came into office just after 1,000 members of the city's 10,000-person work force had been laid off because of a Texas-wide economic downturn. "It had been handled awfully," Camille recalls. "Austin had gone from being an economic dream story to just another municipal nightmare. Most people considered city government too arrogant to listen and too incompetent to act. City government was demoralized and disrespected. People actually referred to the city as bankrupt."

Faced with this crisis, Camille decided to build her administration around two words which she placed prominently in every speech: *service* and *leadership*. "I used these words to every audience I saw that day, and for weeks afterwards. Under 'service,' I said: 'We are here to serve. We are a service organization. We are here to solve problems, not to cause them.' Under 'leadership,' I said: 'You have a right to expect that elected leaders talk about the right things, focus our attention on them, and make decisions.' "

When Camille arrived in office, a rule stipulated that the seven city council members, including the mayor, couldn't talk directly to staff but had to communicate through the city manager's office. "The old system was based on mistrust and control," Camille explains. "The city manager was afraid to lose control if he or she did not control the information flow. I introduced a new belief: control comes from shared values and a system for dealing with differences. I told the department heads that we were all on the same team. We would operate on the basis of trust. Specifically, I told the city council that they no longer had to send memos through the city manager's office. I said, 'You can ask the staff directly whatever you want to ask them about. If we can be helpful, contact us. Otherwise, just contact them.' " Within a few weeks paperwork was reduced, efficiency increased, and working relationships strengthened.

The same mistrust that divided city officials from each other had also divided government from citizen. Council meetings customarily began, for example, with a brief item called "citizen communication." Ten citizens who had signed up the previous week were each given a few minutes to have their views heard. Although well-intentioned, this agenda item assured that every meeting began with angry, accusatory statements hurled at defensive city council members.

Troubled by the repeated and predictable acrimony, Camille took a different approach. She asked the citizens who wished to speak to put down not only their names but their intended subject matter, along with their phone numbers. Her goal was simple: first, to see if she could resolve their concerns by telephone to avoid a public process; and second, to enable her staff to prepare themselves to deal with upcoming issues. But this straightforward change, she soon realized, caused suspicion. "Many citizens wondered why we were calling. Were we trying to intimidate them? Were we trying to collect intelligence in advance so that we could overwhelm them? It was amazing how much mistrust there was."

Ultimately the change worked: citizen concerns were handled more effectively than before and the tone of city council meetings shifted from adversarial to collaborative. "We set it up so that it was much less paternalistic, much more of partnership between the government and the community."

"In the beginning," Camille says, "I didn't know how we were going to do it. I just knew that it all had to be done."[18] Today, after completing five years in office, she still keeps her souvenir in her desk—a stamp that reads "Public Serpent"—as a reminder of the challenges government officials continue to face.

True Public Servants Learn to Be Innovators Who Continually Reinvent and Reinvigorate Government.

"Those of us who work in urban areas have to change the way we do business," says Don Vermillion, the administrator of Montgomery County, Ohio, of which Dayton is the major city. The reason for his concern was the obsolete, overlapping structure of metropolitan government. In a county of just over half a million people, this twenty-year veteran of county government had to cope with thirty-one competing jurisdictions. These "multiple local governments," as Don calls them, all operated in the interests of their particular jurisdictions.

"That means maximizing the tax base for your own community," he explains. "But local officials find it difficult to broaden their definition of the community to which they are responsible. They don't see that the future of their own jurisdiction depends on what happens to those around them. Our fate is tied together, but our governments are disconnected. Social ills do not respect city boundary lines. What happens in the center city of Dayton is eventually going to have an impact on the suburban cities around it. There's no way that an area that has a decaying city center is going to remain economically competitive. Only communities that have found ways of forging partnerships across jurisdictions are going to be competitive in the future."

Under Don's leadership, Montgomery County officials worked for fifteen months to develop a tax-sharing plan for the entire area which involved placing a portion of the income from each jurisdiction's property taxes into a pool to assist other communities which were not developing. "People had a lot of opinions about what was fair and what was not," Don says. The result was a fund receiving $5 million a year, much of which is invested in the inner city because everyone has seen that the investment will pay off, not just for the center of Dayton but for the entire community.

But the other, more far-reaching consequence of the tax-sharing plan was that the county began to see itself as a whole community. Instead of competing with each other for new business, the different parts of the county began working together. They began asking themselves how they could make the region as a whole attractive to corporations. In other words, they began thinking of themselves as partners.

"The most important variables," says R. Scott Fosler, president of the National Academy of Public Administration, "are partnership and collaboration." He first started working on public-private ventures in the 1970s in an effort to break down the wall between government and those it is supposed to serve. "The most important public challenges do not lend themselves to approach by a single institution," Scott concludes. "Since there is almost always more than one player involved, the question becomes: how will they work together?"[19]

The inspiring innovations of Austin, Texas, and Montgomery County, Ohio, may not be typical, but they are certainly not isolated. Across the country—from Oregon's innovative "Benchmarks" program to Chattanooga's extraordinary citywide revisioning of its future—local governments are becoming the cutting edge of innovation and change. "Power is devolving to the states and cities," says Peter Harkness, the former editor of *Congressional Quarterly*, who now edits *Governing*, a magazine that chronicles creative public initiatives all across the country.[20]

New Patriots Don't Just Run Against Their Opponents;
They Campaign for Their Communities.

Washington, D.C.'s, continual boxing match is turning the nation off. Kevin Phillips, one of America's leading political analysts, argues that its expensive, ugly slugfests "aggravate more problems than they solve." Voters, Phillips believes, "want a new arrangement." As to those who are still enamored of a world divided into elephants and donkeys, Phillips informs them that the "twenty-first century will make mincemeat of such thinking."[21]

The good news is that candidates at the local level are breaking through the polarization and actually forging partnerships with their opponents. While there are many examples of such breakthroughs, Daniel Kemmis of Missoula, Montana, is one of the most inspiring. Back in 1985, Democrat Kemmis watched a bitter campaign for mayor of Missoula result in a narrow victory for the Republican candidate. The predictable result, in Dan's words, was "a four-year pitched battle with no quarter given by either side."

To Dan's surprise, he found himself appealing to his fellow Democrats to give some leeway to the Republican mayor. "He *is* the mayor," he reminded his neighbors, "and we will all be better off if we support his capacity to govern our city." But few people listened, and the city government's reputation steadily eroded.

To rebuild civic spirit, Dan and the Republican head of the Chamber of Commerce, David Owen, founded a forum called the Missoula Community Roundtable. "We were looking for a better way to do politics," Dan says. "So we fashioned this roundtable where very diverse and even polarized interests could come together and look for common ground."

In 1989, after two years of working closely with the Roundtable, the two men found themselves running against each other for mayor. To take stock of this surprising turn of events, they had breakfast together. "We compared notes," Daniel recalls, "and we both agreed that neither of us wanted to be mayor under the conditions that prevailed under the current administration. We promised each other two things at that breakfast. First, we pledged that whoever was not elected would do whatever he could to support and assist the winner in governing, and would persuade our supporters to do the same. Second, we agreed to do everything we could to conduct the campaign so as to make the first outcome more likely to happen. We pledged to care for the civic fabric, which was fundamental to the ability of *either* of us to govern.

"The campaign," Daniel says, "was a chore. We were often tempted to break the compact. But we didn't trash each other. We had opportunities to do so, but we refused. We went out of our way to refer respectfully to each other."

Eventually Daniel won the election, and David Owen, who continued to be active in local politics, kept both promises. Countless townsfolk have told them how much they appreciated the way the two men conducted themselves. "As a politician," Daniel says, "the amount of pressure to resort to the negative is absolutely enormous. On all levels of politics, candidates resort to very ugly, divisive campaigning. The electorate consistently say they hate it, but it keeps going on because it's effective. In Missoula, we went against the trend—and we have been rewarded with a tremendous strengthening in our civic culture and a heightened respect for public service."

Missoula is just one small town in a state of less than a million people. But Kemmis's experience shows that it *is* possible for political leaders to turn the tide. "It cannot be done by one side, but requires both," Daniel stresses. "The candidates must partner with each other, and a very active citizenry must support the healing process. They must recognize that their political culture is fragile and must be treated with great care."

Wherever and whenever the poison of polarization appears, the antidote is precisely this kind of new patriotism. When independent candidate Angus King ran for governor of Maine in 1994, his slogan was "partnership, not partisanship." Elected over his Democratic and Republican opponents, King became the only head of a state who was free of party affiliation. Calling the Democratic Party a "mainframe in an age of PCs," the iconoclastic lawyer, businessman, and talk-show host is designing an administration which, like Mayor Kemmis's, will focus on collaboration rather than on confrontation with the "other side."[22]

City managers in Texas and Ohio, ministers and rabbis in South Carolina and Milwaukee, bank presidents and community organizers, newspaper editors and government officials, union leaders and environmentalists—all these men and women are part of the emerging citizenship of the twenty-first century. Multiply their stories a thousandfold and one begins to grasp the vast creative renaissance of civic life that is taking root in communities across America.

But there are not yet enough such people. They need allies. They need you and me. They can't renew democracy *for* us, but they can do so *with* us. To help them, we too must practice the new patriotism.

PRACTICING THE NEW PATRIOTISM

America, America,
God shed His grace on thee
And crown thy good with brotherhood
From sea to shining sea.

FROM *"America the Beautiful,"*
KATHARINE LEE BATES (1895)

THIS CHAPTER IS an invitation to join a campaign—not a Republican or Democratic campaign, but an American campaign; not a campaign for office, but a campaign for our country. It is about the principles of citizenship.

As the two preceding chapters have shown, a new patriotism has taken root in the American soil and scores of men and women are practicing it in their daily lives. The new patriots express their love for America every day in countless ordinary acts that serve their fellow citizens and their communities. While these new patriots do not share the same precise beliefs, they do share many of the same fundamental premises of citizenship. If you put these people in a room together and asked them to discuss a controversial issue, they would no doubt differ about the substance. But they would agree about the *process* by which their divergent beliefs could be explored and how the resolution of their conflicts could be sought.

This level of civic consensus is vital. Democracy is a process, not a product. It is how diverse constituencies coexist. It is the fabric of our civil society. What keeps the United States from disintegrating into the Divided States is our fragile yet enduring compact as fellow citizens. To keep America strong and free, we need more than a bureaucratic system of checks and balances. We also need a vital, engaged citizenry that in its day-to-day dealings with one another respect this civic compact.

Every few years a new political hero emerges, and the press asks: Can he save America? One year it is Bill Clinton; the next it is Newt Gingrich, Bob Dole, Colin Powell, or yet another new face. But clearly no one person can make America fulfill its destiny. "If the problem is the disintegration of civil society," says Senator Bill Bradley, "then charismatic leaders won't make the difference."

We must all take responsibility for leadership. No knight on a white horse will save America; but we and our neighbors can. The great orator and patriot from Virginia, Patrick Henry, called on his fellow citizens to pledge allegiance not just to the former colony in which they lived, but to the union of states that was being born. "I am not a Virginian, but an American," he said two hundred years ago. But what does that mean today? Just as his loyalty to America transcended his loyalty to his geographic state, how do we rise above our loyalty to our belief systems?

As always, all of us as individuals must be true to our faiths, adhere to our own philosophies, support the parties of our choice, and vote our consciences. But to serve America's future we must do all these things within a wider framework. We must respect our neighbors' faith and philosophies too, must work with the opposing parties, must respect others who also vote *their* consciences. This is the challenge of citizenship today. This is twenty-first–century patriotism.

As the lyrics of "America the Beautiful" put it, when we ask God to bless our country, we ask Him to "crown" our blessings "with *brotherhood.*" The measure of our citizenship is our connection to each other—the bonds that make us one people. Today some social scientists give the name "social capital" to the interweaving of trust, social ties, and common concerns that underlies genuine community. It is also called collaboration, engagement, revitalizing of citizenship, community building, and myriad other names.[1] But, in essence, it is simply a feeling of kinship—a "fraternal feeling," as Lincoln put it.

As we have seen, the men and women who are America's new patriots all love their country in their own unique ways. Having listened closely to what they say, and watched even more closely what they do, I have found a pattern in their patriotism. Following their example, here are fifty ways we can show we love our country.

1. Take Stock Before You Take Sides.

As you prepare to get involved in public affairs in your own community or nationally, look before you leap. Issues are often framed in a polarized way, so that right from the start partisans will try to force you to choose sides. "You're either with us or against us" is the line you may often hear.

Don't let yourself be bullied by "true believers." Step back for a moment and look at the conflict from as many sides as you can. Listen to your own doubts. Talk about your options with a friend who is also considering joining the fray. Perhaps ultimately you will join one side or the other. But before you engage yourself, consider alternatives that may suit you better.

Before you get involved, find out the real story—or, more likely, *stories.* You will have a stronger, more lasting, and more positive impact if you take stock before you take action.

2. Tell the Truth As Best You Can.

Is it true, as the Annie E. Casey Foundation reported, that the proportion of American children growing up without fathers in the home has quadrupled since 1950? Is it true, as militant pro-gay spokespersons maintain, that 10 percent of American men are homosexuals—or as anti-gay groups argue, is it 1 percent? Is it true that the richest 1 percent of households in America control 40 percent of the nation's wealth? Is it true that California now spends more to jail adults than to educate them?[2]

Facts matter: so does telling the truth. Playing loose with the truth can sometimes score points in the short run. But in the long run, you'll lose the ball game.

The urge to gain power through deception is seductive. Avoid it. Think of yourself as a witness in a trial. When a witness takes the stand, he or she takes a solemn oath to tell "the truth, the whole truth, and nothing but the truth, so help me God." But in public life, candidates hire "spin doctors" who recast the facts to make their candidate look good and their opponents bad. Resist lying. Don't concoct half-truths or manipulate the facts to persuade others. In the long run, the most effective tool you have as a citizen-leader is your credibility. It will only be enhanced by truth-telling.

3. Think for Yourself.

Even if you know the facts, you still have to decide what they mean. Since you will be bombarded by different interpretations, it is vital that you think things through yourself. Don't believe the first "expert" you hear. Be prepared to do your homework and reach your own conclusions. Remember: our country was started by men and women who thought independently.

In the final section of *The Book of Virtues,* William Bennett includes a letter from Thomas Jefferson to his nephew encouraging the young man both to read the Bible and to maintain an inquiring mind. "Do not be frightened from this inquiry by fear of its consequences," the former president advised the young man. "[L]ay aside all prejudice on both sides, and neither believe nor reject anything just because many other persons . . . have rejected it or believed it. Your own reason is the only oracle given you by heaven, and you are answerable, not for the rightness, but uprightness of the decision."[3]

4. Think Like a Minority—Because You Are One.

Whatever your skin color or ancestral country, let go of the idea that you are the norm. Today no ethnic group is the mainstream; no group is a standard of measure for Americanness; no person is average. Even the notion that we can all be categorized as white, black, or brown is obsolete. The 1990 census identified 300 "races," 600 Indian tribes, 70 different Hispanic groups, and

75 multiracial combinations. And if you think "Caucasian" is a racial majority, think again.

Demographers predict that by the year 2000, Los Angeles will be 60 percent nonwhite; San Francisco County, 65 percent. The same transformation is under way in Illinois, Texas, Florida, and to varying degrees, everywhere else in America—from the hundreds of thousands of Middle Easterners in Detroit to the tens of thousands of Hmong refugees from Laos in St. Paul; from the Hispanics spreading across Oregon and Washington to the Vietnamese boat people fishing the bayous of Louisiana.

"It bothers me," said one woman who moved from a predominantly white neighborhood in St. Louis to a mixed neighborhood in Los Angeles. "I feel it's not *my* country anymore." In Monterey Park, a town on the outskirts of metropolitan Los Angeles which has become three-fourths Asian and Hispanic, some white residents say: "It isn't *our* town anymore" or "It isn't an *American* city anymore."[4]

This kind of thinking hurts ourselves, our neighbors and our country. America belongs to everybody, not just to one race or language group. If you are a white person, don't say "We were here first"—because you weren't.

5. Face Your Own Complexity—and America's.

Recognize the richness of your inner contradictions. Witness the full range of your humanity. Respect your own contradictions—they may be one of the greatest gifts you bring to your citizenship, because they will help you deal with America's diversity.

When you listen to almost any heated political debate, whether it's about the Democrats' position on affirmative action or the GOP's "Contract with America," news coverage of these conflicts quotes leaders on both sides who have clear, unambiguous, and often diametrically opposed views. Don't force your feelings to conform to those of either of the adversaries. If you find merit in both positions it can be to your credit: you are entitled to be confused. Whatever position you finally reach, it will be enriched by your integrity.

6. Watch Your Own Shadow.

When you feel the urge to insult someone, take a deep breath. Check to see if what you despise about others is in fact related to what you dislike about yourself. Don't project what you don't like about yourself onto others.

Shortly before he died of AIDS, gay psychologist Jeff Beane said that what angered him most about straight men's homophobia was its hypocrisy. "I hate it when I hear right-wingers talk about the danger that gays represent to the community," Jeff said. "They make it sound like we are all child molesters. But they never talk about the children molested by straight men, or the children molested by their parents. Instead of turning each other into demons, let's be honest about our own failings—and our own fears."

7. Know Your Adversaries.

Even if you can't (or don't want to) get together with those on the "other side," learn about them. Read what they write. Tune into one of their TV channels for a while. Attend one of their meetings. Listen to one of their favorite speakers on the radio. No one says you have to change your mind.

On the contrary, learn about how *their* minds work so that you can communicate with them more effectively. Even if you consider them your enemies, knowledge about them is better than ignorance.

Don't gather information about them like a prosecutor seeking a conviction; see yourself as a fellow citizen seeking a connection. The vast majority of your opponents are genuinely concerned about the well-being of their families and the values of their community. Treat them as if they are well-motivated—that is, until they prove they are not.

8. Don't Be Trapped by Your Stereotypes.

Being wary of other citizens different from yourself is normal. But keep an open mind. Test your fears: don't be trapped by them. Sometimes your fears pose a greater danger to you than whatever triggered them.

In 1993, a Vietnamese family, including a gray-haired grandmother, was about to cross a set of train tracks in East Los Angeles when the crossing bar malfunctioned. Their car was trapped in the middle of the tracks. A young Latino man, hearing a train approach, looked up and saw the family's plight. He raced to their car to alert them to the danger. The family, however, fearing being robbed, rolled up their windows and locked the doors. Finally, they came to their senses. With his help, they leapt to safety—all of them except the grandmother. The car was dragged several hundred feet before it ignited and the grandmother, still in the car, burned to death.

What seems like a threat may actually prove to be an opportunity. Learn to recognize the difference.

9. Develop Your Public Judgment.

You use your judgment every day in your personal life. You ask yourself who can be trusted, and how much, and why. You use your intuition about whom to befriend and whom to reject; whom to do business with and whom to avoid. Just as you value your private judgment, also learn to develop your public judgment. Take responsibility for honing your knowledge, skills, and intuition about public matters.

None of us is born with the full understanding citizenship requires. That is something we must learn. "The public is not magically endowed with good judgment," says veteran pollster Daniel Yankelovich. "Good judgment is something that must be worked at all the time and with great skill and effort."[5] Obviously you cannot be knowledgeable about every issue of public concern. So pick an area that is of particular interest or relevance to you and begin developing your civic judgment about that. Learn to discriminate between sound arguments and empty rhetoric. Distinguish groups that provide sound, thoughtful leadership in a policy area from those that are inflammatory and self-serving. As you gain confidence in your own judgment, then you can become involved in public affairs yourself.

10. Avoid Exaggeration, Hyperbole, and Other Rhetorical Excess.

"Let us appeal to the sense of patriotism of the people," said Lincoln to the First Republican Convention in Illinois, "and not to their prejudices."[6]

Don't resort to getting attention on the cheap. Speak lean, not fat. Give your fellow citizens credit for being able to handle the truth, unembellished and unvarnished. Overblown rhetoric, whether its political bias is liberal or conservative, is not based on love of country but on a quest for power.

"There is a difference between utterance and conversation," says Senator Bill Bradley, who advocates responsibility—as well as freedom—of speech. "Spinning out racist clichés and stereotypes, scurrilous character attacks, and zingy one-liners is not the talk of a vibrant civil society. They are the yelps of demagogues."[7]

As Rush Limbaugh wisely warned the nation, following the terrorist attack on the federal building in Oklahoma City, "an even greater danger to the nation than the bombing" is the "danger of losing the language—the words that convey thoughts, that lead to ideas, that produce progress." But identifying the problem is only the first step. The next step in dealing with this danger (which as yet Mr. Limbaugh has not taken) is to pledge to stop publicly abusing the language—and each other. The nation will fare better if we debate the issues, not debase each other.[8]

11. *Turn the Desire for Revenge into a Commitment to Change.*

The world is full of vengeance. Instead of seeking it, transmute your fury against your enemy into a fierce commitment to change. In that way you can help the next generation of Americans free themselves from the curse of looking for revenge.

When Nathan McCall and his black brothers used to beat up on whites, they called it "getting some get-back." They were, writes McCall, "securing revenge for all the shit they'd heaped on blacks all these years." After serving time in prison for armed robbery, McCall studied journalism, became a reporter, worked at the *Washington Post,* and finally wrote *Makes Me Wanna Holler: A Young Black Man in America.* He now is not vengeful; he has a voice.

Anyone who has been hurt or whose loved ones have been hurt feels the urge to seek retribution. We want our enemies to suffer just as we (or our ancestors) have suffered. But that only perpetuates the cycle of pain.

If your desire to get involved is rooted primarily in revenge—to "get some get-back"—please don't.

12. *Stand Up Against Bigotry in All Its Forms.*

Protect the public arena. When confronted with demagoguery, name it. Expose it. Challenge it—not with frenzy or fear, but with clarity and firmness.

To say that Democrats are the "enemy of normal Americans" or "traitors" (as Representative Newt Gingrich once did) or to assert that Christian conservatives are uneducated and easily brainwashed (as the *Washington Post* once did) is not patriotic. To borrow a phrase from a bygone era, it is un-American. Liberals complain loudly when conservatives resort to bigotry, but then resort to it themselves. Similarly, blacks and Latinos complain about white racism— as they should. But according to a comprehensive national survey conducted by pollster Louis Harris for the National Conference, "The truth is that minorities are more likely than whites to agree to negative stereotypes about other minority groups."[9]

Whether coming from the Left or the Right, venomous hostility directed at any of our fellow citizens—blacks, Jews, gays, corporate executives, devout Christians, television producers, or government officials—isn't an expression of patriotism, but a violation of it.[10]

In December 1993, a racist group in Billings, Montana, threw a cinder block through the bedroom window of a local elementary school student, Isaac Schnitzer. It was clearly a hate crime, because in that window Isaac had placed a menorah, the candleholder that symbolizes the Jewish holiday of Hanukkah. The townspeople did not call in the national news media or national advocacy groups. Instead, they organized. The local newspaper printed a full-page picture of a menorah, and the editor encouraged readers to place the picture in their own windows. By the end of the month, 10,000 menorahs adorned the homes in this freedom-loving Rocky Mountain town.

If only the few Jews in town had responded, the racist attacks would have continued. Instead, all the people of Billings responded. Thousands of Christians stood by a Jewish family. Together, they put the new patriotism to work, and the hate crimes stopped.[11]

13. Hold Your Own Beliefs Sincerely, but Responsibly.

Norman Vincent Peale once received a phone call from a hospitalized man who told the late Christian leader that he found great comfort in his writings. However, the ailing man said, he was troubled by Peale's constant references to Jesus Christ, because he himself was Jew. "That's no problem," Peale responded. "Just change the word 'Jesus' to 'God.' " When Mrs. Peale recounted this story after her husband's death, she added that Muslims might want to change the word to "Allah" and agnostics might replace it with "Higher Power."

The Peales did *not* say (as others have) that God is deaf to the prayers of Jews or Muslims. They did not say that Jesus Christ is the way to salvation and that all others are destined to eternal damnation. Despite their advanced years and their deep and abiding faith in the Son of God, they opened their hearts to the beliefs of others.[12]

If you want to hang the Ten Commandments in a public building (as Billy Byrne, chairman of the County Commission in Cobb County, Georgia, tried to do), you may be sincere, but you are not acting responsibly. It is not true, as Byrne's supporters argued, that the Ten Commandments are the basis of Western law. They are *one* of its bases. The difference matters. Ultimately, it is the difference between democracy and theocracy, between freedom and fascism.[13]

Your freedom to believe whatever you want involves responsibility, to your neighbors and to your country. If you believe God is a New York Yankees fan, die-hard Red Sox fans will no doubt take exception. More seriously, if you portray the Son of God with long, flowing blond hair and blue eyes, be prepared for trouble. Is it an artist's right to draw him that way? Of course it is. But is that how the historical Jesus actually looked? Not likely.[14]

Until a celestial paparazzi manages to get a snapshot of the Creator, and until the Gallup poll manages to interview the Son of God by phone, we are each left with our own image of how they look and think. We may seek insight from the Bible, the Torah, or the Koran, from the sound of an organ as it fills the sanctuary where we worship, or from the morning sunlight flickering on a newborn baby's face. But as journalist E. J. Dionne has observed: "Although human beings may hope to know 'God's will,' they shouldn't confuse their own ideas with God's."[15]

14. *Respect the Integrity of All Religious Faiths.*

"The Declaration of Independence states that the Creator gave man the right to liberty," said Czech President Vaclav Havel when he accepted the Philadelphia Liberty Medal on July 4, 1994. "It seems man can realize that liberty only if he does not forget the one who endowed him with it."

But worshiping God is different than using Him. Some people seem to be trying to reduce God to the status of a political supporter. They portray God as partial to everything from specific economic policies to social positions and even to certain political candidates. But God is not a lobbyist. The Trinity is not a special interest group and the Bible is not a party platform.

Any church, just like any individual believer, is entitled to be as rigid in its faith as it wishes. What outsiders consider rigid, the faithful may consider devout; and what others may see as intolerance, believers may interpret as sincerity. But when we leave our place of worship and enter the public arena, our private religion must give way to mutual respect.

There are 1,600 denominations in America. If you want to spread the word about your religion, feel free to do so. But in a democracy, your neighbors are under no obligation to listen.

All across the country, local communities are recommitting themselves to tolerance. In Colorado Springs, Rabbi Howard Hirsch of Temple Shalom and the Most Reverend Richard C. Hanifen, a Catholic bishop, chose the phrase "covenant of mutual respect" to be the title of a newspaper advertisement promoting interfaith dialogue which they and ten other religious leaders (including Focus on the Family's Dr. James Dobson) placed in their local paper. Their statement concluded: "We covenant together to conduct our common life by scriptural standards of justice, mercy, righteousness, and peace." In South Orangetown, New York, Catholics, Jews, Protestants, Hindus, Muslims, atheists, and agnostics formed the Religion, Respect, and Diversity Committee. Together they have developed a policy for their schools which respects the diversity of their community. And at Vanderbilt University's Freedom Forum First Amendment Center, eighteen organizations, ranging from the Christian Coalition to People for the American Way, signed a Statement of Principles on Religious Liberty, Public Education, and the Future of American Democracy.

Find out more about how these three groups found common ground, and apply what you learn in your own community.

15. Practice Humility.

Democracy "requires something more than the religious devotion to moral ideals," wrote the distinguished Protestant theologian Reinhold Niebuhr. "It requires religious humility."[16]

No matter how firmly you or I hold our beliefs, neither of us has all the answers. You wouldn't want a carpenter fixing your plumbing, or a barber setting your broken leg. Similarly, in public life, we need each other and the wisdom each of us can offer. Since no one has all the answers, humility is just another word for being honest.

Unfortunately, many of our role models in civic affairs are politicians who pretend that they have answers for everything; that they are experts and we are not; and that those who disagree with them are stupid, selfish, or otherwise unfit for public service. Becoming active in public life does not mean you have to act the way they do.

When you speak publicly, be true to your own personality and your own instincts. People like to hear what you think and what you have learned, and then reach their own conclusions. Citizen-leaders who are down-to-earth and considerate of their audiences fare better in the long run than those who are self-inflated or arrogant. Even if you've done your homework and are more knowledgeable than others, don't act like a know-it-all. You know how unpleasant it feels when someone "talks down" to you; so don't do it to others.

"I do not forget," wrote one of the wisest students of the human mind, C. G. Jung, "that my voice is but one voice, my experience a mere drop in the sea, my knowledge no greater than the visual field in a microscope, my mind's eye a mirror that reflects a small corner of the world. . . ."

16. *Ground Your Citizenship in Learning.*

"Ignorance is preferable to error," Jefferson wrote in his *Notes on the State of Virginia*. "He is less remote from the truth who believes nothing than he who believes what is wrong."

Acknowledge and respect your own ignorance. Not knowing is the first step toward learning, and a vital part of citizenship. Whenever we are willing to admit that we do not know, we open ourselves to learning something new. This means shedding our old skins, which takes courage. It also means discovering that we can sometimes be wrong and that our adversaries, to our amazement, can sometimes be right. The truth, like the offerings in a collection plate passed along church pews, is greater than whatever any one person places in it.

"What people don't understand," observes Peter Senge, founder of MIT's Organizational Learning Center, "is that you can be an advocate and an inquirer at the same time. People think that they either have to be fervent believers who are absolutely convinced that they are right, or a sort of milquetoast, not committed to anything, always interested in the next view or the next poll, always saying on-the-one-hand this and on-the-other-hand that. In fact, you can have convictions, and at the same time be inquiring about your convictions. Most of the situations we face are complex, have many different constituencies, have many different points of view. Our challenge as citizens is to continue learning how to be advocates for the whole."

17. *Speak More than One Language.*

When you are exasperated with someone, you may blurt out angrily: "You're not listening." That may be true. But it is also possible that you are not speaking in the idiom of that person's belief system.

Just because English is the country's official language does not mean that we are speaking it the same way. Some of us speak the language of the Bible. Others speak the language of the law. Still others speak the corporate language of bottom lines, inputs, and outputs; and so on. One reason Americans are losing patience with each other is that there is no single "language" that everybody speaks. When you think you can't stand hearing another word about someone else's point of view, take a deep breath and try to learn the language they speak.

18. *Learn To Listen.*

Although our nation is inundated with talk radio and TV talk shows, we need to listen more carefully to what our fellow citizens are trying to tell us. Listening is just as important as speaking, or more so. Until your adversaries recognize that you are listening to them, they will not listen to you.

Recall for a moment what it feels like to talk when someone is not listening. That is where our nation is today. Everyone wants to "have their say"; but no one wants to "lend an ear." The place to begin changing this is in our own daily lives. Listen carefully to people who talk to you. Expect them to listen carefully to you. When people "tune out," tell them you've noticed. When TV sponsors shouting matches, don't watch. Foster genuine dialogue in your home, your workplace, and your community.

To listen deeply, first practice being still, which means more than just not talking. It means being "empty" inside so that you can truly hear and see another. An old Vietnamese poem, recalled by Thich Nhat Hahn, describes this state: "If the pond of your mind is still/the beautiful light of the moon/will be reflected in it."

19. Beware of Blame.

Don't be seduced by eloquent orators who always hold someone else responsible for America's ills. Ultimately, the blame game will turn against us all.

Immediately after the Oklahoma City bombing, most of the nation leapt to the conclusion that the culprits would be Muslim terrorists like those who attempted to blow up the World Trade Center. Arabs in Oklahoma, like Suhair al-Mosawi, a refugee from Iraq, had to crouch behind locked doors with her children after rocks shattered her living room windows. It was not just ignorant, hate-filled hoodlums who jumped to the wrong conclusion: savvy government officials did, too. Former U.S. Representative Dave McCurdy of Oklahoma announced pompously after the bombing that he had "very clear evidence" pointing to "fundamentalist Islamic terrorist groups."

"Believe me, every heart is the same," said a young Arab immigrant named Khalid on KABC's talk radio "Bob Grant Show" in New York. "So I just beg you to please tell the people, because you have influence, that not everybody is bad, no matter if he's a Muslim or if he's a Christian or he's a Jew."[17]

20. Deal Effectively with Differences.

Whatever the problem, whether it is drugs or the deficit, other people will see it differently. Everybody will have a different opinion—and different solutions. Don't deny the differences; face them. Dealing effectively with differences is as important as the issue itself.

"The single biggest barrier to being able to face the problems in our society—whether it is health care or the environment or poverty—is our inability to deal effectively with our differences," says William Ury, coauthor of *Getting to Yes*. "Do we deal with our differences by excluding others and seeking a unilateral victory that denies their needs? Or do we deal with our differences by including others and seeking a solution that meets our needs and theirs too? We cannot choose to eliminate our differences—nor should we. We *can* choose how we deal with them."

21. Make Criticism Work for You, Rather than Against You.

It doesn't matter who you are: some of those who differ with you will inevitably criticize you. Sooner or later, someone will point a finger at you and say: "*You're the problem*."

Instead of being defensive, take the opportunity to observe your critics. Right or wrong, they are trying to tell you something. They are reminding you that you are not being seen for what you think you are. Listen to them, and turn their attack into an opportunity. Sometimes considering their views can be the catalyst of creativity. Even if they are only partly right, tell them that you recognize the truth in what they say. Sometimes doing so can open their ears, if not their hearts, so that next time *they* will hear *you*.

22. Give Yourself, and Others, Room to Change.

Learning leads inevitably to change. So don't box yourself in. If you watch long enough, you will see that people change.

Sharif Abdullah (a.k.a. Sherwood Sanders), the black activist paralyzed by a police beating in Camden, New Jersey, is today a graduate of Boston University Law School, president of the Forum for Community Transformation in Portland, Oregon, and director of The Common Enterprise's "Three Valleys" project. Becky Delmonico, the young Christian who left her family and joined The Way was kidnapped by deprogrammers hired by her family, rebelled against her family *and* The Way, disappeared for several years to work on a cruise ship, and today will have nothing whatsoever to do with heavy-handed fundamentalists.

The point is, people can change, and often do. This doesn't necessarily mean they are inconsistent. It just means they're learning something.

23. Seek Goals Greater Than Victory.

As you get involved, refocus on your purpose. Do you want to win or to find common ground? To vanquish, or to partner? To have it your way, or find a new way?

Martin Luther King, Jr., had some good advice. In the quest for civil rights in Birmingham, Alabama, King asked all volunteers to sign a pledge that they would follow the ten commandments of nonviolence. Commandment two was: "REMEMBER always that the nonviolent movement in Birmingham seeks justice and reconciliation, not victory."[18]

If your goal is just to gain a victory over opponents on the "other side," then they will seek to undo whatever victory you win. If your goal is justice and reconciliation, they can help you reach your goal.

24. To Fix What's Wrong, Build on What's Right.

As you try to change what's wrong with our country, draw your energy from what's right about America. Don't become obsessed with what's not working, or you will lose your way.

For generations it was considered patriotic to say America is the greatest country on earth. Yet today our evening news seems to consist only of our nation's problems. Acts of violence, cruelty, criminality, wrongdoing, or public conflict are considered newsworthy, but acts of kindness, peacemaking, decency, generosity, or public harmony are ignored.

Don't get lost in the trash. Even as you deal with the bad news, keep yourself rooted in the good news. If the media don't report it, develop your own network for learning what *is* working.

25. Don't Wait for Politicians To Fix It.

Some political leaders are competent; some aren't. But all of them together can't do our job as citizens for us.

For some people, public service is a profession. But for all of us, it must become part of our daily lives. Carolyn Lukensmeyer, who has served as chief of staff for the governor of Ohio and in the chief of staff's office in the White House, compares politics to medicine. "Healing is some people's profession—we call them doctors," she says. "Yet all of us are also responsible for our own health. The same is true in politics. Our elected leaders have responsibility for the body politic, but we as citizens must take responsibility for our own political health."

Every new patriot takes responsibility in his or her own way. Find yours.

26. *Start in Your Own Backyard.*

While your concerns may be national or even global, start closer to home. What-ever the issue on which you focus, it probably has roots in your own commu-nity. It is harder, and more important, to clean up your own backyard than to complain about Washington. "The truth is that there is an army of people who are engaging each other at the local level, creating a sense of community and be-longing," observes Lawrence Chickering, a lifelong conservative and the author of *Beyond Left and Right.* "They all feel cut off from the national inside-the-Beltway debate. They are overcoming a whole range of problems locally, but they are getting very little attention. Because they are cut off from like-minded souls all across the country, they do not know the power they actually have."

If you feel daunted by this challenge, meet Herman Wrice. A Little League coach, Wrice began losing some of his best players to drugs. His Mantua neighborhood in Philadelphia had become infested with crack houses, and no-body could get rid of them because everyone was afraid of the drug dealers. Wrice began organizing demonstrations outside crack houses to expose and to shame the junkies inside as well as the crack heads who came to buy drugs. Be-cause of the activities of his organization, Mantua Against Drugs (MAD), dozens of crack houses have been shut down. The crime rate has declined in Mantua at more than twice the rate in the rest of the city. Wrice has helped train citizens in other communities to achieve similar results, from Tyler, Texas, to Marion, Indiana, to southeast Washington, D.C.

"People can't wait for the system to work," says Wrice. "The [city] can help, but the cops can't be on the block all the time."[19] The only solution to many problems is for citizens, acting within the law, to take responsibility themselves.

27. *Link Your Issues to the Values of Your Community.*

When the churches of East Brooklyn, working with the Industrial Areas Founda-tion, decided to develop housing that people with low incomes could afford to buy, it was a risky move. They were not expert home-builders or real estate de-velopers. But they knew something had to be done to save their community, which was filled with boarded-up, abandoned buildings which were magnets for crime. They did not call their initiative a "housing project," however. They named themselves The Nehemiah Story, after the Old Testament prophet who led his people in the rebuilding of the walls of Jerusalem.

"Once they named themselves The Nehemiah Story," observes Harry Boyte, cofounder of the American Civic Forum, "it stopped being just a housing project. It wasn't about bricks and mortar anymore. It was about rebuilding community and restoring hope."

28. Build Bridges; Don't Blow Them Up.

Confronted by groups opposed to your beliefs, you will often feel tempted to write them off—they seem so hostile, so belligerent, so unreasonable. These feelings are both natural and common. But rather than letting them dominate your behavior, keep your options open. Find ways to meet with those who anger you. In Colorado Springs, one of the capitals of Christian fundamentalism, the Citizens Project hosted potluck dinners in people's homes, bringing together members of activist Christian organizations and those who feared them. Sharing food around a dining room table, the two sides began to know each other as neighbors, not as stereotypes. For many of them, it was the first time they had met face-to-face with the "other side" in a private, personal way. By the time dessert was served, a lot of stereotypes had fallen away. While the rest of the nation polarized, these residents of Colorado Springs began to find common ground.

29. Learn the Art of Collaboration.

"Stick to your guns." "Don't give in." "Fight all the way."

That's what many of us consider to be courage. And at its best, it is. But at its worst, it is inflexibility, rigidity, and an unwillingness to learn or to compromise. Often a compromise is a better outcome than victory by one side or the other. Creative compromises don't always mean "giving in" to the other side, but they do mean giving up "being right." "American agree that, of course, Israelis and Palestinians have to find common ground, and of course black and white South Africans have to get together," says John Marks, founder of Search for Common Ground. "But if you say that we must find common ground here at home, they don't get it. But today's problems are often too complex and interconnected to be settled on a win-lose basis. We're running out of time and money. We have to start optimizing solutions rather than sensationalizing problems."

In sex education, for example, the war has been between those advocating better contraceptive information and availability and those advocating abstinence. Each side argues that their adversary's approach would only make the problem of teen pregnancy worse. According to several studies, however, neither strategy alone is most effective. What seems to work best is *both*. Sexually active teens were more likely to actually use contraception if they participated in a sex education program that included discussion of abstinence. Although it is a small sign and the data still preliminary, it suggests that the best results come when we work together.

30. Focus Small, but Think Big.

Jobs, kids, schools, traffic, crime, the media, local or national elections, etc.—all the pieces fit together. Keep the big picture in mind. Successful projects focus on specific issues, and then connect those issues to others. So if you plan to do something about schools, for example, consider the role of real estate and politics. If you're getting involved in the abortion issue, think about sex education, demographics, health care, maternal and infant nutrition programs. If crime is your concern, familiarize yourself not just with law enforcement but with all of the myriad factors which are involved. The purpose of all this is not to be an expert, but to be an informed citizen. Your knowledge is your insurance policy that your energies will be well spent.

31. Begin with Your Own Power Base.

Recognize your own resources and assets. Develop a strategy for change that builds on these strengths.

We often feel that real power is in other people's hands. So our goal becomes getting *them* to change. Instead, begin where you are: with the people who trust you; the organizations in which you have influence; the networks of which you are a part. If you try to save a neighborhood Little League field from being taken over by developers by yelling at the developers or complaining to the city council, they can just ignore you. But if you get the Little League roster and organize—convene a community meeting and invite the developers and the relevant city officials, and create a power base that compels respect—your kids may still be able to play ball.

32. Engage Unlikely Allies.

Take your cause beyond the borders of your belief system. Test the waters among groups that are not already in your camp.

Besides your like-minded supporters, there are less obvious potential allies who don't expect that you will call on them. Although it may be harder to convince them to join your cause, seek them out. If they don't come aboard, you'll still learn something from their refusal that you need to know. And if they do sign up, they will be able to reach constituencies that would otherwise elude you.

For the last forty-five years, ten cities have been selected annually to be honored as "All-American Cities" for exceptional civic accomplishments, made possible by the collaborative efforts of the city's residents. Again and again, John Parr, former president of the century-old National Civic League, which coordinates the awards program, has observed the crucial role that partnerships have played. "In the past ten years," John says, "projects that won the award have shifted from improving the physical community to dealing with the deeper, more fundamental social problems. Today, the problem that cities are dealing with are much tougher, and the partnerships are consequently much more diverse."[20]

Those who seek to be leaders in the coming century "should be introduced soon to cross-boundary experiences," advises John W. Gardner, chairman of the National Civic League and founder of the Alliance for National Renewal.[21] America is so fragmented into subcultures and subprofessions, he argues, that effective leaders must learn to work with many different groups. More than ever, finding allies "across the border" from one's own belief system will be the key to effective, enlightened citizen action.

33. Mobilize Untapped Resources.

Think fresh. Frame your cause in a new way so that it will appeal to new sources of support.

Good causes almost always lack money, and this breeds discouragement. Start thinking along different lines. Don't approach the predictable sources that are already committed. If your cause is worthy, you should be able to persuade other Americans to contribute time or money. If you cannot persuade enough of your fellow citizens, then reflect on your approach. How we spend money reflects what we care about (or at least what we think we care about). Fund raising is not just a question of money; it's a question of communicating what we care about, and awakening an awareness in others so that they will care about it too.

For example, because he had a vision, Juan Sepulveda, director of The Common Enterprise in San Antonio, received contributions from several corporate funders in Texas. The private sector was concerned about strengthening public education; what they needed was a viable project in which they could invest responsibly. Working with Temple University, Juan tapped a pool of resources that might otherwise have gone elsewhere.

34. Use Your Current Resources More Effectively.

By all means seek support, financial and otherwise, from multiple sources. Submit proposals to foundations; develop revenue-generating projects; apply for government grants; ask wealthy individuals for donations; and so on.

But, in a time of growing need and decreasing funds, start with what you have. Stretch it. Leverage it to secure other in-kind contributions. Demonstrate that you can make one dollar do the work of two. Doing so will help you accomplish more with your existing resources and demonstrate to potential funders that you are a good investment.

35. Seek Durable, Long-Term Solutions.

Think long-term. Focus on underlying causes, not symptoms. Don't invest so much energy in winning a battle that you are unprepared for peace. Avoid quick fixes that unravel almost as fast as they were made.

Sometimes a big rally or a splashy headline can give a quick boost to your efforts, but don't be misled by the noise and the publicity. Think about the day after the event, or the week after the news story. Plan a strategy that is as much as possible self-sustaining and that focuses on fundamental, lasting change.

36. Bring Everybody to the Table.

Make your community work for all its members. Don't get sidetracked by thinking that a small group of like-minded power brokers should set the agenda. In the process of decision-making, include everybody who will be affected by the decision.

Surprisingly, some people are nostalgic for a time when a few city fathers could make all the decisions for a city quickly and clearly; but in the long run, the decisions these "old boys' clubs" made created hosts of problems which our generation and those that follow have to solve.

As you become engaged in your community, bring all relevant parties into the discussion. Make sure all their voices are heard. Listen to dissent. Since an effective policy requires the cooperation of all of them, monitor the discussion to ensure the widest possible agreement. Superficial consensus will produce only superficial change.

It is natural to begin with a like-minded group with similar backgrounds. But don't wait until the major issues are resolved to bring in people with other points of view and life experiences. If your group is too homogeneous, you will scare away people who are different. Seeking diversity is more than being "politically correct"; it is morally right—and often effective.

37. In a Fight, Stake Out the High Ground.

Getting along with one's adversaries is not always possible. There comes a time when we have to choose between one side and the other. "Win/win" solutions are wonderful, but sometimes loss is inevitable. In such circumstances, claim your turf carefully.

If the school board plans to adopt a curriculum you find offensive and a group in your community invites you to join the school board members who favor its adoption, you have every right to stick to your guns and fight. But first ask yourself: what is the higher ground? How do we make the school system serve children better? How do we fight this battle in a way that does not just start another?

As Jim Wallis writes in *The Soul of Politics:* "We can find common ground only by moving to higher ground."

38. Make Sure the Media Serve You.

Just as a food diet loaded with salt, fat, and sugar will affect your physical health, a media diet heavy with hostility, blame, confrontation, and violence will bias your civic outlook for the worse. The point isn't to filter out whatever is uncomfortable or disconcerting, but rather (as Elizabeth Thoman, author of *Citizenship in a Media Age* and founder of the Center for Media and Values puts it) to "navigate more consciously" through the sea of words and images that reach you through the media.

George Abbott, the veteran Broadway writer-director (*A Tree Grows in Brooklyn, Damn Yankees,* et al.) who recently died at the age of 107, believed that people fill the theaters in search of "refreshment of the spirit."[22] If that's not what you're getting from your media diet, then look for a better one.

39. Use Your Own Eyes and Ears.

To be a new patriot, develop sources of information that do not depend on the media. Talk and listen directly to your neighbors. What we need, as Eric Utne, publisher of the *Utne Reader,* puts it, is *dis*-intermediation. "Neighbors need to start meeting again without a newspaper or TV standing in their way," he says.

Form a neighborhood organization or create an informal association on your block. Find the reliable sources of information in your community. Link with other similar groups in your city. Develop personal contacts that allow you to check what you read in the newspaper or see on the TV news against your own sources. Since your time is limited, don't try to do this alone. Get information from a human network, not just the electronic networks and the print media.

40. Monitor Your Children's Storytellers.

If a stranger came to your front door and said he wanted to talk to your children about sex, what would you do? Would you invite him in and leave him alone with your children? Would you question him about his motives? Or would you slam the door and call the police?

Television speaks directly to your children about sex and violence. It tells them stories which are primarily designed not to educate them as family members and as citizens, but to reach a maximum audience. If you don't like what's on the screen or on the radio, speak up. Don't let yourself be intimidated by those who claim it is "Right Wing" or even "fascist" to demand moral standards on what is broadcast: conservatives and liberals alike are becoming outraged. The media are "poisoning the minds of our young people," says Republican Senate leader Bob Dole, with "destructive messages of casual violence and even more casual sex." Scores of liberal lawmakers agree.

Whether you prefer a liberal organization (such as the Citizens Coalition on TV Violence or Action for Children's Television) or one of the more conservative alternatives (such as the American Family Association or the Christian Film and Television Commission), get involved in the debate. If children, as Marian Wright Edelman of the Children's Defense Fund observes, "are God's presence, promise, and hope for humankind," then those who love children must put their interests first—before ratings, before profits, and perhaps hardest of all, before pride. To be new patriots, we must care more about their welfare than about winning, more about children's rights than about being right.[23]

41. Make Schools Safe for Democracy.

Two teachers were fired not long ago for standing up for their beliefs: Carol Marlowe, a liberal white teacher in Arizona who allowed her high school drama class to read a play with controversial ideas and language; and Bishop Knox, a conservative black principal in Alabama who allowed his students to read a prayer over the high school's public address system.

The result of reading the controversial play and the Christian prayer in school was controversy. But Marlowe's and Knox's students began to educate themselves about the matter. They started a debate about freedom of speech. When students see that other people who hold fundamentally different views can engage in respectful dialogue about their differences, they learn something valuable about citizenship.

Conflicts about freedom of speech, separation of church and state, and scores of other old and new issues will not vanish. You can help ensure that those conflicts expand debate rather than constrict it, and serve your children's education, rather than threatening it. Let's not fire teachers who have strong, legitimate beliefs that create controversy, but rather find ways to let those controversies serve our children's education.

42. *Encourage Communicators to Listen to Their Conscience.*

No organization can function for the public good without moral courage and human decency on the part of the individuals within it. Give your support to those in the communications industry who, as an act of conscience, take risks for the public good.

"The great American viewing audience," says veteran TV producer Norman Lear, founder of People for the American Way, "will be far better served the day television decision makers decide to drop [their] numbers-driven mental maps . . . in favor of developing those programs that flow solely from their tastes and sensibilities, from their capacities for awe and wonder and mystery, from their humanity and compassion, and from the voice within that may be saying even now, 'This is right, this is *right.*' "[24]

But they need our help to do this. Write letters rewarding acts of moral courage and condemning moral cowardice. Let your voice be heard.

43. *Remember That* Local *Matters As Much As* National.

While politicians argue about more government versus less government, join your fellow citizens and stand up for self-governance. Let this great nation be "of, by, and for the people." Help lower the political center of gravity so that all the people are empowered.

Whether conservative or liberal, citizens on both sides of the ideological fence have gotten lazy. We have asked politicians to fix things which we know we must deal with ourselves.

In 1975, Neil Pierce began a self-syndicated column focusing on important trends in community life. While other journalists eagerly sought promotions to their Washington bureaus, his goal for the past two decades has been to get closer and closer to the grass roots. Pierce views his job as covering the kinds of community stories that aren't being reported in the national press because they are considered too small.

"I looked at small, unromantic, unspecial places for new and important developments," says Pierce, whose unique "Pierce Reports" have appeared in local newspapers throughout the country. "I believed that social change might emerge among people who were not experts, who were not social theorists, who were not government officials, but who were ordinary citizens. People need to have the experience of making their own decisions and making their own mistakes, rather than focusing only on federal action."

44. Make Time for Citizenship.

Citizenship not only requires courage. It also takes time, and it seems harder than ever nowadays to find a minute to spare. But that's no excuse. "Do basketball fans complain," asks history professor Robert Wiebe, "when their team makes the play-offs, forcing another round of games with a new opponent? Why should control over one's daily life somehow be less engaging?"[25]

You spend time on what matters to you. The fate of your favorite sports team clearly does not matter more than the fate of your neighborhood. Democracy needs fans, too. Right now, the sports arenas at NBA games are full, and the local school board meetings are not. Perhaps that is related to why we have the best basketball players in the world and some of the lowest student test scores. Compute the total time you spend each week with the entertainment media, and devote a fraction of that amount to your civic life.

Even if you in fact have no time to spare, you can still make a difference. Ask someone else with a lighter schedule to be your partner and keep you posted on local affairs. Empower him or her to speak for you.

45. Clean Up Political Campaigns.

While we were waiting for politicians to start cleaning up their campaigns, things just got worse. As long as politicians can win using dirty tactics, they will use them. They will stop using those tactics when they no longer work—and that is *our* job.

Whether you are a Republican, Democrat, or Independent, why not start a "clean campaign" movement in your district? Ask candidates to sign a "clean campaign" pledge with very specific standards of behavior, covering their media advertising as well as statements by their staffs. Tell them that unless they sign the pledge you will not vote for them.

Three out of four Americans who voted in the 1994 election said they disliked negative ads, and six out of ten who did not vote said negative ads were one reason why they stayed home.[26] If enough citizens joined the "clean campaign" movement, the quality of our elections would improve. The change will not happen overnight, but it *will* happen.

Representative Jim Leach (R-Iowa) took a step in the right direction when he called on candidates of both parties to pledge allegiance to a "new political ethic" that would require them not to exploit racial, religious, or ethnic tensions. "For American reality to match American ideals," Leach said, "public officials have a special responsibility to uplift rather than tear down, to unify rather than divide."[27]

It was a good first step. The next step is ours.

46. If You Intend to Push Hard for Change, Protect Yourself.

Change cuts both ways. It threatens people, and when people are threatened, they may try to hurt you. Don't be naive about the risks in going public. Protect yourself—not out of paranoia, but out of prudence.

Whether you are pushing for gun control or against abortion, for sex education or against gay rights, someone else will fear that your proposals threaten them or violate their beliefs. Realize that you may be attacked and be prepared. And the harder you push, the more prepared you must be. Consider ways you can bear witness to your cause that are less frightening for others and less dangerous for you.

Meanwhile, be vigilant. No matter how hard you try, or how widely you open your heart to your fellow citizens, others may hate you if they think it serves their purpose. When you dare to stand for something, you may become a target. Taking action involves risks. And remember: if there were no risk, there would be no call for courage.

47. Let Your Love for Your Country Go Beyond the National Borders.

If you love America and its people, don't let our national borders become a barrier. America's citizens—our neighbors—come from everywhere; and the families and relatives of our fellow citizens live in literally every country of the world. Economically as well as ecologically, our well-being is intertwined with that of millions who are *not* Americans. America is not an island; it is part of the planet. Your water and your air, your job and your children's future, all are affected by what goes on beyond our borders. Foreigners are part of your community, whether you like it or not. Their relatives here pitch for your local baseball team. They are chefs in your local restaurants. They build parts for the car you drive. Foreigners are part of our lives.

48. Be a Respectful Leader.

"The first responsibility of a leader," wrote Max de Pree, CEO of Herman Miller, "is defining reality."[28] And the reality is that if a leader loves this country, he must lead both those who agree with him and those who disagree.

When it was time for the Founding Fathers to draft the Declaration of Independence, they chose a committee which included Benjamin Franklin, the widely admired John Adams, and two other veteran statesmen, Roger Sherman and Robert Livingston. But the man who received the most votes was the committee's fifth member, Thomas Jefferson, who was immediately made chairman and asked to draft the document.

Certainly one of the reasons this young Virginian was elevated so quickly to the top was his character. During his first year in the Continental Congress, he was generally silent while on the floor. But Jefferson listened closely to others and was persuasive in private. As the debate over the country's future swirled around him, Jefferson was firmly on the side of revolution. But he refused to be antagonistic toward those who felt differently. On the contrary, he worked with them and showed respect for their views. It was his decency, as much as his writing skills, that made him so respected. Unlike the revolutionary firebrands who were contemptuous of their timid countrymen, Jefferson knew that, once nationhood became a reality, they would all be partners in the grand experiment. If they wanted a truly *United* States of America, they had to treat each other with respect.[29]

It was true two hundred years ago. And it is true today.

49. Have Faith in Democracy.

Forces are at work in our nation that make us anxious. If you are a fundamentalist Christian, the secular humanists frighten you; and if you are a secular humanist, the Religious Right seems dangerous. Almost everyone feels that one group or another is out to destroy our country. Often things seem out of control.

Don't despair. Democracy is a remarkable invention. A free society is resilient and capable of rebalancing itself. When secularism pulls us as a people too far away from spiritual values, some of our fellow citizens organize to pull us back. And if they go too far and become dogmatic and authoritarian, another group will sooner or later emerge to challenge them and limit their power. But this process of checks and balances does not happen by magic, and it does not happen just inside the Beltway. It depends on you and me and every one of us who call ourselves Americans. Keep the faith—in democracy.

50. (Fill in the Blank.)

This list of suggestions, gleaned from conversations with new patriots from all across the country, is my list, not yours. I will not complete it, because the truth is that the way you show your love for your country is up to you. Don't sit back and think about whether you like my list or not. Make your own. Contact one of the organizations you have read about in this book. Decide for yourself how you will love your country. Create your own agenda for repairing this magnificent house we call America.

The privilege of being an American citizen is having freedom. The challenge of being an American is using it.

Resource List

THE FOLLOWING organizations are resources for citizens who wish to explore further dimensions of the new patriotism.

For reasons of space, this list includes only a few of the many organizations that are working to reunite the Divided States of America. Obviously many other organizations that should be included were not listed because they could not handle direct inquiries from the public. In addition, many other groups that do excellent work are not included here because their orientation remains primarily partisan.

Although this resource list is limited, it provides an excellent starting point for citizens eager to become involved in revitalizing America.

In addition to the research of Matt Moseley, I especially appreciate the assistance of Millennium Communications, the staff of Senator Bill Bradley, the Alliance for National Renewal, and the Center for Living Democracy.

All-America City and Community Award Program
National Civic League
1445 Market St., Suite 300
Denver, CO 80202-1728
1-800-223-6004
Designates ten cities each year for their civic excellence and their success in meeting the challenges of difficult and complex problems through innovative and collaborative ways.

Alliance for Community Media/ Minneapolis Television Network
125 South East Main St.
Minneapolis, MN 55414
612-331-8575

MTN provides community access to communication and information networks. We strengthen community by encouraging creation of and access to programs and information using electronic technology. We support freedom of expression for all.

Alliance for National Renewal
1445 Market St., Suite 300
Denver, CO 80202
1-800-223-6004
ANR is a collaborative initiative of more than 120 organizations that gives a national voice to diverse community-building projects. Its goal, in the words of John Gardner, its founder, is "to give national attention to local innovators . . . and to spread the good news about the successes of their projects."

Alliance for Redesigning Government/ NAPA
1120 G St., NW, Suite 850
Washington, D.C. 20005
202-347-3190
The mission of the Alliance for Redesigning Government is to generate a more effective system of governing in the United States.

The American Project
One Copenhill Ave.
Atlanta, GA 30307
404-881-3400
The America Project serves as a catalyst and link between communities that are striving to create a collaborative, holistic project.

America Speaks
Citizens Revitalizing Democracy
915 15th St., NW, Suite 600
Washington, DC 20005
Its mission is to create a meaningful connection between citizen voices and the institutions that shape public policy at the local, state, and national levels.

Center for Civic Networking
P.O. Box 53152
Washington, DC 20009
202-362-3831
CCN is a research, education, consulting, and applications development group that puts information infrastructure to work to sustain healthy communities and help people of differing viewpoints and values to coexist better.

Center for Community Change
1000 Wisconsin Ave., NW
Washington, DC 20007
202-342-0519
The Center helps build the capacity of low-income and minority community organizations to solve critical problems. Through technical assistance and training, the Center addresses the unique needs and requests of

each community, and helps residents improve their local economic and social conditions.

Center for Consensual Democracy
35 Old Powerhouse Road
Falmouth, ME 04105
207-781-2604
The Center cooperates with and encourages networks between organizations and communities that uphold the principles of consensual democracy. The Center is active in fifty-two communities in seven countries.

Center for Living Democracy
RR#1 Black Fox Road
Brattleboro, VT 05301
802-254-1234
The Center works to promote democracy—not as something we have, but as what we *do*, as a rewarding way of life, instead of merely a structure of government. It distributes a newsletter and "learning tools" catalog to assist citizens in becoming effectively involved in addressing public problems. Its American News Service helps to make widely visible the unseen stories of citizen problem solving.

Center for Media and Values
1962 S. Shenandoah
Los Angeles, CA 90034
310-559-2944
http://www.earthlink.net/~cml
The Center produces and distributes material that educates citizens on media literacy. Their flagship video, *Beyond Blame*, teaches citizens how to be consumers of the media; that all people take responsibility for media that we create, and not blame the "media" for society's problems.

Center for Neighborhood Technology
2125 W. North Ave.
Chicago, IL 60647
312-278-4800
An environmental policy organization that

makes connections with different organizations and also publishes *Neighborhood Works*.

Citizen Magazine
Focus on the Family
P.O. Box 3550
Colorado Springs, CO 80935-3550
Written from a conservative religious perspective, this magazine profiles citizens who have taken action to promote their beliefs. It provides a valuable perspective for those who wish to better understand the values and concerns of conservative Christian activists.

Citizens Jury™
7101 York Ave., South
Minneapolis, MN 55435
612-333-5300
The Jefferson Center originates the Citizens Jury™, which brings together a microcosm of the community to study an issue. Emphasis is placed on bringing together a balanced group of witnesses, conducting the process in a fair way, and being sure the jurors are empowered to speak with an authentic voice on the issue.

Civic Forum
The Hubert Humphrey Institute of Public Affairs
University of Minnesota
Minneapolis, MN 55455
612-625-0142
The institute of Public Affairs' Center for Democracy and Citizenship supports several citizenship-building and civic education programs, including Project Public Life and the New Citizenship.

Civic Practices Network
Pearlman Hall
Brandeis University
Waltham, MA 02254-9110
617-492-1949
http://cpn.journalism.wisc.edu
A network chronicling stories of successful citizen problem solving, they provide an ex-tensive database of other programs as well as tools and services that provide direction for effective community problem solving.

The Civil Society Project
Don E. Eberly, Founder/Director
3544 North Progress Ave., Suite 101
Harrisburg, PA 17110
717-671-1908
The purpose of the project is to foster the broadest possible public understanding of what civil society is, why it matters, and what all Americans must do to help recover it. Toward this end they publish essays on civil society and conduct bipartisan conferences and high-profile town hall meetings.

Coalition for Improving City, State Government
University of Texas at Arlington
School of Urban Affairs
P.O. Box 19588
Arlington, TX 76019-0588
817-273-2145
The Coalition works to strengthen democratic, effective, and trusted government on the local, state, and federal levels.

The Common Enterprise
c/o Rockefeller Foundation
420 Fifth Ave.
New York, NY 10018-2702
(Program Office: 303-939-8605)
Dedicated to revitalizing democracy and citizenship through collaborative problem-solving efforts. In particular, it promotes public dialogue about solving community problems and bridging societal gulfs such as race, ideology, economics, gender, generations, and religion.

Common Ground Network for Life and Choice
1601 Connecticut Ave., NW, Suite 200
Washington, DC 20009
202-265-4300

The Common Ground Network for Life and Choice offers a "meeting place" for pro-choice and pro-life people to dialogue in a nonadversarial manner and to explore ways to address issues and shared concerns, such as teenage pregnancy and inadequate resources for women and children. The Network staff offers facilitation, training, and resource materials.

Community Self-Leadership Project
Campus Box 308 (Davis 144)
Trinidad State Junior College
Trinidad, CO 81082
719-846-5240
This project helps communities set up a dialogue process that enables citizens to form their own leadership network and determine their own civic priorities.

The Dialogue Project
Organizational Learning Center
Massachusetts Institute of Technology
E60-319 Sloan School of Management
30 Memorial Drive
Cambridge, MA 02142
617-253-1549
The Organizational Leaning Center is a consortium of innovative projects working with MIT researchers to build state-of-the-art learning organizations through collaborative research and practice.

Do Something
35 James St.
Newark, NJ 07102
201-643-6373
Do Something is a youth-serving nonprofit targeted at creating community for inner-city youth of Newark. Through diverse neighborhood programs, they are enhancing the leadership skills on the most local level.

The Enterprise Foundation
American City Building
10227 Wincopin Circle, Suite 500
Columbia, MD 21044

410-964-1230
The goal of the Enterprise Foundation is to see that all low-income people in the United States have the opportunity for affordable housing, and to enter the mainstream of American Life.

Freedom Forum First Amendment Center at Vanderbilt University
1207 18th Ave., South
Nashville, TN 37212
615-321-9588
The Center promotes understanding and appreciation of First Amendment values. They also produce "Freedom Speaks" on PBS and publish a monthly newsletter *Freedom First*.

Funder's Committee for Citizen Participation
Carnegie Corporation of New York
437 Madison Ave.
New York, NY 10022
212-371-3200
The Committee was brought together in 1984 to address the alarming decline in voter turnout rates. The Committee convenes to discuss the barriers to electoral participation, with a special interest in lower-income areas and minorities, who find themselves underrepresented in the electorate.

HandsNet
20195 Stevens Creek Boulevard,
Suite 120
Cupertino, CA 95014
408-257-4500
Its mission is to support the human services and public interest community by enhancing its communications, information-sharing, and collaboration capabilities. HandsNet's 3,000 members include national clearinghouses and research centers, community-based service providers, foundations, local and state government agencies, public-policy advocates, legal-services programs, and grassroots coalitions.

Highlander Research and Education Center
Route 3, Box 370
New Market, TN 37820
615-933-3443
Works toward social change through education of social justice issues by conducting a wide variety of activities, including youth and environmental programs.

Humphrey Institute
301 19th Ave. S.
Minneapolis, MN 55455
612-625-8330
Host several conferences each year. Selects 30 fellows to participate in program each year to research public policy and ways to strengthen civil engagement. The Institute houses a number of diverse programs, most notably the Center for Population Control, and Women and Public Policy.

Independent Sector
1828 L St., NW, Suite 1200
Washington, DC 20036
202-223-8100
IS is a nonprofit coalition of more than 800 voluntary organizations, foundations, and corporations with national interest and impact in philanthropy and voluntary action. The organization's mission is to create a national forum that could encourage the giving, volunteering, and not-for-profit initiatives that help all of us better serve people, communities, and causes.

Institute for Self-Governance
720 Market Street
San Francisco, CA 94102
415-981-5353, ext 242
Promoting self-governance and an entrepreneurial way of life through workshops and literature.

Institute for the Study of Civic Values
1218 Chesnut St., 702
Philadelphia, PA 19107
215-238-1434

The Institute helps organize CDCs, civic associations, and citywide coalitions around the ideals of the American democratic tradition. The Institute uses telecommunications to inform people around the country about their efforts and to engage activists and educators in an ongoing dialogue over the strengthening of democracy in the year ahead.

Institute of Faith and Politics
110 Maryland Ave. NE, Suite 306
Washington, DC 20002
An interfaith multicultural, non-partisan organization, the Institute of Faith and Politics provides spiritual guidance for members of Congress, and coordinates race relations in North Carolina and the Southeast.

International City/County Management Association
777 N. Capitol St., NE, Suite 500
Washington, DC 20002-4201
202-962-3612
ICMA is composed of administrators of boroughs, cities, counties, towns, and villages. Its goals include enhancing the quality of local government and supporting and assisting local administrators.

International Healthy Cities Foundation
One Kaiser Plaza, Suite 1930
Oakland, CA 94612
510-271-2660
The purpose of IHCF is to improve communications and develop strategic projects to increase and enhance Healthy Cities–Healthy Communities initiatives worldwide. They are committed to a systemic, participatory, community-oriented, multi-dimensional approach to urban and health issues.

Kettering Foundation
200 Commons Rd.
Dayton, OH 45459
513-434-7300
The Kettering Foundation is a research institute

concerned with politics in the broadest sense, especially democratic politics, to prepare materials for people to use to be effective citizens.

National Association of Community Leadership
200 South Meridian St., Suite 340
Indianapolis, IN 46225
317-637-7408

Through training seminars and educational publications, NACL seeks to inspire and encourage community leadership programs across the country, and to help them address issues of vital importance to their respective communities.

The National Community Building Network
c/o Urban Strategies Council
672 13th St., Suite 200
Oakland, CA 94612
510-893-2404

The National Community Building Network is an alliance of locally driven urban initiatives in more than twenty cities that utilize diverse approaches to building community, expanding economic opportunity, and fighting poverty.

The National Conference
71 Fifth Avenue
New York, NY 10003
212-206-0006

The National Conference is a human relations organization dedicated to fighting bias, bigotry, and racism in America. The National Conference promotes understanding and respect among all races, religions and cultures through advocacy, conflict resolution and public education.

National Federation of Community Broadcasters
666 11th St., NW, Suite 805
Washington, DC 20001
202-393-2355

The National Federation of Community Broad-casters is a nonprofit membership organization representing community radio groups throughout the United States. The Federation offers many services to its members, including technical assistance, system-wide programming support, as well as publications on community broadcasting.

National Institute for Dispute Resolution
1726 M St., NW, Suite 500
Washington, DC 20036
202-466-4764

NIDR fosters the development of innovative conflict-resolution processes. Their goal is to provide those in conflict with the skills and understanding to productively solve problems with a special focus on underrepresented ethnic, economic, and cultural groups.

The New Citizenship Project
1150 17th St., NW, Suite 510
Washington, DC 20036
202-822-8333

NCP helps to forge a cohesive agenda for reinvigorating citizenship. They offer a principled alternative to revitalize civil society and consolidate the historic opportunity for reform.

Pew Center for Civic Journalism
601 13th St. NW, Suite 310 S.
Washington, DC 20005
202-331-3200

The Pew Center administers grants to media partnerships who engage in civic journalism projects.

Points of Light Foundation
1737 H Street, NW
Washington, DC 20006
202-223-9186

The Foundation develops and promotes strategies and methods to recruit and engage more volunteers, and works to increase public awareness of how community service helps to build healthier communities.

Program for Community Problem Solving
915 15th St., NW
Washington, DC 20005
202-783-2961
PCPS assists communities in using collaborative approaches for a wide array of undertakings, such as long-range planning, service delivery, conflict resolution, and program implementation as well as problem solving. PCPS offers training, technical assistance, consultation, and publications for community leaders.

Project on Public Life and the Press— New York University
New York University Department of Journalism
10 Washington Place
New York, NY 10003
212-998-3793
This project is a clearinghouse for information on civic journalism, its theory, and practical applications. Periodic reports describe specific initiatives undertaken by media across the country.

Public Agenda Foundation
6 East 39th St.
New York, NY 10016-0112
212-686-6610
PA works to help citizens better understand critical policy issues and to help the nation's leaders better understand the public's point of view. Its research on how citizens think about policy forms the basis for its extensive citizens education work.

Public Conversations Project
Family Institute of Cambridge
51 Kondazian St.
Watertown, MA 02172
617-924-4400
The Public Conversations Project explores the possibility that family therapists have ways of working with conflict that can be fruitfully applied to the political arena.

Resolving Conflict Creatively Program National Center
163 Third Ave., #103
New York, NY 10003
212-387-0225
RCCP, an initiative of Educators for Social Responsibility (ESR), is a comprehensive K-12 school-based program in conflict resolution and intergroup relations that provides a model for preventing violence and creating caring learning communities. The RCCP model includes in-depth training, curricula, and staff development support for teachers, peer mediation programs, and parent and administrator components.

Search for Common Ground
1601 Connecticut Ave., NW, Suite 200
Washington, DC 20009
202-265-4300
SCG is dedicated to finding workable solutions to domestic and international disputes. Domestically, the Common Ground Network for Life and Choice brings together pro-life and pro-choice supporters to discover areas of common ground.

Study Circles Resource Center
P.O. Box 203
697 Pomfret St.
Pomfret, CT 06258
203-928-2616
A project of the Topfield Foundation, Study Circles promotes deliberative democracy. Its mission is to create involved and educated citizens through small, intensive study groups composed of citizens from diverse backgrounds to discuss crucial and difficult issues.

Who Cares
1511 K St., NW, Suite 1042
Washington, DC 20005
202-628-1691
A national nonprofit magazine that covers community service and activism which aims to educate, challenge, and inspire a new generation of leaders. The web site contains more than 150 youth-led programs.

❧

NOTES

PREFACE

1. America's Talking/Gallup survey of 1,013 adults eighteen years or older conducted June 17–19, 1994. The margin of error is plus or minus three percentage points. In response to the first question, 28 percent consider themselves "somewhat" patriotic, and only 7 percent say they are "not especially" patriotic; 1 percent had no opinion. In response to the second question, 26 percent said "more," 7 percent said "the same," and 4 percent had no opinion.
2. Cited in John Gardner, *On Leadership* (New York, 1990), p. 160.
3. These figures, cited by Harry Boyte ("To Keep the U.S. from Going Adrift . . . ," *Minneapolis Star Tribune*, 10/30/94), can of course have another entirely different meaning. They can be seen as evidence that citizens are no longer willing to be blind to government shortcomings, but have woken up to their responsibility to be self-governing and therefore vigilant. We explore this more fully in Part II.
4. From a speech by Daniel Yankelovich at the National Civic League's "Summit for Community Builders," November 11, 1994. The "veteran political observer" is Knight-Ridder's Bill Bishop: "What Happened to Citizenship?" *Daily Camera* (hereafter referred to as *DC*), 11/20/94.
5. Newt Gingrich's widely reprinted and frequently repeated statement was discussed thoughtfully in "Spiro Agnew With Brains," by Jonathan Alter, *Newsweek*, 11/28/94.

INTRODUCTION

1. "Candidates Respond to Voter Impatience, Cynicism," *DC*, 10/23/94.

PART I

1. A variety of similar phrases that are used interchangeably with "belief systems." Sometimes they are called "paradigms" (following the outline of Thomas Kuhn's *The Structure of Scientific Revolutions*). Others call them "myths" (following the work of Joseph Campbell and others.) Still others prefer the simple word "stories" (as popularized in Daniel Quinn's award-winning novel *Ishmael*). In *A Conflict of Visions,* Thomas Sowell, the distinguished African-American conservative scholar, uses the term "visions." We rely on our visions, according to Sowell, for "our sense of how the world works," because reality itself is too com-

plex for any of us to understand fully. We therefore adopt visions that help us make sense out of our experience. We use them "like maps that guide us through a tangle of bewildering complexities." Thomas Sowell, *A Conflict of Visions,* pp. 14–15.

CHAPTER 1

For their personal interviews, I am grateful to Marlene Elwell, Jim Rohlfsen, Mel Gabler, John Higgins, Tom Minnery, and several other Patrians. "Becky Delmonico" and "Warren Miller" are pseudonyms used at the subjects' request. Some of Ms. Elwell's comments are from Mark Hartwig, "Learning from Our Victories," *Citizen,* published by *Focus on the Family,* 3/15/95.

1. James Davison Hunter, *Evangelicalism; The Coming Generation* (University of Chicago: 1987). National Survey of Religion and Politics 1992, and the University of Akron Survey Research Center, as cited in *Time,* 1/30/95.
2. Harvey Cox, *Fire From Heaven: The Rise of Penecostal Spirituality and the Reshaping of Religion in the Twenty-first Century* (Reading, MA, 1995).
3. "Gingrich Vows to Pursue Christian Coalition Agenda," *Washington Post,* 5/18/95, p. 1. At the press conference announcing the "Contract with the American Family," Gingrich said that "75, 80, 85 percent of the country believes in the same general direction." He cited no evidence to support these figures.
4. "Taking Your City for Christ" by Nate Krupp, appearing in *Crosswinds: The Reformation Digest,* Winter 1992, p. 42.
5. "The Right Hand of God," *Time,* cover story, 5/15/95, p. 35.
6. Developed by the Coalition on Revival, Inc., P. O. Box A, Sunnyvale, California 94087, and endorsed by a cross section of Christian leaders.
7. David Harrell, Jr. *Pat Robertson: A Personal Religious and Political Portrait* (New York: Harper & Row, 1987).
8. Ibid. pp. 203–4.
9. "Growing Mormon Church Faces Dissent by Women and Scholars," by Dirk Johnson, *New York Times* (hereinafter referred to as *NYT*), 10/2/93, p. 1.
10. *DC,* 10/1/93.
11. Martin Marty, "For Better or for Worse, *Time,* 5/24/93.
12. "Church Keeps Gay-Pastor Ban," by Peter Steinfels, *NYT,* 6/9/93.
13. Cited in James Davison Hunter, *Culture Wars* (New York, 1991), pp. 183, 189.
14. Quoted in "Christian Charm School," by Lynda Edwards, reprinted in the *Indianapolis Star,* 6/2/93.
15. " 'True Love Waits' for Some Teen-Agers," *NYT,* 6/21/92.
16. "Clinic Firebombed in Pennsylvania," by Tamar Lewin, *NYT* 9/30/93, p. A12.
17. Paul Vitz, "Religion and Traditional Values in Public School Textbooks: An Empirical Study," a report submitted to National Institute of Education, 1985. Cited in Hunter, *Culture Wars* (1991), p. 204. Dan Quayle quoted in *DC,* 6/17/95.
18. In 1978, IRS agents and government lawyers, arguing that Christian schools were nothing more than monuments to racial segregation, threatened to withdraw their tax-exempt status, a move which pushed many schools to the edge of extinction. Many Christian parents interpreted this as an attack on their faith.
19. Incident recounted in Mel and Norma Gabler, *What Are They Teaching Our Children?* (Wheaton, IL: Victor Books, 1985).

20. Article by Tal Brooke in *Crosswinds: The Reformation Digest,* Winter 1992, p. 39.

21. Pat Robertson, "New Order for the New Age," *The New World Order,* chapter 8, p. 174.

22. "Beating the Big City Bureaucrats," *Citizen,* vol. 7, no. 4.

23. *San Diego Union,* 9/21/91. Since then, the community, disturbed by its national reputation as a stronghold of the Christian Right, voted in a more moderate school board.

24. After weeks of uproar, City Attorney David Levin was called in to render a legal opinion. His determination was unequivocal: religious invocations were permissible only if they did not include "references to any particular religious symbol." He based his decision on the legal precedent of two Supreme Court cases: *Marsh* v. *Chambers,* 103 S. Ct. 3330 (1983), in which the court upheld the constitutionality of a chaplain's opening each session of the Nebraska legislature; and *County of Allegheny* v. *American Civil Liberties Union* (1989), a case triggered by the presence of a nativity scene in front of a county courthouse. "The fullest realization of true religious liberty requires that government . . . effect no favoritism among sects or between religion and nonreligion," wrote Levin, quoting from the 1989 ruling. Levin stressed that, according to the Supreme Court, prayers "in the Judeo–Christian tradition" were considered nonsectarian. Therefore, Levin concluded, the commissioners were certainly permitted to pray, but were not permitted to make references to "particular religious symbols," such as Jesus Christ.

25. "Reclaiming Lost Territory," by Ted Baehr, in *Crosswinds: The Reformation Digest,* Winter 1992, p. 85.

26. Harrel, *Pat Robertson,* p. 205.

27. "The Quiet Man Who Tripped Up Donahue," by Tom Hess, *Citizen,* vol. 6, no. 11.

28. Ron Scherer, "Religionist Sees a 'Christophobic' Elite," *Christian Science Monitor,* 3/22/94, p. 13.

29. Hunter, *Culture Wars* (1991), pp. 227–29.

30. Harrell, *Pat Robertson,* chapter 15.

31. "Heedless of Scorners, a G-Rated Las Vegas Booms in the Ozarks" (Branson, Missouri), by Peter Applebome, *NYT,* 6/1/93; and "Middle America's Music Mecca," by Ed Will, *Denver Post.*

32. The article referred to is by Greg Goldin, "The 15 Per Cent solution: How the Christian Right is Building from Below to Take Over From Above," *Village Voice,* April 6, 1993.

33. Reprinted in *CFV Report,* (Colorado for Family Values) vol. 3, April 1993.

34. Cited in E. J. Dionne, Jr. "Bush and Dukakis with Anger Debate Leadership and Issues from Abortion to Iran-Contra," *NYT,* 9/26/88.

35. The meteoric rise of Michael Farris in Virginia is just such a case. Until very recently, his primary public involvement was in the home-schooling movement. The fact that all eight of his children were being educated at home and that he was an outspoken critic of the public school system (which he calls a "Godless monstrosity"), gave him some public visibility. An attorney, Farris won a highly publicized case in which he argued that the use of such stories as *The Wizard of Oz* and *The Diary of Anne Frank* constituted an infringement of fundamentalist religious beliefs. (A federal appeals court later overturned the decision.) But in 1993 he was a nominee for lieutenant governor at the Republican convention in Richmond, where 5,000 of the 13,000 delegates were Christian activists.

36. *Citizen,* Newsletter, vol. 7, no. 3, March 15, 1993.

37. Philip Weiss, "Outcasts Digging in for the Apocalypse," *Time,* 5/1/95, pp. 48–49; "Patriot Movement: Confederation of Anti-government Groups," Keith Schneider, *NYT* 4/24/95; "Ready For War: Inside the World of the Paranoid," *NYT* Week in Review, 4/30/95.

38. "Red-Hot Anger Across the West," Jon Christensen, Pacific News Service, April 24–28, 1995; reprinted in *High Country News*, Paonia, CO, 4/3/95.
39. ABC News, American Agenda, "In God's Name," 5/3/95.

CHAPTER 2

For their personal interviews, I am grateful to H. Don Nelson, Rich Tosi, John Abele, Compton Chase-Lansdale, Ray Vaughn, Brenda French, Joel Kotkin, and many other citizens of Corporatia. The staff of *Inc.* magazine and the American Association of University Research Parks were generous in their assistance.

1. "The New Millionaires: Making It in Tough Times," James Barron, *NYT*, 9/15/93.
2. This point is frequently made by Robert Reich, Secretary of Labor in the Clinton Administration.
3. George Gilder, *The Spirit of Enterprise* (New York: 1984), pp. 9, 254.
4. For instance: Zip Quality #1: "Blue Blood Estates." Median income $70,000; home value $200,000+; college grads; 50.7 percent. Examples: McLean, Virginia, and Westchester County in the east; Malibu, California, and San Diego's Rancho Sante Fe in the West. Zip Quality #2: "Money and Brains" (in Claritas typology), which includes communities such as Georgetown (Washington) D.C.; Palo Alto, California; and Princeton, New Jersey. Not far away, in Zip Quality #3 ("Furs and Station Wagons"), other Corporatians live in executive bedroom communities like Plano, Texas; Needham, Massachusetts; Pomona, California; or the Dunwoody area of Atlanta, Georgia, and other similar communities. See Michael J. Weiss, *The Clustering of America* (New York, 1988), pp. 60, 269–87.
5. Weiss, *The Clustering of America*, p. 393.
6. Thomas V. DiBacco, *Made in the USA* (New York, 1987), chapter 14.
7. "Town Ready to Cash in on Mercedes Plant," *USA Today* 10/11/93, p. 10B. Conversely, nothing makes the advantages of life in Corporatia clearer than the experience of losing one's citizenship in this privileged state. Whatever companies call it—"downsizing," "delayering," "belt tightening" or some other euphemism for firing their employees—the experience of unemployment is torture for many former executives. Unlike previous eras, when losing an executive position simply meant finding another, in a tightening economy it now means forfeiting access to the Capitalist State. In the seventies, 90 percent of laid-off white collar employees found comparable work fairly soon. In the late eighties, only 50 percent were so fortunate. By the early nineties, only one out of four could find work with similar pay and perks. "Executives the Economy Left Behind," *NYT*, 11/22/92, p. B1.
8. Interview, 11/10/9.
9. James B. Stewart, *Den of Thieves* (New York, 1991), p. 223.
10. *Forbes* cover story, 10/22/9.
11. Because war and economics are so closely tied in the Corporatian belief system, it was not a surprise when Sears, Roebuck announced that it was hiring Lieutenant General William G. Pagonis, fifty-two, to be its new senior vice-president in charge of logistics for its department stores. General Pagonis had distinguished himself in the Persian Gulf War by overcoming shipping bottlenecks, blinding sandstorms, cultural misunderstandings, and hostile adversaries to achieve the biggest military operation since the Allied invasion of France in World War II. His new job is to make sure that Sears's 800 department stores around the country stay stocked, and that they continue to be more effective than their

competitors. In his book entitled *Moving Mountains: Lessons in Leadership and Logistics from the Gulf War,* General Pagonis was clear about his intentions. "Our colleagues in the private sector," he wrote in the introduction, "may now get some good guidance from us." "Sears Hires Army Logistics Expert" by Barnaby Feder, *NYT,* 9/21/93, p. B1.

12. Interview, 10/3/93.
13. Gilder, *The Spirit of Enterprise,* p. 160.
14. "Chrysler's Driving Wheel Bids Farewell," *Washington Post,* 12/27/92.
15. Near Austin, Texas, 450 new companies have created 55,000 jobs. In Orlando's "Laser Lane," 35 companies have created 5,000 new jobs in electro-optics and laser photonics. Meanwhile in the Princeton, New Jersey, area, new companies in biotechnology and telecommunications have created more than 130,000 new jobs. "Medical Alley," in the Minneapolis–St. Paul area, has led to 500 new companies and 40,000 jobs. Similar successes have occurred in Boise, Idaho, where semiconductor chips and laser printers are now in production, and in the "Biomed Mountains" outside Salt Lake City, where medical devices and artificial organs have created an economic boom.
16. "West of Wall Street," *Newsweek,* 5/24/93.
17. Interviews with AAURP staff, 10/16/93.
18. "Pros Seek 'Easy Money' in Risky Biotech Sector," Dan Dorfman, *USA Today,* 11/12/93.
19. Interview.
20. Interview; and "Hillary Raps Insurance Industry," *DC,* 11/2/93.
21. "U.S. Study of Drug Makers Criticizes 'Excess Profits,' " *NYT,* 2/26/93, p. C1.
22. "Now: The Brick Wall," *Newsweek,* 8/24/92.
23. Jack D. Schwager, *Market Wizards: Interviews with Top Traders,* (New York: New York Institute of Finance, 1989).
24. From a Corporatian perspective, inheritance is an irritating contradiction. Unlike liberal economists (such as Lester Thurow in *Generating Inequality)* who argue that inheritance is "the dominant factor" in producing America's millionaires, Corporatians minimize its relevance. They marshal facts to prove that, for most wealthy families, money has been earned, not inherited. "Families of zero wealth built America," Gilder confidently asserts. According to his data, among those with roughly $2 million dollars net worth, more than two-thirds reported no inherited assets at all. George Gilder, *Wealth and Poverty* (New York, 1981), p. 99.
25. Kristol writes: "Today, businessmen, and especially corporate executives, are just about the only class of people which a television drama will feel free to cast as pure villains. Jews and blacks and teachers and journalists and social workers and politicians and trade union leaders and policemen and just about everyone else . . . are given protective coloration on the television screen. Where one of them goes bad, there is sure to be a good one nearby. . . . The business executive gets no such dramatic compensation." Kristol was reprinted in *The Corporation in a Democratic Society,* ed. Wedward J. Bander (New York, 1975), p. 38.

CHAPTER 3

I am grateful to the many citizens of Disia who shared their lives with me. Several who wanted to remain anonymous will find their views reflected in the text. I acknowledge the contributions of Sharif Abdullah, who shared experiences from his early years. The chapter benefited greatly from an early reading by Jim Gibson, a senior fellow at the Urban Institute and former director of the Equal Opportunity Division at the Rockefeller Foundation.

1. Lyrics from Tracy Chapman's song "Subcity."
2. "Clinton Trying to Make a Break from Party of Losers," David Broder, *DC*, 11/21/93.
3. Lawrence M. Mead, *New Politics of Poverty: The Nonworking Poor in America* (New York, 1992).
4. Howard Zinn, *A People's History of the United States* (New York, 1980).
5. "Same Passion, New Tactics," *NYT*, 11/18/93.
6. Manning Marable, *Colorado Daily*, 10/17/94.
7. Russell Means, public lecture, Boulder, Colorado, 10/11/93; *DC*, 10/12/93. When Means asks for questions, the first raised hand belongs to a young Korean-American woman. "It seems strange to me that everybody who comes to America tries to be like the Americans," she asks, slowly rising to her feet. "But you, the Native Americans, were here first. You don't want to be like them. How come?"
8. Dee Brown, *Bury My Heart at Wounded Knee* (New York, 1970), chapter 19.
9. Zinn, Howard. op. cit., p. 29.
10. Ellis Cose, "The Rage of a Privileged Class," reprinted in *Newsweek*, 11/15/93.
11. Cornel West, *Race Matters* (New York, 1993), p. 35.
12. *Los Angeles Times*, 11/16/92, article by Jesse Katz.
13. Interview with Thelma Malone, 11/8/93. At the NAACP's national convention in Indianapolis, Benjamin F. Chavis, Jr., said that his organization must play a crucial role in the battle against "the lingering vestiges of American apartheid." It was a well-chosen phrase because a guest at the NAACP convention was Nelson Mandela, the South African leader who had led the African National Congress for many years, from both inside and outside of prison. Also "Getting Real at the NAACP," *Newsweek*, 6/1/93.
14. "The decisions about what happens to the people who use drugs or the people who are in prisons are being made by people who live in virtually another world," says Aaron Kipnis, who is working on a major book about the prison system to be called *The American Gulag*. "One part of society has, in effect, outlawed the behavior of citizens of another. They have said that their culture is illegal."
15. "Gangs Go Public in New Fight for Respect," *Los Angeles Times*, 5/2/93.
16. Arthur Schlesinger, Jr., *The Disuniting of America* (New York, 1992).
17. Asian-Americans' status in Disia is complex. Often called a "model minority," the group tends to advance more quickly economically than blacks or Latinos. Yet, they too are caught in the dilemma of Disia. Angela Oh, a prominent Korean-American lawyer in Los Angeles, complained after the Los Angeles riots that Americans, instead of confronting the real problems blacks face, point to Koreans and say, "How come blacks aren't more like you guys? Why don't they help each other more? Why don't they work as hard as you do?" Miss Oh, who has served as a mediator in disputes between Korean and African-Americans, concludes: "We stand between the African-Americans, who are really at the bottom rung, and the white community, which is the top rung. I hate the term model minority. It really makes me blanch. It translates into being a human shield." "Giving Voice to the Hurt and Betrayal of Korean–Americans," *NYT*, 5/2/93.
18. "Race," by Thomas Byrne Edsall and Mary D. Edsall, *Atlantic Monthly*, May 1991.
19. Michael Harrington, *The Other America* (New York, 1962).
20. Based on U.S. Census data analyzed by Greater Washington's Research Center's Committee on Strategies to Reduce Chronic Poverty, reported by Associated Press, *DC*, 3/19/93.
21. William Julius Wilson, *The Truly Disadvantaged: The Inner City, the Underclass, and Public Policy* (Chicago, 1987); and "Forget the Stereotypes of Young Black Males," Omar Tyree, *DC*, 7/25/93.

22. U.S. Bureau of Labor Statistics, *Newsweek*, 2/22/93.

23. Jonathan Freedman, *From Cradle to Grave* (New York, 1993), pp. 137–38.

24. "Schools Become More Segregated," William Eaton, *Los Angeles Times* article reprinted in *DC* 12/13/93; Cornel West, *Race Matters* (New York, 1993); Philadelphia, PA: *WILFP Resources* (Women's International League for Peace and Freedom), 1992.

25. Audre Lord, *Sister Outside* (Berkeley, California: 1984), p. 100.

26. If the New York City schools were funded at the level of the highest-spending suburbs of Long Island, points out Jonathan Kozol in *Savage Inequalities: Children in America's Schools* (New York, 1991), a class in the ghetto with thirty-six children would receive $200,000 more per year in education from public funds than it presently does. With this money, Kozol points out, they could have hired "two extraordinary teachers at enticing salaries of $50,000 each, divided the class into two classes of some eighteen children each, provided them with computers, carpets, air-conditioning, new texts and reference books and learning games, and still have money left over to pay for administration."

27. Jonathan Kozol, op cit.

28. *The Thin Red Line: How the Poor Still Pay More*, written by David Dante Trout for a project of the West Coast regional office of the Consumers Union. In a poor neighborhood of West Oakland, California, Consumers Union found that 48,000 residents functioned without a single bank within their borders. Just up in the hills, however, where middle and upper income families live, there were 31 bank branches, one for every 2,300 residents. The Consumers Union study showed that banks made five loans in the highest income area for every loan in the lowest income area. Even when they compared neighborhoods, one black and one white, with the same median income, they found that loans were granted twice as often in the white neighborhood as in the minority neighborhood.

29. "Youth Joblessness in NY City Soars to 40%, Worst on Record," *NYT*, 6/4/93, p. A20.

30. Moreover, the health gap between the affluent and well-educated and the poor and poorly educated has been widening for three decades. According to Gregory Pappas, an epidemiologist at the National Center for Health Statistics, "the inequality in mortality rates among people of different educational levels also increased over that period [1960–1986]." "Why Health Gap Linked to Income," *NYT*, 7/18/93.

31. *Poverty and Race*, vol. 2, no. 3, May/June 1993. Published by Poverty and Race Research Action Council (PRRAC), 1875 Connecticut Avenue NW, Suite 714, Washington, D.C.

32. Alex Kotlowitz, *There Are No Children Here* (New York: 1991), p. 25.

33. Interview. Kotlowitz added that the *New York Times* bureau in the South Bronx is the exception rather than the rule.

34. When Disians themselves commit acts of violence, they tend to blame "the system" rather than the individual perpetrators. "Houston Knows Murder, But This . . ." *NYT*, 7/9/93.

35. "Black America: Multicultural Democracy in the age of Clarence Thomas and David Duke," *Amsterdam: Open Magazine Series*, 1992: 5.

36. "Houston Knows Murder, But This . . ." *NYT*, 7/9/93.

37. " 'Tougher' is Dumber," Todd R. Clear, *NYT*, 12/4/93.

38. "Drug Gang Leader Gets Life, Admonishes Court," by Michael York, *Washington Post*, 5/15/93.

39. Julia Agwin, "GOP's 'war on women' decried," States News Service, DC 8/4/95.

40. Susan Faludi, *Backlash: The Undeclared War on American Women* (New York: Crown Publishers, 1991), pp. 49ff.

41. In such Disian periodicals as *Race and Class*, which calls itself "a journal for black and Third World liberation," women scholars attack even Disia's own heroes for their anti-

woman bias. Malcolm X's thinking, for example, is considered by Disian feminists to have been "pervaded by masculinist assumptions" which "impoverished his version of black nationalism." According to such critics, Malcolm X's views on women were nothing more than a reflection of the "dominant views of white manhood and womanhood" prevalent in America. Similarly, highly regarded rap groups such as Public Enemy and Arrested Development are taken to task for lyrics which "uncritically accept the dominant society's patriarchal model of gender and family relations."

42. Elijah Anderson, "Sex Codes in the Inner City," a paper presented at the Public Enterprise Institute, pp. 14–15.

43. Lawrence H. Fuchs, *The American Kaleidoscope: Race, Ethnicity and the Civic Culture* (Hanover, N.H., 1990); Pokalow, *Lives on the Edge: Single Mothers and Their Children in the Other America* (Chicago, 1993), pp. 55, 59, 80; and U.S. Census Bureau, 1992, *Newsweek,* 8/30/93.

44. Pokalow, *Lives on the Edge,* pp. 68, 73, 94.

45. "The Glass Ceiling Theory," *Newsweek* 3/27/95, p. 24.

46. Faludi, op. cit., p. xiii.

47. Betty Friedan, *The Feminine Mystique* (New York, 1963), pp. 296, 325.

48. In Vivian Gornick and Barbara K. Moran, *Woman In Sexist Society* (New York, 1971), 684. According to Disian feminists, fear of women's sexuality is as pervasive among men as fear of gay sexuality. In "Organs and Orgasms," Alix Shulman argues that the exploitation of women is so pervasive that it affects the way they experience their own bodies, even their own sexuality. Women have been persuaded by patriarchal experts that they should only experience sexual orgasm from vaginal penetration. In fact, she argues, they rarely do. Although men would like to think that the pleasure they have in reaching orgasm automatically ensures that women will also experience pleasure, that is a lie. The entire view of male-defined heterosexual intercourse as "normal sexuality" is a travesty foisted on women who (until feminism) were "hopelessly isolated in their cells in a male-dominated society. . . ." She concludes her essay with the revolutionary bumper sticker aphorism: "Think clitoris." Similarly, Caroline Bird, author of *Born Female,* believes that human relationships are now caught in a "stranglehold of reproduction." Only by breaking that stranglehold will other, more humane lifestyles be possible.

    Women are kept "from being in control of their own sexual experience," concurs Naomi Wolf, a heterosexual feminist, Rhodes Scholar, and author of *The Beauty Myth.* In her discussion of contemporary sexual mores, she cites study after study that demonstrate that men are overwhelmingly domineering and aggressive in their behavior toward women. In one study of college-age men, nine out of ten men said that they wanted to "dominate a woman," more than eight of ten believed that some women "look like they're just asking to be raped," and more than six out of ten said they enjoy it "when a woman struggles over sex" and that it is "exciting to use force to subdue a woman." Although in her latest book *Fire With Fire* she calls on women to reject "victim feminism," her allusions to the Holocaust (when discussing anorexia) and to "gender apartheid" (when discussing discrimination against women in the mass media) underscore her conviction that women, indeed, are an oppressed and exploited class. Abbott and Love, in Gornick et. al, op. cit., and Naomi Wolf, *The Beauty Myth* (New York, 1991) and *Fire With Fire* (New York, 1993).

49. Sonia Johnson, *Going Out of Our Minds: The Metaphysics of Liberation* (Freedom, 1987).

50. The genocide committed against women in Europe who were called "witches" was a direct result of this patriarchal view. Thousands were killed for no reason except that male church authorities, afraid of women's spiritual powers, wanted them to be destroyed. When the Pope

in 1468 defined witchcraft as *crimen exceptum* and removed all legal limits to torture, he not only ensured that unspeakable crimes would be committed throughout the Christian world; he also ensured that women forever after would consider the church their enemy. See, as an example of this extensive literature, Susan Griffin, *Woman and Nature* (New York, 1978).

51. Miedzian, *Boys Will Be Boys* (New York, 1991).

52. Helen Caldicott, *Missile Envy* (New York, 1984).

53. James B. Stewart, *Den of Theives* (New York, 1991), 120.

54. "Amid Women a Male Outpost Falls," *New York Times*, 1/6/93.

55. Reverend Troy D. Perry and Thomas L. P. Swicegood, *Profiles in Gay and Lesbian Courage* (New York, 1991).

56. Philip L. Berman, *The Search for Meaning* (New York, 1990), 141.

57. Vivian Gornick and Barbara K. Moran, "Is Women's Liberation A Lesbian Plot," *Woman In Sexist Society* (New York, 1971).

58. Ben Hamper, *Rivethead: Tales from the Assembly Line* (New York, 1992); Thomas Geoghegan, *Which Side Are You On? Trying to Be for Labor When It's Flat on Its Back* (New York, 1992); and Patricia Cayo Sexton, *The War on Labor and the Left* (Boulder, 1991).

59. William Manchester, "Conspiracy Theory of JFK Assassination Based on Quicksand," *DC*, 11/21/93.

60. "Increasingly, Two-Career Family Means Illegal Immigrant Help," *NYT*, 2/24/93.

61. Cornell West, *Race Matters*, pp. 6, 17.

62. Michael Parenti makes these arguments in *Inventing Reality* (New York, 1986).

63. These statistics are from a speech by Jesse Jackson at the University of Colorado, *DC*, 2/11/95.

CHAPTER 4

I am grateful to citizens of Media (and its critics) who appear in this chapter or whose comments have strengthened it, including Geneva Overholser, Howard Kurtz, Claudia Gurtzman, Ellen Hume, Jim Fallows, Gene Stone, and M. Scott Peck.

1. The "electronic superhighway" now opening up across the nation and the world is extending participation to levels that the Founding Fathers could never have imagined. Although the leaders of Media have tended historically to be concentrated in New York and Los Angeles, today they are ubiquitous. Ted Turner's CNN empire is in Atlanta, a once sleepy southern town. John Malone's Tele-Communications, Inc., is based in Denver, a mountain town formerly known for rodeos, not fiber optics. Some well-known Medians, like pop icons Madonna and Michael Jackson or Creative Artists Agency deal-maker Michael Ovitz, may still reside in Malibu or Beverly Hills. But many others, like director Steven Spielberg or actor Harrison Ford, may live in a hacienda in Santa Fe or a mountain ranch in Montana.

The ordinary citizens of Media, however, are not famous. They work for the innumerable companies that own, operate, and program the media of communications.

2. Cited in J. Laurent Scharff, "Needed; A First-Class First Amendment for Television Journalism," *Television Quarterly*, vol. 25, no. 1, 1990.

3. *Entertainment Weekly*, cover story, 4/9/93; and *Rolling Stone*.

4. "Culture Wars: No End In Sight," Mary Otto, Knight-Ridder, *DC*, 9/5/93, p. E1.

5. "The Selling of Sex" *Newsweek*, 11/2/92.

6. J. Laurent Scharff, op. cit.

7. Howard Kurtz, "Top Editor Gives Up Paper Chase," *Washington Post* 2/15/95, p. D1.
8. Interview, March 27, 1995.
9. Excerpted from *American Inquisitors* (1928); cited by Ellen Hume, "The News Media and the National Interest: Lectures on Moral Values in a Free Society," University of Texas at Dallas, November 11, 1992.
10. Bill Carter, "GM Suspends Ad on NBC News Despite Apology For Truck Report," *NYT*, 2/11/93.
11. Statistics from a *Los Angeles Time* poll cited in "MBAs Now Rule the Newsroom," *Utne Reader*, September/October 1993, p. 44.
12. Elizabeth Kolbert, "Covering Gay Rights: Can Journalists be Marchers?" *NYT*, 4/24/93.
13. "Black Journalists Feel Exiled in Newsrooms," by Terry Langford, Associated Press, *DC*, 7/24/93.
14. Transcript of "Dateline NBC," August 3, 1993, no. 59.
15. *Unreliable Sources*, by Martin A. Lee and Norman Solomon. Both are associated with F.A.I.R.
16. William A. Rusher, *The Coming Battle for the Media* (New York: 1988), p. 22.
17. See *The Media Elite*, by S. Robert Lichter, et al. (Hastings: 1990), chapter 2, "Group Portrait."
18. "After Killing, Hard Questions for Talk Shows," by Bill Carter, *NYT* 3/14/95, p. A8.
19. Data from Recording Industry Association of America.
20. "Murder, Mayhem Stalk TV," by Jeff Silverman, *NYT*, 11/22/92.
21. J. Laurent Scharff, op. cit.
22. "Police Drama Under Fire for Sex and Violence," by Bill Carter, *NYT*, 6/22/93.
23. "Bochco Chides Affiliates Who Won't Run 'Blue,' " *USA Today*, 9/14/93, p. 3D.
24. "Breaking the TV Taboos" and "Interview," *TV Guide*, 8/14/93, pp. 10, 15.
25. "TV Executives Assess Impact of the Violence They Portray," by Elizabeth Kolbert, *NYT*, 8/3/93.
26. "Gory Video Game Racks Up Big Sales on Its Opening Day," William M. Bulkeley, *Wall Street Journal*, 9/14/93, p. B8.
27. "Execs Vow to Cut TV Violence," by Diane Duston, Associated Press, *DC*.
28. Phillip Elmer DeWitt, "Electronic Superhighway," *Newsweek*, 4/12/93.
29. "The Ultimate Mogul," by Janice Castro, *Time*, 4/19/93.
30. Fiber optics cables will be for Media what the church has been for Patria—the thread which holds the state together. With fiber optic connections, which carry more than 100 times more information than conventional copper wires, four signals—telephone, television, radio, and computer data—can be carried simultaneously. In 1991 5.6 million miles of fiber optic cable were run in the United States. By 1992 the highway was 16 million miles long, and continues to expand rapidly today. By the year 2000, 40 million homes are likely to be linked to a fiber optics network, and soon afterward, like television today, it will be in virtually every home that wants it (and can afford it) in America. "Eyes on the Future," *Newsweek*, 5/31/93.
31. David A. Kaplan, "Believe in Magic," *Newsweek*, June 14, 1993; and "The Force of an Idea Is With Him," *Newsweek*, 5/31/93.
32. "Virtual News and Virtual Truths: News Reporting in the New Media," John Henry Clippinger III, November 6, 1992, for Twentieth Century Fund publication.
33. Howard Rheingold, *Virtual Reality: The Revolutionary Technology of Computer-Generated Artificial Worlds and How It Promises to Transform Society* (New York, 1991), pp. 131–2 and 386.

CHAPTER 5

I am grateful to the citizens of Gaia, most notably Bill McKibben, Stephanie Clarke, Barbara Bernstein, Jeffery Duvall, and Mary McHenry, as well as scores of others who agreed to be interviewed for this chapter. I also appreciate the assistance of Stephen Bendixson.

1. Stanislav Grof, M.D., *The Holotropic Mind: The Three Levels of Human Consciousness and How They Shape Our Lives* (New York: HarperCollins, 1993).
2. See *Whole Earth Catalog,* ed. Howard Rheingold (New York, 1994), and "How Stewart Brand Learns," by Katherine Fulton, *Los Angeles Times Magazine,* 10/30/94.
3. Fritjof Capra, "A Systems Approach to the Emerging Paradigm," in *The New Paradigm in Business,* ed. Michael Ray and Alan Rinzler (Los Angeles, 1993), p. 237.
4. Data from National Survey of Religion and Politics, 1992, University of Akron Survey Research Center, and as reported in *Time,* 1/30/95.
5. James Lovelock, in *Gaia: A Way of Knowing,* ed. William Irwin Thompson (Great Barrington, MA: Lindisfarne Press, 1987) p. 88.
6. Interview, Spring 1993.
7. *As Above, So Below,* ed. Ron Miller (Los Angeles, 1992), p. 11.
8. "Planet Water: The Spirituality of H_2O," reprinted in *Utne Reader,* May/June 1993.
9. "Gaia—She's Alive: A Conversation with James Lovelock," *Orion Nature Quarterly* 8:1, p. 58.
10. "The Gaian Agenda," Tal Brooke, *Crosswinds: The Reformation Digest,* Winter 1992.
11. Bill McKibben, *The End of Nature* (New York, 1989), part 2.
12. McKibben illustrates his point with a story of his recent trip to Thailand, "the most environmentally devastated country on earth." His conclusion: "It took about five years for television to overturn 3,000 years of a stable Buddhist society." While he admits that other factors besides television were involved, he nevertheless stands by his statement that television, "the linch-pin of the consumer society," is the crucial catalyst in the destruction of ecologically friendly human cultures.
13. Thomas Berry, *Dream of the Earth* (San Francisco, 1990), pp. 37–38.
14. *As Above, So Below,* p. 260.
15. Richard Leviton, "It's the New Age Again," *Yoga Journal,* May/June 1993.
16. David Spangler, *Emergence,* pp. 81, 84.
17. Charles Reich, *The Greening of America* (New York, 1970), pp. 229, 304.
18. Quoted in Capra, "A Systems Approach to the Emerging Paradigm," in *The New Paradigm in Business,* ed. Michael Ray and Alan Rinzler (Los Angeles, 1993), p. 237.
19. Ferguson, 289.
20. Henderson, in *Gaia: A Way of Knowing,* p. 160.
21. Ferguson, 212–13.
22. Michael Ray and Alan Rinzler, in Capra, *The New Paradigm in Business.*
23. *Gaia: A Way of Knowing,* cited above, p. 27
24. Parliament of the World's Religions program catalogue; and Peter Steinfels, "Religious Leaders Hold a World Parliament," *NYT,* 8/30/93.
25. Based on interviews with those present, who reconstructed the Dalai Lama's remarks.
26. *Creativism,* by Harry Palmer (Longwood, Fla.: Star's Edge International).
27. *NYT Book Review,* 9/12/93.
28. Since then, Dr. Chopra, to his credit, has regained control over the promotional material and toned down his claims.
29. *Superlife* (Published by Zygon International, Inc., 18368 Redmond Way, Redmond, WA 98052), February 1990.

30. "Have We Outgrown the Age of Heroes?" *Utne Reader,* May/June 1993.

31. *NYT,* 2/17/93.

32. David Brower, in "Greedlock Threatening Earth," by Chris Roberts, *DC,* 22/6/93, p. C1.

33. Thomas Berry, *Dream of the Earth,* pp. 157–58.

34. Jerry Mander, *In the Absence of the Sacred: The Failure of Technology* (San Francisco, 1991), p. 136.

35. "Environmentalism or Stewardship: What Is the Christian's Responsibility?" by E. Calvin Beisner, *Crosswinds,* Fall 1992.

36. *Greenpeace,* April/May/June 1993, p. 1; "Thunder of Debate on Owls . . . ," Timothy Egad, *NYT,* 4/2/93; "Fear and Loathing in the Adirondacks," *E Magazine,* September/October 1992, p. 28.

CHAPTER 6

Many thanks to Claudine Schneider, Tim Honey, and Ellen Baer, who were interviewed "on the record." Many more were not. I appreciate their candor and their courage. I also want to thank John Parr, Carolyn Lukensmeyer, and Peter Goldmark for their useful comments regarding this chapter.

1. President Bill Clinton, "What Good Is Government . . . ," *Newsweek,* 4/10/95, pp. 20–22.

2. CBS/*New York Times* poll, September 12, 1994; reported on the CBS Evening News.

3. "Seven Days," *Newsweek,* 7/12/93.

4. *Reinventing Government,* by David Osborne and Ted Gaebler (Reading, MA, 1992), p. xxi; and "Why Uncle Sam Isn't a Better Landlord," by Michael Wines, *NYT,* 7/4/93.

5. Times Mirror Study of the American Electorate, conducted by the Gallup Organization, September 1987 pp. 4–5.

6. Mark Green, ed., *Changing America: Blueprints for the New Administration* (New York, 1992).

7. Robert N. Bellah, et al. *The Good Society* (New York, 1991), p. 113.

8. *Changing America,* Introduction.

9. Robert C. Vaughn, *The Spoiled System: A Call for Civil Service Reform* (New York, 1975), chapter 3.

10. "Minority Caucuses Count on New Clout," by Leslie Phillips, *USA Today,* 12/9/92; "High-level Grumbling Over Pace of Appointments," by Douglas Jehl, *NYT,* 2/25/93.

11. "Female Candidates Overcome the 'Credibility' Gap," by Ellen R. Malcolm, *NYT* 8/5/92.

12. "Opposition to Baird Grows as Senators Hear the People," by Adam Clymer, *NYT,* 1/22/93; "What Many Say About Baird: What She Did Wasn't Right," by Felicity Barringer, *NYT,* 1/22/93.

13. "Senators Attack Housing Nominee," by Clifford Krauss, *NYT,* 5/21/93; "Tate Withdraws Name from RTC," *USA Today,* 12/1/93.

14. "Ron Brown Says He Is Canceling His Gala Party," by Stephen Labaton, *NYT,* 1/14/93.

15. "Mr. Clinton Spins the Lobby Door," *NYT,* 12/9/93, op ed page.

16. Robert Kuttner, *The End of Laissez-Faire* (New York, 1991), pp. 262–63.

17. Michael Wines, "Tax's Demise Illustrates First Rule of Lobbying: Work, Work, Work," *NYT,* 6/14/93 (Sources: Ways and Means Committee report; interviews; Steven Greenhouse, "The White House Struggles to Save Energy Tax Plan," *NYT,* National Journal, 5/10.93); *Odessa American,* cited in *Daily Corners,* 5/22/93; Diana Simeon, "Many in Congress Favor Spending Cuts," *Lincoln Star,* 5/19/93.

18. "Lawmaker Calls Security on Protester," *Sarasota Herald-Tribune,* 3/23/93.

19. "Senate Votes to Ban Attacks on Abortion Clinics," *NYT,* 11/17/93.

20. "For Armed Forces, Policing Sex Is Nothing New," by Jane Gross, *NYT,* 7/17/93.

21. John Frohnmayer, *Leaving Town Alive: Confessions of an Arts Warrior* (New York, 1993).

22. "Clinton and the Challenges of the Arts Endowment," by Kim Masters, *Washington Post,* 12/27/92.

23. "Health Leaders Target Smoking," Associated Press story, *DC,* 1/12/94.

24. As this goes to press, the battle between the tobacco industry and the Clinton administration has just begun.

25. "I.R.S. Outlines New Rules to Govern Executives' Pay," by Robert D. Hershey, Jr., *NYT,* 12/16/93; and Derek Bok, *The Cost of Talent* (New York, 1993).

26. "Wealthiest Taxpayers Would Take It on the Chin," by Kevin Maney, *USA Today,* 2/18/93.

27. "Housing Secretary Eulogizes a Homeless Woman," *NYT,* 12/10/93.

28. "Where to Prune and Where to Hack Away," *Business Week,* 9/13/93.

29. David Osborne and Ted Gaebler, *Reinventing Government* (Reading, MA, 1992), p. 198.

30. "Unfetterd by Past, He's Set to Govern," *NYT,* 11/18/94, p. A7.

31. "President Presses Business Leaders on Tax-rise Plan," by David E. Rosenbaum, *NYT,* 2/12/93; "Taxes vs. Growth," by Jack Kemp, *NYT,* 2/19/93.

32. "Clinton Wants Corporations to Pay More" by Owen Ullmann, *DC,* 2/12/93; "There They Go Again," by Ronald Reagan, *NYT,* 2/18/93.

33. "Jobless Rate Underestimated, U.S. Says, Citing Survey Bias," *NYT,* 11/17/93.

34. "Report to Clinton Sees Vast Extent of Homelessness," *NYT,* 2/27/94.

35. ABC "Nightline" transcript, May 13, 1993; "That Was Then and This Is Now for David Gergen," by Ruth Marcus, *Washington Post,* National Weekly Edition, 6/7–13/93.

36. Kenneth Keniston, *All Our Children: The Report of the Carnegie Council on Children* (New York, 1977).

37. *The Common Good: Social Welfare and the American Future,* Ford Foundation (New York, 1989).

38. "Text of the President's Address to a Joint Session of Congress," *NYT,* 2/18/93.

39. "Disrespect Stings Boulder City Council," by C. Rusnock Hoover, *DC,* 10/17/93.

40. "Money Talks Louder Than Ever in Congress," Frank Greene (Knight-Ridder), *DC,* 6/18/95.

41. "Clinton Tells Cabinet to Cut Work Force and Privileges," by Thomas L. Friedman, *NYT,* 2/11/93; "Washington Takes Leaf from Business Manuals," by Steve Lohr, *NYT,* 9/8/93.

42. "Remaking Government," by David E. Rosenbaum, *NYT,* 9/8/93; "The Latest Reinvention," *NYT,* 9/8/93, op ed page.

43. This statement is based on the author's review of transcripts of the major networks' evening news programs as well as direct viewing.

44. Neal Baxter, *Opportunities in Federal Government Careers* (Lincolnwood, IL: VGM Career Horizons, 1980).

45. "Calls Mount for Ethics Reform in Congress," by John Dillin, *Christian Science Monitor,* 3/2/93.

46. The networks (CNN, ABC, NBC, CBS) combined forces to interview 15,874 voters as they exited from the polls last November. The interviews were analyzed in "A Review of the Exit Polls in the 1992 Election," by Francis E. Smith, for the Future Fund, May 1993.

PART II

1. Letter to James H. Van Allen, April 14, 1865, printed in Mario Cuomo and Harold Holzer, *Lincoln on Democracy* (New York, 1990), p. 349.

CHAPTER 7

This chapter could not have been written without the counsel and cooperation of countless colleagues who are active in the new "citizenship movement." I particularly want to thank my colleagues at the Rockefeller Foundation, the site leaders of The Common Enterprise, the staff of the National Civic League and the Alliance for National Renewal, the Civic Television Network, and the Civic Forum. This chapter also benefited from the advice of participants at several meetings, particularly "Revitalizing Citizenship" at the American Enterprise Institute (1994) and "The Citizenship Movement" at the Center for the Study of Community (1995).

1. Until 1892, the Pledge did not exist. It was written for part of a National School Celebration that year commemorating the 400th anniversary of Columbus's voyage to this continent, but it did not become official until an act of Congress made it part of our salute to the flag. It has been modified several times over the years—most recently in 1954, when anticommunist passions fueled a movement to add the words "under God." But even without the reference to divinity, the Pledge has been opposed by groups who felt the entire hand-over-the-heart exercise was chauvinistic. Its popularity has therefore waxed and waned along with public concepts of patriotism.

   The Pledge reiterates that we are committing ourselves "to the republic for which it [the flag] stands, one nation, under God, *indivisible . . .*" We pledge allegiance to "the *flag* of the United States of America"—that is, to a symbol of the whole of which the states are but a part. The flag, like the "republic for which it stands," constantly changes. Every time a state is added to the union, a star is added. If read at this deeper level, the Pledge of Allegiance is not a call to mindless, flag-waving chauvinism. It is a call to the new patriotism.

2. *Roget's II: The New Thesaurus* (Boston, 1980).

3. George H. Gallup International Institute, November 1994: data from sampling of 1,025; margin of error plus or minus 3 percent. DYG, Inc., survey, February 1994. Confidence in religious leaders dropped from 57 to 40 percent between 1990 and 1994. Data provided by the National Civic League.

4. Peter Berger and Richard John Neuhaus, "To Empower People: The Role of Mediating Structures in Public Policy" (Washington, D.C. American Enterprise Institute).

5. DYG, Inc., survey February 1994: figure 14, "Obstacles to a Healthy Community." Data provided by the National Civic League.

6. "How Everybody Lost in a Textbook Trial," *Woodrow Wilson Center Report,* vol. 5, no 4, February 1994.

7. Cited by Kevin Phillips, *Arrogant Capital* (Boston, 1994) p. 133.

8. "US Likely to See More Gridlock," Knight-Ridder column by Robert Rankin and David Hess, *DC,* 11/9/94.

9. *NYT,* 10/10/94

10. Associated Press national poll of 1,006 adults taken from October 28 to November 2, 1994, by ICR Survey Research Group of Media, PA, part of AUS Consultants.

11. The first definitions are from *Oxford English Dictionary;* the final definition is from *American Heritage Dictionary of the English Language.*

12. Lincoln, at a post-election celebration in Springfield, Illinois, November 20, 1860, cited in Cuomo and Holzer, *Lincoln on Democracy.*

13. It is worth noting here what it means to be "religious," in the original sense of the word. The origin of the word religion is *re* ("again") and *ligare* (to "bind," "bond," "bridge"). Being religious, in the deepest sense, means to join the different parts of life together in a sacred whole. To be religious means to connect ourselves, again and again, to what we have been disconnected from; to bond what has been broken apart; to bridge what has been torn asunder. Thus defined, spirituality is not a thorn in the side of democracy, it is a civic necessity. Robert A. Johnson, a Jungian analyst who has delved deeply into both myth and politics, writes: "The religious faculty is the art of taking the opposites and binding them back together again, surmounting the split that has been causing so much suffering. It helps us move from contradiction . . . to the realm of paradox, where we are able to entertain simultaneously two contradictory notions and give them equal dignity. Then, and only then, is there the possibility of grace, the spiritual experience of contradictions brought into a coherent whole." Robert A Johnson, *Owning Your Own Shadow* (San Francisco, 1993), p. 85.

14. This often-cited statement by Jefferson was reprinted recently in the Civic Forum prospectus, October 1994.

15. Interview; All-America Cities Program, Oakland, CA, June 1994.

16. Lawrence Fuchs, *The American Kaleidoscope* (Hanover, NH, 1990), p. 277.

17. Cited in *DC,* 11/27/94.

18. Ellis Cose, *A Nation of Strangers* (New York, 1992), p. 11.

19. I am grateful to Matt Moseley for the research which produced this demographic data. If not otherwise indicated, it is based on Taeuber and Taeuber, *The Changing Population of the United States* (New York, 1958); Margo J. Anderson, *The American Census: A Social History* (New Haven, 1988); and Lawrence Fuchs, *The American Kaleidoscope.*

20. "Group Plans to Exploit G.O.P. Rise," *NYT,* 11/27/94.

21. These concepts are developed by Robert Fuller cited in McLaughlin and Davidson, *Spiritual Politics* (New York, 1994), p. 81.

CHAPTER 8

The scores of "new patriots" who appear in these pages graciously shared their lives with me. I am profoundly grateful to them, and to the scores of others whose interviews unfortunately could not be included for reasons of space. Also, special thanks to Robert Levi, John Steiner, and Millennium Communications for their assistance in the writing of this chapter.

1. Peter Drucker, *Post-Capitalist Society* (New York, 1995), chapter 9.

2. "The False Gods of Earth Day," *Wall Street Journal,* 4/22/94.

3. Focus group conducted in Plano, Texas, near Dallas, August 1994. Comments from James Kunde at a meeting of America's Future in Denver, CO, September 1994.

4. Robert DeMoss, *Learn to Discern* (Grand Rapids MI, 1992); video by same name available from Focus on the Family, Colorado Springs, CO.

5. Together with George Downs, the African-American pastor of Ebenezer Baptist Church, Reverend Clay Turner is now developing the Stop The Violence Collaboration. "It's a

group of about four hundred citizens, concerned about the violence that comes out of our community particularly the public housing projects which are surrounded by crack houses. There are virtually no fathers there because it violates the regulations. We're trying to look at the violence systemically—drugs, housing, family violence, school dropout rates, teen pregnancy." While it is too soon to tell where this collaboration will be successful, those who are involved in it know that the clinic was the springboard for these new relationships. Just as the clinic "built bridges across the old turf battles," Turner believes the Stop the Violence Collaboration can do the same.

6. Comments are from interviews with Marjorie Kelley, except for the final passage, which is from her interview in James Liebig, *Merchants of Vision* (San Francisco: World Business Academy, 1994).

7. As Willis Harman, president of the Institute of Noetic Sciences, argued in a speech to the World Business Academy, Boston, May 12–14, 1994, most of Corporatia's hallowed beliefs—that productivity must be increased in order for a business to remain competitive; that profits measure progress; that the benefits of technology outweigh the risks; that competition is fundamental; that self-interest leads to the larger social good; et al.—must be reopened to question. When these beliefs lead to polarization rather than partnership, they splinter society rather than support it. Reprinted in *Noetic Sciences Review,* Autumn 1994.

8. "Social entrepreneurs" is a widely used term, particularly popular among the members of the Social Venture Network, a group of "socially responsible" business people. "Merchants of vision" is the phrase used by James Liebig in his book by that title, published by the World Business Academy, which profiles business leaders with deep social involvements. "Virtuosi of the market" is Daniel Yanekelovich's phrase, cited in private correspondence with John Steiner and shared with the author.

9. Citations from the economic press are from Kevin Phillips, *Arrogant Capital* (Boston, 1994) chapter 4, "The Financialization of America."

10. It is worth noting that money, while necessary, is not sufficient. Less than $1 million in seed money was invested by the Enterprise Foundation during its first three years of operation. The real value was in community energy, or what social scientists call "social capital." Based on interviews and on presentations on the occasion of the National Civic League's 100th anniversary, "A Summit of Community Builders," Philadelphia, November 10–12, 1994.

11. Interview, December 1994.

12. Carl Bernstein, "Talk Show Nation," *New Perspectives Quarterly,* Summer 1994, based on a speech Bernstein delivered at New York University.

13. "Up Front, Here's Our Election Bias," Davis Merritt, Jr. *Wichita Eagle,* September 9, 1990, p. 13A.

14. Frances Lappe and Paul Du Bois, *The Quickening of America* (New York, 1993).

15. See Lappe and Du Bois, chapter 6, for further details.

16. "Against the Wind," by John Marks, *Nieman Reports,* Winter 1989 (Harvard University). The National Public Radio citation is from a transcript of the program.

17. *U.S. News & World Report,* November 7, 1994; p. 35.

18. This comment appeared in *Austin, Texas: The City as a Teaching Firm,* by Teresa Parker, published by Institute for Education and Empowerment, Education Development Center, Inc, 55 Chapel Street, Newton, MA 02158–1060, February 1994.

19. Interview. I am grateful to James Kunde for the introduction to Don Vermillion, whom Kunde calls one of the truly visionary local officials at work in America today.

20. He made these comments at a meeting of the Alliance for Redesigning Government, Den-

ver, CO, 1994. *Governing,* he believes, "wouldn't have been possible ten years ago. I know—I brought it up to my company and they wouldn't consider it." The company he referred to was the Times Publishing Co., which owns the *St. Petersburg Times* and *Congressional Quarterly.*

21. Kevin Phillips, *Arrogant Capital,* pp. 113, 120.
22. "Unfettered by Past, He's Set To Govern," *NYT* 11/18/94, p. A7.

CHAPTER 9

This chapter is based on my own synthesis of what I have learned from the many of the projects and individuals who are rebuilding America. The following footnotes acknowledge my indebtedness to some of them. They cannot do justice to all the wisdom that has been shared with me. To all the new patriots who contributed to this chapter, I give my thanks. I particularly appreciate the critique and encouragement of Michael Lerner and John Parr.

1. The term "social capital" was developed by Robert Putnam, *Making Democracy Work* (Princeton, 1993). For other dimensions of the new patriots see a bibliography compiled by the National Civic League, including Madelyn Burley Allen, *Listening: The Forgotten Skill;* Benjamin Barber, *Strong Democracy: Participatory Politics for a New Age;* Hans Bleiker and Anne Marie Bleiker, *Citizen Participation Handbook for Public Officials and Other Professionals;* Robert Bolton, *People Skills: How to Assert Yourself, Listen to Others and Resolve Conflicts;* Harry C. Boyte, *Commonwealth: A Return to Citizen Politics;* Community Board of San Francisco, *Conciliation Handbook: Neighbors Helping Neighbors Resolve Conflicts That Keep Us Apart;* Molly Roth Hamaker and Cynthia Cusick, *Town Meeting Tool Kit;* Frances Moore Lappe, *The Quickening of America;* National Congress of Neighborhood Women, *The Neighborhood Women's Training Manual;* Elizabeth Thoman, *Citizenship in a Media Age;* and John Javna, *Time to Get Involved.* See also Michael Briand, *Practical Politics* (forthcoming) and Ronald Heifetz, *Leadership Without Easy Answers.*
2. Annie E. Casey Foundation study reported in *DC,* 4/34/95. Competing data on homosexuals taken from materials produced by advocacy groups on both sides. Data on economic inequality is from research by Professor Edward Wolff of New York University and reported in many newspapers, including the *New York Times.* For example, see *NYT* editorial 4/18/95, "The Rich Get Richer Faster." California prison spending data is from "Prison-Building Binge in California Casts Shadow on Higher Education," *NYT* 4/12/95.

   To the best of my knowledge, the answers to the four factual questions are: (1) True. (2) Both choices are false. A more accurate estimate is 4 to 7 percent. (3) True. (4) True.
3. Representative John Kasich (D-N.Y.) made a similar point when he said, "Democrats are supposed to be knee-jerks for welfare, and Republicans are supposed to be knee-jerks for defense. Well, I don't think we should be knee-jerk for anything. I think we should do what's right." "Jefferson Urges an Examination of Faith" is in William Bennett, *The Book of Virtues* (New York, 1993).
4. Lawrence Fuchs, *The American Kaleidoscope: Race, Ethnicity, and the Civic Culture* (Hanover, NH, 1990), pp. 374, 461.
5. Daniel Yankelovich, *Coming to Public Judgment* (Syracuse University Press, 1991), p. 11.
6. John Gabriel Hunt, ed., *The Essential Abraham Lincoln* (Avenel, N.J.: 1933).
7. Speech at the National Civic League's 50th Anniversary Meeting, November 1994, Philadelphia.

8. Rush Limbaugh, "Blame the Bombers—Only," *Newsweek*, 5/8/95, p. 39.

9. "Taking America's Pulse," a summary report of the National Conference Survey on Inter-Group Relations, issued by the National Conference, 71 Fifth Avenue, New York, NY 10003.

10. "Media Mum on Liberals' Crude Remarks," Linda Chavez, *USA Today*, 4/12/95.

11. Documented in *Not in Our Town*, a film distributed by the California Working Group, 5867 Ocean View Drive, Oakland, CA 94618.

12. "Today" show (TV), June 9, 1994.

13. "Cobb County War of Beliefs is Heating Up," *Atlanta Constitution*, Wednesday, June 1, 1994.

14. "The Man Who Rendered Jesus for the Age of Publication," *NYT* 10/12/94, p. B1.

15. E. J. Dionne, "The Necessary Tension Between Faith and Politics," *Washington Post*, 12/26/93.

16. Reinhold Niebuhr, "Democratic Toleration and the Groups of the Community," in *The Children of Light and the Children of Darkness* (New York, 1944).

17. "Muslims Continue to Feel Apprehensive, *NYT*, 4/24/95, p. A9; "Way More than Two Cents Worth," John Tierney, *NYT*, 4/30/95.

18. Coretta Scott King, ed, *The Words of Martin Luther King* (New York, 1984), p. 74.

19. "Smoking Them Out," *Policy Review*, Winter 1995, p. 56; published by the Heritage Foundation, Washington, D.C.

20. Interview, November 1994.

21. John W. Gardner, *On Leadership* (New York, 1990), p. 175.

22. "Mister Broadway," *Newsweek*, 2/13/95, p. 61.

23. Marian Wright Edelman, *The Measure of Our Success* (Boston, 1992), p. 11.

24. "A TV Pioneer Says the Industry Has Lost Its Way," *Christian Science Monitor*, 5/23/95.

25. Robert Wiebe, *Self-Rule: A Cultural History of American Democracy* (Chicago, 1995) pp. 260–61.

26. Reginald K. Brack, Jr., chairman of Time, Inc., and the Advertising Council cite this data in "How to Clean Up Gutter Politics," *NYT*, 12/27/94.

27. Cited by Marian Wright Edelman in *The Measure of Our Success*, p. 55.

28. Max de Pree, *Leadership Is an Art* (New York, 1989).

29. Jefferson's character remained true even as president. To his lasting credit, he never used his respected status to dominate. Unlike George Washington, who traveled regally in a cream-colored carriage pulled by six horses and attended by servants in lily-white uniforms trimmed with scarlet, Jefferson rode to his inauguration alone, dismounted, and quietly hung the bridle of his horse on a fence outside the Capitol. From Claud G. Bowers, *The Young Jefferson, 1743–1789* (Boston, 1945); and Carl Binger, *Thomas Jefferson: A Well-tempered Mind* (New York, 1970).

INDEX

❧

About the Author

MARK GERZON has spent most of his life exploring conflicting beliefs. Working with the Rockefeller Foundation, he has created and designed innovative programs to help American communities creatively confront the challenge of their own diversity. As codirector of the Campaign for Common Ground, a project to revitalize political discourse during the 1996 election, he is working to ensure that political campaigns serve rather than undermine the public interest.

After his best-selling *The Whole World Is Watching: A Young Man Looks at Youth's Dissent,* published in 1969 during his senior year at Harvard, he began working with many educational, business, and philanthropic organizations dealing with the conflict between generations. In the seventies, as cofounder and managing editor of *WorldPaper,* a global newspaper with circulation on four continents, he assembled and coordinated a team of associate editors who reflected the diversity of the world's major cultures. As the author of *A Choice of Heroes: The Changing Faces of American Manhood,* he fostered constructive dialogue between feminism and the emerging men's movement. As founder of the "Entertainment Summit," a Moscow-Hollywood citizen diplomacy project that built partnerships between the Soviet and American film industries, he contributed to deeper understanding between the superpowers.

A consultant to both public and private organizations dealing with conflict and diversity issues, he is also president of Mediators Foundation, a nonprofit educational organization dedicated to furthering this work. For further information about the author and his programs, please contact Mediators Foundation, 9 Bowser Road, Lexington, MA 02173.